CAMBRIDGE ENGLISH CLASSICS

The Poetical Works
of
Giles Fletcher
and
Phineas Fletcher

In Two Volumes

GILES FLETCHER
(The Younger)

Born, *circa* 1585

Died, 1623

PHINEAS FLETCHER

Born, 1582

Died, 1650

>   Richard Marsham & Elizabeth Grove wear   } 1 of November
>   married
>   Edmund the Sonn of William Freman & his   } 9 of December
>   wife Alice was buried
>   Kath'yan the daughter of John Dipher & his } 9 of December
>   wife Isabel was baptised
>   Margaret the daughter of William   } 16 of December
>   Bradbery & Frances his wife was baptised
>   Elizabeth ye daughter of Phineas Fletcher } 16 of December
>   & Elizabeth his wife was baptised
>   Widow Akers was buried   } 17 of Decemb.
>   Katherin Elom ye wife of George Elom buried} Mar: 8
>   Thomas the sonn of Stephan Bloyes   } Mar: 15
>   Winifred his wife was buried
>
> An:Do: Ursala the daughter of Thomas Goddard   } Mar: 31
> 1622   & Cicelie his wife was baptised
>   Margaret ye daughter of Christopher   } 7 of April
>   Turner & Elizabeth his wife baptised
>   Jeremie Colleyn was buried   } April 14
>   Elizabeth the daughter of Richard Marsham } April 14
>   & Elizabeth his wife was baptized
>   Christopher Steward & Margaret   } April 29
>   Buglass wear married
>   Robert Toppin & Elizabeth Pigot   } May 1
>   wear married
>   Bright the daughter of Mark Walter   } May 19
>   & Margaret his wife was baptised
>   at Southrie by permission of mr
>   Phinees Fletcher Rector of Hilgay
>
>   p mr: Phin: Fletcher
>   Rector

Part of a leaf of the Register of All Saints' Church, Hilgay, containing the earliest entries in the Register by Phineas Fletcher, 1621-2.

GILES AND PHINEAS FLETCHER

POETICAL WORKS

EDITED BY

FREDERICK S. BOAS, M.A.,

Formerly Professor of English Literature in Queen's College, Belfast,
and Clark Lecturer in Trinity College, Cambridge

Volume I

CAMBRIDGE:
at the University Press
1908
reprinted
1970

Published by the Syndics of the Cambridge University Press
Bentley House, 200 Euston Road, London, N.W.1
American Branch: 32 East 57th Street, New York, N.Y. 10022

PUBLISHER'S NOTE

Cambridge University Press Library Editions are re-issues of out-of-print standard works from the Cambridge catalogue. The texts are unrevised and, apart from minor corrections, reproduce the latest published edition.

Standard Book Number: 521 07773 7
Library of Congress Catalogue Card Number: 70-108103

First published 1908
Reprinted 1970

PR
2271
.A24
1970
v.1

First printed in Great Britain at the University Press, Cambridge
Reprinted in Great Britain by John Dickens & Co. Ltd, Northampton

PREFACE.

THE present volume contains all the extant poetical works of Giles Fletcher, and those of his brother Phineas[1], including the piscatorial play *Sicelides*, which were published before 1633. A second volume will contain the poems of Phineas Fletcher published in or after that year.

The only editions of the collected poems of the two brothers hitherto issued are those by the Rev. A. B. Grosart. He printed for private circulation in *The Fuller Worthies' Library* the *Poems* of Giles Fletcher in one volume in 1868, and the *Poems* of Phineas Fletcher in four volumes in 1869. He published a revised edition of Giles Fletcher's *Poems* (Chatto and Windus) in 1876; a similar publication of those of Phineas was contemplated but not carried out. Every later editor must pay tribute to Grosart's industry and enthusiasm. His volumes marked a great advance upon the modernised and incomplete reprints which had preceded them, and they have done much to revive the study of the two writers. But Grosart's limitations as editor and critic are well known, and a reproduction of the poems, in convenient form, from the original texts and MSS. is a need of English scholarship which the present edition endeavours to supply.

In this volume appear (in addition to some fragments of translation) five poems by Giles Fletcher, two

[1] The accepted spelling of the name has been retained in this edition, though Fletcher himself always uses the form *Phinees*.

PREFACE

of which, an English and a Latin elegy on Henry, Prince of Wales, have not hitherto been reprinted. The first poem, *A Canto on the death of Eliza*, originally formed part of the academic miscellany, *Sorrowes Joy. Or, A Lamentation for our late deceased Soveraigne Elizabeth, with a triumph for the prosperous succession of our gratious King, James*, published at Cambridge by John Legat in 1603. It was reprinted by Nichols in his *Progresses of Queen Elizabeth*, vol. III. 257—9 (1805), and his *Progresses of James I.*, vol. I. 17—19 (1828). Grosart adopted the text used in the *Progresses of James I.*, but with some inaccuracies. The poem is here reproduced from the original version in *Sorrowes Joy*.

Christs Victorie and Triumph is reprinted from the Quarto published at Cambridge by Cantrell Legge in 1610. This was the only edition which appeared in the author's lifetime, and it has therefore been taken as the basis of the present text. But the edition issued at Cambridge in 1632 by Francis Green must have had the authority, and probably the supervision, of Phineas Fletcher, who appended to his original commendatory stanzas (cf. p. 14 and Notes) a couplet addressed *Defuncto fratri*.

> Think (if thou canst) how mounted on his spheare,
> In heaven now he sings: thus sung he here.

Its readings, therefore, claim special consideration, and, in some cases, indicated by square brackets, they have been adopted in preference to those of the earlier edition. All variants are recorded in the Notes.

The Quarto of 1640, printed by Roger Daniel for Richard Royston is merely a reissue of that of 1632, with a different title-page, and with the addition of seven engravings, by George Yate, of scenes from the

PREFACE

Gospel narrative. Two of these engravings, representing the Nativity and the Temptation in the Wilderness, are reproduced in this volume, and in the Notes I have given a detailed description of all the engravings, including the curious miniatures, which, in each case, accompany the principal scenes.

The short poem in couplets, for which I have suggested as title *A Description of Encolpius*, is transcribed from the Bodleian *Tanner MSS.*, 465, f. 42, in Archbishop Sancroft's handwriting. It was printed by Grosart in *Miscellanies of the Fuller Worthies' Library*, vol. III. pp. 510—12 (1872), and later in his revised edition of Giles Fletcher's *Poems* in 1876, but very inaccurately. Moreover from his remarks Grosart seems to have thought that *Encolpus*, as the name is misspelt in the MS., was a work of Petronius, instead of a character in his prose satire.

The two *Elegies on Henry, Prince of Wales*, are here for the first time reproduced since they appeared in 1612[1], though Thomas Fuller in *The Church-History of Britain* (1655), Bk. x. p. 67, stated that the prince "was generally lamented of the whole Land, both *Universities* publishing their Verses in print," and quoted the last four lines of the *Carmen Sepulchrale* (cf. p. 270) "made by *Giles Fletcher* of Trinity Colledge in Cambridge on this PRINCES plain grave, because wanting an inscription." Fuller adds an English version of his own:

> *If wise, amaz'd depart this* holy Grave ;
> *Nor these* New-ashes, *ask what* Names *they have.*
> *The* Graver *in concealing them was* wise.
> *For, who so knows, straight melts in tears and dies.*

This passage in the *Church-History* is alluded to by Joseph Hunter in his *Chorus Vatum*, vol. I. p. 124

[1] They are printed in the Appendix, pp. 266—70, as I came upon their track after the earlier part of this volume had passed through the press.

PREFACE

(British Museum *Addit. MSS.*, 24,487), but Hunter does not appear to have known anything of Fletcher's poem except the lines quoted by Fuller. I have succeeded in finding the epitaph and the Latin elegy by which it is preceded in *Epicedium Cantabrigiense, In obitum immaturum, semperq, deflendum, Henrici, Illustrissimi Principis Walliæ*, &c., a collection of memorial verses on Prince Henry by members of the University, published by Cantrell Legge in 1612. They occur on pp. 12—14 of the volume and are signed G[iles] F[letcher] T[rinity] C[ollege]. The collection, in its original form, consisted of 112 pages, and its contents were in classical or foreign languages. But in another issue, also of 1612, there is a supplementary sheaf of English poems on pages numbered, by some confusion, from 97 to 110. The first of these additions, signed in the same manner as the Latin verses, is the elegy by Giles Fletcher, *Upon the most lamented departure of the right hopefull, and blessed Prince Henrie Prince of Wales*[1]. It is gratifying to be able to enlarge the too slender store of Fletcher's poetry by this set of verses, which are additionally interesting as written not in the eight-line stanza of *A Canto upon the death of Eliza* and *Christs Victorie and Triumph*, but in "the rhyme royal" which the author has hitherto not been known to have used. The verses also claim attention as being the last that we possess from Giles Fletcher's pen, and as forming another link in the chain of literary associations connected with Prince Henry[2].

The Appendix also includes the fragmentary translations from Greek and Latin verse in Fletcher's prose

[1] In one of the copies of *Epicedium Cantabrigiense* in the British Museum (161. b. 22) there is a Latin MS. note indicating Giles Fletcher as the author of this elegy, but this has hitherto escaped attention.

[2] For a new link between the Prince and Phineas Fletcher see below on *Locustæ*.

PREFACE

tract, *The Reward of the Faithfull* (1623). These have already been reprinted by Grosart.

Unless he has been wrongly credited with a work belonging to his father, a much more important specimen of Giles Fletcher's powers as a translator was formerly extant, but has now apparently disappeared. One of the oldest catalogues of King's College Library contains the entry: *Lamentationes Jeremiæ per metaphrasin. Authore A. Fletcher.* Additional information is supplied by William Cole, the antiquary, who became a member of King's College in 1736. In his MS. *Athenæ Cantabrigienses* he has a short account of Giles Fletcher (British Museum *Addit. MSS.*, 5869, f. 24 *verso*) which includes the following statement: "In the library of King's Coll. is a small MS. given to it Febr. 2. 1654–5 by S. Th. Socius, wch I take to be Saml Thoms who gave other books also to it, with this Title *Ægidii Fletcheri Versio Poetica Lamentationum Jeremiæ.* It is dedicated in 19 Hex[ameter] & Pen[tameter] verses to *Ornatissimo doctissimoq, viro D° Doctori Whytgyfte Ægidius Fletcherus Salutem.*" Probably Cole had good grounds for ascribing the MS. to the younger Giles Fletcher. Otherwise if Dr "Whytgyfte," to whom the translation is dedicated, be John Whitgift, Master of Trinity from 1567–77, and later Archbishop of Canterbury, who died in 1604, there would seem a presumption in favour of the father's authorship. The elder Giles was himself a member of King's College, and he and Whitgift were in residence at the University together for a number of years.

Unfortunately the manuscript cannot now be traced. It is not entered in a King's College Library catalogue compiled between 50 and 60 years ago, or in any catalogue of more recent date. An appeal for information concerning it has hitherto proved fruitless (cf.

PREFACE

Mr A. R. Waller's letter in *The Athenaeum*, June 9, 1906, p. 701).

The first poem of Phineas Fletcher in this volume was, like Giles' *Canto upon the death of Eliza*, one of the contributions to *Sorrowes Joy*. As, however, it has no separate title, I have grouped it, for convenience of reference, under the heading *Verses of Mourning and Joy on the Death of Elizabeth and Accession of James*, with some Latin verses by Fletcher on the same theme. These verses were contributed by him to another academic miscellany, also issued at Cambridge in 1603 by John Legat, and entitled *Threno-thriambeuticon. Academiae Cantabrigiensis ob damnum lucrosum, & infœlicitatem fœlicissimam, luctuosus triumphus*. Both the English and the Latin lines were reprinted by Grosart in his edition of Phineas Fletcher's *Poems*, with the exception of the twenty hexameters on pp. 95—96 of the present volume. These were omitted because Grosart misunderstood the method of marking off the various contributors' work in *Threno-thriambeuticon*, and did not realise that the signature at the foot of the lines headed *In eosdem* was intended to include the preceding set of hexameters.

Locustæ vel Pietas Jesuitica and *The Locusts or Apollyonists* are reprinted from the only edition published in the author's lifetime. This is the Quarto of 1627, issued at Cambridge by Thomas and John Bucke, in which both poems are included, though with separate title-pages. Of *The Apollyonists*[1] no other text exists, but *Locustæ*, as is for the first time set forth fully in the Notes to this volume, went through a series of remarkable changes before it appeared in book form.

---

[1] I have followed Grosart in adopting this as the short title of the poem, as it distinguishes it more clearly for purposes of reference from *Locustæ*.

PREFACE

Three autograph manuscripts of it are extant which differ materially from one another and from the printed version. As only one of these manuscripts has hitherto been collated, and that imperfectly, it is necessary to set forth in some detail their relation to one another and to the Quarto, and to place their authenticity beyond question.

The earliest in date, as is proved by internal evidence, is the British Museum *Sloane MSS.*, 444, entitled *Pietas Jesuitica*. It was mentioned in *Chorus Vatum*, vol. I. f. 115, by Joseph Hunter, who gives a short abstract of its dedicatory letter. It is doubtful, however, whether he can have read the poem, even cursorily, or he would scarcely have set down the query (f. 125) "how far is this the same with the satire against the Jesuits published by him in 1627 entitled Locustes or Apolyonists?" Grosart did not know of this MS. when he edited the poem in 1869, but he mentions it in his *Miscellanies of the Fuller Worthies' Library* (1872), vol. III. p. 509. He there also states that he had secured "another MS. (wholly autograph) of the Locustæ, with an interesting Epistle-dedicatory to Henry, Prince of Wales," and that he hoped to use both MSS. in his "intended facsimile edition of Milton." This design was, however, never carried out, and on Grosart's death in 1899, his manuscript passed into the hands of Mr Bertram Dobell, who has kindly given me facilities for collating it for the present volume. The third manuscript, *Harleian MSS.*, 3196, is better known, as it was collated by Grosart for his edition, though his variants contain a number of inaccuracies. On the fly-leaf of this MS. is an entry by Wanley, Harley's librarian, 13 *die Augusti*, A.D. 1724. This entry is confirmed and explained by Wanley's *Diary* (*Lansdowne MSS.*, 772,

xiii

PREFACE

f. 33 b), in which it is recorded that the manuscript is one of a number bought from Nathaniel Noel, the bookseller, on that date, and which had either belonged to Simon Harcourt of Penley or had "come from beyond the sea." It had probably been one of those in Simon Harcourt's collection.

At the head of the fly-leaf in the *Harleian* MS. is written in an unknown hand the name, *P: Fletcher.* In the frontispiece to Volume I. of the large paper copies of his edition of Phineas Fletcher's poems Grosart reproduced this in facsimile as Fletcher's "autograph." In the same frontispiece he also reproduced the signature to the dedicatory epistle in this MS., which he declared elsewhere (P. Fletcher's *Poems,* vol. II. p. 3) to be "in the handwriting of the Author," though it was manifestly impossible that both signatures could have been written by one person. Furthermore in vol. IV. p. 20 of his edition Grosart stated that there was an autograph inscription in Fletcher's presentation copy of *The Purple Island* to Benlowes (now c. 34, g. 33 in the British Museum), which he quotes in the following form:

"Nec mare nec venti nec quod magis omnibus Angli
    Horruimus Te tergeminus non fortior armis.
                                         Phinees ffletcher."

As a fact there are two entries in this copy of *The Purple Island.* Close to the top of the page are the verse lines quoted by Grosart, with no signature following, and probably inserted by some later owner of the book. Nearer the middle of the page, in a different hand, are the words, *Ex dono Phineæ ffletcheri authoris.* This inscription (as my investigations have since proved) was not written by Fletcher himself. It seems probable therefore that it is in Benlowes' hand, but

PREFACE

I have found it impossible to verify this. What is, however, material to the present subject is that both these handwritings are entirely different from the signature on the fly-leaf of the *Harleian* MS. and from the script in the MS. itself.

It was evident, therefore, that Grosart had made reckless and mutually destructive statements, and that the only method of solving the questions of authenticity thus raised was to compare the MSS. of *Locustæ* with authentic specimens of Fletcher's handwriting. This I have been able to do through the kindness of the Rev. J. H. Maude, Rector of All Saints' Church, Hilgay, where Fletcher was the incumbent from 1621 till 1650. Mr Maude was good enough to send to the British Museum vol. I. of the *Register of Baptisms, Burials and Marriages*, which includes the entries made by Phineas Fletcher as Rector, that they might be compared with the handwriting in the MSS. of *Locustæ*[1]. Dr G. F. Warner, the Keeper of the Manuscripts, very kindly examined the entries in the Register together with the *Sloane* and *Harleian* MSS. and Mr Dobell's manuscript, and I have his authority for stating that the three versions of the poem, with the accompanying dedicatory epistles, are unquestionably in Fletcher's own hand. By Mr Maude's kind permission Fletcher's earliest entries in the Hilgay Register, including two signatures, are reproduced in facsimile as the frontispiece to this volume, and facsimiles are also given of leaves from each of the three MSS. of *Locustæ*.

A full collation of the variants in the MSS. will

---

[1] This volume of the Register covers the period 1583 to 1673. The entries by Phineas Fletcher are continuous from November 1621 to November 1645. From that date the entries in his hand are intermittent till early in 1650, when they cease.

PREFACE

be found in the Notes, but a few general points bearing on the evolution of the poem during a period of about seventeen years require notice here. The *Sloane* MS. must have been written early in 1611, for in the dedicatory letter to Montagu, Bishop of Bath and Wells, Fletcher speaks of it as "*carmen hoc Cantabrigiæ nuper inchoatum, inter urbanos strepitus, parentisq illius quidem exspirantis singultus...confectum.*" The death of Giles Fletcher, the elder, here alluded to, took place in Fenchurch Street, London, in March, 1610–11, and the poem was evidently finished in haste (*properatum tibi munus*) in the hope of attracting some substantial token of Montagu's appreciation of it. This hope, apparently, was disappointed, for Fletcher penned a second version, Mr Dobell's manuscript, which differs only in slight details from the *Sloane* MS., except that it omits the letter to Montagu and substitutes a dedicatory poem in hexameters to Henry, Prince of Wales. This version must therefore have been written later than March, 1611, and before Prince Henry's death on November 6, 1612. At some period after this event Fletcher, still seeking for royal patronage, wrote a third draft, the *Harleian* MS., in which, with a judicious economy of his material for panegyrics, he transferred to Prince Charles, with the minimum of necessary change, the dedicatory verses previously addressed to Prince Henry[1]. These were, however, now preceded by a prose epistle to Prince Charles' tutor, Thomas Murray, afterwards Provost of Eton. As Fletcher speaks of being driven to appeal to Murray

---

[1] Even in the Quarto edition of the poem, in which these dedicatory verses disappeared, he could not resist the temptation to use some of them for the third time by inserting them near the close of the work (cf. notes on pp. 122—3).

PREFACE

by a "*dura et planè ferrea necessitas*," this recension of *Locustæ* must have been made previously to his appointment to the living of Hilgay in 1621. How much nearer to the close of 1612 it is to be placed is doubtful. On the one hand it would seem natural for Fletcher to have sought a new patron as soon as was at all becoming after Prince Henry's death. On the other he speaks of dragging the poem again into the light of day out of the dust in which it had long been buried: "*situ diuturno sepulta, et hac tandem necessitate resuscitata, in lucem (tanquam Musarum umbræ) desuetam prodeuntia.*" There is, doubtless, some rhetorical exaggeration in this statement, and it is followed by another which is demonstrably incorrect. For Fletcher proceeds to describe his lines as roughly fashioned and never revised: "*versus...malè tornati neq; unquam incudi postea redditi.*" Yet when we compare the *Harleian* MS. with the two earlier versions of the poem, we find that it differs from them materially. Apart from minor verbal variants throughout, and from the addition or omission of passages ranging from one line to nine, it inserts 37 continuous new lines (cf. notes on pp. 114—15) and rearranges and greatly enlarges the important section of the work dealing with the Gunpowder Plot (cf. notes on pp. 116—19). The *Harleian* MS. in fact represents the principal stage in the revision of *Locustæ*, as the satire is for the first time entitled in this MS. But the printed edition of 1627 embodies some further changes. As Thomas Murray was now dead, and Charles was on the throne, the dedications to them were omitted, and an epistle to Sir Roger Townshend was substituted. And in the body of the poem a number of variants in detail from the *Harleian* MS. are found, including the omission, and, more frequently, the addition of passages of a few lines. Nevertheless

PREFACE

in their main features the MS. and the text of 1627 are akin.

The last work of Phineas Fletcher included in this volume, *Sicelides*, also requires somewhat detailed observations. In dealing with it I have had, for reasons stated immediately below, to depart in one respect from the customary practice in the *Cambridge English Classics* series. Owing to the absence of any authoritative version of the "piscatory," I have given what, in a carefully restricted sense of the word, is an "eclectic" text.

This fisher-play, which was performed at King's College, Cambridge, on 13 March, 1614–15, is extant in three different forms. There is the Quarto edition of 1631 printed in London for William Sheares. Though this was issued in Fletcher's lifetime, it cannot have had his authority, for his name does not appear on the title-page, and the text is full of misprints and corruptions. It was reproduced, with a number of emendations, by Grosart in vol. III. of his edition of Phineas Fletcher's poetical works. There are also two manuscripts of the play, one in the *Birch* collection in the British Museum (*Addit. MSS.* 4453) and the other in the Bodleian (*Rawlinson Poet.* 214). The British Museum MS. is mentioned by Mr F. G. Fleay (*Biographical Chronicle of the English Drama*, vol. I. p. 230), and in Mr W. C. Hazlitt's *Manual of Old English Plays*, but otherwise both manuscripts seem to have been unknown to editors and biographers of Fletcher. I have to acknowledge my special obligation to my friend, Professor G. C. Moore-Smith, of the University of Sheffield, who drew my attention to the manuscripts, and who has also been kind enough to furnish me with some new *data* (as will appear below) bearing on Fletcher as a dramatist.

PREFACE

I have found the work of collation alike unusually heavy and interesting. The manuscripts, as is evident from the Notes, have proved remarkably different from one another. They both also vary widely from the Quarto, though they stand in definitely contrasted relations to it. The texts of the *Birch* MS. and of the Quarto, in spite of their numerous differences, belong to a common type, and internal evidence clearly shows that the MS. often preserves the correct reading where the Quarto is corrupt. In most of these cases the *Rawlinson* MS. agrees with the *Birch* MS. But in some places where the *Birch* MS. and the Quarto differ, and in hundreds of instances where they are at one, the *Rawlinson* MS. has a variant reading. A considerable number of these variants are, in themselves, comparatively insignificant, but occurring, as they do, *passim* throughout a very long play, their cumulative effect is great. Moreover, among the multitudinous minor variants there are others more substantial. The stage-directions in the *Rawlinson* MS. are fewer and more concise than in the other texts, where they are virtually identical, and from Act III. Sc. 2 onwards it adopts, in the main, a different division of scenes. It omits here and there verse passages of one or two lines; on rare occasions it makes additions, the chief being of six lines in Act III. Sc. 5. In some of the prose scenes, notably Act II. 6, it rearranges and slightly shortens part of the dialogue, and it omits the songs at the beginning of Act II. 5, and Act V. 6, and the Choruses at the end of Acts III. and IV. The *Rawlinson* MS. therefore contains a unique version of the play, but whether this is an earlier or a later draft than the two other allied texts is, I think, difficult to determine. On the whole

PREFACE

it makes the impression of a version revised and slightly cut down for some special performance[1].

Unlike the MSS. of *Locustæ* those of *Sicelides* give no clue to their date or *provenance*. Neither of them is in the handwriting of Fletcher, though the *Birch* MS., alone among the three texts, names him as author of the "piscatory." The script, however, though not Fletcher's, is in both cases of the earlier seventeenth century. The penman of the *Birch* MS. appears to have copied his original, though his writing is neat and clear, somewhat hurriedly, for he occasionally puts down, and then erases, a word before it is due, as if his eye had travelled faster than his pen. The writer of the *Rawlinson* MS. also makes occasional slips. He omits short passages and then adds them on the blank leaf opposite. In the Chorus at the end of Act II. (cf. p. 213, l. 13, of this volume) he leaves a blank where the word *natures* is found in the other two texts,

---

[1] It is noticeable, however, that in all three versions of the play the incidents are exactly the same. This has a bearing on a curious and interesting problem raised by Mr W. W. Greg in his *Pastoral Poetry and Pastoral Drama* (p. 347, and note). He there states that "the stealing of the Hesperian apples, and the penalty entailed [*Sicelides*, Act I. 3 and Act II. 4], appear to be imitated from the breaking of Pan's tree in Browne's *Britannia's Pastorals*, as does also the devotion and rescue of Perindus" [*Sicelides*, Act V. 3 and 5]. It is true that Fletcher and Browne place the episodes here alluded to in very different settings, but I agree with Mr Greg that one of them must have imitated the other. There are similarities of situation and of language, especially between *Sicelides*, Act V. 5, pp. 259—60, and the later sections of *Britannia's Pastorals*, Book II. Song V., which cannot be fortuitous. But, as Mr Greg points out, "Book II. of Browne's work...was not printed till 1616." Hence he concludes that "Fletcher had seen Browne's poem in manuscript, or else the play, as originally performed, differed from the printed version. I think it unlikely that the borrowing should have been the other way." But the fact that the episodes are found in three different versions of the play makes it probable that they were not later additions, and indeed they seem necessary to the framework of the plot. If, therefore, Fletcher was the borrower, I believe that he must have seen Book II. of *Britannia's Pastorals* before it was printed. But may not, on the other hand, Browne have made use of a manuscript of *Sicelides* which, from its performance in connection with a royal visit, is likely to have attracted special notice outside Cambridge?

PREFACE

as if it were either missing or undecipherable in his source. In both MSS. there are numerous corrections in different ink. In the *Rawlinson* MS. these appear to have been added later by the original scribe; in the *Birch* MS. I think that they are by another hand.

It is evident from what has been said that neither in the printed or written copies of *Sicelides* is an authoritative text to be found. Under the circumstances I have taken the Quarto which, with all its imperfections, was issued at a known date within Fletcher's lifetime, as the basis of the text in this volume. But where it is manifestly corrupt, I have substituted, within square brackets, the readings of the allied *Birch* MS., which are frequently supported by the *Rawlinson* MS. I have also in a much smaller number of cases adopted within brackets the readings of the *Rawlinson* MS. alone, when considerations of meaning or of metre strongly suggested that these were not peculiar to it, but belonged to the original text of the play. As, however, in every case the source of my text is indicated, and the alternative version or versions recorded in the Notes, any reader who may think me guilty of undue "subjectivity" in my method has the materials at hand for checking its results. I venture to think, however, that, unless the *Rawlinson* MS. is taken as the basis of the text, the margin for differences of opinion is not very wide. And I may perhaps be allowed to add the hope that this "piscatory," which even in the imperfect Quarto version has won the suffrages of discerning critics, may have its merits yet more widely recognised in its emended form.

It is, moreover, almost certain that *Sicelides* was not Fletcher's only contribution to the academic drama. Professor Moore-Smith informs me that in examining the Account Books of King's College he has found

PREFACE

the following entries under the year 1607, *Termino Annuniationis* (i.e. between Easter and Midsummer):

It^m. solut[um] D[omi]no ffletcher
  pro variis circa Comediam vt patet   xlv^s ij^d
  ....
It. solut. eidem [sc. Elam]
  pro watching the comodie night about the porters lodge   x^d
It. solut. pro expensis
  circa le englishe Comodye   iii^{li}

The entries all apparently refer to the same play. That concerning Elam (who was probably, as Prof. Moore-Smith suggests, a college servant) is doubtless explained by the fact that a short time previously, on 20 February, 1606–7, there had been "foul & great disorder committed at the time of a comedy in King's College" (Cooper, *Annals of Cambridge*, III. p. 24).

It is just possible that this "englishe Comodye" of Fletcher performed in 1607 was *Sicelides*, and that the play was revived in honour of the King's visit to Cambridge in March, 1615. But this is far from probable. All the existing versions of the "piscatory" must, at the very earliest, date from 1612, as they contain the satirical allusion to Thomas Coryat hanging up the shoes, in which he had walked from Venice, in Odcombe Church (Act III. 4, p. 222). Moreover, the contemporary account of the royal visit in the *Dering MSS.* seems to imply that *Sicelides* was specially written for the occasion. "The Piscatory, an English comedy, was acted before the University in King's Colledge, which Master Fletcher of that Colledge had provided if the King should have tarried another night[1]." There

---

[1] Prof. Moore-Smith tells me that there is no reference to this performance in the King's College Account Books, but that he has been informed by Mr F. L. Clarke, Bursar's Clerk, of the following entry in the *Liber Communarum* for the thirteenth week (March 11–17) of the *Terminus Nativitatis*, 1614–15: "The cause of the extra ordinary expence was entertainment of strangers and the Comedy."

PREFACE

can be little doubt that Fletcher's "englishe Comodye" of 1607 is one of those numerous products of the academic stage concerning which College Bursars in the faithful discharge of their office have recorded every item involved in their production, but with lofty detachment from literary considerations have not even mentioned their name.

In addition to the acknowledgments already made in the course of this Preface, I have to thank my brother-in-law, Mr S. G. Owen, Senior Student and Tutor of Christ Church, for reading through the proofs of *Locustæ*, and making valuable suggestions; the Rev. Professor H. Kynaston, of the University of Durham, for tracing the source of Fragment III. on p. 271; and Mr J. A. Herbert of the MSS. department of the British Museum for information on various points. And I have, finally, to express my acknowledgments to the Syndics of the Cambridge University Press for facilitating my work in every possible way; and especially to Mr A. R. Waller, of the University Press, for much valuable advice on questions both large and small.

F. S. BOAS.

BICKLEY
10 *April*, 1908

CONTENTS.

GILES FLETCHER
PAGE
- A Canto upon the Death of Eliza . . . 1
- Christs Victorie, and Triumph 5
- A Description of Encolpius 89

PHINEAS FLETCHER
- Verses of Mourning and Joy on the Death of Elizabeth and Accession of James . . 92
- Locustæ, vel Pietas Jesuitica 97
- The Locusts, or Apollyonists 125
- Sicelides, A Piscatory 187

APPENDIX TO THE POEMS OF GILES FLETCHER
- Elegies on Henry, Prince of Wales . . . 266
- Fragmentary Verse Translations in *The Reward of the Faithfull* 271

NOTES 274

CORRIGENDA 310

PLATES
- Part of a leaf of the Register of All Saints' Church, Hilgay . . . . *Frontispiece*
- The Nativity . . . . . *to face p.* 18
- The Temptation in the Wilderness . ,, ,, 44
- Facsimiles of the handwriting of Phineas Fletcher *between pp.* 96, 97

GILES FLETCHER

A CANTO UPON THE DEATH
OF ELIZA.

THe earely Houres were readie to unlocke
   The doore of Morne, to let abroad the Day,
When sad *Ocyroe* sitting on a rocke,
Hemmd in with teares, not glassing as they say
Shee woont, her damaske beuties (when to play
   Shee bent her looser fancie) in the streame,
   That sudding on the rocke, would closely seeme
To imitate her whitenesse with his frothy creame.

But hanging from the stone her carefull head,
That shewed (for griefe had made it so to shew)
A stone it selfe, thus onely differed,
That those without, these streames within did flow,
Both ever ranne, yet never lesse did grow,
   And tearing from her head her amber haires,
   Whose like or none, or onely Phæbus weares,
Shee strowd thē on the flood to waite upō her teares.

About her many Nymphes sate weeping by,
That when shee sang were woont to daunce & leape.
And all the grasse that round about did lie,
Hung full of teares, as if that meant to weepe,
Whilest, th' undersliding streames did softly creepe,
   And clung about the rocke with winding wreath,
   To heare a *Canto* of Elizaes death: (her breath.
Which thus poore nymph shee sung, whilest sorrowe lent

Tell me ye blushing currols that bunch out,
To cloath with beuteous red your ragged sire,
So let the sea-greene mosse curle round about
With soft embrace (as creeping vines doe wyre
Their loved Elmes) your sides in rosie tyre,
   So let the ruddie vermeyle of your cheeke
   Make staind carnations fresher liveries seeke,
So let your braunched armes grow crooked, smooth, & sleeke.

GILES FLETCHER

So from your growth late be you rent away,
And hung with silver bels and whistles shrill,
Unto those children be you given to play
Where blest Eliza raignd: so never ill
Betide your canes nor them with breaking spill,
   Tell me if some uncivill hand should teare
   Your branches hence, and place them otherwhere;
Could you still grow, & such fresh crimson ensignes beare?

Tell me sad Philomele that yonder sit'st
Piping thy songs unto the dauncing twig,
And to the waters fall thy musicke fit'st,
So let the friendly prickle never digge
Thy watchfull breast with wound or small or bigge,
   Whereon thou lean'st, so let the hissing snake
   Sliding with shrinking silence never take
Th'unwarie foote, whilst thou perhaps hangst halfe awake.

So let the loathed lapwing when her nest
Is stolne away, not as shee uses, flie,
Cousening the searcher of his promisd feast,
But widdowd of all hope still *Itis* crie,
And nought but *Itis*, *Itis*, till shee die.
   Say sweetest querister of the airie quire
   Doth not thy *Tereu*, *Tereu* then expire,
When winter robs thy house of all her greene attire?

Tell me ye velvet headed violets
That fringe the crooked banke with gawdie blewe,
So let with comely grace your prettie frets
Be spread, so let a thousand *Zephyrs* sue
To kisse your willing heads, that seeme t'eschew
   Their wanton touch with maiden modestie,
   So let the silver dewe but lightly lie
Like little watrie worlds within your azure skie,

So when your blazing leaves are broadly spread
Let wandring nymphes gather you in their lapps,
And send you where Eliza lieth dead,
To strow the sheete that her pale bodie wraps,
Aie me in this I envie your good haps:
   Who would not die, there to be buried?
   Say if the sunne denie his beames to shedde
Upon your living stalkes, grow you not withered?

UPON THE DEATH OF ELIZA

Tell me thou wanton brooke, that slip'st away
T'avoid the straggling bankes still flowing cling,
So let thy waters cleanely tribute pay
Unmixt with mudde unto the sea your king,
So never let your streames leave murmuring
   Untill they steale by many a secret furt
   To kisse those walls that built Elizaes court,   (durt?
Drie you not when your mother springs are choakt with

Yes you all say, and I say with you all,
Naught without cause of joy can joyous bide,
Then me unhappie nymph whome the dire fall
Of my joyes spring, But there aye me shee cried,
And spake no more, for sorrow speech denied.
   And downe into her watrie lodge did goe;
   The very waters when shee sunke did showe
With many wrinckled ohs they sympathiz'd her woe.

The sunne in mourning cloudes inveloped
Flew fast into the westearne world to tell
Newes of her death. Heaven it selfe sorrowed
With teares that to the earthes danke bosome fell;
But when the next Aurora gan to deale
   Handfuls of roses fore the teame of day
   A sheapheard drove his flocke by chance that way
& made the nymph to dance that mourned yesterday.

G. Fletcher. Trinit.

CHRISTS
VICTORIE, AND TRI-
umph in Heaven, and Earth,
over, and after death.

*A te principium, tibi desinet, accipe jussis
Carmina c[œ]pta tuis, atque hanc sine tempora circum
Inter victrices hederam tibi serpere lauros.*

CAMBRIDGE
Printed by C. LEGGE. 1610.

TO THE RIGHT
WORSHIP[F]ULL, AND REVEREND
M^r. Doctour NEVILE, Deane of CANTERBURIE,
and the Master of TRINITIE Colledge
in CAMBRIDGE.

R*Ight worthie, and reverend Syr:*
    As I have alwaies thought the place wherein I live, after heaven, principally to be desired, both because I most want, and it most abounds with wisdome, which is fled by some with as much delight, as it is obtained by others, and ought to be followed by all: so I cannot but next unto God, for ever acknowledge myselfe most bound unto the hand of God, (I meane yourselfe) that reacht downe, as it were out of heaven, unto me, a benefit of that nature, and price, then which, I could wish none, (onely heaven itselfe excepted) either more fruitfull, and contenting for the time that is now present, or more comfortable, and encouraging for the time that is alreadie past, or more hopefull, and promising for the time that is yet to come.
    For as in all mens judgements (that have any judgement) Europe is worthily deem'd the Queene of the world, that Garland both of Learning, and pure Religion beeing now become her crowne, and blossoming upon her head, that hath long since laine withered in Greece *and* Palestine; *so my opinion of this Island hath alwaies beene, that it is the very face, and beautie of all* Europe, *in which both true Religion is faithfully professed without superstition, and (if on earth) true Learning sweetly flourishes without ostentation: and what are the two eyes of this Land, but the two Universities; which cannot but prosper in the time of such a Prince, that is a Prince of Learning, aswell as of People: and truly I should forget myselfe, if I should not call* Cambridge

GILES FLETCHER

the right eye: and I thinke (King Henrie *the* 8. *beeing the uniter,* Edward *the* 3. *the Founder, and your selfe the Repairer of this Colledge, wherein I live) none will blame me, if I esteeme the same, since your polishing of it, the fairest sight in* Cambridge: *in which beeing placed by your onely favour, most freely, without either any meanes from other, or any desert in my selfe, beeing not able to doe more, I could doe no lesse, then acknowledge that debt, which I shall never be able to pay, and with old* Silenus, *in the Poet (upon whome the boyes—*injiciunt ipsis ex vincula sertis, *making his garland, his fetters) finding my selfe bound unto you by so many benefits, that were given by your selfe for ornaments, but are to me as so many golden cheines, to hold me fast in a kind of desired bondage, seeke (as he doth) my freedome with a song, the matter whereof is as worthie the sweetest Singer, as my selfe, the miserable Singer, unworthie so divine a subject: but the same favour, that before rewarded no desert, knowes now as well how to pardon all faults, then which indulgence, when I regard my selfe, I can wish no more; when I remember you, I can hope no lesse.*

So commending these few broken lines unto yours, and your selfe into the hands of the best Physitian, Jesus Christ, *with whome, the most ill affected man, in the midst of his sicknes, is in good health, and without whome, the most lustie bodie, in his greatest jollitie, is but a languishing karcase, I humbly take my leave, ending with the same wish, that your devoted Observer, and my approoved Friend doth, in his verses presently sequent, that your passage to heaven may be slow to us, that shall want you here, but to your selfe, that cannot want us there, most secure and certeyne.*

Your Worships, in all

dutie, and service

G. Fletcher.

Thomas Nevyle.
Most Heavenly.

AS when the Captaine of the heavenly host,
   Or else that glorious armie doth appeare
In waters drown'd, with surging billowes tost,
We know they are not, where we see they are;
   We see them in the deepe, we see them moove,
   We know they fixed are in heaven above:
So did the Sunne of righteousnesse come downe
Clowded in flesh, and seem'd be in the deepe:
So doe the many waters seeme to drowne
The starres his Saints, and they on earth to keepe,
   And yet this Sunne from heaven never fell,
   And yet these earthly starres in heaven dwell.
What if their soules be into prison cast
In earthly bodies? yet they long for heaven:
What if this wordly Sea they have not past?
Yet faine they would be brought into their haven.
   They are not here, and yet we here them see,
   For every man is there, where he would be.
Long may you wish, and yet long wish in vaine,
Hence to depart, and yet that wish obtaine.
Long may you here in heaven on earth remaine,
And yet a heaven in heaven hereafter gaine.
   Go you to heaven, but yet O make no hast,
   Go slowly slowly, but yet go at last.

      But when the Nightingale so neere doth sit,
      Silence the Titmouse better may befit.
                            F. Nethersole.

To the Reader.

THear are but fewe of many that can rightly judge of Poetry, and yet thear ar many of those few, that carry so left-handed an opinion of it, as some of them thinke it halfe sacrilege for prophane Poetrie to deale with divine and heavenly matters, as though *David* wear to be sentenced by them, for uttering his grave matter upon the harpe: others something more violent in their censure, but sure lesse reasonable (as though Poetrie corrupted all good witts, when, indeed, bad witts corrupt Poetrie) banish it with *Plato* out of all well-ordered Commonwealths. Both theas I will strive rather to satisfie, then refute.

And of the first I would gladlie knowe, whither they suppose it fitter, that the sacred songs in the Scripture of those heroicall Sainɔts, *Moses, Deborah, Jeremie, Mary, Simeon, David, Salomon*, (the wisest Scholeman, and wittiest Poet) should bee ejected from the canon, for wante of gravitie, or rather this erroure eraced out of their mindes, for wante of truth. But, it maye bee, they will give the Spirit of God leave to breath through what pipe it please, & will confesse, because they must needs, that all the songs dittied by him, must needs bee, as their Fountaine is, most holy: but their common clamour is, who may compare with God? true; & yet as none may compare without presumption, so all may imitat, and not without commendation: which made *Nazianzen*, on[e] of the Starrs of the Greeke Church, that nowe shines as bright in heaven, as he did then on earth, write so manie divine Poems of the Genealogie, Miracles, Parables, Passion of Christ, called by him his χριστὸς πάσχων, which when *Basil*, the Prince of the Fathers, and his Chamberfellowe, had seene, his opinion of them was, that he could have devised nothing either more

TO THE READER

fruitfull to others: because it kindely woed them to Religion, or more honourable to himselfe, οὐδὲν γὰρ μακαριώτερόν ἐστι τοῦ τὴν ἀγγέλων χορείαν ἐν γῇ μιμεῖσθαι, because by imitating the singing Angels in heav'n, himselfe became, though before his time, an earthly Angel. What should I speake of *Juvencus, Prosper*, & the wise *Prudentius*? the last of which living in *Hieroms* time, twelve hundred yeares agoe, brought foorth in his declining age, so many, & so religious poems, straitly charging his soule, not to let passe so much as one either night or daye without some divine song, *Hymnis continuet dies, Nec nox ulla vacet, quin Dominum canat.* And as sedulous *Prudentius*, so prudent *Sedulius* was famous in this poeticall divinity, the coetan of *Bernard*, who sung the historie of *Christ* with as much devotion in himself, as admiration to others; all which wear followed by the choicest witts of *Christendome*: *Nonnius* translating all Sainct *Johns* Gho[s]pel into Greek verse, *Sanazar*, the late-living Image, and happy imitator of *Virgil*, bestowing ten yeares upon a song, onely to celebrat that one day when Christ was borne unto us on earth, & we (a happie change) unto God in heav'n: thrice-honour'd *Bartas*, & our (I know no other name more glorious then his own) Mr. *Edmund Spencer* (two blessed Soules) not thinking ten years inough, layeing out their whole lives upon this one studie: Nay I may justly say, that the Princely Father of our Countrey (though in my conscience, God hath made him of all the learned Princes that ever wear the most religious, and of all the religious Princes, the most learned, that so, by the one, hee might oppose him against the Pope, the peste of all Religion, and by the other, against *Bellarmine* the abuser of all good Learning) is yet so far enamour'd with this celestiall Muse, that it shall never repent mee—*calamo trivisse labellum,* whensoever I shall remember *Hæc eadem ut sciret quid non faciebat Amyntas?* To name no more in such plenty, whear I may finde how to beginne, sooner then to end, Saincte Paule, by the Exāple of Christ, that wente singing to mounte Olivet, with his Disciples, after his last supper, exciteth the Christians to solace themselves with hymnes, and Psalmes, and spirituall songs; and thearefore, by their leav's, be it an error for *Poets* to be Divines, I had rather err with the Scripture, then be rectifi'd by them: I had rather adore the stepps of *Nazianzen*,

GILES FLETCHER

Prudentius, Sedulius, then followe their steps, to bee misguided: I had rather be the devoute Admirer of *Nonnius, Bartas,* my sacred Soveraign, and others, the miracles of our latter age, then the false sectarie of these, that have nothing at all to follow, but their own naked opinions: To conclude, I had rather with my Lord, and his most divine Apostle sing (though I sing sorilie) the love of heaven and earthe, then praise God (as they doe) with the woorthie guift of silence, and sitting still, or think I dispraisd him with this poetical discourse. It seems they have either not read, or clean forgot, that it is the dutie of the Muses (if wee maye beeleeue *Pindare,* and *Hesiod*) to set allwaies under the throne of *Jupiter, ejus & laudes, & beneficia* ὑμνειούσας, which made a very worthy German writer conclude it *Certò statuimus, proprium atq̃ peculiare poetarum munus esse, Christi gloriam illustrare,* beeing good reason that the heavenly infusion of such Poetry, should ende in his glorie, that had beginning from his goodnes, *fit orator, nascitur Poeta.*

For the secound sorte thearfore, that eliminat Poets out of their citie gates; as though they wear nowe grown so bad, as they could neither growe woorse, nor better, though it be somewhat hard for those to bee the onely men should want cities, that wear the onely causers of the building of them, and somewhat inhumane to thrust them into the woods, to live among the beasts, who wear the first that call'd men out of the woods, from their beastly, and wilde life, yet since they will needes shoulder them out for the onely firebrands to inflame lust (the fault of earthly men, not heavenly Poetrie) I would gladly learne, what kind of professions theas men would bee intreated to entertaine, that so deride and disaffect Poesie: would they admit of Philosophers, that after they have burnt out the whole candle of their life in the circular studie of Sciences, crie out at length, *Se nihil prorsus scire?* or should Musitians be welcome to them, that *Dant sine mente sonum—* bring delight with them indeede, could they aswell expresse with their instruments a voice, as they can a sound? or would they most approve of Soldiers that defend the life of their countrymen either by the death of themselves, or their enemies? If Philosophers please them, who is it, that knowes not, that all the lights of Example, to cleare their precepts, are borowed

TO THE READER

by Philosophers from Poets; that without *Homers* examples, *Aristotle* would be as blind as *Homer:* If they retaine Musitians, who ever doubted, but that Poets infused the verie soule into the inarticulate sounds of musique; that without *Pindar*, & *Horace* the Lyriques had beene silenced for ever: If they must needes entertaine Soldiers, who can but confesse, that Poets restore againe that life to soldiers, which they before lost for the safetie of their country; that without *Virgil*, *Æneas* had never beene so much as heard of. How then can they for shame deny commonwealths to them, who wear the first Authors of them; how can they denie the blinde Philosopher, that teaches them, his light; the emptie Musitian that delights them, his soule; the dying Soldier, that defends their life, immortalitie, after his owne death; let Philosophie, let *Ethiques*, let all the Arts bestowe upon us this guift, that we be not thought dead men, whilest we remaine among the living: it is onely Poetrie that can make us be thought living men, when we lie among the dead, and therefore I thinke it unequall to thrust them out of our cities, that call us out of our graves, to thinke so hardly of them, that make us to be so well thought of, to deny them to live a while among us, that make us live for ever among our Posteritie.

So beeing nowe weary in perswading those that hate, I commend my selfe to those that love such Poets, as *Plato* speakes of, that sing divine and heroical matters. οὐ γὰρ οὗτοι εἰσὶν, οἱ ταῦτα λέγοντες, ἀλλ' ὁ Θεὸς, αὐτός ἐστιν ὁ λέγων, recommending theas my idle howers, not idly spent, to good schollers, and good Christians, that have overcome their ignorance with reason, and their reason, with religion.

GILES FLETCHER

Fond ladds, that spend so fast your poasting time,
(Too poasting time, that spends your time as fast)
To chaunt light toyes, or frame some wanton rime,
Where idle boyes may glut their lustfull tast,
Or else with praise to cloath some fleshly slime
With virgins roses, and faire lillies chast:
   While itching bloods, and youthfull eares adore it,
But wiser men, and once your selves will most abhorre it.

But thou (most neere, most deare) in this of thine
Hast proov'd the Muses not to Venus bound,
Such as thy matter, such thy muse, divine.
Or thou such grace with Merci's selfe hast found,
That she her selfe deigns in thy leaves to shine:
Or stol'n from heav'n, thou brought['st] this verse to ground,
   Which frights the nummed soule with fearefull thunder,
And soone with honied dewes melts it twixt joy, and wonder.

Then doe not thou malitious tongues esteeme,
The glasse, through which an envious eye doth gaze,
Can easily make a molehill mountaines seeme;
His praise dispraises, his dispraises, praise.
Enough if best men best thy labours deem,
And to the highest pitch thy merit raise,
   While all the Muses to thy song decree
Victorious Triumph, Triumphant Victorie.

Phin. Fletcher Regal.

COMMENDATORY VERSES

Quid ô, quid *Veneres*, *Cupidines*q̃,
*Turtures*q̃, *iocos*q̃, *passeres*q̃
   Lascivi canitis greges, *poëtæ?*
Etiam languidulos amantum ocellos,
Et mox turgidulas sinu papillas,
*Jam risus teneros, lachrymulas*q̃,
*Mox suspiria, morsiunculas*q̃,
Mille basia ; mille, mille nugas?
Et vultus pueri, puellululæve
*(Heu fusci pueri, puellulæ*q̃*)*
*Pingitis nivibus, rosunculis*q̃,
*(Mentitis nivibus, rosunculis*q̃*)*
Quæ vel primo hyemis rigore torpent,
Vel Phæbi intuitu statim relanguent.
Heu stulti nimiùm greges poëtæ!
Ut, quas sic nimis, (ah!) nimis stupetis,
(Nives candidulæ & rosæ pudentes)
Sic vobis pereunt statim labores :
Et solem fugiunt severiorem,
Vel solem gelidâ rigent senectâ :
   At tu qui clypeo, haud inane nomen
*(Minervæ clypeo Jovis*q̃*) sumens*
Victrices resonas dei Triumphos,
*Triumphos lachrymis metu*q̃ *plenos,*
Plenos lætitiæ, & spei triumphos,
*Dum rem carmine, Piero*q̃ *dignam*
Aggrederis, tibi res decora rebus
*Præbet carmina, Piero*q̃ *digna.*
Quin ille ipse tuos legens triumphos,
Plenos militia, labore plenos,
Tuo propitius parat labori
Plenos lætitiæ, & spei triumphos.

Phin. Fletcher Regal.

GILES FLETCHER

Ἡ Μαριὰμ
Μὴ μιαρά.

BEatissima virginum Maria,
 Sed materq́ simul beata, per quam
Qui semper fuit ille cœpit esse:
Quæ Vitæ dederisq́ inire vitam:
Et Luci dederis videre lucem:
Quæ fastidia, morsiunculasq́
Passa es quas gravidæ solent, nec unquam
Audebas propior viro venire,
Dum clusus penetralibus latebat
Matricis tunicâ undiq́ involutus,
Quem se posse negant tenere cœli.
Quæ non virgineas premi papillas
Passa, virgineas tamen dedisti
Lactandas puero tuo papillas.
Eia, dic age, dic beata virgo,
Cur piam abstineas manum, timesq́
Sancta tangere, Sanctuariumq́
Insolens fugias? an inquinari
Contactu metuis tuo sacrata?
Contactu metuit suo sacrata
Polluipia, cernis (en!) ferentem,
Lenimenta Dei furentis, illa
Fœdatas sibi ferre quæ jubebat.
Sis felix nova virgo-mater opto,
Quæ mollire Deum paras amicum.
Quin hic dona licet licet reliquas,
Agnellumq́ repone, turturemq́,
Audax ingrediare inanis ædes
Dei, tange Deo sacrata, tange.
Quæ non concubitu coinquinata
Agnellum peperitq́, Turturemq́
Exclusit, facili Deo litabit
Agno cum Deus insit, & columbæ.

COMMENDATORY VERSES

Nor can I so much say as much I ought,
   Nor yet so little can I say as nought,
In praise of this thy worke, so heavenly pend,
That sure the sacred Dove a quill did lend
From her high-soaring wing: certes I know
No other plumes, that makes man seeme so low
In his owne eyes, who to all others sight
Is mounted to the highest pitch of height:
Where if thou seeme to any of small price,
The fault is not in thee, but in his eyes:
But what doe I thy flood of wit restreine
Within the narrow bankes of my poore veyne?
More I could say, and would, but that to praise
Thy verses, is to keepe them from their praise.
For them who reades, and doth them not advance,
Of envie doth it, or of ignorance.   *F. Nethersole.*

CHRISTS VICTORIE
in Heaven.

1

The Argument propounded in generall: Our redemption by Christ.

THe birth of him that no beginning knewe,
  Yet gives beginning to all that are borne,
And how the Infinite farre greater grewe,
By growing lesse, and how the rising Morne,
That shot from heav'n, did backe to heaven retourne,
  The obsequies of him that could not die,
  And death of life, ende of eternitie,
How worthily he died, that died unworthily;

2

How God, and Man did both embrace each other,
Met in one person, heav'n, and earth did kiss,
And how a Virgin did become a Mother,
And bare that Sonne, who the worlds Father is,
And Maker of his mother, and how Bliss
  Descended from the bosome of the High,
  To cloath himselfe in naked miserie,
Sayling at length to heav'n, in earth, triumphantly,

3

The Authors Invocation, for the better handling of it.

Is the first flame, wherewith my whiter Muse
Doth burne in heavenly love, such love to tell.
O thou that didst this holy fire infuse,
And taught'st this brest, but late the grave of hell,
Wherein a blind, and dead heart liv'd, to swell
  With better thoughts, send downe those lights that lend
  Knowledge, how to begin, and how to end
The love, that never was, nor ever can be pend.

The Nativity.
From an engraving by George Yate in *Christs Victorie and Triumph* (1640).

CHRISTS VICTORIE IN HEAVEN

4

Ye sacred writings in whose antique leaves
The memories of heav'n entreasur'd lie,
Say, what might be the cause that Mercie heaves
The dust of sinne above th' industrious skie;
And lets it not to dust, and ashes flie?
   Could Justice be of sinne so over-wooed,
   Or so great ill be cause of so great good,
That bloody man to save, mans Saviour shed his blood?

5

Or did the lips of Mercie droppe soft speech   *The Argument, Mans redemption, expounded from the cause. Mercie*
For traytrous man, when at th' Eternalls throne
Incensed Nemesis did heav'n beseech
With thundring voice, that justice might be showne
Against the Rebells, that from God were flowne;
   O say, say how could Mercie plead for those
   That scarcely made, against their Maker rose?
Will any slay his friend, that he may spare his foes?

6

There is a place beyond that flaming hill   *Dwelling in heaven*
From whence the starres their thin apparance shed,
A place, beyond all place, where never ill,
Nor impure thought was ever harboured,
But Sainctly Heroes are for ever s'ed
   To keepe an everlasting Sabbaoths rest,
   Still wishing that, of what th' ar still possest,
Enjoying but one joy, but one of all joyes best.

7

Here, when the ruine of that beauteous frame,   *And pleading for mā now guiltie,*
Whose golden building shin'd with everie starre
Of excellence, deform'd with age became,
MERCY, remembring peace in midst of warre,
Lift up the musique of her voice, to barre
   Eternall fate, least it should quite erace
   That from the world, which was the first worlds grace,
And all againe into their nothing, Chaos chase.

GILES FLETCHER

8

For what had all this All, which Man in one
Did not unite; the earth, aire, water, fire,
Life, sense, and spirit, nay the powrefull throne
Of the divinest Essence, did retire,
And his owne Image into clay inspire:
   So that this Creature well might called be
   Of the great world, the small epitomie,
Of the dead world, the live, and quicke anatomie.

9

with Justice, described

But Justice had no sooner Mercy seene
Smoothing the wrinkles of her Fathers browe,
But up she starts, and throwes her selfe betweene.
As when a vapour, from a moory slough,
Meeting with fresh Eous, that but now
   Open'd the world, which all in darkenesse lay,
   Doth heav'ns bright face of his rayes disaray,
And sads the smiling orient of the springing day.

10

by her qualities.

She was a Virgin of austere regard,
Not as the world esteemes her, deafe, and blind,
But as the Eagle, that hath oft compar'd
Her eye with heav'ns, so, and more brightly shin'd
Her lamping sight: for she the same could winde
   Into the solid heart, and with her eares,
   The silence of the thought loude speaking heares,
And in one hand a paire of even scoals she weares.

11

No riot of affection revell kept
Within her brest, but a still apathy
Possessed all her soule, which softly slept,
Securely, without tempest, no sad crie
Awakes her pittie, but wrong'd povertie,
   Sending his eyes to heav'n swimming in teares,
   With hideous clamours ever struck her eares,
Whetting the blazing sword, that in her hand she beares.

CHRISTS VICTORIE IN HEAVEN

12

The winged Lightning is her Mercury,   *Her Retinue.*
And round about her mightie thunders sound:
Impatient of himselfe lies pining by
Pale Sicknes, with his kercher'd head upwound,
And thousand noysome plagues attend her round,
   But if her clowdie browe but once growe foule,
   The flints doe melt, and rocks to water rowle,
And ayrie mountaines shake, and frighted shadowes howle.

13

Famine, and bloodles Care, and bloodie Warre,
Want, and the Want of knowledge how to use
Abundance, Age, and Feare, that runnes afarre
Before his fellowe Greefe, that aye pursues
His winged steps; for who would not refuse
   Greefes companie, a dull, and rawebon'd spright,
   That lankes the cheekes, and pales the freshest sight,
Unbosoming the cheerefull brest of all delight;

14

Before this cursed throng, goes Ignorance,
That needes will leade the way he cannot see:
And after all, Death doeth his flag advaunce,
And in the mid'st, Strife still would roaguing be,
Whose ragged flesh, and cloaths did well agree:
   And round about, amazed Horror flies,
   And over all, Shame veiles his guiltie eyes,
And underneth, Hells hungrie throat still yawning lies.

15

Upon two stonie tables, spread before her,   *Her Subject.*
She lean'd her bosome, more then stonie hard,
There slept th' unpartiall judge, and strict restorer
Of wrong, or right, with paine, or with reward,
There hung the skore of all our debts, the card
   Whear good, and bad, and life, and death were painted:
   Was never heart of mortall so untainted,
But when that scroule was read, with thousand terrors fainted.

GILES FLETCHER

16

Witnes the thunder that mount Sinai heard,
When all the hill with firie clouds did flame,
And wandring Israel, with the sight afeard,
Blinded with seeing, durst not touch the same,
But like a wood of shaking leaves became.
   On this dead Justice, she, the Living Lawe,
   Bowing herselfe with a majestique awe,
All heav'n, to heare her speech, did into silence drawe.

17

Her accusation of Mans sinne.
Dread Lord of Spirits, well thou did'st devise
To fling the worlds rude dunghill, and the drosse
Of the ould Chaos, farthest from the skies,
And thine owne seate, that heare the child of losse,
Of all the lower heav'n the curse, and crosse,
   That wretch, beast, caytive, monster Man, might spend,
   (Proude of the mire, in which his soule is pend)
Clodded in lumps of clay, his wearie life to end.

18

And 1. of Adams first sinne.
His bodie dust: whear grewe such cause of pride?
His soule thy Image: what could he enuie?
Himselfe most happie: if he so would bide:
Now grow'n most wretched, who can remedie?
He slewe himselfe, himselfe the enemie.
   That his owne soule would her owne murder wreake,
   If I were silent, heav'n and earth would speake,
And if all fayl'd, these stones would into clamours breake.

19

How many darts made furrowes in his side,
When she, that out of his owne side was made,
Gave feathers to their flight? whear was the pride
Of their newe knowledge; whither did it fade,
When, running from thy voice into the shade,
   He fled thy sight, himselfe of sight bereav'd;
   And for his shield a leavie armour weav'd,
With which, vain mā, he thought Gods eies to have deceav'd?

CHRISTS VICTORIE IN HEAVEN

20

And well he might delude those eyes, that see,
And judge by colours: for who ever sawe
A man of leaves, a reasonable tree?
But those that from this stocke their life did drawe,   Then of his
Soone made their Father godly, and by lawe   posterities,
   Proclaimed Trees almightie: Gods of wood,   of Idolatrie.
   Of stocks, and stones with crownes of laurell stood
Templed, and fed by fathers with their childrens blood.

21

The sparkling fanes, that burne in beaten gould,
And, like the starres of heav'n in mid'st of night,
Blacke Egypt, as her mirrhours, doth behould,
Are but the denns whear idoll-snakes delight
Againe to cover Satan from their sight:
   Yet these are all their gods, to whome they vie
   The Crocodile, the Cock, the Rat, the Flie.
Fit gods, indeede, for such men to be served by.

22

The Fire, the winde, the sea, the sunne, and moone,
The flitting Aire, and the swift-winged How'rs,
And all the watchmen, that so nimbly runne,
And centinel about the walled towers
Of the worlds citie, in their heav'nly bowr's.
   And, least their pleasant gods should want delight,
   Neptune spues out the Lady Aphrodite,
And but in heaven proude Junos peacocks skorne to lite.

23

The senselesse Earth, the Serpent, dog, and catte,
And woorse then all these, Man, and woorst of men
Usurping Jove, and swilling Bacchus fat,
And drunke with the vines purple blood, and then
The Fiend himselfe they conjure from his denne,
   Because he onely yet remain'd to be
   Woorse then the worst of men, they flie from thee,
And weare his altar-stones out with their pliant knee.

GILES FLETCHER

24

All that he speakes (and all he speakes are lies)
Are oracles, 'tis he (that wounded all)
Cures all their wounds, he (that put out their eyes)
That gives them light, he (that death first did call
Into the world) that with his orizall,
   Inspirits earth: he heav'ns al-seeing eye,
  He earths great Prophet, he, whom rest doth flie,
That on salt billowes doth, as pillowes, sleeping lie.

25

How hope-
lesse any
patronage
of [i]t.

But let him in his cabin restles rest,
The dungeon of darke flames, and freezing fire,
Justice in heav'n against man makes request
To God, and of his Angels doth require
Sinnes punishment: if what I did desire,
   Or who, or against whome, or why, or whear,
  Of, or before whom ignorant I wear,
Then should my speech their sands of sins to mountaines rear.

26

Wear not the heav'ns pure, in whose courts I sue,
The Judge, to whom I sue, just to requite him,
The cause for sinne, the punishment most due,
Justice her selfe the plaintiffe to endite him,
The Angells holy, before whom I cite him,
   He against whom, wicked, unjust, impure;
  Then might he sinnefull live, and die secure,
Or triall might escape, or triall might endure,

27

The Judge might partiall be, and over-pray'd,
The place appeald from, in whose courts he sues,
The fault excus'd, or punishment delayd,
The parties selfe accus'd, that did accuse,
Angels for pardon might their praiers use:
   But now no starre can shine, no hope be got.
  Most wretched creature, if he knewe his lot,
And yet more wretched farre, because he knowes it not.

CHRISTS VICTORIE IN HEAVEN

28

What should I tell how barren earth is growne,   All the
All for to sterve her children, didst not thou   Creatures
                                                               having
Water with heav'nly showers her wombe unsowne,   disleagued
                                                               themselves
And drop downe cloudes of flow'rs, didst not thou bowe   with him
Thine easie eare unto the plowmans vowe,
    Long might he looke, and looke, and long in vaine
    Might load his harvest in an emptie wayne,
And beat the woods, to finde the poore okes hungrie graine.

29

The swelling sea seethes in his angrie waves,
And smites the earth, that dares the traytors nourish,
Yet oft his thunder their light corke outbraves,
Mowing the mountaines, on whose temples flourish
Whole woods of garlands, and, their pride to cherish,
    Plowe through the seaes greene fields, and nets display
    To catch the flying winds, and steale away,
Coozning the greedie sea, prisning their nimble prey.

30

How often have I seene the waving pine,
Tost on a watrie mountaine, knocke his head
At heav'ns too patient gates, and with salt brine
Quench the Moones burning hornes, and safely fled
From heav'ns revenge, her passengers, all dead
    With stiffe astonishment, tumble to hell?
    How oft the sea all earth would overswell,
Did not thy sandie girdle binde the mightie well?

31

Would not the aire be fill'd with steames of death,
To poyson the quicke rivers of their blood,
Did not thy windes fan, with their panting breath,
The flitting region? would not the hastie flood
Emptie it selfe into the seas wide wood,
    Did'st not thou leade it wandring from his way,
    To give men drinke, and make his waters strey,
To fresh the flowrie medowes, through whose fields they play?

GILES FLETCHER

32

Who makes the sources of the silver fountaines
From the flints mouth, and rocky valleis slide,
Thickning the ayrie bowells of the mountaines?
Who hath the wilde heards of the forrest tide
In their cold denns, making them hungrie bide
    Till man to rest be laid? can beastly he,
    That should have most sense, onely senseles be,
And all things else, beside himselfe, so awefull see?

33

Wear he not wilder then the salvage beast,
Prowder then haughty hills, harder then rocks,
Colder then fountaines, from their springs releast,
Lighter then aire, blinder then senseles stocks,
More changing then the rivers curling locks,
    If reason would not, sense would soone reproove him,
    And unto shame, if not to sorrow, moove him,
To see cold floods, wild beasts, dul stocks, hard stones out-love him.

For his extreame ungratefulnes.

34

Under the weight of sinne the earth did fall,
And swallowed Dathan; and the raging winde,
And stormie sea, and gaping Whale, did call
For Jonas; and the aire did bullets finde,
And shot from heav'n a stony showre, to grinde
    The five proud Kings, that for their idols fought,
    The Sunne it selfe stood still to fight it out,
And fire frō heav'n flew downe, when sin to heav'n did shout.

35

Should any to himselfe for safety flie?
The way to save himselfe, if any were,
Wear to flie from himselfe: should he relie
Upon the promise of his wife? but there,
What can he see, but that he most may feare,
    A Syren, sweete to death: upon his friends?
    Who that he needs, or that he hath not lends?
Or wanting aide himselfe, ayde to another sends?

So that beeing destitute of all hope, or any remedie,

CHRISTS VICTORIE IN HEAVEN

36

His strength? but dust: his pleasure? cause of paine:
His hope? false courtier: youth, or beawtie? brittle:
Intreatie? fond: repentance? late, and vaine:
Just recompence? the world wear all too little:
Thy love? he hath no title to a tittle:
   Hells force? in vaine her furies hell shall gather:
   His Servants, Kinsmen, or his children rather?
His child, if good, shall judge, if bad, shall curse his father.

37

His life? that brings him to his end, and leaves him:
His ende? that leaves him to beginne his woe:
His goods? what good in that, that so deceaves him?
His gods of wood? their feete, alas, are slowe
To goe to helpe, that must be help't to goe:
   Honour, great woorth? ah, little woorth they be
   Unto their owners: wit? that makes him see
He wanted wit, that thought he had it, wanting thee.

38

The sea to drinke him quicke? that casts hi[m] dead:
Angells to spare? they punish: night to hide?
The world shall burne in light: the heav'ns to spread
Their wings to save him? heav'n it selfe shall slide,
And rowle away like melting starres, that glide
   Along their oylie threads: his minde pursues him:
   His house to shrowde, or hills to fall, and bruse him?
As Seargeants both attache, and witnesses accuse him:

39

What need I urge, what they must needs confesse?
Sentence on them, condemn'd by their owne lust;
I crave no more, and thou canst give no lesse,
Then death to dead men, justice to unjust;
Shame to most shamefull, and most shameles dust:
   But if thy Mercie needs will spare her friends,
   Let Mercie there begin, where Justice endes.
Tis cruell Mercie, that the wrong from right defends.

He can look for nothing, but a fearful sentence.

GILES FLETCHER

40

<small>The effect of Justice her speech: the inflammation of the heavenly Powers</small>
She ended, and the heav'nly Hierarchies,
Burning in zeale, thickly imbranded weare:
Like to an armie, that allarum cries,
And every one shakes his ydraded speare,
And the Almighties selfe, as he would teare
    The earth, and her firme basis quite in sunder,
    Flam'd all in just revenge, and mightie thunder,
Heav'n stole it selfe from earth by clouds that moisterd under.

41

<small>Appeased by Mercie, who is described by her cherfulnes to defend Man.</small>
As when the cheerfull Sunne, elamping wide,
Glads all the world with his uprising raye,
And wooes the widow'd earth afresh to pride,
And paint[s] her bosome with the flowrie Maye,
His silent sister steales him quite away,
    Wrap't in a sable clowde, from mortall eyes,
    The hastie starres at noone begin to rise,
And headlong to his early roost the sparrowe flies.

42

But soone as he againe dishadowed is,
Restoring the blind world his blemish't sight,
As though another day wear newely ris,
The cooz'ned birds busily take their flight,
And wonder at the shortnesse of the night:
    So Mercie once againe her selfe displayes,
    Out from her sisters cloud, and open layes   (dayes.
Those sunshine lookes, whose beames would dim a thousand

43

<small>Our inabilitie to describe her.</small>
How may a worme, that crawles along the dust,
Clamber the azure mountaines, thrown so high,
And fetch from thence thy faire Idea just,
That in those sunny courts doth hidden lie,
Cloath'd with such light, as blinds the Angels eye;
    How may weake mortall ever hope to file
    His unsmooth tongue, and his deprostrate stile?
O raise thou from his corse, thy now entomb'd exile.

CHRISTS VICTORIE IN HEAVEN

44

One touch would rouze me from my sluggish hearse,
One word would call me to my wished home,
One looke would polish my afflicted verse,
One thought would steale my soule from her thicke lome,
And force it wandring up to heav'n to come,
    Thear to importune, and to beg apace
    One happy favour of thy sacred grace,
To see, (what though it loose her eyes?) to see thy face.

45

If any aske why roses please the sight,   *Her beautie,*
Because their leaves upon thy cheekes doe bowre;   *resembled by the crea-*
If any aske why lillies are so white,   *tures, which are all fraile*
Because their blossoms in thy hand doe flowre: *shadows of her essentiall*
Or why sweet plants so gratefull odours shoure;   *perfection.*
    It is because thy breath so like they be:
    Or why the Orient Sunne so bright we see;
What reason can we give, but from thine eies, and thee?

46

Ros'd all in lively crimsin ar thy cheeks,
Whear beawties indeflourishing abide,
And, as to passe his fellowe either seekes,
Seemes both doe blush at one anothers pride:
And on thine eyelids, waiting thee beside,
    Ten thousand Graces sit, and when they moove   *Her*
    To earth their amourous belgards from above,   *Attendants.*
They flie from heav'n, and on their wings convey thy love.

47

All of discolour'd plumes their wings ar made,
And with so wondrous art the quills ar wrought,
That whensoere they cut the ayrie glade,
The winde into their hollowe pipes is caught:
As seemes the spheres with them they down have brought:
    Like to the seaven-fold reede of Arcadie,
    Which Pan of Syrinx made, when she did flie
To Ladon sands, and at his sighs sung merily.

GILES FLETCHER

48

Her perswasive power.

As melting hony, dropping from the combe,
So still the words, that spring between thy lipps,
Thy lippes, whear smiling sweetnesse keepes her home,
And heav'nly Eloquence pure manna sipps,
He that his pen but in that fountaine dipps,
 How nimbly will the golden phrases flie,
 And shed forth streames of choycest rhetorie,
Welling celestiall torrents out of poësie?

49

Like as the thirstie land, in summers heat,
Calls to the cloudes, and gapes at everie showre,
As though her hungry clifts all heav'n would eat,
Which if high God into her bosome powre,
Though much refresht, yet more she could devoure:
 So hang the greedie ears of Angels sweete,
 And every breath a thousand cupids meete,
Some flying in, some out, and all about her fleet.

50

Upon her breast, Delight doth softly sleepe,
And of eternall joy is brought abed,
Those snowie mountelets, through which doe creepe
The milkie rivers, that ar inly bred
In silver cesternes, and themselves doe shed
 To wearie Travailers, in heat of day,
 To quench their fierie th[ir]st, and to allay
With dropping nectar floods, the furie of their way.

51

Her kind offices to Man.

If any wander, thou doest call him backe,
If any be not forward, thou incit'st him,
Thou doest expect, if any should growe slacke,
If any seeme but willing, thou invit'st him,
Or if he doe offend thee, thou acquit'st him,
 Thou find'st the lost, and follow'st him that flies,
 Healing the sicke, and quickning him that dies,
Thou art the lame mans friendly staffe, the blind mans eyes.

CHRISTS VICTORIE IN HEAVEN

52
So faire thou art that all would thee behold,
But none can thee behold, thou art so faire,
Pardon, O pardon then thy Vassall bold,
That with poore shadowes strives thee to compare,
And match the things, which he knowes matchlesse are;
   O thou vive mirrhour of celestiall grace,
     How can fraile colours pourtraict out thy face,
Or paint in flesh thy beawtie, in such semblance base?

53
Her upper garment was a silken lawne,   *Her Garments,*
With needle-woorke richly embroidered,   *wrought by*
Which she her selfe with her owne hand had drawne,   *her owne hands, wher-*
And all the world therein had pourtrayed,   *with shee cloaths her*
With threads, so fresh, and lively coloured,   *selfe, com-*
   That seem'd the world she newe created thear,   *pos'd of all*
     And the mistaken eye would rashly swear   *the Crea-*
The silken trees did growe, and the beasts living wear.   *tures,*

54
Low at her feet the Earth was cast alone,   *The Earth,*
(As though to kisse her foot it did aspire,
And gave it selfe for her to tread upon)
With so unlike, and different attire,
That every one that sawe it, did admire
   What it might be, was of so various hewe;
     For to it selfe it oft so diverse grewe,
That still it seem'd the same, and still it seem'd a newe.

55
And here, and there few men she scattered,
(That in their thought the world esteeme but small,
And themselves great) but she with one fine thread
So short, and small, and slender wove them all,
That like a sort of busie ants, that crawle
   About some molehill, so they wandered:
     And round about the waving Sea was shed,   *Sea,*
But, for the silver sands, small pearls were sprinkled.

GILES FLETCHER

56

So curiously the underworke did creepe,
And curling circlets so well shadowed lay,
That afar off the waters seem'd to sleepe,
But those that neere the margin pearle did play,
Hoarcely enwaved wear with hastie sway,
   As though they meant to rocke the gentle eare,
   And hush the former that enslumbred wear,
And here a dangerous rocke the flying ships did fear.

57

Ayre, High in the ayrie element there hung
Another clowdy sea, that did disdaine
(As though his purer waves from heaven sprung)
To crawle on earth, as doth the sluggish maine:
But it the earth would water with his raine,
   That eb'd, and flow'd, as winde, and season would,
   And oft the Sun would cleave the limber mould
To alabaster rockes, that in the liquid rowl'd.

58

Beneath those sunny banks, a darker cloud,
Dropping with thicker deaw, did melt apace,
And bent it selfe into a hollowe shroude,
On which, if Mercy did but cast her face,
A thousand colours did the bowe enchace,
   That wonder was to see the silke distain'd
   With the resplendance from her beawtie gain'd,
And Iris paint her locks with beames, so lively feign'd.

59

The celestiall bodies, About her head a cyprus heav'n she wore,
Spread like a veile, upheld with silver wire,
In which the starres so burn't in golden ore,
As seem'd, the azure web was all on fire,
But hastily, to quench their sparkling ire,
   A flood of milke came rowling up the shore,
   That on his curded wave swift Argus bore,
And the immortall swan, that did her life deplore.

CHRISTS VICTORIE IN HEAVEN

60

Yet strange it was, so many starres to see
Without a Sunne, to give their tapers light:
Yet strange it was not, that it so should be:
For, where the Sunne centers himselfe by right,
Her face, and locks did flame, that at the sight,
   The heavenly veile, that else should nimbly moove,
   Forgot his flight, and all incens'd with love,
With wonder, and amazement, did her beautie proove.

61

Over her hung a canopie of state,   *The third heaven.*
Not of rich tissew, nor of spangled gold,
But of a substance, though not animate,
Yet of a heav'nly, and spirituall mould,
That onely eyes of Spirits might behold:
   Such light as from maine rocks of diamound,
   Shooting their sparks at Phebus, would rebound,
And little Angels, holding hands, daunc't all around.

62

Seemed those little sprights, through nimbless bold,
The stately canopy bore on their wings,
But them it selfe, as pendants, did uphold,
Besides the crownes of many famous kings,
Among the rest, thear David ever sings,
   And now, with yeares growne young, renewes his layes
   Unto his golden harpe, and ditties playes,
Psalming aloud in well tun'd songs his Makers prayse.

63

Thou self-Idea of all joyes to come,
Whose love is such, would make the rudest speake,
Whose love is such, would make the wisest dumbe,
O when wilt thou thy too long silence breake,
And overcome the strong to save the weake!
   If thou no weapons hast, thine eyes will wound
   Th' Almighties selfe, that now sticke on the ground,
As though some blessed object thear did them empound.   *Her Objects.*

GILES FLETCHER

64

Repentance.
    Ah miserable Abject of disgrace,
    What happines is in thy miserie?
    I both must pittie, and envie thy case.
    For she, that is the glorie of the skie,
    Leaves heaven blind, to fix on thee her eye.
        Yet her (though Mercies selfe esteems not small)
        The world despis['d], they her Repentance call,
    And she her selfe despises, and the world, and all.

65

Deepely, alas empassioned she stood,
To see a flaming brand, tost up from hell,
Boyling her heart in her owne lustfull blood,
That oft for torment she would loudely yell,
Now she would sighing sit, and nowe she fell
    Crouching upon the ground, in sackcloath trust,
    Early, and late she prayed, and fast she must,
And all her haire hung full of ashes, and of dust.

66

Of all most hated, yet hated most of all
Of her owne selfe she was; disconsolat
(As though her flesh did but infunerall
Her buried ghost) she in an arbour sat
Of thornie brier, weeping her cursed state,
    And her before a hastie river fled,
    Which her blind eyes with faithfull penance fed,
And all about, the grasse with tears hung downe his head.

67

Her eyes, though blind abroad, at home kept fast,
Inwards they turn'd, and look't into her head,
At which shee often started, as aghast,
To see so fearfull spectacles of dread,
And with one hand, her breast shee martyred,
    Wounding her heart, the same to mortifie,
Faith.
    The other a faire damsell held her by,
Which if but once let goe, shee sunke immediatly.

CHRISTS VICTORIE IN HEAVEN

68

But Faith was quicke, and nimble as the heav'n,
As if of love, and life shee all had been,
And though of present sight her sense were reaven,
Yet shee could see the things could not be seen:
Beyond the starres, as nothing wear between,
  She fixt her sight, disdeigning things belowe,
  Into the sea she could a mountaine throwe,
And make the Sun to stande, and waters backewards flowe.

69

Such when as Mercie her beheld from high,
In a darke valley, drownd with her owne tears,
One of her graces she sent hastily,
Smiling Eirene, that a garland wears
Of guilded olive, on her fairer hears,
  To crowne the fainting soules true sacrifice,
  Whom when as sad Repentance comming spies,
The holy Desperado wip't her swollen eyes.

70

But Mercie felt a kinde remorse to runne   *Her deprecative speech for Man, in which*
Through her soft vaines, and therefore, hying fast
To give an end to silence, thus begunne.
Aye-honour'd Father, if no joy thou hast
But to reward desert, reward at last
  The Devils voice, spoke with a serpents tongue,
  Fit to hisse out the words so deadly stung,
And let him die, deaths bitter charmes so sweetely sung.

71

He was the father of that hopeles season,   *She trāslates the principal fault unto the Devill.*
That to serve other Gods, forgot their owne,
The reason was, thou wast above their reason:
They would have any Gods, rather then none,
A beastly serpent, or a senselesse stone:
  And these, as Justice hates, so I deplore:
  But the up-plowed heart, all rent, and tore,
Though wounded by it selfe, I gladly would restore.

GILES FLETCHER

72

<small>And repeating Justice her aggravation of mans sinne,</small>

He was but dust; Why fear'd he not to fall?
And beeing fall'n, how can he hope to live?
Cannot the hand destroy him, that made all?
Could he not take away, aswell as give?
Should man deprave, and should not God deprive?
   Was it not all the worlds deceiving spirit,
   (That, bladder'd up with pride of his owne merit,
Fell in his rise) that him of heav'n did disinherit?

73

<small>Mittigates it 1. by a cōtrarie inference.</small>

He was but dust: how could he stand before him?
And beeing fall'n, why should he feare to die?
Cannot the hand that made him first, restore him?
Deprav'd of sinne, should he deprived lie
Of grace? can he not hide infirmitie
   That gave him strength? unworthy the forsaking,
   He is, who ever weighs, without mistaking,
Or Maker of the man, or manner of his making.

74

Who shall thy temple incense any more;
Or to thy altar crowne the sacrifice;
Or strewe with idle flow'rs the hallow'd flore;
Or what should Prayer deck with hearbs, and spice,
Her vialls, breathing orisons of price?

<small>2. By interessing her selfe in the cause, and Christ.</small>

   If all must paie that which all cannot paie?
   O first begin with mee, and Mercie slaie,
And thy thrice-honour'd Sonne, that now beneath doth strey.

75

But if or he, or I may live, and speake,
And heav'n can joye to see a sinner weepe,
Oh let not Justice yron scepter breake
A heart alreadie broke, that lowe doth creep,
And with prone humblesse her feets dust doth sweep.
   Must all goe by desert? is nothing free?
   Ah, if but those that onely woorthy be,
None should thee ever see, none should thee ever see.

CHRISTS VICTORIE IN HEAVEN

76

What hath man done, that man shall not undoe,   *That is as*
Since God to him is growne so neere a kin?   *sufficient to*
Did his foe slay him? he shall slay his foe: *satisfie, as*
Hath he lost all? he all againe shall win;   *Man was impotent.*
Is Sinne his Master? he shall master sinne:
  Too hardy soule, with sinne the field to trie:
  The onely way to conquer, was to flie,
But thus long death hath liv'd, and now deaths selfe shall die.

77

He is a path, if any be misled,
He is a robe, if any naked bee,
If any chaunce to hunger, he is bread,
If any be a bondman, he is free,
If any be but weake, howe strong is hee?
  To dead men life he is, to sicke men health,
  To blinde men sight, and to the needie wealth,
A pleasure without losse, a treasure without stealth.

78

Who can forget, never to be forgot,   *Whom shee*
The time, that all the world in slumber lies,   *celebrates*
When, like the starres, the singing Angels shot   *from the*
To earth, and heav'n awaked all his eyes,   *time of his*
To see another Sunne, at midnight rise,   *nativitie.*
  On ear[t]h? was never sight of pareil fame,
  For God before Man like himselfe did frame,
But God himselfe now like a mortall man became.

79

A Child he was, and had not learn't to speake,   *From the*
That with his word the world before did make,   *effects of it*
His Mothers armes him bore, he was so weake,   *in himselfe.*
That with one hand the vaults of heav'n could shake,
See how small roome my infant Lord doth take,
  Whom all the world is not enough to hold.
  Who of his yeares, or of his age hath told?
Never such age so young, never a child so old.

GILES FLETCHER

80

And yet but newely he was infanted,
And yet alreadie he was sought to die,
Yet scarcely borne, alreadie banished,
Not able yet to goe, and forc't to flie,
But scarcely fled away, when by and by,
   The Tyrans sword with blood is all defil'd,
   And Rachel, for her sonnes with furie wild,
Cries, O thou cruell King, and O my sweetest child.

81

Egypt, Egypt his Nource became, whear Nilus springs,
Who streit, to entertaine the rising sunne,
The hasty harvest in his bosome brings;
But now for drieth the fields wear all undone,
And now with waters all is overrunne,
   So fast the Cynthian mountaines powr'd their snowe,
   When once they felt the sunne so neere them glowe,
That Nilus Egypt lost, and to a sea did growe.

82

The Angels, The Angells caroll'd lowd their song of peace,
The cursed Oracles wear strucken dumb,
Men. To see their Sheapheard, the poore Sheapheards press,
To see their King, the Kingly Sophies come,
And them to guide unto his Masters home,
   A Starre comes dauncing up the orient,
   That springs for joye over the strawy tent,
Whear gold, to make their Prince a crowne, they all present.

83

Young John, glad child, before he could be borne,
Leapt in the woombe, his joy to prophecie,
Old Anna though with age all spent, and worne,
Proclaimes her Saviour to posteritie,
And Simeon fast his dying notes doeth plie.
   Oh how the blessed soules about him trace.
   It is the fire of heav'n thou doest embrace,
Sing, Simeon, sing, sing Simeon, sing apace.

CHRISTS VICTORIE IN HEAVEN

84

With that the mightie thunder dropt away
From Gods unwarie arme, now milder growne,
And melted into teares, as if to pray
For pardon, and for pittie, it had knowne,
That should have been for sacred vengeance throwne:
   Thereto the Armies Angelique dev[ow'd]
   Their former rage, and all to Mercie b[ow'd],
Their broken weapons at her feet they gladly strow'd.

The effect of Mercies speech.

85

Bring, bring ye Graces all your silver flaskets,
Painted with every choicest flowre that growes,
That I may soone unflow'r your fragrant baskets,
To strowe the fields with odours whear he goes,
Let what so e're he treads on be a rose.
   So downe shee let her eyelids fall, to shine
   Upon the rivers of bright Palestine,
Whose woods drop honie, and her rivers skip with wine.

A Transition to Christs second victorie.

CHRISTS VICTORIE

on Earth.

1

<small>Christ brought into the place of combat, the wildernes, among the wilde beasts. Mark 1. 13.</small>

THear all alone she spi'd, alas the while;
   In shadie darknes a poore Desolate,
That now had measur'd many a wearie mile,
Through a wast desert, whither heav'nly fate,
And his owne will him brought; he praying sate,
    And him to prey, as he to pray began,
    The Citizens of the wilde forrest ran,
And all with open throat would swallowe whole the man.

2

<small>Described by his proper Attribute, The Mercie of God.</small>

Soone did the Ladie to her Graces crie,
And on their wings her selfe did nimbly strowe,
After her coach a thousand Loves did flie,
So downe into the wildernesse they throwe,
Whear she, and all her trayne that with her flowe
    Thorough the ayrie wave, with sayles so gay,
    Sinking into his brest that wearie lay,
Made shipwracke of themselves, and vanish't quite away.

3

Seemed that Man had them devoured all,
Whome to devoure the beasts did make pretence,
But him their salvage thirst did nought appall,
Though weapons none he had for his defence:
What armes for Innocence, but Innocence?
    For when they saw their Lords bright cognizance
    Shine in his face, soone did they disadvaunce,
And some unto him kneele, and some about him daunce.

CHRISTS VICTORIE ON EARTH

4

Downe fell the Lordly Lions angrie mood, *Whom the*
And he himselfe fell downe, in congies lowe; *creatures*
Bidding him welcome to his wastfull wood, *cannot but*
Sometime he kist the grasse whear he did goe, *adore.*
And, as to wash his feete he well did knowe,
   With fauning tongue he lickt away the dust,
   And every one would neerest to him thrust,
And every one, with new, forgot his former lust.

5

Unmindfull of himselfe, to minde his Lord,
The Lamb stood gazing by the Tygers side,
As though betweene them they had made accord,
And on the Lions back the goate did ride,
Forgetfull of the roughnes of the hide,
   If he stood still, their eyes upon him bayted,
   If walk't, they all in order on him wayted,
And when he slep't, they as his watch themselves conceited.

6

Wonder doeth call me up to see, O no, *By his unitie*
I cannot see, and therefore sinke in woonder, *with the*
The man, that shines as bright as God, not so, *Godhead.*
For God he is himselfe, that close lies under
That man, so close, that no time can dissunder
   That band, yet not so close, but from him breake
   Such beames, as mortall eyes are all too weake
Such sight to see, or it, if they should see, to speake.

7

Upon a grassie hillock he was laid, *His proper*
With woodie primroses befreckeled, *place.*
Over his head the wanton shadowes plaid
Of a wilde olive, that her bowgh's so spread,
As with her leav's she seem'd to crowne his head,
   And her greene armes [t'] embrace the Prince of peace,
   The Sunne so neere, needs must the winter cease,
The Sunne so neere, another Spring seem'd to increase.

GILES FLETCHER

8

<small>The beutie of his bodie.
Cant. 5. 11.
Psalm 45. 2.</small>

His haire was blacke, and in small curls did twine,
As though it wear the shadowe of some light,
And underneath his face, as day, did shine,
But sure the day shined not halfe so bright,
Nor the Sunnes shadowe made so darke a night.
    Under his lovely locks, her head to shroude,
    Did make Humilitie her selfe growe proude,
Hither, to light their lamps, did all the Graces croude.

9

One of ten thousand soules I am, and more,
That of his eyes, and their sweete wounds complaine,
Sweete are the wounds of love, never so sore,
Ah might he often slaie mee so againe.
He never lives, that thus is never slaine.
    What boots it watch? those eyes, for all my art,
    Mine owne eyes looking on, have stole my heart,
In them Love bends his bowe, and dips his burning dart.

10

As when the Sunne, caught in an adverse clowde,
Flies crosse the world, and thear a new begets,
The watry picture of his beautie proude,
Throwes all abroad his sparkling spangelets,
And the whole world in dire amazement sets,
    To see two dayes abroad at once, and all
    Doubt whither nowe he rise, or nowe will fall:
So flam'd the Godly flesh, proude of his heav'nly thrall.

11

<small>Gen. 49. 12.
Cant. 5. 10.</small>

His cheekes as snowie apples, sop't in wine,
Had their red roses quencht with lillies white,
And like to garden strawberries did shine,
Wash't in a bowle of milke, or rose-buds bright
Unbosoming their brests against the light:
    Here love-sicke soules did eat, thear dranke, and made
    Sweete-smelling posies, that could never fade,
<small>Isa. 53. 2.</small> But worldly eyes him thought more like some living shade.

CHRISTS VICTORIE ON EARTH

12

For laughter never look't upon his browe,
Though in his face all smiling joyes did bide,
No silken banners did about him flowe,
Fooles make their fetters ensignes of their pride:
He was best cloath'd when naked was his side,
   A Lambe he was, and wollen fleece he bore,
   Wove with one thread, his feete lowe sandalls wore,
But bared were his legges, so went the times of yore.

13

As two white marble pillars that uphold
Gods holy place whear he in glorie sets,
And rise with goodly grace and courage bold,
To beare his Temple on their ample jetts,
Vein'd every whear with azure rivulets,
   Whom all the people on some holy morne,
   With boughs and flowrie garlands doe adorne,
Of such, though fairer farre, this Temple was upborne.

14

Twice had Diana bent her golden bowe,   *By preparing himself to the combate*
And shot from heav'n her silver shafts, to rouse
The sluggish salvages, that den belowe,
And all the day in lazie covert drouze,
Since him the silent wildernesse did house,
   The heav'n his roofe, and arbour harbour was,
   The ground his bed, and his moist pillowe grasse.
But fruit thear none did growe, nor rivers none did passe.

15

At length an aged Syre farre off he sawe   *With his Adversarie, that seemd what he was not,*
Come slowely footing, everie step he guest
One of his feete he from the grave did drawe,
Three legges he had, the woodden was the best,
And all the waie he went, he ever blest
   With benedicities, and prayers store,
   But the bad ground was blessed ne'r the more,
And all his head with snowe of Age was waxen hore.

GILES FLETCHER

16

<small>Some devout Essene.</small> A good old Hermit he might seeme to be,
That for devotion had the world forsaken,
And now was travailing some Saint to see,
Since to his beads he had himselfe betaken,
Whear all his former sinnes he might awaken,
   And them might wash away with dropping brine,
   And almes, and fasts, and churches discipline,
And dead, might rest his bones under the holy shrine.

17

But when he neerer came, he lowted lowe
With prone obeysance, and with curt'sie kinde,
That at his feete his head he seemd to throwe;
What needs him now another Saint to finde?
Affections are the sailes, and faith the wind,
   That to this Saint a thousand soules conveigh
   Each hour': O happy Pilgrims thither strey!
What caren they for beasts, or for the wearie way?

18

Soone the old Palmer his devotions sung,
Like pleasing anthems, moduled in time,
For well that aged Syre could tip his tongue
With golden foyle of eloquence, and lime,
And licke his rugged speech with phrases prime.
   Ay me, quoth he, how many yeares have beene,
   Since these old eyes the Sunne of heav'n have seene!
Certes the Sonne of heav'n they now behold I weene.

19

Ah, mote my humble cell so blessed be
As heav'n to welcome in his lowely roofe,
And be the Temple for thy deitie!
Loe how my cottage worships thee aloofe,
That under ground hath hid his head, in proofe
   It doth adore thee with the feeling lowe,
   Here honie, milke, and chesnuts wild doe growe,
The boughs a bed of leaves upon thee shall bestowe.

The Temptation in the Wilderness.
From an engraving by George Yate in *Christs Victorie and Triumph* (1640).

CHRISTS VICTORIE ON EARTH

20

But oh, he said, and therewith sigh't full deepe,
The heav'ns, alas, too envious are growne,
Because our fields thy presence from them keepe;
For stones doe growe, where corne was lately sowne:
(So stooping downe, he gather'd up a stone)
   But thou with corne canst make this stone to eare.
   What needen we the angrie heav'ns to feare?
Let them envie us still, so we enjoy thee here.

(Closely tempting him to despaire of Gods providence, and provide for himselfe.)

21

Thus on they wandred, but those holy weeds
A monstrous Serpent, and no man did cover.
So under greenest hearbs the Adder feeds:
And round about that stinking corps did hover
The dismall Prince of gloomie night, and over
   His ever-damned head the Shadowes err'd
   Of thousand peccant ghosts, unseene, unheard,
And all the Tyrant feares, and all the Tyrant fear'd.

But was what he seemed not, Satan, & would faine have lead him

22

He was the Sonne of blackest Acheron,
Whear many frozen soules doe chattring lie,
And rul'd the burning waves of Phlegethon,
Whear many more in flaming sulphur frie,
At once compel'd to live and forc't to die,
   Whear nothing can be heard for the loud crie
   Of oh, and ah, and out alas that I
Or once againe might live, or once at length might die.

23

Ere long they came neere to a balefull bowre,
Much like the mouth of that infernall cave,
That gaping stood all Commers to devoure,
Darke, dolefull, dreary, like a greedy grave,
That still for carrion carkasses doth crave.
   The ground no hearbs, but venomous did beare,
   Nor ragged trees did leave, but every whear
Dead bones, and skulls wear cast, and bodies hanged wear.

1. To Desperation, charaĉterd by his place,

GILES FLETCHER

24

Upon the roofe the bird of sorrowe sat
Elonging joyfull day with her sad note,
And through the shady aire, the fluttring bat
Did wave her leather sayles, and blindely flote,
While with her wings the fatall S[c]reechowle smote
   Th' unblessed house, thear, on a craggy stone,
   Celeno hung, and made his direfull mone,
And all about the murdered ghosts did shreek, and grone.

25

Countenance, Apparell, horrible apparitions, &c.

Like clowdie moonshine, in some shadowie grove,
Such was the light in which DESPAIRE did dwell,
But he himselfe with night for darkenesse strove.
His blacke uncombed locks dishevell'd fell
About his face, through which, as brands of hell,
   Sunk in his skull, his staring eyes did glowe,
   That made him deadly looke, their glimpse did showe
Like Cockatrices eyes, that sparks of poyson throwe.

26

His cloaths wear ragged clouts, with thornes pind fast,
And as he musing lay, to stonie fright
A thousand wilde Chimera's would him cast:
As when a fearefull dreame, in mid'st of night,
Skips to the braine, and phansies to the sight
   Some winged furie, strait the hasty foot,
   Eger to flie, cannot plucke up his root,
The voyce dies in the tongue, and mouth gapes without boot.

27

Now he would dreame that he from heaven fell,
And then would snatch the ayre, afraid to fall;
And now he thought he sinking was to hell,
And then would grasp the earth, and now his stall
Him seemed hell, and then he out would crawle,
   And ever, as he crept, would squint aside,
   Lest him, perhaps, some Furie had espide,
And then, alas, he should in chaines for ever bide.

CHRISTS VICTORIE ON EARTH

28

Therefore he softly shrunke, and stole away,
Ne ever durst to drawe his breath for feare,
Till to the doore he came, and thear he lay
Panting for breath, as though he dying were,
And still he thought, he felt their craples teare
   Him by the heels backe to his ougly denne,
   Out faine he would have leapt abroad, but then
The heav'n, as hell, he fear'd, that punish guilty men.

29

Within the gloomie hole of this pale wight
The Serpent woo'd him with his charmes to inne,
Thear he might baite the day, and rest the night,
But under that same baite a fearefull grin
Was readie to intangle him in sinne.
   But he upon ambrosia daily fed,
   That grew in Eden, thus he answered,
So both away wear caught, and to the Temple fled.

30

Well knewe our Saviour this the Serpent was,
And the old Serpent knewe our Saviour well,
Never did any this in falshood passe,
Never did any him in truth excell:
With him we fly to heav'n, from heav'n we fell
   With him: but nowe they both together met
   Upon the sacred pinnacles, that threat
With their aspiring tops, Astræas starrie seat.

31

Here did PRESUMPTION her pavillion spread,   *2. To Presumption, characterd by her place,*
Over the Temple, the bright starres among,
(Ah that her foot should trample on the head
Of that most reverend place!) and a lewd throng
Of wanton boyes sung her a pleasant song   *Attendants, &c.*
   Of love, long life, of mercie, and of grace,
   And every one her deerely did embrace,
And she herselfe enamour'd was of her owne face.

GILES FLETCHER

32

A painted face, belied with vermeyl store,
Which light Eüëlpis every day did trimme,
That in one hand a guilded anchor wore,
Not fixed on the rocke, but on the brimme
Of the wide aire she let it loosely swimme:
   Her other hand a sprinkle carried,
   And ever, when her Ladie wavered,
Court-holy water all upon her sprinkeled.

33

Poore foole, she thought herselfe in wondrous price
With God, as if in Paradise she wear,
But, wear shee not in a fooles paradise,
She might have seene more reason to despere:
But him she, like some ghastly fiend, did feare,
   And therefore as that wretch hew'd out his cell
   Under the bowels, in the heart of hell,
So she above the Moone, amid the starres would dwell.

34

Her Tent with sunny cloudes was seel'd aloft,
And so exceeding shone with a false light,
That heav'n it selfe to her it seemed oft,
Heav'n without cloudes to her deluded sight,
But cloudes withouten heav'n it was aright,
   And as her house was built, so did her braine
   Build castles in the aire, with idle paine,
But heart she never had in all her body vaine.

35

Like as a ship, in which no ballance lies,
Without a Pilot, on the sleeping waves,
Fairely along with winde, and water flies,
And painted masts with silken sayles embraves,
That Neptune selfe the bragging vessell saves,
   To laugh a while at her so proud aray;
   Her waving streamers loosely shee lets play,
And flagging colours shine as bright as smiling day:

CHRISTS VICTORIE ON EARTH

36

But all so soone as heav'n his browes doth bend,
Shee veils her banners, and pulls in her beames,
The emptie barke the raging billows send
Up to th' Olympique waves, and Argus seemes
Againe to ride upon our lower streames:
    Right so PRESUMPTION did her selfe behave,
    Tossed about with every stormie wave,
And in white lawne shee went, most like an Angel brave.

37

Gently our Saviour shee began to shrive,   *And by her Temptation.*
Whither he wear the Sonne of God, or no;
For any other shee disdeign'd to wive:
And if he wear, shee bid him fearles throw
Himselfe to ground, and thearwithall did show
    A flight of little Angels, that did wait
    Upon their glittering wings, to latch him strait,
And longed on their backs to feele his glorious weight.

38

But when she saw her speech prevailed nought,
Her selfe she tombled headlong to the flore:
But him the Angels on their feathers caught,
And to an ayrie mountaine nimbly bore,
Whose snowie shoulders, like some chaulkie shore,
    Restles Olympus seem'd to rest upon
    With all his swimming globes: so both are gone,
The Dragon with the Lamb. Ah, unmeet Paragon.   *3. To Vaine-Glorie.*

39

All suddenly the hill his snowe devours,   *Poetically described from the place where her court stood, A garden.*
In liew whereof a goodly garden grew,
As if the snow had melted into flow'rs,
Which their sweet breath in subtill vapours threw,
That all about perfumed spirits flew.
    For what so ever might aggrate the sense,
    In all the world, or please the appetence,
Heer it was powred out in lavish affluence.

GILES FLETCHER

40

Not lovely Ida might with this compare,
Though many streames his banks besilvered,
Though Xanthus with his golden sands he bare,
Nor Hibla, though his thyme depastured,
As fast againe with honie blossomed.
   Ne Rhodope, ne Tempes flowrie playne,
   Adonis garden was to this but vayne,
Though Plato on his beds a flood of praise did rayne.

41

For in all these, some one thing most did grow,
But in this one, grew all things els beside,
For sweet varietie herselfe did throw
To every banke, here all the ground she dide
In lillie white, there pinks eblazed wide;
   And damask't all the earth, and here shee shed
   Blew violets, and there came roses red,
And every sight the yeelding sense, as captive led.

42

The garden like a Ladie faire was cut,
That lay as if shee slumber'd in delight,
And to the open skies her eyes did shut;
The azure fields of heav'n wear sembled right
In a large round, set with the flo[w'r]s of light,
   The flo[w'r]s-de-luce, and the round sparks of deaw,
   That hung upon their azure leaves, did shew
Like twinkling starrs, that sparkle in th[e] eav'ning blew.

43

Upon a hillie banke her head shee cast,
On which the bowre of Vaine-Delight was built,
White, and red roses for her face wear plac't,
And for her tresses Marigolds wear spilt:
Them broadly shee displaid, like flaming guilt,
   Till in the ocean the glad day wear drown'd,
   Then up againe her yellow locks she wound,
And with greene fillets in their prettie calls them bound.

CHRISTS VICTORIE ON EARTH

44

What should I here depeint her lillie hand,
Her veines of violets, her ermine brest,
Which thear in orient colours living stand,
Or how her gowne with silken leaves is drest;
Or how her watchmen, arm'd with boughie crest,
   A wall of prim hid in his bushes bears,
   Shaking at every winde their leavie spears,
While she supinely sleeps, ne to be waked fears?

45

Over the hedge depends the graping Elme,
Whose greener head, empurpuled in wine,
Seemed to wonder at his bloodie helme,
And halfe suspect the bunches of the vine,
Least they, perhaps, his wit should undermine.
   For well he knewe such fruit he never bore:
   But her weake armes embraced him the more,
And with her ruby grapes laught at her paramour.

46

Under the shadowe of these drunken elmes
A Fountaine rose, where Pangloretta uses,
(When her some flood of fancie overwhelms,
And one of all her favourites she chuses)
To bath herselfe, whom she in lust abuses,
   And from his wanton body sucks his soule,
   Which drown'd in pleasure, in that shaly bowle,
And swimming in delight, doth am[o]rously rowle.

47

The font of silver was, and so his showrs
In silver fell, onely the guilded bowles
(Like to a fornace, that the min'rall powres)
Seem'd to have moul't it in their shining holes:
And on the water, like to burning coles,
   On liquid silver, leaves of roses lay:
   But when PANGLORIE here did list to play,
Rose water then it ranne, and milke it rain'd they say.

GILES FLETCHER

48

The roofe thicke cloudes did paint, from which three boyes
Three gaping mermaides with their eawrs did feede,
Whose brests let fall the streame, with sleepie noise,
To Lions mouths, from whence it leapt with speede,
And in the rosie laver seem'd to bleed.
    The naked boyes unto the waters fall,
      Their stonie nightingales had taught to call,
When Zephyr breath'd into their watry interall.

49

And all about, embayed in soft sleepe,
A heard of charmed beasts aground wear spread,
Which the faire Witch in goulden chaines did keepe,
And them in willing bondage fettered,
Once men they liv'd, but now the men were dead,
    And turn'd to beasts, so fabled Homer old,
      That Circe, with her potion, charm'd in gold,
Us'd manly soules in beastly bodies to immould.

50

From her Court, and Courtiers.
1. Pleasure in drinking.

Through this false Eden, to his Lemans bowre,
(Whome thousand soules devoutly idolize)
Our first destroyer led our Saviour.
Thear in the lower roome, in solemne wise,
They daunc't a round, and powr'd their sacrifice
    To plumpe Lyæus, and among the rest,
      The jolly Priest, in yvie garlands drest,
Chaunted wild Orgialls, in honour of the feast.

51

Others within their arbours swilling sat,
(For all the roome about was arboured)
With laughing Bacchus, that was growne so fat,
That stand he could not, but was carried,
And every evening freshly watered,
    To quench his fierie cheeks, and all about
      Small cocks broke through the wall, and sallied out
Flaggons of wine, to set on fire that spueing rout.

CHRISTS VICTORIE ON EARTH

52

This their inhumed soules esteem'd their wealths,
To crowne the bouzing kan from day to night,
And sicke to drinke themselves with drinking healths,
Some vomiting, all drunken with delight.
Hence to a loft, carv'd all in yvorie white, *in Luxurie.*
   They came, whear whiter Ladies naked went,
   Melted in pleasure, and soft languishment,
And sunke in beds of roses, amourous glaunces sent.

53

Flie, flie thou holy child that wanton roome,
And thou my chaster Muse those harlots shun,
And with him to a higher storie come, *2. Avarice.*
Whear mounts of gold, and flouds of silver run,
The while the owners, with their wealth undone,
   Starve in their store, and in their plentie pine,
   Tumbling themselves upon their heaps of mine.
Glutting their famish't soules with the deceitfull shine.

54

Ah, who was he such pretious perills found?
How strongly Nature did her treasures hide;
And threw upon them mountains of thicke ground,
To darke their orie lustre; but queint Pride
Hath taught her Sonnes to wound their mothers side,
   And gage the depth, to search for flaring shells,
   In whose bright bosome spumie Bacchus swells,
That neither heav'n, nor earth henceforth in safetie dwells.

55

O sacred hunger of the greedie eye,
Whose neede hath end, but no end covetise,
Emptie in fulnes, rich in povertie,
That having all things, nothing can suffice,
How thou befanciest the men most wise?
   The poore man would be rich, the rich man great,
   The great man King, the King, in Gods owne seat
Enthron'd, with mortal arme dares flames, and thunder threat.

GILES FLETCHER

56

3. Ambitious honour.

Therefore above the rest Ambition sat:
His Court with glitterant pearle was all enwall'd,
And round about the wall in chaires of State,
And most majestique splendor, wear enstall'd
A hundred Kings, whose temples wear impal'd
 In goulden diadems, set here, and thear
 With diamonds, and gemmed every whear,
And of their golden virges none disceptred wear.

57

From her throne.

High over all, *Panglories* blazing throne,
In her bright turret, all of christall wrought,
Like Ph[œ]bus lampe in midst of heaven, shone:
Whose starry top, with pride infernall fraught,
Selfe-arching columns to uphold wear taught:
 In which, her Image still reflected was
 By the smooth christall, that most like her glasse,
In beauty, and in frailtie, did all others passe.

58

A Silver wande the sorceresse did sway,
And, for a crowne of gold, her haire she wore,
Onely a garland of rosebuds did play
About her locks, and in her hand, she bore
A hollowe globe of glasse, that long before,
 She full of emptinesse had bladdered,
 And all the world therein depictured,
Whose colours, like the rainebowe, ever vanished.

59

Such watry orbicles young boyes doe blowe
Out from their sopy shells, and much admire
The swimming world, which tenderly they rowe
With easie breath, till it be waved higher,
But if they chaunce but roughly once aspire,
 The painted bubble instantly doth fall.
 Here when she came, she gan for musique call,
And sung this wooing song, to welcome him withall.

CHRISTS VICTORIE ON EARTH

Love is the blossome whear thear blowes *From her temptation.*
Every thing, that lives, or growes,
Love doth make the heav'ns to move,
And the Sun doth burne in love;
Love the strong, and weake doth yoke,
And makes the yvie climbe the oke,
Under whose shadowes Lions wilde,
Soft'ned by Love, growe tame, and mild;
Love no med'cine can appease,
He burnes the fishes in the seas,
Not all the skill his wounds can stench,
Not all the sea his fire can quench;
Love did make the bloody spear
Once a levie coat to wear,
While in his leaves thear shrouded lay
Sweete birds, for love, that sing, and play;
And of all loves joyfull flame,
I the bud, and blossome am.
   Onely bend thy knee to me,
   Thy wooeing, shall thy winning be.

See, see the flowers that belowe,
Now as fresh as morning blowe,
And of all, the virgin rose,
That as bright Aurora showes,
How they all unleaved die,
Loosing their virgin[i]tie:
Like unto a summer-shade,
But now borne, and now they fade.
Every thing doth passe away,
Thear is danger in delay,
Come, come gather then the rose,
Gather it, or it you lose.
All the sande of Tagus shore
Into my bosome casts his ore;
All the valleys swimming corne
To my house is yeerely borne;
Every grape, of every vine
Is gladly bruis'd to make me wine,

GILES FLETCHER

While ten thousand kings, as proud,
To carry up my traine, have bow'd,
And a world of Ladies send me
In my chambers to attend me:
All the starres in heav'n that shine,
And ten thousand more, are mine:
   Onely bend thy knee to mee,
   Thy wooing shall thy winning bee.

60

Thus sought the dire Enchauntress in his minde
Her guilefull bayt to have embosomed,
But he her charmes dispersed into winde,
And her of insolence admonished,
The effect of this victorie in Satan. And all her optique glasses shattered.
   So with her Syre to hell shee tooke her flight,
   (The starting ayre flew from the damned spright,)
Whear deeply both aggriev'd, plunged themselves in night.

61

The Angels. But to their Lord, now musing in his thought,
A heavenly volie of light Angels flew,
And from his Father him a banquet brought,
Through the fine element, for well they knew,
After his lenten fast, he hungrie grew,
   And, as he fed, the holy quires combine
   To sing a hymne of the celestiall Trine;
All thought to passe, and each was past all thought divine.

62

The Creatures. The birds sweet notes, to sonnet out their joyes,
Attemper'd to the layes Angelicall,
And to the birds, the winds attune their noyse,
And to the winds, the waters hoarcely call,
And Eccho back againe revoyced all,
   That the whole valley rung with victorie.
   But now our Lord to rest doth homewards flie:
See how the Night comes stealing from the mountains high.

CHRISTS
TRIUMPH O-
ver and after death.

Vincenti dabitur.

Printed by C. LEGGE. 1610.

CHRISTS TRIUMPH
over Death.

1

<small>Christs Tryumph over death, on the crosse, exprest 1. in generall by his joy to undergoe it: singing before he went to the garden, Mat. 26. 30.</small>

SO downe the silver streames of Eridan,
On either side bank't with a lilly wall,
Whiter then both, rides the triumphant Swan,
And sings his dirge, and prophesies his fall,
Diving into his watrie funerall:
  But Eridan to Cedron must submit
  His flowry shore, nor can he envie it,
If when Apollo sings, his swans doe silent sit.

2

That heav'nly voice I more delight to heare,
Then gentle ayres to breath, or swelling waves
Against the sounding rocks their bosomes teare,
Or whistling reeds, that rutty Jordan laves,
And with their verdure his white head embraves,
  To chide the windes, or hiving bees, that flie
  About the laughing bloosms of sallowie,
Rocking asleepe the idle groomes that lazie lie.

3

And yet, how can I heare thee singing goe,
When men incens'd with hate, thy death foreset?
Or els, why doe I heare thee sighing so,
When thou, inflam'd with love, their life doest get?
That Love, and hate, and sighs, and songs are met;
  But thus, and onely thus thy love did crave,
  To sende thee singing for us to thy grave,
While we sought thee to kill, and thou sought'st us to save.

CHRISTS TRIUMPH OVER DEATH

4

When I remember Christ our burden beares,   *By his griefe*
I looke for glorie, but finde miserie;   *in the under-*
I looke for joy, but finde a sea of teares;   *going it.*
I looke that we should live, and finde him die;
I looke for Angels songs, and heare him crie:
    Thus what I looke, I cannot finde so well,
    Or rather, what I finde, I cannot tell,
These bankes so narrowe are, those streames so highly swell.

5

Christ suffers, and in this, his teares begin,
Suffers for us, and our joy springs in this,
Suffers to death, here is his Manhood seen,
Suffers to rise, and here his Godhead is.
For Man, that could not by himselfe have ris,
    Out of the grave doth by the Godhead rise,
    And God, that could not die, in Manhood dies,
That we in both might live, by that sweete sacrifice.

6

Goe giddy braines, whose witts are thought so fresh,
Plucke all the flo[w'r]s that Nature forth doth throwe,
Goe sticke them on the cheekes of wanton flesh;
Poore idol, (forc't at once to fall and growe)
Of fading roses, and of melting snowe:
    Your songs exceede your matter, this of mine,
    The matter, which it sings, shall make divine,
As starres dull puddles guild, in which their beauties shine.

7

Who doth not see drown'd in Deucalions name,   *By the*
(When earth his men, and sea had lost his shore)   *obscure*
Old Noah; and in Nisus lock, the fame   *fables of the*
Of Sampson yet alive; and long before   *Gentiles,*
In Phaethons, mine owne fall I deplore: *typing it.*
    But he that conquer'd hell, to fetch againe
    His virgin widowe, by a serpent slaine,
Another Orpheus was then dreaming poets feigne.

8

That taught the stones to melt for passion,
And dormant sea, to heare him, silent lie,
And at his voice, the watrie nation
To flocke, as if they deem'd it cheape, to buy
With their owne deaths his sacred harmonie:
    The while the waves stood still to heare his song,
    And steadie shore wav'd with the reeling throng
Of thirstie soules, that hung upon his fluent tongue.

9

By the cause of it in him, his Love.
What better friendship, then to cover shame?
What greater love, then for a friend to die?
Yet this is better to asself the blame,
And this is greater, for an enemie:
But more then this, to die, not suddenly,
    Not with some common death, or easie paine,
    But slowly, and with torments to be slaine,
O depth, without a depth, farre better seene, then saine!

10

By the effect it should have in us.
And yet the Sonne is humbled for the Slave,
And yet the Slave is proude before the Sonne:
Yet the Creator for his creature gave
Himselfe, and yet the creature hasts to runne
From his Creator, and self-good doth shunne:
    And yet the Prince, and God himselfe doth crie
    To Man, his Traitour, pardon not to flie,
Yet Man his God, and Traytour doth his Prince defie.

11

Who is it sees not that he nothing is,
But he that nothing sees; what weaker brest,
Since Adams Armour fail'd, dares warrant his?
That made by God of all his creatures best,
Strait made himselfe the woorst of all the rest:
    "If any strength we have, it is to ill,
    "But all the good is Gods, both pow'r, and will":
The dead man cannot rise, though he himselfe may kill.

CHRISTS TRIUMPH OVER DEATH

12

But let the thorny schools these punctualls
Of wills, all good, or bad, or neuter diss;
Such joy we gained by our parentalls,
That good, or bad, whither I cannot wiss,
To call it a mishap, or happy miss
   That fell from Eden, and to heav'n did rise:
   Albee the mitred Card'nall more did prize
His part in Paris, then his part in Paradise.

13

A Tree was first the instrument of strife,   *By the instrument,*
Whear Eve to sinne her soule did prostitute,   *the cursed Tree,*
A Tree is now the instrument of life,
Though ill that trunke, and this faire body suit:
Ah, cursed tree, and yet O blessed fruit!
   That death to him, this life to us doth give:
   Strange is the cure, when things past cure revive,
And the Physitian dies, to make his patient live.

14

Sweete Eden was the arbour of delight,   *2. exprest in particular,*
Yet in his hony flo[w'r]s our poyson blew;   *1. by his fore-passion*
Sad Gethseman the bowre of balefull night,   *in the Garden.*
Whear Christ a health of poison for us drewe,
Yet all our hony in that poyson grewe:
   So we from sweetest flo[w'r]s, could sucke our bane,
   And Christ from bitter venome, could againe
Extract life out of death, and pleasure out of paine.

15

A Man was first the author of our fall,
A Man is now the author of our rise,
A Garden was the place we perisht all,
A Garden is the place he payes our price,
And the old Serpent with a newe devise,
   Hath found a way himselfe for to beguile,
   So he, that all men tangled in his wile,
Is now by one man caught, beguil'd with his owne guile.

GILES FLETCHER

16

The dewie night had with her frostie shade
Immant'led all the world, and the stiffe ground
Sparkled in yce, onely the Lord, that made
All for himselfe, himselfe dissolved found,
Sweat without heat, and bled without a wound:
   Of heav'n, and earth, and God, and Man forlore,
   Thrice begging helpe of those, whose sinnes he bore,
And thrice denied of those, not to denie had swore.

17

Yet had he beene alone of God forsaken,
Or had his bodie beene imbroyl'd alone
In fierce assault, he might, perhaps, have taken
Some joy in soule, when all joy els was gone,
But that with God, and God to heav'n is flow'n;
   And Hell it selfe out from her grave doth rise,
   Black as the starles night, and with them flies,
Yet blacker then they both, the Sonne of blasphemies.

18

As when the Planets, with unkind aspect,
Call from her caves the meager pestilence,
The sacred vapour, eager to infect,
Obeyes the voyce of the sad influence,
And vomits up a thousand noysome sents,
   The well of life, flaming his golden flood
   With the sicke ayre, fevers the boyling blood,
And poisons all the bodie with contagious food.

19

The bold Physitian, too incautelous,
By those he cures, himselfe is murdered,
Kindnes infects, pitie is dangerous,
And the poore infant, yet not fully bred,
Thear where he should be borne, lies buried:
   So the darke Prince, from his infernall cell,
   Casts up his griesly Torturers of hell,
And whets them to revenge, with this insulting spell.

CHRISTS TRIUMPH OVER DEATH

20

See how the world smiles in eternall peace;
While we, the harmles brats, and rustie throng
Of Night, our snakes in curles doe pranke, and dresse:
Why sleepe our drouzie scorpions so long?
Whear is our wonted vertue to doe wrong?
   Are we our selves; or are we Graces growen?
   The Sonnes of hell, or heav'n? was never knowne
Our whips so over-moss't, and brands so deadly blowne.

21

O long desired, never hop't for howre,
When our Tormentour shall our torments feele!
Arme, arme your selves, sad Dires of my pow'r,
And make our Judge for pardon to us kneele,
Slise, launch, dig, teare him with your whips of steele:
   My selfe in honour of so noble prize,
   Will powre you reaking blood, shed with the cries
Of hastie heyres, who their owne fathers sacrifice.

22

With that a flood of poyson, blacke as hell,
Out from his filthy gorge, the beast did spue,
That all about his blessed bodie fell,
And thousand flaming serpents hissing flew
About his soule, from hellish sulphur threw,
   And every one brandisht his fierie tongue,
   And woorming all about his soule they clung,
But he their stings tore out, and to the ground them flung.

23

So have I seene a rocks heroique brest,
Against proud Neptune, that his ruin threats,
When all his waves he hath to battle prest,
And with a thousand swelling billows beats
The stubborne stone, and foams, and chafes, and frets
   To heave him from his root, unmooved stand;
   And more in heaps the barking surges band,
The more in pieces beat, flie weeping to the strand.

GILES FLETCHER

24

So may wee oft a vent'rous father see,
To please his wanton sonne, his onely joy,
Coast all about, to catch the roving bee,
And stung himselfe, his busie hands employ
To save the honie, for the gamesome boy:
   Or from the snake her rank'rous teeth erace,
   Making his child the toothles Serpent chace,
Or, with his little hands, her tum'rous gorge embrace.

25

Thus Christ himselfe to watch, and sorrow gives,
While, deaw'd in easie sleepe, dead Peter lies:
Thus Man in his owne grave securely lives,
While Christ alive, with thousand horrours dies,
Yet more for theirs, then his owne pardon cries:
   No sinnes he had, yet all our sinnes he bare,
   So much doth God for others evills care,
And yet so careles men for their owne evills are.

26

[2.] By his passion it selfe, amplified, 1. from the general causes.

See drouzie Peter, see whear Judas wakes,
Whear Judas kisses him whom Peter flies:
O kisse more deadly then the sting of snakes!
False love more hurtfull then true injuries!
Aye me! how deerly God his Servant buies?
   For God his man, at his owne blood doth hold,
   And Man his God, for thirtie pence hath sold.
So tinne for silver goes, and dunghill drosse for gold.

27

Yet was it not enough for Sinne to chuse
A Servant, to betray his Lord to them;
But that a Subject must his King accuse,
But that a Pagan must his God condemne,
But that a Father must his Sonne contemne,
   But that the Sonne must his owne death desire,
   That Prince, and People, Servant, and the Sire,
Gentil, and Jewe, and he against himselfe conspire?

CHRISTS TRIUMPH OVER DEATH

28

Was this the oyle, to make thy Saints adore thee,   Parts, and
The froathy spittle of the rascall throng?
Ar these the virges, that ar borne before thee,
Base whipps of corde, and knotted all along?
Is this thy golden scepter, against wrong,
   A reedie cane? is that the crowne adornes
   Thy shining locks, a crowne of spiny thornes?
Ar theas the Angels himns, the Priests blasphemous scornes?

29

Who ever sawe Honour before asham'd;   Effects of it.
Afflicted Maiestie, debased height;
Innocence guiltie, Honestie defam'd;
Libertie bound, Health sick, the Sunne in night?
But since such wrong was offred unto right,
   Our night is day, our sicknes health is growne,
   Our shame is veild, this now remaines alone
For us, since he was ours, that wee bee not our owne.

30

Night was ordeyn'd for rest, and not for paine,   [2]. From
But they, to paine their Lord, their rest contemne,   the particu-
Good lawes to save, what bad men would have slaine,   lar causes.
And not bad Judges, with one breath, by them
The innocent to pardon, and condemne:
   Death for revenge of murderers, not decaie
   Of guiltles blood, but now, all headlong sway
Mans Murderer to save, mans Saviour to slaie.

31

Fraile Multitude, whose giddy lawe is list,
And best applause is windy flattering,
Most like the breath of which it doth consist,
No sooner blowne, but as soone vanishing,
As much desir'd, as little profiting,
   That makes the men that have it oft as light,
   As those that give it, which the proud invite,
And feare: the bad mans friend, the good mans hypocrite.

GILES FLETCHER

32

It was but now their sounding clamours sung,
Blessed is he, that comes from the most high,
And all the mountaines with Hosanna rung,
And nowe, away with him, away they crie,
And nothing can be heard but crucifie:
   It was but now, the Crowne it selfe they save,
   And golden name of King unto him gave,
And nowe, no King, but onely Cæsar, they will have:

33

It was but now they gathered blooming May,
And of his armes disrob'd the branching tree,
To strowe with boughs, and blossomes all thy way,
And now, the branchlesse truncke a crosse for thee,
And May, dismai'd, thy coronet must be:
   It was but now they wear so kind, to throwe
   Their owne best garments, whear thy feet should goe,
And now, thy selfe they strip, and bleeding wounds they show.

34

See whear the author of all life is dying:
O fearefull day! he dead, what hope of living?
See whear the hopes of all our lives are buying:
O chearfull day! they bought, what feare of grieving?
Love love for hate, and death for life is giving:
   Loe how his armes are stretch't abroad to grace thee,
   And, as they open stand, call to embrace thee,
Why stai'st thou then my soule; ô flie, flie thither hast thee.

35

His radious head, with shamefull thornes they teare,
His tender backe, with bloody whipps they rent,
His side and heart, they furrowe with a spear,
His hands, and feete, with riving nayles they tent,
And, as to disentrayle his soule they meant,
   They jolly at his griefe, and make their game,
   His naked body to expose to shame,
That all might come to see, and all might see, that came.

CHRISTS TRIUMPH OVER DEATH

36

Whereat the heav'n put out his guiltie eye,   *Effects of it in heaven.*
That durst behold so execrable sight,
And sabled all in blacke the shadie skie,
And the pale starres strucke with unwonted fright,
Quenched their everlasting lamps in night:
   And at his birth as all the starres heav'n had,
   Wear not enough, but a newe star was made,
So now both newe, and old, and all away did fade.

37

The mazed Angels shooke their fierie wings,   *[I]n the heavenly Spirits.*
Readie to lighten vengeance from Gods throne,
One downe his eyes upon the Manhood flings,
Another gazes on the Godhead, none
But surely thought his wits wear not his owne:
   Some flew, to looke if it wear very hee,
   But, when Gods arme unarmed they did see,
Albee they sawe it was, they vow'd it could not bee.

38

The sadded aire hung all in cheerelesse blacke,   *[I]n the Creatures sub-cœlestiall.*
Through which, the gentle windes soft sighing flewe,
And Jordan into such huge sorrowe brake,
(As if his holy streame no measure knewe,)
That all his narrowe bankes he overthrewe,
   The trembling earth with horrour inly shooke,
   And stubborne stones, such griefe unus'd to brooke,
Did burst, and ghosts awaking from their graves gan looke.

39

The wise Philosopher cried, all agast,
The God of nature surely lanquished,
The sad Centurion cried out as fast,
The Sonne of God, the Sonne of God was dead,
The headlong Jew hung downe his pensive head,   *In the wicked Jewes.*
   And homewards far'd, and ever, as he went,
   He smote his brest, halfe desperately bent,
The verie woods, and beasts did seeme his death lament.

GILES FLETCHER

40

In Judas.   The gracelesse Traytour round about did looke,
(He lok't not long, the Devill quickely met him)
To finde a halter, which he found, and tooke,
Onely a gibbet nowe he needes must get him,
So on a wither'd tree he fairly set him,
   And helpt him fit the rope, and in his thought
   A thousand furies, with their whippes, he brought,
So thear he stands, readie to hell to make his vault.

41

For him a waking bloodhound, yelling loude,
That in his bosome long had sleeping layde,
A guiltie Conscience, barking after blood,
Pursued eagerly, ne ever stai'd,
Till the betrayers selfe it had betray'd.
   Oft chang'd he place, in hope away to winde,
   But change of place could never change his minde,
Himselfe he flies to loose, and followes for to finde.

42

Thear is but two wayes for this soule to have,
When parting from the body, forth it purges,
To flie to heav'n, or fall into the grave,
Where whippes of scorpions, with the stinging scourges,
Feed on the howling ghosts, and firie Surges
   Of brimstone rowle about the cave of night,
   Where flames doe burne, and yet no sparke of light,
And fire both fries, and freezes the blaspheming spright.

43

Thear lies the captive soule, aye-sighing sore,
Reck'ning a thousand yeares since her first bands,
Yet staies not thear, but addes a thousand more,
And at another thousand never stands,
But tells to them the starres, and heapes the sands,
   And now the starres are told, and sands are runne,
   And all those thousand thousand myriads done,
And yet but now, alas! but now all is begunne.

CHRISTS TRIUMPH OVER DEATH

44

With that a flaming brand a Furie catch't,
And shooke, and tost it round in his wilde thought,
So from his heart all joy, all comfort snatch't,
With every starre of hope, and as he sought,
(With present feare, and future griefe distraught)
   To flie from his owne heart, and aide implore
   Of him, the more he gives, that hath the more,
Whose storehouse is the heavens, too little for his store.

45

Stay wretch on earth, cried Satan, restles rest,
Know'st thou not Justice lives in heav'n; or can
The worst of creatures live among the best;
Among the blessed Angels cursed man?
Will Judas now become a Christian?
   Whither will hopes long wings transport thy minde;
   Or canst thou not thy selfe a sinner finde;
Or cruell to thy selfe, wouldst thou have Mercie kinde?

46

He gave thee life: why shouldst thou seeke to slay him?
He lent thee wealth: to feed thy avarice?
He cal'd thee friend: what, that thou shouldst betray him?
He kist thee, though he knew his life the price:
He washt thy feet: should'st thou his sacrifice?
   He gave thee bread, and wine, his bodie, blood,
   And at thy heart to enter in he stood,
But then I entred in, and all my snakie brood.

47

As when wild Pentheus, growne madde with fear,
Whole troups of hellish haggs about him spies,
Two bloodie Sunnes stalking the duskie sphear,
And twofold Thebes runs rowling in his eyes:
Or through the scene staring Orestes flies,
   With eyes flung back upon his Mothers ghost,
   That, with infernall serpents all embost,
And torches quencht in blood, doth her stern sonne accost.

GILES FLETCHER

48

Such horrid gorgons, and misformed formes
Of damned fiends, flew dauncing in his heart,
That now, unable to endure their stormes,
Flie, flie, he cries, thy selfe, what ere thou art,
Hell, hell alreadie burnes in every part.
   So downe into his Torturers armes he fell,
   That readie stood his funeralls to yell,
And in a clowd of night to waft him quick to hell.

49

Yet oft he snacht, and started as he hung:
So when the senses halfe enslumb'red lie,
The headlong bodie, readie to be flung,
By the deluding phansie, from some high,
And craggie rock, recovers greedily,
   And clasps the yeelding pillow, halfe asleepe,
   And, as from heav'n it tombled to the deepe,
Feeles a cold sweat through every trembling member creepe.

50

Thear let him hang, embowelled in blood,
Whear never any gentle Sheapheard feed
His blessed flocks, nor ever heav'nly flood
Fall on the cursed ground, nor holesome seed
That may the least delight or pleasure breed:
   Let never Spring visit his habitation,
   But nettles, kixe, and all the weedie nation,
With emptie elders grow, sad signes of desolation.

51

Thear let the Dragon keepe his habitance,
And stinking karcases be throwne avaunt,
Faunes, Sylvans, and deformed Satyrs daunce,
Wild-cats, wolves, toads, and s[c]reechowles direly chaunt,
Thear ever let some restles spirit haunt,
   With hollow sound, and clashing cheynes, to scarr
   The passenger, and eyes like to the starr,
That sparkles in the crest of angrie Mars afarr.

CHRISTS TRIUMPH OVER DEATH

52

But let the blessed deawes for ever showr
Upon that ground, in whose faire fields I spie
The bloodie ensigne of our Saviour:
Strange conquest, whear the Conquerour must die,
And he is slaine, that winns the victorie:
   But he, that living, had no house to owe it,
   Now had no grave, but Joseph must bestowe it,
O runne ye Saints apace, and with sweete flo[w'r]s bestrowe it.

In the blessed Joseph, &c.

53

And ye glad Spirits, that now sainted sit
On your cœlestiall thrones, in beawtie drest,
Though I your teares recoumpt, O let not it
With after-sorrowe wound your tender brest,
Or with new griefe unquiet your soft rest:
   Inough is me your plaints to sound againe,
   That never could inough my selfe complaine,
Sing then, O sing aloude thou Arimathean Swaine.

54

But long he stood, in his faint armes upholding
The fairest spoile heav'n ever forfeited,
With such a silent passion griefe unfoulding,
That, had the sheete but on himselfe beene spread,
He for the corse might have beene buried:
   And with him stood the happie theefe, that stole
   By night his owne salvation, and a shole
Of Maries drowned, round about him, sat in dole.

55

At length (kissing his lipps before he spake,
As if from thence he fetcht againe his ghost)
To Mary thus, with teares, his silence brake.
Ah woefull soule! what joy in all our cost,
When him we hould, we have alreadie lost?
   Once did'st thou loose thy Sonne, but found'st againe,
   Now find'st thy Sonne, but find'st him lost, and slaine.
Ay mee! though he could death, how canst thou life sustaine?

GILES FLETCHER

56

Whear ere, deere Lord, thy Shadowe hovereth,
Blessing the place, wherein it deigns abide,
Looke how the earth darke horrour covereth,
Cloathing in mournfull black her naked side,
Willing her shadowe up to heav'n to glide,
    To see and if it meet thee wandring thear,
    That so, and if her selfe must misse thee hear,
At least her shadow may her dutie to thee bear.

57

See how the Sunne in daytime cloudes his face,
And lagging Vesper, loosing his late teame,
Forgets in heav'n to runne his nightly race,
But, sleeping on bright Oetas top, doeth dreame
The world a Chaos is, no joyfull beame
    Looks from his starrie bowre, the heav'ns doe mone,
    And Trees drop teares, least we should greeve alone,
The windes have learnt to sigh, and waters hoarcely grone.

58

And you sweete flow'rs, that in this garden growe,
Whose happie states a thousand soules envie,
Did you your owne felicities but knowe,
Your selves unpluckt would to his funerals hie,
You never could in better season die:
    O that I might into your places slide,
    The gate of heav'n stands gaping in his side,
Thear in my soule should steale, and all her faults should hide.

59

Are theas the eyes, that made all others blind;
Ah why ar they themselves now blemished?
Is this the face, in which all beawtie shin'd;
What blast hath thus his flowers debellished?
Ar these the feete, that on the watry head
    Of the unfaithfull Ocean passage found;
    Why goe they now so lowely under ground,   (wound?
Wash't with our woorthles teares, and their owne precious

CHRISTS TRIUMPH OVER DEATH

60
One hem but of the garments that he wore,
Could medicine whole countries of their paine,
One touch of this pale hand could life restore,
One word of these cold lips revive the slaine:
Well the blinde man thy Godhead might maintaine,
   What though the sullen Pharises repin'd?
   He that should both compare, at length would finde
The blinde man onely sawe, the Seers all wear blinde.

61
Why should they thinke thee worthy to be slaine?
Was it because thou gav'st their blinde men eyes;
Or that thou mad'st their lame to walke againe;
Or for thou heal'dst their sick mens maladies;
Or mad'st their dumbe to speake; and dead to rise?
   O could all these but any grace have woon,
   What would they not to save thy life have done?
The dumb man would have spoke, and lame man would have
                                                        (runne.

62
Let mee, O let me neere some fountaine lie,
That through the rocke heaves up his sandie head,
Or let me dwell upon some mountaine high,
Whose hollowe root, and baser parts ar spread
On fleeting waters, in his bowells bred,
   That I their streames, and they my teares may feed,
   Or, cloathed in some Hermits ragged weed,
Spend all my daies, in weeping for this cursed deed.

63
The life, the which I once did love, I leave,
The love, in whi[c]h I once did live, I loath,
I hate the light, that did my light bereave,
Both love, and life, I doe despise you both,
O that one grave might both our ashes cloath!
   A Love, a Life, a Light I now obteine,
   Able to make my Age growe young againe,
Able to save the sick, and to revive the slaine.

GILES FLETCHER

64

Thus spend we teares, that never can be spent,
On him, that sorrow now no more shall see:
Thus send we sighs, that never can be sent,
To him, that died to live, and would not be,
To be thear whear he would; here burie we
   This heav'nly earth, here let it softly sleepe,
   The fairest Sheapheard of the fairest sheepe.
So all the bodie kist, and homewards went to weepe.

65

So home their bodies went, to seeke repose,
But at the grave they left their soules behinde;
O who the force of love cœlestiall knowes!
That can the cheynes of natures selfe unbinde,
Sending the Bodie home, without the minde.
   Ah blessed Virgin, what high Angels art
   Can ever coumpt thy teares, or sing thy smart,
When every naile, that pierst his hand, did pierce thy heart?

66

So Philomel, perch't on an aspin sprig,
Weeps all the night her lost virginitie,
And sings her sad tale to the merrie twig,
That daunces at such joyfull miserie,
Ne ever lets sweet rest invade her eye:
   But leaning on a thorne her daintie chest,
   For feare soft sleepe should steale into her brest,
Expresses in her song greefe not to be exprest.

67

So when the Larke, poore birde, afarre espi'th
Her yet unfeather'd children (whom to save
She strives in vaine) slaine by the fatall sithe,
Which from the medowe her greene locks doeth shave,
That their warme nest is now become their grave;
   The woefull mother up to heaven springs,
   And all about her plaintive notes she flings,
And their untimely fate most pittifully sings.

CHRISTS TRIUMPH
after Death.

1

BUt now the second Morning, from her bowre,
   Began to glister in her beames, and nowe
The roses of the day began to flowre
In th' easterne garden ; for heav'ns smiling browe
Halfe insolent for joy begunne to showe :
  The early Sunne came lively dauncing out,
  And the bragge lambes ranne wantoning about,
That heav'n, and earth might seeme in tryumph both to shout.

Christs Triumph after death.
1. [I]n his Resurrection, manifested by the effects of it in the Creatures.

2

Th' engladded Spring, forgetfull now to weepe,
Began t' eblazon from her leavie bed,
The waking swallowe broke her halfe-yeares sleepe,
And everie bush lay deepely purpured
With violets, the woods late-wintry head
  Wide flaming primroses set all on fire,
  And his bald trees put on their greene attire,
Among whose infant leaves the joyeous birds conspire.

3

And now the taller Sonnes (whom Titan warmes)
Of unshorne mountaines, blowne with easie windes,
Dandled the mornings childhood in their armes,
And, if they chaunc't to slip the prouder pines,
The under Corylets did catch the shines,
  To guild their leaves, sawe never happie yeare
  Such joyfull triumph, and triumphant cheare,
As though the aged world anew created wear.

GILES FLETCHER

4

Say Earth, why hast thou got thee new attire,
And stick'st thy habit full of dazies red?
Seems that thou doest to some high thought aspire,
And some newe-found-out Bridegroome mean'st to wed:
Tell me ye Trees, so fresh apparelled,
  So never let the spitefull Canker wast you,
  So never let the heav'ns with lightening blast you,
Why goe you now so trimly drest, or whither hast you?

5

Answer me Jordan, why thy crooked tide
So often wanders from his neerest way,
As though some other way thy streame would slide,
And faine salute the place where something lay?
And you sweete birds, that shaded from the ray,
  Sit carolling, and piping griefe away,
  The while the lambs to heare you daunce, and play,
Tell me sweete birds, what is it you so faine would say?

6

And, thou faire Spouse of Earth, that everie yeare,
Gett'st such a numerous issue of thy bride,
How chance thou hotter shin'st, and draw'st more neere?
Sure thou somewhear some worthie sight hast spide,
That in one place for joy thou canst not bide:
  And you dead Swallowes, that so lively now
  Through the flit aire your winged passage rowe,
How could new life into your frozen ashes flowe?

7

Ye Primroses, and purple violets,
Tell me, why blaze ye from your leavie bed,
And wooe mens hands to rent you from your sets,
As though you would somewhear be carried,
With fresh perfumes, and velvets garnished?
  But ah, I neede not aske, 'tis surely so,
  You all would to your Saviours triumphs goe,
Thear would ye all awaite, and humble homage doe.

CHRISTS TRIUMPH AFTER DEATH

8

Thear should the Earth herselfe with garlands newe   In himselfe.
And lovely flo[w'r]s embellished adore,
Such roses never in her garland grewe,
Such lillies never in her brest she wore,
Like beautie never yet did shine before:
   Thear should the Sunne another Sunne behold,
   From whence himselfe borrowes his locks of gold,
That kindle heav'n, and earth with beauties manifold.

9

Thear might the violet, and primrose sweet
Beames of more lively, and more lovely grace,
Arising from their beds of incense meet;
Thear should the Swallowe see newe life embrace
Dead ashes, and the grave unheale his face,
   To let the living from his bowels creepe,
   Unable longer his owne dead to keepe: (sleepe.
Thear heav'n, and earth should see their Lord awake from

10

Their Lord, before by other judg'd to die,
Nowe Judge of all himselfe, before forsaken
Of all the world, that from his aide did flie,
Now by the Saints into their armies taken,
Before for an unworthie man mistaken,
   Nowe worthy to be God confest, before
   With blasphemies by all the basest tore,
Now worshipped by Angels, that him lowe adore.

11

Whose garment was before indipt in blood,
But now, imbright'ned into heav'nly flame,
The Sun it selfe outglitters, though he should
Climbe to the toppe of the celestiall frame,
And force the starres go hide themselves for shame:
   Before that under earth was buried,
   But nowe about the heav'ns is carried,
And thear for ever by the Angels heried.

12

So fairest Phosphor the bright Morning starre,
But neewely washt in the greene element,
Before the drouzie Night is halfe aware,
Shooting his flaming locks with deaw besprent,
Springs lively up into the orient,
    And the bright drove, fleec't all in gold, he chaces
    To drinke, that on the Olympique mountaine grazes,
The while the minor Planets forfeit all their faces.

13

2. In his Ascention to heaven, whose joyes are described.

So long he wandred in our lower spheare,
That heav'n began his cloudy starres despise,
Halfe envious, to see on earth appeare
A greater light, then flam'd in his owne skies:
At length it burst for spight, and out thear flies
    A globe of winged Angels, swift as thought,
    That, on their spotted feathers, lively caught
The sparkling Earth, and to their azure fields it brought.

14

The rest, that yet amazed stood belowe,
With eyes cast up, as greedie to be fed,
And hands upheld, themselves to ground did throwe,
So when the Trojan boy was ravished,
As through th' Idalian woods they saie he fled,
    His aged Gardians stood all dismai'd,
    Some least he should have fallen back afraid,
And some their hasty vowes, and timely prayers said.

15

Tosse up your heads ye everlasting gates,
And let the Prince of glorie enter in:
At whose brave voly of sideriall States,
The Sunne to blush, and starres growe pale wear seene,
When, leaping first from earth, he did begin
    To climbe his Angells wings; then open hang
    Your christall doores, so all the chorus sang
Of heav'nly birds, as to the starres they nimbly sprang.

CHRISTS TRIUMPH AFTER DEATH

16

Hearke how the floods clap their applauding hands,
The pleasant valleyes singing for delight,
And wanton Mountaines daunce about the Lands,
The while the fieldes, struck with the heav'nly light,
Set all their flo[w'r]s a smiling at the sight,
   The trees laugh with their blossoms, and the sound
   Of the triumphant shout of praise, that crown'd   (found.
The flaming Lambe, breaking through heav'n, hath passage

17

Out leap the antique Patriarchs, all in hast,   1. By the
To see the po[w'r]s of Hell in triumph lead,   accesse of
And with small starres a garland interchast   blessed
Of olive leaves they bore, to crowne his head,   Societie of
That was before with thornes degloried,   the Saints,
   After them flewe the Prophets, brightly stol'd
   In shining lawne, and wimpled manifold,
Striking their yvorie harpes, strung all in chords of gold.

18

To which the Saints victorious carolls sung,
Ten thousand Saints at once, that with the sound,
The hollow vaults of heav'n for triumph rung:
The Cherubins their clamours did confound   Angels, &c.
With all the rest, and clapt their wings around:
   Downe from their thrones the Dominations flowe,
   And at his feet their crownes, and scepters throwe,
And all the princely Soules fell on their faces lowe.

19

Nor can the Martyrs wounds them stay behind,
But out they rush among the heav'nly crowd,
Seeking their heav'n out of their heav'n to find,
Sounding their silver trumpets out so loude,
That the shrill noise broke through the starrie cloude,
   And all the virgin Soules, in pure araie,
   Came daunsing forth, and making joyeous plaie;
So him they lead along into the courts of day.

GILES FLETCHER

20

<small>The sweete quiet and peace, injoyed under God.</small>
So him they lead into the courts of day,
Whear never warre, nor wounds abide him more,
But in that house, eternall peace doth plaie,
Acquieting the soules, that newe before
Their way to heav'n through their owne blood did skore,
   But now, estranged from all miserie,
   As farre as heav'n, and earth discoasted lie,
Swelter in quiet waves of immortalitie.

21

<small>Shadowed by the peace we enjoy under our Soveraigne.</small>
And if great things by smaller may be ghuest,
So, in the mid'st of Neptunes angrie tide,
Our Britan Island, like the weedie nest
Of true Halcyon, on the waves doth ride,
And softly sayling, skornes the waters pride:
   While all the rest, drown'd on the continent,
   And tost in bloodie waves, their wounds lament,
And stand, to see our peace, as struck with woonderment.

22

The Ship of France religious waves doe tosse,
And Greec[e] it selfe is now growne barbarous,
Spains Children hardly dare the Ocean crosse,
And Belges field lies wast, and ruinous,
That unto those, the heav'ns ar invious,
   And unto them, themselves ar strangers growne,
   And unto these, the Seas ar faithles knowne,
And unto her, alas, her owne is not her owne.

23

Here onely shut we Janus yron gates,
And call the welcome Muses to our springs,
And ar but Pilgrims from our heav'nly states,
The while the trusty Earth sure plentie brings,
And Ships through Neptune safely spread their wings.
   Goe blessed Island, wander whear thou please,
   Unto thy God, or men, heav'n, lands, or seas,
Thou canst not loose thy way, thy King with all hath peace.

CHRISTS TRIUMPH AFTER DEATH

24

Deere Prince, thy Subjects joy, hope of their heirs,
Picture of peace, or breathing Image rather,
The certaine argument of all our pray'rs,
Thy Harries, and thy Countries lovely Father,
Let Peace, in endles joyes, for ever bath her
    Within thy sacred brest, that at thy birth
    Brought'st her with thee from heav'n, to dwell on earth,
Making our earth a heav'n, and paradise of mirth.

25

Let not my Liege misdeem these humble laies,
As lick't with soft, and supple blandishment,
Or spoken to disparagon his praise;
For though pale Cynthia, neere her brothers tent,
Soone disappeares in the white firmament,
    And gives him back the beames, before wear his,
    Yet when he verges, or is hardly ris,
She the vive image of her absent brother is.

26

Nor let the Prince of peace his beadsman blame,
That with his Stewart dares his Lord compare,
And heav'nly peace with earthly quiet shame:
So Pines to lowely plants compared ar,
And lightning Phœbus to a little starre:
    And well I wot, my rime, albee unsmooth,
    Ne, saies but what it meanes, ne meanes but sooth,
Ne harmes the good, ne good to harmefull person doth.

27

Gaze but upon the house, whear Man embo[w'r]s: *The beauty of the place*
With flo[w'r]s, and rushes paved is his way,
Whear all the Creatures ar his Servitours,
The windes doe sweepe his chambers every day,
And cloudes doe wash his rooms, the seeling gay,
    Starred aloft the guilded knobs embrave:
    If such a house God to another gave,
How shine those glittering courts, he for himselfe will have?

GILES FLETCHER

28

<small>The C[l]aritie (as the schoole cals it) of the Saints bodies.</small>

And if a sullen cloud, as sad as night,
In which the Sunne may seeme embodied,
Depur'd of all his drosse, we see so white,
Burning in melted gold his watrie head,
Or round with yvorie edges silvered,
   What lustre superexcellent will he
     Lighten on those, that shall his sunneshine see,
In that all-glorious court, in which all glories be

29

If but one Sunne, with his diffusive fires,
Can paint the starres, and the whole world with light,
And joy, and life into each heart inspires,
And every Saint shall shine in heav'n, as bright
As doth the Sunne in his transcendent might,
   (As faith may well beleeve, what Truth once sayes)
     What shall so many Sunnes united rayes
But dazle all the eyes, that nowe in heav'n we praise?

30

Here let my Lord hang up his conquering launce,
And bloody armour with late slaughter warme,
And looking downe on his weake Militants,
Behold his Saints, mid'st of their hot alarme,
Hang all their golden hopes upon his arme.
   And in this lower field dispacing wide,
     Through windie thoughts, that would thei[r] sayles misguide,
Anchor their fleshly ships fast in his wounded side.

31

Here may the Band, that now in Tryumph shines,
And that (before they wear invested thus)
In earthly bodies carried heavenly mindes,
Pitcht round about in order glorious,
Their sunny Tents, and houses luminous,
   All their eternall day in songs employing,
     Joying their ende, without ende of their joying,
While their almightie Prince Destruction is destroying.

CHRISTS TRIUMPH AFTER DEATH

32

Full, yet without satietie, of that   *The imple-*
Which whetts, and quiets greedy Appetite,   *tion of the*
Whear never Sunne did rise, nor ever sat,   *Appetite.*
But one eternall day, and endles light
Gives time to those, whose time is infinite,
   Speaking with thought, obtaining without fee,
   Beholding him, whom never eye could see,
And magnifying him, that cannot greater be.

33

How can such joy as this want words to speake?
And yet what words can speake such joy as this?
Far from the world, that might their quiet breake,
Here the glad Soules the face of beauty kisse,
Powr'd out in pleasure, on their beds of blisse.
   And drunke with nectar torrents, ever hold
   Their eyes on him, whose graces manifold,
The more they doe behold, the more they would behold.

34

Their sight drinkes lovely fires in at their eyes,   *The joy of*
Their braine sweete incense with fine breath accloyes, *the senses,*
That on Gods sweating altar burning lies,   *&c.*
Their hungrie cares feede on their heav'nly noyse,
That Angels sing, to tell their untould joyes;
   Their understanding naked Truth, their wills
   The all, and selfe-sufficient Goodnesse fills,
That nothing here is wanting, but the want of ills.

35

No Sorrowe nowe hangs clowding on their browe,   *2. By the*
No bloodles Maladie empales their face,   *amotion of*
No Age drops on their hayrs his silver snowe,   *all evill.*
No Nakednesse their bodies doeth embase,
No Povertie themselves, and theirs disgrace,
   No feare of death the joy of life devours,
   No unchast sleepe their precious time deflowrs,
No losse, no griefe, no change waite on their winged hour's.

GILES FLETCHER

36

But now their naked bodies skorne the cold,
And from their eyes joy lookes, and laughs at paine,
The Infant wonders how he came so old,
And old man how he came so young againe;
Still resting, though from sleepe they still refraine,
 Whear all are rich, and yet no gold they owe,
 And all are Kings, and yet no Subjects knowe,
All full, and yet no time on foode they doe bestowe.

37

For things that passe are past, and in this field,
The indeficient Spring no Winter feares,
The Trees together fruit, and blossome yeild,
Th' unfading Lilly leaves of silver beares,
And crimson rose a skarlet garment weares:
 And all of these on the Saints bodies growe,
 Not, as they woont, on baser earth belowe;

By the accesse of all good againe Three rivers heer of milke, and wine, and honie flowe.

38

in the glorie of the Holy Cittie. About the holy Cittie rowles a flood
Of moulten chrystall, like a sea of glasse,
On which weake streame a strong foundation stood,
Of living Diamounds the building was,
That all things else, besides it selfe, did passe.
 Her streetes, in stead of stones, the starres did pave,
 And little pearles, for dust, it seem'd to have,
On which soft-streaming Manna, like pure snowe, did wave.

39

[I]n the beatificall vision of God. In mid'st of this Citie cœlestiall,
Whear the eternall Temple should have rose,
Light'ned th' Idea Beatificall:
End, and beginning of each thing that growes,
Whose selfe no end, nor yet beginning knowes,
 That hath no eyes to see, nor ears to heare,
 Yet sees, and heares, and is all-eye, all-eare,
That no whear is contain'd, and yet is every whear.

CHRISTS TRIUMPH AFTER DEATH

40

Changer of all things, yet immutable,
Before, and after all, the first, and last,
That mooving all, is yet immoveable,
Great without quantitie, in whose forecast,
Things past are present, things to come are past,
   Swift without motion, to whose open eye
   The hearts of wicked men unbrested lie,
At once absent, and present to them, farre, and nigh.

41

It is no flaming lustre, made of light,
No sweet concent, or well-tim'd harmonie,
Ambrosia, for to feast the Appetite,
Or flowrie odour, mixt with spicerie.
No soft embrace, or pleasure bodily,
   And yet it is a kinde of inward feast,
   A harmony, that sounds within the brest,
An odour, light, embrace, in which the soule doth rest.

42

A heav'nly feast, no hunger can consume,
A light unseene, yet shines in every place,
A sound, no time can steale, a sweet perfume,
No windes can scatter, an intire embrace,
That no satietie can ere unlace,
   Ingrac't into so high a favour, thear
   The Saints, with their Beaw-peers, whole worlds outwear,
And things unseene doe see, and things unheard doe hear.

43

Ye blessed soules, growne richer by your spoile,   *And of Christ.*
Whose losse, though great, is cause of greater gaines,
Here may your weary Spirits rest from toyle,
Spending your endlesse eav'ning, that remaines,
Among those white flocks, and celestiall traines,
   That feed upon their Sheapheards eyes, and frame
   That heav'nly musique of so woondrous fame,
Psalming aloude the holy honours of his name.

GILES FLETCHER

44

Had I a voice of steel to tune my song,
Wear every verse as smoothly fil'd as glasse,
And every member turned to a tongue,
And every tongue wear made of sounding brasse,
Yet all that skill, and all this strength, alas,
   Should it presume to guild, wear misadvis'd,
   The place, whear David hath new songs devis'd,
As in his burning throne he sits emparadis'd.

45

Most happie Prince, whose eyes those starres behould,
Treading ours under feet, now maist thou powre
That overflowing skill, whearwith of ould
Thou woont'st to combe rough speech, now maist thou showr
Fresh streames of praise upon that holy bowre,
   Which well we heaven call, not that it rowles,
   But that it is the haven of our soules.
Most happie Prince, whose sight so heav'nly sight behoulds.

46

Ah foolish Sheapheards, that wear woont esteem,
Your God all rough, and shaggy-hair'd to bee;
And yet farre wiser Sheapheards then ye deeme,
For who so poore (though who so rich) as hee,
When, with us hermiting in lowe degree,
   He wash't his flocks in Jordans spotles tide,
   And, that his deere remembrance aie might bide,
Did to us come, and with us liv'd, and for us di'd?

47

But now so lively colours did embeame
His sparkling forehead, and so shiny rayes
Kindled his flaming locks; that downe did streame
In curles, along his necke, whear sweetly playes
(Singing his wounds of love in sacred layes)
   His deerest Spouse, Spouse of the deerest Lover,
   Knitting a thousand knots over, and over,
And dying still for love, but they her still recover.

CHRISTS TRIUMPH AFTER DEATH

48

Faire Egliset, that at his eyes doth dresse
Her glorious face, those eyes, from whence ar shed
Infinite belamours, whear to expresse
His love, high God all heav'n as captive leads,
And all the banners of his grace dispreads,
   And in those windowes, doth his armes englaze,
   And on those eyes, the Angels all doe gaze,
And from those eies, the lights of heav'n do gleane their blaze.

49

But let the Kentish lad, that lately taught
His oaten reed the trumpets silver sound,
Young Thyrsilis, and for his musique brought
The willing sphears from heav'n, to lead a round
Of dauncing Nymphs, and Heards, that sung, and crown'd
   Eclectas hymen with ten thousand flowrs
   Of choycest prayse, and hung her heav'nly bow'rs
With saffron garlands, drest for Nuptiall Paramours,

50

Let his shrill trumpet, with her silver blast,
Of faire Eclecta, and her Spousall bed,
Be the sweet pipe, and smooth Encomiast:
But my greene Muse, hiding her younger head
Under old Chamus flaggy banks, that spread
   Their willough locks abroad, and all the day
   With their owne watry shadowes wanton play,
Dares not those high amours, and love-sick songs assay.

51

Impotent words, weake sides, that strive in vaine,
In vaine, alas, to tell so heav'nly sight,
So heav'nly sight, as none can greater feigne,
Feigne what he can, that seemes of greatest might,
   Might any yet compare with Infinite?
   Infinite sure those joyes, my words but light,
Light is the pallace whear she dwells. O blessed wight!

GILES FLETCHER

RUina Cœli pulchra; iam terris decus,
  Deusq̇: proles matris innuptæ, & pater:
Sine matre natus, sine patre excrescens caro:
Quem nec mare, æther, terra, non cœlum capit,
Utero puellæ totus angusto latens;
Æquævus idem patri, matre antiquior:
Heu domite victor, & triumphator; tui
Opus opifexq̇, qui minor quàm sis, eò
Major resurgis: vita, quæ mori velis,
Atq̇ ergo possis: passa finem Æternitas.
Quid tibi rependam, quid tibi rependam miser?
Ut quando ocellos mollis invadit quies,
Et nocte membra plurimus Morpheus premit,
Avidè videmur velle de tergo sequens
Effugere monstrum, & plumbeos frustra pedes
Celerare; media succidimus ægri fugâ;
Solitum pigrescit robur, os quærit viam,
Sed proditurus moritur in lingua sonus:
Sic stupeo totus, totus hæresco, intuens
Et sæpe repeto, forte si rependerem:
Solus rependit ille, qui repetit bene.
          G. Fletcher.

Τέλειόν ἐστι, καὶ τελῶν Θεὸς τέλος.

A DESCRIPTION OF ENCOLPIUS

[MS. Tanner 465, fol. 42.]

Nisus amore pio pueri &c.

    'Tis Encol-
p[i]us in
Petronius.
I had it of
Mr. Blois.

IT was at evening, & in Aprill mild,
  Of twelve sonnes of the yeare the fairest child,
When night, & day their strife to peace doe bring,
To have an æquall interest in the Spring,
The Sunne being Arbiter: I walkt to see,
How Nature drew a meddow, & a tree
In orient colo[rs]; & to smell what sent
Of true perfume the winds the aire had lent.
When with a happy-carelesse glance I spy
One pace a shade; Encolp[i]us cry'd 'tis I;
And soe unmask't his forehead branch't more faire,
Than locks of grasse, our mother Rheas haire.
I had mine eyes soe full of such a freind,
That Flora's pride was dimmd; & in the end
I askt some time, before I could perswade
My senses it was spring; The silken blade
Of Cowslips lost their grace; the speckled Pancie,
Came short to flatter, though he smil'd, my fancie.
If later seasons had the Roses bredd,
I doubt the modest Damaske had turn'd redd,
Stain'd with a parallel: but it was good
They swadled were, like infants, in the bud.
Solsequium, gladd of this excuse, begunne
To close his blushes with the setting sunne.
Thrice chanting Philomel beganne a song,
Thrice had noe audience for Encolp[i]us tongue.
This thorne did touch her brest to be rejected,
And tun'd a moane, not heard, she was neglected.
I thought uncurteous Time would wait; but Night
Appear'd, Orions whelpes had chas'd the light

GILES FLETCHER

Into the Westerne coverts; Judge from hence,
How farre a beauty commands reverence.
The neighbour starres in love were waxen clearer,
The farthest shott, me thought, to view him neerer.
My Uranoscopy said, the Moone did cast
Faint beames, & sullen glimpses; when at last
I spy'd in her a new, & uncouth spott,
Doubtles through Envy all the rest she gott.
And then she hidd her palenes in a shrowd,
Borrowing the pleighted curtaines of a clowd.
Flowers, birds, & starres, all to Encolp[i]us yeelds,
As to Adonis doe Adonis feilds.
Oh had some other this describ'd, and seene!
I came a partiall Judge to praise the screene.

  G. Fletcher.

PHINEAS FLETCHER

[VERSES OF MOURNING AND JOY ON THE DEATH OF ELIZABETH AND ACCESSION OF JAMES.]

[I]

[From *Sorrowes Joy*, pp. 27—30.]

NOw did the sunne like an undaunted Hart,
  Even in his fall enlarge his ample browe;
Now his last beames on Spanish shore did dart,
Hurrying to Thetis his all-flaming cart,
When th' Atticke maid pearched on bared bowe,
Unhappie Atticke maide sang the sad treason
    Of *Tereus* most wicked man,
    And well as her renu'd tongue can,
Tempered her tragicke laies unto the sulleine season.

When *Coridon* a cruel heardgroomes boy,
Yet somewhat us'd to sing, and with his peeres
Carroll of love, and lovers sad annoy;
Wearie of passed woe, and glad of present joy,
Having instal'd his sunn'd, and ful fed steeres,
Thus to the river his blisse signified
      Well as he couth, and turning all
      Unto the humming rivers fall,
The woods and Eccho his song goodly dignified.

Ye goodly nymphes that with this river dwell,
All daughters of the yellow-sanded Chame,
Which deepe in hollow rockes frame out your cell,
Tell me ye nymphes, for you can surely tell;
Is death the cause of life? or can that same
Be my great'st blisse, which was my great'st annoy?
      Eliza's dead, and can it be
      Eliza's death brings joy to me?
Hell beeing the cause, why heavenly is the joy?

VERSES OF MOURNING AND JOY

With floods of teares I waile that deadly houre,
When as Eliza, Eliza blessed maide,
Was married to death, and we giv'n as her dowre,
And low descending into *Plutoes* bower,
Scarce fils an earthen pot beeing loosely laid.
Ah is there such power, such crueltie in fate?
    Can one Sunne one man see
    Without, and worse then miserie?
Then farewell glorious pompe, and fickle mortals state.

And yet ten thousand times I blesse that time,
When that good Prince, that Prince of endles fame,
Both in the yeares and our joyes springing prime,
Strucke my glad eares and raisd my rugged rime
To carroll lowd and herie his honor'd name.
Ah is there such power, such bountie in fate?
    Can one Sunne one man see
    Worse, and without all miserie?
Then welcome constant joy, & never-changing state.

Thou blessed spirit, sit thou ever there
Where thou nowe sit'st, in heav'n, the worlds late wonder,
Now heavens joy, and with that God yfere,
Who still to-thee, thou stil to him wast deare,
Leave us unto the world and fortunes thunder;
Or where thou dost that blessedness enjoy,
    Bid me, O quickly bid me
    Come there where thou hast hid thee,
In Joves all-blessed lap without, and bove annoy.

If not; ile live under thy sunshine rayes,
And while the Fates afoard me vitall breath
Ile spend it as thy tribute in thy praise.
Dighting, such as I can, light virelaies,
To thee, great Prince, whose life paies for her death,
Thereto doe thou my humble spirit reare,
    And with thy sacred fire
    My frozen heart inspire:
Chasing from thy high spirit all imperious feare.

PHINEAS FLETCHER

Then will I sing, and yet who better sings
Of thee, then thine owne oft-tride Muse?
Which when into thy heroicke spirit springs,
The fields resound, and neighbour forrest rings,
And sacred Muses leaving their woont use
Of carroling, flying their loathed cell,
    Run to thy silver sound,
    And lively dauncen round:
What caren they for *Helicon*, or their *Pegasean* well?

Then thou thy selfe thy selfe historifie,
But I in willow shade will chaunt thy name,
And sing I will, though I sing sorrily,
And thee, though little, I will glorifie,
And shrilly pipe aloud, the whilst my Chame
Shall answer all againe, thy name aye lives,
    While th' Oceans froathie hoare
    Beats on thy Brittish shore,
And Albion threats the heavē with high whited clives.

By this the old nights head gan to be gray,
And dappled round with many a whited spot,
So that the boy through ruinous nights decay,
Saw the first birth of the new infant day,
So up he rose and to his home he got;
And all the way of *James* he lowdly sang,
    And all the way the plaine,
    Answered *James* againe:
That all the woods of *James* & th' heaven lowdly rāg.

                      Phin. Fletcher. Regalis.

VERSES OF MOURNING AND JOY

[II]

[From *Threno-thriambeuticon*, pp. 2—3 and 5—7.]

Quæ, sicut rutilis Cynthia curribus,
    Lucebat solio splendida patrio,
        Sub lætho, (hei mihi lætho
        Fas tantum scelus est?) jacet.
Qui, sicut Clarius nube deus nigra,
Occultus tenebris delituit suis :
        Jam nuper Boreali
        Sol nobis oritur plaga.
Hanc si specto, nihil sum nisi lachrymæ ;
Hunc si specto, nihil sum nisi gaudium ;
        Nil sum, si simul uno
        Utrunq̨ intuitu noto.
Sic navem retrahunt æstus, & æstui
Robustè aura reflans ; stat dubia, & nimis
        Dum parebit utriq̨,
        Neutri sedula paruit.
Si, regina, tuo plausero funeri,
Eheu parce precor ; debita sunt meo,
        Sunt & prima Jacobo
        Plausus, quos fero, munera.
Si sceptrum lachrymis sparsero, rex, novū,
Eheu parce precor ; debita sunt meæ,
        Heu sunt ultima Elizæ
        Fletus, quos fero, munera.
                Phin. Fletcher. Regalis.

*   *   *   *   *   *   *   *

Flebilis Elizam deserta Thamesis unda
Ingemuit, virides tollens è gurgite crines,
Quà pater Oceanus solitum bibit ore tributum
Impiger, extremasq̨ tridente reverberat undas.
Crebraq̨ cum verbis immiscens verbera, nocte
Elizam veniente, Elizam abeunte canebat.
Et tantùm Elizam dilectaq̨ nomina clamans

PHINEAS FLETCHER

(Magna stupet, levis est quæcunq̧ est garrula cura)
Ad miseram Elizam fluvio labente vocabat.
Elizam pulsæ ingeminant ad sydera ripæ.
Sic quando obscurâ siluerunt omnia nocte,
Ignes flet noctem tristes, ruptosq̧ hymenæos,
Jamq̧ novam pellex admirans Attica linguam,
Terea voce, eheu crudelem Terca clamat.
At cùm Jacobi sceptrum cum nomine fama
Miscuerat, verso ad melius, quod funera nuper
Elizæ ingemuit lachrymans, & inania regna,
Jacobum inclamat, Jacobum concinit ore:
Ab faustum læto Jacobum murmure cantat:
Jacobum toto resonabat flumine lympha.

In eosdem.

Quisquis triumphos lachrymis componere
  Novit, dolorem risui,
 Te canat Eliza, te canat, & mortem tuam,
  Fletusq̧ morti debitos:
Simulq̧ te celebret Jacobe, te & tuo
  Gaudia triumpho debita.
Mea cùm tumentes Musa turgescens subit
  Repletq̧ leniter sinus,
Tota est dolor, tota est lachrymæ, dum te dolet
  Eliza, dum te lachrymat.
At cùm madidos Jacobe deflectit oculos
  In te, serenans nubila
Tota est triumphus, tota plausus, dum tibi
  Triumphat, & plaudit tibi.
Sic cùm te Eliza defleo, tantùm fleo;
  Stupescit immensus dolor.
Cùm tibi Jacobe gratuler, sileo stupens;
  Levia loquuntur gaudia.
Hoc tantùm, Eliza, vix & hoc, dico tibi:
  Eliza perpetuum vale;
Hoc tibi Jacobe, (nil mihi si non hoc deest)
  Ad sydera serus avoles.

       Phin. Fletcher. Regal.

*Facsimiles
of the handwriting of
Phineas Fletcher
from the MSS of
Locustæ,
vel
Pietas Jesuitica.*

> Sororumq́; lachrymas confectum (properatum tibi munus) quo soles oculo perlegas.
>
> Inttrim qui te maximæ Ecclesiæ vtilitati ad hanc dignitatem evexit Deus, ejdem Ecclesiæ, Principi, Patriæ, bonis deniq́; omnibus florentissimum diu conservet.
>
> Tibi, et dignitati tuæ
>
> devotissimus
>
> Phin: Fletcher
> Coll: Regal:

A leaf of *Pietas Jesuitica* (afterwards called *Locustæ*) in Sloane MSS., 444, containing part of the Dedication to James Montagu, Bishop of Bath and Wells, in Phineas Fletcher's handwriting.

Iesuitica

Qum etiam sacri vulgata Scientia scripti
Invenit Superos terris, et luce corusca
Dissoluit tenebras, noctemq excussit mortem.
Et nunc illa quidem, gentes emensa supremas,
Imperium terris æquat, cæloq profundo.
Crescit in immensum pietas, finesq recusat
Relligionis amor; fugit Ignorantia, lucis
Impatiens, fugit Impietas, arcusq pudendos
Nuda Superstitio, et nunquam non devius Error.
Nunc etiam gentes multa olim nocte sepultas,
Virginiam nostras umbræ, tot sæcula sedes,
Aggreditur; mox et manes, Stygiasq paludes
Tranabit, vix hunc nobis Acheronta relinquet
At nos lethæo per tuta silentia, somno
Sternimur interea, et media iam luce supini
Ster—

A leaf of *Pietas Jesuitica* (afterwards called *Locustæ*) in Mr Dobell's MS, in Phineas Fletcher's handwriting.

et malè tornati, neq: unquam mundi posteà redditi, et multa inter (immixa Musis) negotia descripti sunt. Siquid erratum est, pro humanitate tua ignoscas, versusq: ipsos, eorúq: authorem in tutelam tuam, famulitiúmq: recipies. Sic te, spémq: nostram tibi auspicato comissam fortunet deus. Sic Carolus noster (ut diximus olim ille puellus) annis, virtutibus, gratiâq: apud deum, hominésq: quotidie accrescat.

E familiâ tibi maximè
devinctâ, et devotâ
natu maximus.

Phinees Fletcher.

A leaf of *Locustæ* in Harl. MSS., 3196, containing part of the Dedication to Thomas Murray, in Phineas Fletcher's handwriting.

LOCUSTÆ,
VEL
PIETAS JE-
SUITICA.

Per
PHINEAM FLETCHER
Collegii Regalis
CANTABRIGIÆ,

Apud THOMAM & JOANNEM BUCKE,
celeberrimæ Academiæ Typographos.
Ann. Dom. MDCXXVII.

Rogero Townshend,

Equiti Baron.

Musarum omnium Patrono,

verè nobili, mihíque

amicissimo.

M*Agnum illud (optime Musarum pridem Alumne, nunc Patrone) imò planè maximum nobis vitium inest, altiùs naturæ (penitiùs corruptæ) defixum, & defossum, cùm injurias imo, & memori sub corde, beneficia summâ tantùm linguâ, & primoribus vix labris reponimus. In illis retinendis quàm tenaces, pertinaces? In his (præsertim divinis) quàm lubrici, & prorsus elumbes? Illa Gentis Israeliticæ tyrannide plusquam ferreâ (ad vitæ tædium) depressæ in libertatem vindicatio (Proh Deus immortalis!) qualis, quanta? Ægyptios, Regémq̃ adeò ipsum tumentem odiis ferocémque plurimis, cruentísque admodum plagis maceratos, quàm lenes viderant, & humanos? Maximos hostium exercitus (totúmque adeò Ægypti robur) sine hoste devictos, sine ferro deletos conspexerant: Fluctuum ipsi mœnibus vallati, illos molibus depressos & demersos spectaverant: Rupem sitientibus in flumina liquatam, solum esurientibus pane cœlesti, epulísq̃ instructissimis constratum, imò (ut nunc moris est) ferculis in cubitos coacervatis planè contectum degustârant. Quàm subitâ tamen oblivione hæc omnia prorsus evanuerunt? Miracula sanè magna, & stupenda; sed (ut nobis in Proverbio est) non ad triduum durantia. Id nobis hodie vitii est: Celebris illa anni Octogesimi Octavi pugna, imò potiùs sine pugnâ victoria, penitus nobis excidit. Hui! quàm citò! Vidimus Hispanos ante prælium ovantes, dictísque, imò scriptis ἐπινικίοις priusquam solverent triumphantes: Sed quod nos de Martio dici-*

mus, rabie plusquàm leoninâ mensem auspicari, abire vel agnellâ leniorem, id divino adjutorio classi Invictæ contigit. Quin & sulphurea quidem illa, Tartarea imò sanè nullo unquam dæmone vel sperata machinatio divinis solùm oculis patens, divinâ solùm manu patefacta quàm citò, quàm prorsus intercìdit! Vix ulla (atque illa certè exesa, penitùsque contempta) proditionis tam horrendæ, liberationis tam stupendæ monumenta restant. Negant impudentes Papistæ, pernegant, ejurántque. Quin & nos diem tanto beneficio illustrem quàm pigri & enervosi ab illorum mendaciis, calumniisque vindicamus! Ignoscent igitur mihi æqui judices, si Poetarum minimus scelerum omnium longè maximum, crassâ (ut aiunt) Minervâ contextum ad perpetuam Jesuiticæ Pietatis memoriam, ad animos Britannorum excitandos, honorêmque Deo Servatori restaurandum, in lucem emiserim.

Ignoscent alii, Tu verò Equitum nobilissime, aliquod fraterni, sive paterni potiùs genii vestigium agnosces, & vultu non illæto munusculum accipies ab homunculo

Tuæ dignitati devotissimo

Phin. Fletcher.

Ad P. F.

Pro approbatione Redargutio,
sed amica atque honora.

Quid istoc esse *Phinea* dixerim rei
   Fletchere, Vatum *Sanguis*, & Vatum *Caput*,
     Hostem ut professus sceleris atrocissimi
Stylóque pectoréque proditorii,
Eóusque carmine alite & fama vehas,
Cœlóque tradas, inserásque *Seculo*
Ferè ut pigendam feceris nobis *Fidem*,
Quicunque patriæ nil sinistrè movimus,
Stetimúsque sol'da vividùm *Constantia*,
Quam nemo simili cecinit, aut clanget tuba?
An fortè quale *Mæonidem* ferunt patrem,
Genuinus ut sciare ab illo Surculus?

    Διεξιὼν, Ὅμηρε, τὴν κεκαυμένην
    Φθονεῖν ἀφῆκας τὰς ἀπορθήτους πόλεις.

                  Tui faventissimus
                         S. Collins.

LOCUSTÆ,
VEL
PIETAS JESU-
ITICA.

PAnditur Inferni limen, patet intima Ditis
   Janua, concilium magnum, Stygiósq; Quirites
Accitos, Rex ipse nigra in penetralia cogit.
Olli conveniunt, volitant umbrosa per auras
Numina, Tartareóq; tumet domus alta Senatu.
Confidunt, numeróq; omnes subsellia justo
(Concilium horrendum) insternunt, causámq; fluendi
Intenti expectant: solio tum Lucifer alto
Insurgens, dictis umbras accendit amaris,
Manésq; increpitans cunctantes; Cernitis, inquit,
(Cœlo infensa cohors, exosa, expulsáq; cœlo)
Cernitis, ut superas mulcet Pax aurea gentes?
Bella silent, silet injectis oppressa catenis
Inque Erebum frustra è terris redit exul Erinnys.
Divino interea resonant Sacraria verbo,
Indomitus possessa tenet suggesta Minister,
Et victus, victórq; novos vocat impiger hostes:
Et nunc ille minis stimulans, nunc læta reponens,
Scitè animos flectit monitis, & corda remulcet.
   Quin etiam sancti vulgata Scientia Scripti
Invexit superos terris, & luce coruscâ
Dissolvit tenebras, noctémq; excussit inertem.
Crescit in immensum Pietas, finésque recusat
Relligionis amor: fugit Ignorantia, lucis
Impatiens, fugit Impietas, artúsque pudendos
Nuda Superstitio, & nunquam non devius Error:
Vim patitur, gaudétq; trahi cœleste rapíque

LOCUSTÆ

Imperium. Quin & gentes emensa supremas,
Virginiam (nostras, Umbræ, tot secula sedes)
Aggreditur, mox Cocytum, Stygiásque paludes
Tranabit, vix hunc nobis Acheronta relinquet.
  Nos contrà immemori per tuta silentia somno
Sternimur interea, & mediâ jam luce supini
Stertentes, festam trahimus, pia turba, quietem.
Quòd si animos sine honore acti sine fine laboris
Pœnitet, & proni imperii regníque labantis
Nil miseret, positis flagris, odiísque remissis
Oramus veniam, & dextras præbemus inermes.
Fors ille audacis facti, & justæ immemor iræ,
Placatus, facilísq; manus & fœdera junget.
Fors solito lapsos (peccati oblitus) honori
Restituet, cœlum nobis soliúmq; relinquet.
At me nulla dies animi, cœptíque prioris
Dissimilem arguerit: quin nunc rescindere cœlum,
Et conjurato victricem milite pacem
Rumpere, ferventíq; juvat miscere tumultu.
  Quò tanti cecidere animi? Quò pristina virtus
Cessit, in æternam quâ mecum irrumpere lucem
Tentâstis, trepidúmq; armis perfringere cœlum?
Nunc verò indecores felicia ponitis arma,
Et toties victo imbelles conceditis hosti.
Per vos, per domitas cœlesti fulmine vires,
Indomitúmq; odium, projecta resumite tela;
Dum fas, dum breve tempus adest, accendite pugnas,
Restaurate acies, fractúmq; reponite Martem.
Ni facitis, mox soli, & (quod magis urit) inulti
Æternùm (heu) vacuo flammis cruciabimur antro.
Ille quidem nullâ, heu, nullâ violabilis arte,
Securum sine fine tenet, sine milite regnum;
A nullo p[e]titur, nullo violatur ab hoste.
Compatitur tamen, ínque suis violabile membris
Corpus habet: nunc ô totis consurgite telis,
Quà patet ad vulnus nudum sine tegmine corpus,
Imprimite ultrices, pen[i]túsque recondite flammas.
Accelerat funesta dies, jam limine tempus
Insistit, cùm nexa ipso cum vertice membra
Naturam induerint cœlestem, ubi gloria votum,

PHINEAS FLETCHER

Atque animum splendor superent, ubi gaudia damno
Crescant, deliciǽque modum, finémque recusent.
At nos supplicio æterno, Stygiísque catenis
Compressi, flammis & vivo sulphure tecti
Perpetuas duro solvemus carcere pœnas.
Hîc anima, extremos jam tum perpessa dolores,
Majores semper metuit, queritúrque remotam,
Quam toto admisit præsentem pectore, mortem;
Oráque cæruleas perreptans flamma medullas
Torquet anhela siti, fibrásque atque ilia lambit.
Mors vivit, moritúrque inter mala mille superstes
Vita, vicésque ipsâ cum morte, & nomina mutat.
Cùm verò nullum moriendi conscia finem
Mens reputat, cùm mille annis mille addidit annos,
Præteritúmque nihil venturo detrahit ævum,
Mox etiam stellas, etiam superaddit arenas,
Jámque etiam stellas, etiam numeravit arenas;
Pœna tamen damno crescit, per flagra, per ignes,
Per quicquid miserum est, præceps ruit, anxia lentam
Provocat infelix mortem; si fortè relabi
Possit, & in nihilum rursus dispersa resolvi.
Æquemus meritis pœnas, atque ultima passis
Plura tamen magnis exactor debeat ausis;
Tartareis mala speluncis, vindictáque cœlo
Deficiat; nunquam, nunquam crudelis inultos,
Immeritósve Erebus capiet: meruisse nefandum
Supplicium medios inter solabitur ignes,
Et, licèt immensos, factis superâsse dolores.
Nunc agite, ô Proceres, omnésque effundite technas,
Consulite, imperióque alacres succurrite lapso.
Dixerat, insequitur fremitus, trepidantiáque inter
Agmina submissæ franguntur murmure voces.
Qualis, ubi Oceano mox præcipitandus Ibero
Immineat Phœbus, flavíque ad litora Chami
Conveniunt, glomerántque per auras agmina muscæ,
Fit sonitus; longo crescentes ordine turbæ
Buccinulis voces acuunt, sociósque vocantes,
Undas nube premunt; strepitu vicinia rauco
Completur, resonántque accensis litora bombis.
Postquam animi posuere, soníque relangüit æstus,

LOCUSTÆ

Excipit Æquivocus, quo non astutior alter
Tartareos inter technas effingere Patres.
Illi castra olim numero farcibat inerti
Crescens in ventrem Monachus, simul agmine junčti
Tonsi ore, & tonsi lunato vertice Fratres:
At nunc felici auspicio Jesuitica Princeps
Agmina ducebat, veteranóque omnia laté
Depopulans, magnas passim infert milite clades.
Illum etiam pugnantem, illum admirata loquentem
Circuit, & fremitu excepit plebs vana secundo.
Composuere animos omnes, tacitíque quiêrunt;
Surgit, & haud læto Æquivocus sic incipit ore;
  O Pater, ô Princeps umbrarum, Erebíque potestas,
Ut rebare, omnes nequicquam insumpsimus artes:
Nil tanti valuere doli; nihil omnibus actum
Magnorum impensis operum, verùm omnia retrò
Deteriùs ruere, ínque bonum sublapsa referri.
  Non secùs adverso pictum tenet amne phaselum
Anchora, si funem, aut mordaces fibula nexus
Solverit, atque illum pronâ trahit alveus undâ.
Nec quenquam accusa, tentatum est quicquid apertâ
Vi fieri, aut pressâ potuit quod tectiùs arte.
Ille Pater rerum, cui frustra obnitimur omnes
(Sed frustra juvat obniti) vim magnus inanem
Discutit, & cœlo fraudes ostendit aprico.
Quin soliti lento Reges torpescere luxu,
Palladiis nunc tecti armis, Musísque potentes,
In nos per mediam meditantur prælia pacem.
Nec tamen æternos obliti, absiste timere,
Unquam animos, fessíque ingentes ponimus iras.
Nec fas, non sic deficimus, nec talia tecum
Gessimus, in cœlos olim tua signa sequuti.
Est hîc, est vitæ, & magni contemptor Olympi,
Quíque oblatam animus lucis nunc respuat aulam,
Et domiti tantùm placeat cui Regia cœli.
Ne dubita, nunquam fractis hæc pectora, nunquam
Deficient animis: priùs ille ingentia cœli
Atria, desertósque æternæ lucis alumnos
Destituens, Erebum admigret, noctémque profundam,
Et Stygiis mutet radiantia lumina flammis.

PHINEAS FLETCHER

Quòd si acies, fractásque iterum supplere catervas
Est animus, scitéque malas dispergere fraudes;
Non ego consilii, armorum non futilis author:
Nec veteres frustra, Genitor, revocabimus artes,
Sed nova, sed nulli prorsus speranda priorum
Aggredienda mihi conamina; Non ego lentos
Nequicquam adstimulem Fratres, alvúmque sequentes
Distentām Monachos: dum nox, dum plurima terris
Incumbens caligo animos sopivit inertes,
Non ingratus erat Fratrum labor, omnia nobis
Artibus ignavis dederat secura, trahénsque
Invisam coelo lucem, tenebrísve nitentem
Involvens, jam nube diem, jam nocte premebat.
   At nebulas postquam Ph[oe]bus dimovit inanes,
T[ar]tareæ immisso patuerunt lumine sordes,
Nec patitur lucem miles desuetus apertam.
Nunc alio imbelles tempus supplere cohortes
Milite, & emeritos castris emittere Fratres:
Nunc Jesuitarum sanctum prodentia nomen
Arma, manúsque placent: juvat ipsum invadere coelum,
Sideráque hærentémque polo detrudere solem.
Jam mihi sacratos felici milite Reges
Protrahere, atque ipsum coeli calcare tyrannum
Sub pedibus videor: nihil isto milite durum,
Nil sanctum, clausúmque manet, quin oppida latè
Præsidiis, urbésque tenent; jam limina Regum,
Jámque adyta irrumpunt, vel mollibus intima blandi
Corda dolis subeunt, vel ferro & cæde refringunt.
Hi vetulæ fucum Romæ, pigméntaq; rugis
Aptantes, seros effoetæ nuper amores
[C]onciliant, lapsúmque decus, formámq; reponunt.
Ni facerent (noctem coelíque inamabile lumen
Testor) mox aliæ sedes, nova regna per orbem
Exulibus querenda, solóque atque æthere pulsis:
Cocytus tantùm nobis, Erebúsque pateret.
Quin tu (magne Pater) Stygias reclude cavernas,
Ac barathrum in terras, Orcúmq; immitte profundum;
Insueti totum Superi mirentur Avernum.
   Hic solita infidis inspiret prælia Turcis;
Sarmatas hic, gelidósque incendat Marte Polonos,

LOCUSTÆ

Germanósque duces, hic Reges inflet Iberos;
Regnorúmque sitim, & nullo saturabile pectus
Imperio stimulet, diróque intorqueat æstu.
Ite foras Stygiæ (Princeps jubet) ite catervæ,
Vipereas inferte manus, serite arma per agros,
Et scelerum, & fœti dispergite semina belli:
Ast ego Tarpeium Tiberina ad flumina Patrem,
Conciliúmque petam solus, mea regna, Latinum,
Murice vestitum, rubeóque insigne galero.
Mox scelere ingenti, atque ingenti cæde peractâ
Regrediar, Stygiásque domus, & inania latè
Undique collectis supplebo regna colonis.
At tu, magne Pater, fluitantes contrahe manes;
Præcipitésque vias, latósque extende meatus;
Ut patulo densùm volitantes Orcus hiatu
Corripiat rabidus mentes, intúsque recondat.
 Dixit; & illæti perfracto limine Averni
Exiliit primus, lucémque invasit apertam.
Insequitur deforme Chaos; ruit omne barathrum,
Fœda, horrenda cohors: trepidant pallentia cœli
Lumina, & incerto Tellus tremit horrida motu.
Ipse pater pronos laxatis Ph[œ]bus habenis
Præcipitat currus, & cœlo territus exit.
Succedit nox umbrarum, cœlúmque relictum
Invadit, multáque premit caligine terras.
 Non secùs Æoliis emissi finibus Austri
Omnia corripiunt, terrásque undásque tumultu
Miscent; arboreos fœtus, segetémque resectam
Turbine convellunt rapido, verrúntque per auras.
Ast oculis longè mœstus sua vota colonus
Insequitur, totóque trahit suspiria corde.
Senserat adventum, subitóque inferbuit æstu
Terra, odiísque tumet, fœto jam turgida bello:
Circùm umbræ volitant, fraudésque, & crimina spargunt.
 Hic gelidos semper nivibus, glaciéque Polonos
Exacuit, tacitéque subit Jesuitica totus
Pectora, jámque dolos, cædésque inspirat; at illa
Arripiunt avidè flammas, notǽque per ossa
Discurrunt furiæ, ínque sinus ínque ilia serpunt.
 Jámque in cognatos meditantur bella Suëvos,

PHINEAS FLETCHER

Sarmaticásque ardent Romano adnectere gentes
Pontifici, & Graecas templis expellere leges.
Fictitiam Regis sobolem, consutáque belli
Crimina supponunt vafri, mentitáque veris
Texunt, Sarmaticósque implent rumoribus agros.
Caedibus accrescit bellum, regníque medullis
Haeret inexpletùm: semper nova praelia victus
Integrat: erubuere nives jam sanguine tinctae
Purpureo, & tepidâ solvuntur frigora caede.
Ast alii Graias olim cognomine terras,
Graias Pieriis gratissima nomina Musis:
Nunc domitos tutus consedit Turca per agros.
Invisunt alacres bello loca foeta perenni,
Et tenero caedem inspirant & praelia Regi.
Nunc oculo, nunc voce ferox, nunc fronte minatur,
Non epulis luxúve puer, non ille paternâ
Desidiâ gaudet; sed bella, sed aspera cordi
Ira sedent, saevámque superbia Turcica mentem
Inflat, & ingentes volvit sub pectore motus.
Aut is linigeras aptabit classibus alas,
Aut galeas finget, clypeósque, & (fulmina belli)
Tormenta, impositis strident incudibus aera.
Et nunc ille ferox Persas Asiámque rebellem
Subjiciens, totum spirat de pectore Martem,
Exultánsque animis multâ se suscitat irâ.
Heu quae Christicolis caedes, quàm debita pestis
Imminet? Heu quantus tanto timor instat ab hoste,
Ni tu, Christe, malum avertas, tu fulmina, Christe,
Dispergas, & vana manu conamina ludas?
   Interea toto dum bella seruntur in orbe,
Italiam Æquivocus magnam, & Tiberina fluenta
Adveniens, intrat feralis moenia Romae.
Nec mora, nota subit mitrati tecta Tyranni,
Quáque incedit ovans, adytísque vagatur opacis,
I[n]sperata Erebo vel aperto crimina sole
Gaudet ubique tuens, messémque expectat opimam.
Dicite, Pierides, quis nunc tenet Itala primus
Arva? Quibus tandem gradibus, quo principe Reges
Exuit, & pingues aptans sibi Roma cucullos,
Subjicitur raso modò facta Sororcula Fratri?

LOCUSTÆ

Siccine decrepiti puerascunt tempore mores,
Pontifice Augustum ut mutent, Monachóq; Monarcham?
   Postquam res Latii totum porrecta per orbem
Creverat, & terras Urbi subjecerat uni,
Substitit, & justo librata in pondere sedit.
At mox prona ruens, in se conversa, relabi
Cœpit, & effœtam vix jam, vix sustinet urbem.
Haud secùs alternis crescentes fluctibus undæ
Incedunt, facilésq; Actæ superantia clivos
Æquora prorepunt tacitè, mox litora complent,
Subjectásq; procul despectant vertice terras:
Jámq; viarum incerta hærent, mox prona recedunt,
Defervénsq; undis paulatim in se ipse residit
Nereus, & nulli noto caput abdidit alveo.
Interea Patrum manibus cœlestia passim
Semina sparguntur, surgit cum fœnore campis
Læta seges, plenísq; albescunt messibus arva.
At simul hirsutis horrebat carduus agris,
Et tribuli lolíq; nemus, simul aspera lappæ
Sylva, & lethæos operata papavera somnos.
Quippe hominum cœlíq; hostis, dum membra colonis
Fessa quies laxat, tritico vilémq; faselum
Miscuit infestus, viciásq; aspersit inanes.
Mirantur lolium agricolæ, mirantur avenas,
Mortiferásq; horrent mediis in messibus herbas.
   Quin etiam imperio Christi Pro-christus eodem
Parvus adhuc, clausúsq; utero succrevit opaco:
Jámq; vias trudens tentaverat, integra Romæ
Auspicia impediunt, ausísq; ingentibus obstant.
At Latiis postquam imperium segnesceret arvis,
Inq́; Bisantinas sensim concederet urbes,
Exilit, & justo prodit jam firmior ævo.
Mox etiam laxis paulatim assuetus habenis,
Mauricio scelere extincto, duce, & auspice Phoca,
Excutit aurigam, ínque rotas succedit inanes.
Et nunc rasorum longus producitur ordo
Pontificum, magicâque rudem, Stygiâque popellum
Arte ligans, Italâ solus dominatur in aula.
Jámque furens animis, & torquens fulmina, sceptrum
Paulus habet, clavésque manu violentus inanes

PHINEAS FLETCHER

Projiciens Petri, gladio succinctus acuto
Intonat, & longè distantes territat urbes.
Stulte, quid æterni crepitantia fulmina Patris,
Cœlestésque minas, & non imitabile numen
Ignibus, ah, fatuis simulas? Venetósque sagaces,
Et non fictitio terrendos igne Britannos
Exagitas? Ast hi contrà, cùm debita poscunt
Tempora (non illi voces, verbosáque chartæ
Fulmina) tela alacres, verásque in mœnia Romæ
Incutient flammas, carnésque, & viscera mandent.
   Arma foris Regum Meretrix vetula, arma dolósque
Exercet, Circæa domi sed carmina, & artes
Infandas magicis dirùm miscendo susurris
Irritat flammis, durósque obtrudit amores.
At cùm feralis languet saturata libido,
In facies centum, centum in miracula rerum
Corpora Lethæo transformat adultera cantu.
Aut Asini fiunt, Vulpésve, hirtíve Leones,
Atque Lupi, atque Sues, atque exosæ omnibus Hydræ.
Illi capta quidem dextro, sed acuta sinistro
Lumine, deformis cæcæ Ignorantia portæ
Excubat, & nebulis aditus, & limen opacat.
Filius huic Error comes assidet; ille vagantes
Excipit hospitio, & longis circum undique ducit
Porticibus, veterúmque umbras, simulacráque rerum
Mirantes, variis fallit per inania ludis.
Intrantem prensat mores venerata vetustos
Stulta superstitio, properantéque murmura voce
Præcipitans, votis Superos, precibúsque fatigat.
   Interiùs scelus imperitat, fœcundáque regnant
Flagitia, & mentes trudunt, rapiúntque nefandas.
Inficit hic cœlos audax, Christúmque venenans
Porrigit immistis Regi sacra tanta cicutis.
Lethalem ille Deum, atque imbutam morte salutem
Ore capit, multóque lavat peccata veneno.
Hic clavos, virgásque, crucémque, tua (optime Jesu)
Supplicia, hastámque innocuo sub corde refixam,
Hic truncum, hic saxum (saxo contemptior ipso)
Propitium implorat supplex, Stygiísque ululantes
Speluncis flexo veneratur poplite manes.

LOCUSTÆ

Hic Cereri, & fluido procumbit stultus Jaccho,
Quósque colit vorat ipse Deos, & numina plenus
(Ah scelus!) abscondit venis, alvóque reponit.
Hic caligantes, cœlum execratus apertum,
Te magicos, Jesu, te immittens Sagus in ignes,
Umbras imperiis audax, Stygiúmque nefando
Ore Jovem, totúmque vocat de sedibus Orcum.
Romulidûm ille Patrum, primæque haud immemor urbis,
Et fovet ipse lupas, atque ipse fovetur ab illis.
Hic sobolem impurus prohibens, castósque hymenæos,
Ah, pathicos ardet pueros, & mascula turpis
Scorta alit; (heu facinus terris, cœlóque pudendum
Ausus!) purpureo quin mox Pater ille galero
Emeritos donat, procerésque, oviúmque magistros
Esse jubet, mox dura Pater, Musísque tremenda
Laudat, & incestis tutatur crimina Musis.
 Nec requies, fervent nova crimina, fervet honorum
Nummorúmque infanda sitis; tumet improba fastu
Conculcans stratos immensa Superbia Reges.
Venerat huc, lætúsque animi vetera agmina lustrans
Æquivocus falsi subiit penetralia Petri:
Quem super Anglorum rebus, Venetóque tumultu
Ardentem curæ, & semper nova damna coquebant.
Huic Stygias sub corde faces, omnésque nefando
Pectore succendit furias, ille improbus irâ
Concilium vocat. Agglomerant imberbia Fratrum
Agmina, concurrunt veteranis ordine longo
Insignes ducibus Jesuitæ, animísque parati,
Sive dolo libeat, seu Marti fidere aperto.
Discumbunt, sedet in mediis diademate Paulus
Tempora præfulgens triplici, vultúque dolorem
Præfatus, sic tandem iras, atque ora resolvit.
 Nil pudet incepto victos desistere? fessos
Deficere, extremóq; ferè languere sub actu,
Nec posse instantem Romæ differre ruinam?
Fata vetant: méne incertis concedere fatis?
Inclusus latebris Monachus tot vertere prædas,
Tot potuit Patri Romano avellere gentes?
Ast ego, quem strato venerantur corpore, sacris
Blanda etiam pedibus libantes oscula Reges:

PHINEAS FLETCHER

Quem Superi, quem terra tremit, manésq; profundi,
Qui solio Christi assideo, Christo æmulus ipsi,
Tot mala quotidie, & semper crescentia inultus
Damna fero: & quisquam Romanum numen adoret?
Aut vigiles supplex munus suspendat ad aras?
Jam Veneti juga detrectant, & jussa superbi
Destituunt, Batavus nulla revocabilis arte
Effugit, longéq; escas laqueósque recusat.
Gallia tot compressa malis, tot cladibus acta
Deficit, & jam dimidiâ plus parte recessit.
Ille Navarrenâ infelix ex arbore ramus
(Exosum genus, & divis hostile Latinis)
Quanquam oculos fingens placidos, vultúsq; serenat,
Aggerat ingentem memori sub corde dolorem.
 Et velut ille fame, & vinclis infractus ahenis,
Oblitúsq; leo irarum, caudámq; remulcens
Porrectas manibus captabit leniter escas:
Si semel insueto saturaverit ora cruore,
Mox soliti redeunt animi: fremit horridus irâ,
Vincula mox & claustra vorat, rapit ore cruento
Custodem, & primas domitor lacer imbuit iras.
Quid referam totâ divisos mente Britannos,
Quos neque blanditiæ molles, non aspera terrent
Jurgia, non ipsos sternentia fulmina Reges?
Heu sobolem invisam, & fatis majora Latinis
Fata Britannorum! Centum variata figuris
Proditio flammis, ferróque, atróq; veneno
Nil agit: insensum detorquet vulnera numen.
Nil Hispana juvat pubes, nil maxima classis,
Quam Tellus stupuit, stupuit Neptunus euntem,
Miratus liquidum sylvescere pinibus æquor.
Quin toto disjecta mari fugit æquore prono,
Jámq; relaxatos immittens navita funes,
Increpitat ventos properans, Eurósq; morantes.
Tot precibus properata ægrè, frustráq; redempta
Quid læti tulit illa dies, quâ sidus Elisæ
Occidit, & longo solvit se Roma dolore?
Occidit illa quidem, qua nullam Roma cruentam
Nostra magis vidit, faustámve Britannia stellam.
Sed simul exoritur, quem nos magis omnibus unum

LOCUSTÆ

Horremus, gelidâ consurgens Phœbus ab Arĉto:
Quem Pallas, quem Musæ omnes comitantur euntem,
Pax simul incedit læto Saturnia vultu,
Lora manu laxans, trahitur captiva catenis
Barbaries: positóq; gemens Bellona flagello.
Non me nequicquam junĉtum uno fœdere triplex
Imperium terret, terret fatale Jacobi,
Nec frustra impositum Luĉtantis ab omine nomen.
Quin similis Patri soboles inimica Latino
Nomina Pontifici assumens, radiante superbos
Henricos puer, & Fredericos exprimit ore.
Nunc & equos domitare libet, spumantiáque ora
Colligere in nodum, sinuosáque fleĉtere colla,
Et teneris hastam jam nunc jaĉtare lacertis.
Quin etiam ille minor, sed non minùs ille timendus
Carolus, haud læto turbat nos omine, cujus
Mortiferam accepit primò sub nomine plagam
Roma, & lethali languens in vulnere, lentâ
Peste cadit, certámque videt moribunda ruinam.
Illa etiam inferior sexu, non peĉtore, terret,
Quæ reducem nobis fœcundam ostentat Elisam,
Invisum, majus fatis, ac cladibus auĉtum
Nomen, & inviĉtam spondens post prælia pacem.
Nec me vanus agit terror, quippe illius ore
Prævideo multas nobis, nisi fallor, Elisas.
 Quæ mihi spes ultra? Vel me præsaga mali mens
Abstulit, & veris majora pavescere jussit,
Vel calamo Pater, & Musis, sed filius armis
Sternet, & extremis condet mea mœnia flammis.
 Hei mihi! sidereæ turres, túque æmula cœli
Urbs, antiqua Deûm sedes, reginàque terræ,
Quam lana Assyrio pingit fucata veneno,
Quam vestes auro, stellásque imitante pyropo
Illusæ decorant, ostro, coccóque pudentes,
Cui tantum de te licuit? Quæ dextera sacras
Dilacerare arces potuit? Quo numine turres
Dejicere, ingentíque vias complere ruina?
 Conticuit: tristísque diu stupor omnibus ora
Defixit, mistóque sinus premit ira dolore.
Ut rediere animi, strepitus, junĉtæque querelis

PHINEAS FLETCHER

Increbuere minæ: dolor iras, ira dolorem
Aggerat, alternísque incendunt pectora flammis:
Tota minis, mistóque fremunt subsellia luctu.
   At sonitus inter medios, & maximus ævo,
Et sceptris Jesuita potens, cui cætera parent
Agmina, consurgens ultro sese obtulit: illo
Conspecto siluere omnes, atque ora tenebant
Affixi. Verba Æquivocus versuta loquenti
Suggerit, & cordi custos, oríque residit.
   O Pater, ô hominum Princeps, ô maxime divûm
Conditor, haud minor ipse Deo, jam parva caduco
Spes superest regno, neque te sententia fallit:
Mœnia præcipitem spondent sublapsa ruinam.
Nullum igitur lacrymis tempus, quin ocyus omnes
Sarcimus veteres, aliásque reponimus arces.
Quid prohibet quin arte diu tua Roma supersit,
Qua vel nunc superest? Fatum sibi quisque supremum est,
Et sortis faber ipse suæ. Nunc, optime, nostram
Quà fieri possit paucis, Pater, accipe mentem.
   Ut qui armis hostile parat rescindere vallum,
Non ubi confertis armantur mœnia turmis,
Aut altis cinguntur aquis, sed quà aggere raro,
Atque humiles tenui muros cinxere coronâ,
Irruit, incautámque malis premit artibus urbem:
Non secus infirmi nutantia pectora sexus
Blanditiis tentanda, dolóque adeunda procaci.
In tenui labor, at lucrum non tenue sequetur.
Vincitur, & vincit citiùs; citò fœmina discit
Errores, scitéque docet: gremio illa virili
Infusa, & niveis cunctantem amplexa lacertis,
Blanda sinus leviter molles, & pectora vellit,
Mox domitæ imperitat menti, bibit ille venenum,
Et rapit errores animo, penitúsque recondit.
Qui toties septus, toties invictus ab hoste
Constitit, armatum qui dente, atque ungue leonem
Manoides dextrâ impavidus lacerabat inermi,
Pellicis in gremio crinem, robúrque relinquens,
Fœmineâ infelix (nullis superandus ab armis)
Arte, sine ense jacet, sine vi, sine vulnere victus.
His, Pater, haud levibus visum est præludere telis.

LOCUSTÆ

Et quoniam illecebris flecti, frangíve recusat
Vi Batavus, technis subeundus, & arte domandus.
 Apta nec ansa deest: manet illic fortè, scholísque
Imperitat vafri ingenii, fidelque labantis
Arminius, quem magna stupet sequitúrque caterva,
Amphibium genus, & studiis hostile quietis.
Hi suetis stimulandi odiis, scitísque fovendi
Laudibus, ac donis onerandi, rebus Iberis
Ut faveant, sceptrum Hispano obsequiúmque reponant.
 Proximus in Gallos labor est, quos agmine pleno
Aversos, iterum ad Romam matrémq; reducam.
Parisios vobis facilè succidere flores,
Liliáque Hispano dabimus calcanda Leoni;
Et trunca, ad solitum decusso vertice morem,
Stemmata, radicémq; arvis transferre Granatis.
Illa Navarrenâ infelix ex arbore planta
Ense recidenda est, flammísque urenda supremis.
Dúmque tener flectíque potest, nescítque reniti
Surculus, in truncum mox immittatur Iberum:
Oblitus primi Hispanum propagine succum
Imbibat, Hispanis excrescant germina ramis.
Quin modo qui sectâ viduus manet arbore ramus,
Hispano discat, si fas, inolescere libro,
Et duplex pietas duplicato crescat amore.
 Hic tragicæ prologus scenæ: majora paramus,
Non facinus vulgare sero: quod nulla tacebit,
Credet nulla dies, magnum populísq; tremendum
Omnibus incepto: nequicquam verba, minásq;
Conterimus, nequicquam artes projecimus omnes:
Tempora nos urgent mortis suprema, supremum
Tentandum scelus est: tollatur quicquid iniqui
Obstiterit; nec te larvati nomen honesti
Terreat, aut sceleris; quin tu moderator honesti,
Regula tu justi: per fas, Pater optime, nobis
Pérq; nefas tentanda via est, qua frangere duros
Possimus, Latiúmq; ipsis inferre Britannis.
Illi hostes, illi telísque dolísque petendi,
Vindictam reliqui tantam videántq;, tremántq;.
Nec mihi mens solum gelidis auferre cicutis,
Aut armis Regem, cultróve invadere: magnum,

PHINEAS FLETCHER

Sed priùs auditum est facinus; certissimus ultor
Et sceptris odiísque puer succedet avitis.
Sed Regem pariter, paritérque inflexile semen,
Sed Proceres, Patrésque Equitésque & quicquid ubique
Prudentis vulgi est, ictu truncabimus uno.
Quin domitos sine telo omnes, sine vulnere victos
Flagitio, Pater, una uno dabit hora Britannos.
Quà facere id possim, paucis adverte, docebo.
 Stat bene nota domus, saxo constructa vetusto,
Marmore cælato, & Pariis formosa columnis,
Quà celebris Thamo generatus & Iside nymphâ
Thamisis inflexo Ludduni mœnia fluctu
Alluit, ingentémque excurrere mœnibus urbem,
Crescentésque videt semper splendescere turres.
Quáque Austros patulis immittit aperta fenestris,
Fronte superba alte submissas despicit undas.
 Huc fluere, & primis omnes concurrere regnis
Et Proceres terræ & Patres Plebémque Britannæ.
Ipse etiam primum tota cum prole Senatum
Reginâ simul ingreditur comitante Jacobus.
 Hîc lapsos revocant mores, Romæque cruentas
Imponunt leges, & pœnas sanguine poscunt.
At latebræ subter cæcæ, magnísq; cavernæ
Excurrunt spatiis, multo loca fœta Lyæo.
His tacitè nitrum & viventia sulphura tectis
Subjiciam, Stygióque implebo pulvere sedes.
 Ut numero primùm crescunt subsellia justo,
Et semel intumuit pleno domus alta Senatu,
Tecta ruam: juvat horrendos procul aure fragores
Excipere, & mistas latoribus aëre leges
Correptas spectare: juvat semusta virorum
Membra, omnésque supra volitantes æthere Reges
Cernere: rupta gemet Tellus, & territa cœli
Dissilient spatia; ast alto se gurgite præceps
Thamisis abscondet, mirabitur æthera Pluto,
Et trepidi fugient immisso lumine manes.
Dixerat: applaudunt omnes, magis omnibus ipse
Consilium laudat sanctus Pater, ipse labantis
Patronum Romæ læto sic ore salutat:
Dii Patribus fausti semper, cultíque Latinis,

LOCUSTÆ

Non omnino tamen moriturae moenia Romae
Deseritis, tales cùm animos, & tanta tulistis
Pectora, jam versis Latium florescere fatis
Aspicio, effoetámque iterum juvenescere Romam.
   Ast ego quas tandem laudes pro talibus ausis,
Quae paria inveniam? Quin tu mox aureus aede
Stabis, victrici succinctus tempora lauro.
Ipse ego marmoreas, meritis pro talibus, aras
Adjiciam, ipse tibi vota, & pia thura frequenter
Imponam, & summos jam nunc meditabor honores.
   Salve praesidium fidei columénque Latinae:
Incipe jam coelo assuesci, stellásque patentes
Ingreditor, manibúsque coli jam disce supinis.
   Interea Æquivocus manes, atq; infima Ditis
Regna petens, magnis Erebum rumoribus implet,
Inventum facinus, cujus caelúmque solúmque,
Atque umbras pudeat steriles, quod cuncta, quod ipsas
Vicerit Eumenidas, totóque à crimine solvat.
   At Jesuita memor sceleris, coeptíque nefandi,
Lucifugae devota Jovi, Patríque Latino
Pectora de tota excerpit lectissima gente:
Digna quidem proles Italâ de matre Britanna.
Hic dirum à Facibus certo trahit omine nomen,
Ille Hyemes referens, magnos portenderat imbres,
Raptáque perpetuâ minitatur lumina nocte.
Hic trahit à Fossis, raucis hic nomina Corvis:
His Jesuita nefas aperit, totúmque recludens
Consilium, horrendísque ligans Acherontica diris
Vota, truces ipso caedes obsignat Jësu.
   Jámque illi, ruptae media inter viscera matris,
Accelerant, duros (agrestia tela) ligones
Convectant, orco vicini, dirius orco
Infodiunt altè scelus, interiúsque recondunt.
Dúmque operi incumbunt alacres, crescúntque ruinae,
Nescio quos multâ visi sub nocte susurros
Percipere, & tenui incertas cum murmure voces.
Vicinos illi manes, Erebúmque timentes
Diffugiunt trepidi, refluunt cum sanguine mentes:
Jamque umbris similes ipsi vitantur, ut umbrae,
Et vitant, ipsíque timent, ipsíque timentur.

PHINEAS FLETCHER

Hic medio lapsus cursu immotúsque recumbens
Pressâ animâ, clausísque oculis, jam flagra sequentis
Tisiphones, uncásque manus, & verbera sperat.
Ille cavas quærit latebras, cupáque receptus
Nitrosâ, trepidos intra se contrahit artus.
Sic cùm membra silent placidâ resoluta quiete,
Terrenus nigra inficiens præcordia fumus
Invadit mentem, jàmque umbram effingit inanem,
Tædâ umbram Stygiâ armatam, saniéque madentem:
Omnia turbantur subitò, volat ille per auras
Exanimis deménsque metu, frustráque refixos
Increpat usque pedes; præsens insultat imago,
Jam tergum calcémque terens: vox ore sepulta
Deficit, & dominum fallaci prodit hiatu.

Ut reduci mox corde metus sedantur inertes,
Paulatim apparent rari latebrásque relinquunt:
Incertíque metus tanti, sed pergere certi,
Cautiùs arrectâ captabant aure susurros.
Ut tandem humanam agnoscunt ex murmure vocem,
Læti abeunt, ortóque die vicina Lyæo
Sacrata ediscunt latis excurrere cellis.
Conducunt, nitrúmque avidè, sulphúrque recondunt,
Et ligno scelus & conjecto vimine celant.
Jámque nefas felix stabat, promptúmque seniles
Temporis increpitant gressus, lucémque morantem.

Sed quid ego nullo effandum, nullóque tacendum
Tempore flagitium repeto? Quid nomina Diris
Vota, & perpetuis repeto celebranda tenebris?
At frustra celabo tamen quod terra stupescit,
Quod Superi exhorrent, quod Tartarus ipse recusat,
Ejurátque nefas: incisum marmore crimen
Vivet in æternum, pariter Jesuitica longùm
Simplicitas vivet, rerúmque piissima Roma.

Jámque optata dies aderat, quâ more vetusto
Conveniunt magno Procerésque Patrésque Senatu:
Ipse sacris Princeps devinctus tempora gemmis,
Aut phalerato insignis equo, currúve superbus
Ingreditur, laterîque hæret pulcherrima Conjux,
Et sobole & formâ fortunatissima princeps.
Proximus incedit facie vultùque sereno

LOCUSTÆ

Ille animum ostentans patrium matrísque decores,
Mistáque concordi felicia prælia paci,
Henricus, placidóque refulgens Carolus ore.
Virgineásque simul, Magnatum incendia, turmas,
Insignes formâ nymphas, formosior ipsa
Flagrantes perfusa genas inducit Elisa,
Et nivibus roseum commiscuit ore pudorem.
Haud secus innumeris cœlo stipata sereno
Ignibus incedit, radiósque argentea puros
Dijaculans, cunctis præfulget Cynthia stellis.
Mox Procerum accrescunt multo splendentia luxu
Agmina, gemmísque insignes & murice fulgent,
Conciliúmque petunt conferti, effusus euntes
Prosequitur plausúsque virûm, clangórque tubarum,
Et faustis mistus precibus ferit ardua clamor
Sidera, tota fremit festis urbs quassa triumphis.
Nox erat, & Facii Titan scelerísque propinqui
Avolat impatiens, stimulísque minísque jugales
Exagitans, latet adverso jam tutus in orbe;
Quáque volat, patulæ lustrans tot crimina terræ,
Nullum æquale videt, Thracésque Getásque cruentos,
Quíq; Platam, Gangem, rapidum qui potat Oraxem,
Qui Phlegetonta, omnes omni jam crimine solvit.
Diffugiunt stellæ, nequicquam impervia tentans
Æquora collectis nebulis extinguitur Ursa.
Manibus, & sceleri nox apta, at nigrior ipsâ
Nocte facem plumbo septam, tædámque latentem
Veste tegens, cellam Facius criménq; revisit.
Dúmq; opus effingit tragicum, facinúsq; retexit,
Multa timet sperátq;: hinc pœna, hinc præmia pectus
Sollicitant, dubio desciscunt viscera motu.
Jámque vacillantem Æquivocus cœnámq; precésq;
Cœcúmq; obsequium menti, Papámq; reponens
Fulcit, & injectis obfirmat pectora Diris.
Ast oculos summo interea deflexit Olympo
Ille Pater rerum, certo qui sidera cursu
Magna rotat, terrásq; manu, & maria improba claudit.
Confectásque videns fraudes, cæcísque cavernis
Crimina vicino matura tumescere partu;
Mox Aquilam affatur, solio quæ sternitur imo

PHINEAS FLETCHER

Advigilans, liquidásq; alis mandata per auras
Præcipitat: Confestim Anglos pete nuncia clivos,
Et Proceres summis curam de rebus habentes
Aggressa, ambiguo fraudes sermone recludas,
Atque acres cœco turbes ænigmate sensus.
Ipse ego dum voces alto sub pectore versant,
Ipse oculos mentémq; dabo, qua infanda Jacobus
Ausa, & Tarpeii evolvat conamina Patris.
   Dixerat: at levibus volucris secat æthera pennis,
Ocyor & vento, & rapido Jovis ocyor igne.
Jámq; simul niveas Ludduni assurgere longè
Aspicit, aspectásq; simul tenet impigra turres.
   Penniger hic primùm contractis nuncius alis
Constitit, & formosa videns fulgescere tecta,
Coctilibus muris, parilíq; rubentia saxo,
Ingreditur, magno posuit quæ splendida sumptu
Qui patriis major succrevit laudibus heros,
Prudentis soboles patris prudentior ipse.
Hunc, ubi consilium pleno de pectore promit,
Mirantur Britones læti, mirantur Iberi,
Et laudant animos trepidi, metuúntque sagaces.
Ille etiam gazam (major tamen ipse) B[r]itannam,
Ille etiam Musas tutatur, & otia Musis,
Chamus ubi angustas tardo vix flumine ripas
Complet, decrepitóque pater jam deficit amne.
Ille mihi labro teretes trivisse cicutas,
Ille modos faustus calamo permisit agresti.
Huc ubi perventum est, mutato nuntius ore
Perplexâ attonito descriptas arte tabellas
Tradidit heroi, & mediæ sese ocyus urbi
Proripiens, suetis iterum se condidit astris.
   Ille legens cæci stupuit vestigia scripti,
Atque iterum voces iterúmque recolligit omnes,
Jámque hoc, jámque illud, jam singula pectore versat,
Quid te frustra, heros, angis? Non si Oedipus author
Spondeat, hos animo speres rescindere nodos.
Non minimum est crimen crimen præsumere tantum,
Nec virtus minima est scelus ignorâsse profundum,
Quod bene cùm scieris, non sit tibi credere tantum.
Postquam fessa oculos nihil ipsa excerpere nigris

LOCUSTÆ

Suspicio scriptis potuit, nihil omnibus actum
Consiliis, ipsi referunt ænigmata Regi.
   Ille oculo nodos facili, scelerúmque nefandas
Percurrens animo ambages (dum nubila spargit
Lux lucis, mentémque aperit) mox omnia pandit
Monstra, aperítque nefas solus, tenebrásque resolvit.
   Quin medias inter [t]echnas jam nocte profundâ
Artificem sceleris prendunt, patet alta nitroso
Pulvere fœta domus, penitúsque recondita Soli
Crimina miranti, & cœlo ostenduntur aperto.
   Non secus atque Euris media inter viscera pressis
Rupta patet Tellus, magnóque fatiscit hiatu,
Dissultant pavidi montes, penitúsque cavernis
Immittunt Ph[œ]bum, furiásque, umbrásque recludunt.
Apparet deforme Chaos Stygiíque penates,
Apparet barathrum, & diri penetralia Ditis,
Mirantúrque diem perculso lumine Manes.
Jámque ipso pariter cum crimine, criminis author
Protrahitur, circum populus fluit omnis euntem :
Expleri nequeunt animi frontémque tuendo
Torvam, squalentésque genas, nemorosáque setis
Ora, & Tartareas referentia lumina tædas.
   Ille autem audenti similis, similísque timenti,
Nunc fremitu turbam, & dictis ridere superbis,
Diductísque ferox inhiantem illudere labris ;
Nunc contrà trepidare metu, tremulósque rotare
Circùm oculos, jam flagra miser, dextrámque parati
Carnificis medios inter sævire cruores
Sentit, jámque Erebum spectat furibundus hiantem :
Et semesa inter labentes membra dracones
Percipiens, æternæ horret primordia pœnæ.
   O Pater, ô terræ, & summi Regnator Olympi,
Quas tibi pro meritis laudes, quæ munera læti
Tantâ servati dabimus de clade Britanni?
Non nos, non miseri, (nec tanta superbia lapsis)
Sufficimus meritis : sed quas priùs ipse dedisti,
Quas iterum solas repetis, Pater, accipe mentes.
Dum domus æterno stabit pulcherrima saxo,
Pulvere sulphureo, & tantis erepta ruinis,
Dum tumidis Nereus undarum mœnibus Anglos

PHINEAS FLETCHER

Sospitet, & tundat liventes æquore clivos,
Semper honos, sempérque tuum solenne Britannis
Nomen erit; te, Magne Pater, te voce canemus,
Factáque per seros dabimus memoranda nepotes.
Tu, Pater, Æolia fratres sub rupe furentes
Tu premis, inmensóque domas luctantia claustro
Pectora, tu vastos turbata ad litora montes
Frangis, aquásque inhibes, Rector, retrahísque rebelles:
Tu, Pater, hibernæ, tu laxas vincula nocti,
Et lenta æstivo tardas vestigia Soli.
Te reduces iterum flores, te terra jubente
Pubescit, virides crinescunt vertice Fagi.
Imperiis Sol ipse tuis immitior ignes
Dijaculat Nemeum medius, Cancrúmque rubentem
Inter, & effœtas tumido de semine fruges
Evocat, ac teneras duro coquit aridus æstu.
Mox iterum ignoto dilapsus tramite Phœbus
Declinat, jámque Æthiopes, Nilíque fluenta,
Desertásque Libum propior despectat arenas.
Nos anni premit effœti properata senectus;
Flavent pampineæ frondes, salicésque recurvæ,
Decrepitæ fluxis calvescunt crinibus ulmi.
 Tu, Pater, invictas quas jactat Iberia classes
Frangis, & ingentes dispergis in æthera motus,
Jámque etiam ereptâ (sacro mihi nomine) Elisâ,
Ingentem meritos cladem, ingentémque timentes
Restituis, placidóque ferens tria septra Jacobo,
Multiplicem nobis reddis placatus Elisam.
 Salve, summe Heros, ætatis gloria nostræ,
O Decus Anglorum, Princeps, patriæque beatus
Musarúmque pater, placidam tu pacis olivam
Angligenis infers felix, majoráque votis
Gaudia, & æternos firmas in prole triumphos.
Tu bifidum clauso nobis premis obice Janum,
Pieridúmque potens armis, feralia sacræ
Mœnia prosternis Romæ, Regúmque lupanar
Diruis, & nimio meretricem vulnere figis.
Accipe pubentem tenerâ lanugine Musam,
Quæ salices inter spretas, ulvámque palustrem,
(Non lauros palmásque ambit) proludere discit,

LOCUSTÆ

Et tentans sese innatos depascitur ignes,
Quà Pater externis Chamus vix cognita rivis
Flumina demulcens, Regales alluit hortos,
Templáq; submissis veneratur Regia lymphis.
Mox ubi pennatis crevit maturior alis,
Te canere audebit, tua (Princeps) condere facta :
Exhaustóq; tumens Helicone, undantia pleno
Carmina diffundet fluvio; cœlum audiet omne,
Audiet omne nemus : resonabilis accinet Eccho.

FINIS.

THE
LOCUSTS,
OR
APOLLYO-
NISTS.

By
PHINEAS FLETCHER
of
Kings Colledge
in
CAMBRIDGE.

Printed by THOMAS BUCKE and JOHN BUCKE,
Printers to the *Universitie* of
CAMBRIDGE.
1627.

To the right noble Lady TOWNSHEND.

Excellent Lady, as the Roote from which you sprang, those ever by me honoured, and truly honourable Parents; so the Stocke into which you are newly grafted (my most noble friend) challenge at my hand more honour, then I can, not more then I would give you. It may perhaps seeme strange, that I have consecrated these uncombed verses to your hands, yet unknowne; unknowne I confesse, if knowledge were by sight onely. But how should he not know the Branch, who knowes the Tree? How should I but see your ingenuous nature in their noble Genius? Who can be ignorant of the Science, who knowes as well the Roote that bare, and nourish it, as the Stocke into which it is grafted? Marvell not then, that in the dedication of this little Pamphlet, I durst not separate you, who are so neere by Gods owne hand united. And not for mine (who cannot aspire to deserve any respect from you) but his sake, who is (my heart) your head, accept this poore service. So may you still enjoy on earth the joyes and fruites of a chaste, and loving bed; and at length the most glorious embraces of that most excellent Spouse in heaven.

Your unknowne servant in all
Christian love,
P. F.

To my Friend the Author.

WHen after-times read in thy living Muse
    The Shame of ours, it will be thought th' Abuse
Of this blacke age, and that this matchlesse Crime
Is th' issue of thy Braine, not of the Time.
And though the Actors in this dismall Vow
Had their deserts, yet dy'de they not till now.
Thou giv'st them life: the life thy Verses give
Is the reward of those that ought not live,
But where their Plot and they may naked ly,
And be made o're to lasting Infamy.
Begin, and who approove not thy relation,
Lik[e] Them and It, forfeit their preservation.

                                        H. M.

THE
LOCUSTS,
OR
APOLLYONISTS.

CANTO I.

1

OF Men, nay Beasts: worse, Monsters: worst of all,
　　Incarnate Fiends, English Italianat,
Of Priests, O no, Masse-Priests, Priests-Cannibal,
Who make their Maker, chewe, grinde, feede, grow fat
With flesh divine: of that great Cities fall, 　　　　(sat,
Which borne, nurs't, growne with blood, th' Earth's Empresse
　　Clens'd, spous'd to Christ, yet backe to whoordome fel,
　　None can enough, something I faine would tell. 　(hell.
How black are quenched lights! Fa[l'n]e Heaven's a double

2

Great Lord, who grasp'st all creatures in thy hand,
Who in thy lap lay'st downe proud Thetis head,
And bind'st her white curl'd locks in caules of sand,
Who gather'st in thy fist, and lay'st in bed
The sturdy winds; who ground'st the floting land
On fleeting seas, and over all hast spread
　　Heaven's brooding wings, to foster all below;
　　Who mak'st the Sun without all fire to glow,
The spring of heat and light, the Moone to ebbe and flow:

THE APOLLYONISTS

3

Thou world's sole Pilot, who in this poore Isle
(So small a bottome) hast embark't thy light,
And glorious selfe: and stear'st it safe, the while
Hoarse drumming seas, and winds lowd trumpets fight,
Who causest stormy heavens here onely smile:
Steare me poore Ship-boy, steare my course aright;
   Breath gracious Spirit, breath gently on these layes,
   Be thou my Compasse, Needle to my wayes,
Thy glorious work's my Fraught, my Haven is thy prayse.

4

Thou purple Whore, mounted on scarlet beast,   *Revel.* 17. 2.
Gorg'd with the flesh, drunk with the blood of Saints,   3. 4. 6.
Whose amorous golden Cup, and charmed feast
All earthly Kings, all earthly men attaints;
See thy live pictures, see thine owne, thy best,
Thy dearest sonnes, and cheere thy heart, that faints.
   Harke thou sav'd Island, harke, and never cease
   To prayse that hand which held thy head in peace.
Else had'st thou swumme as deep in blood, as now in seas.

5

The cloudy Night came whirling up the skie,
And scatt'ring round the dewes, which first shee drew
From milky poppies, loads the drousie eie:
The watry Moone, cold Vesper, and his crew
Light up their tapers: to the Sunne they fly,
And at his blazing flame their sparks renew.
   Oh why should earthly lights then scorne to tine
   Their lamps alone at that first Sunne divine?
Hence as false falling starres, as rotten wood they shine.

6

Her sable mantle was embroydered gay
With silver beames, with spangles round beset:
Foure steedes her chariot drew, the first was gray,
The second blue, third browne, fourth blacke as jet.
The hollowing Owle her Post prepares the way,

PHINEAS FLETCHER

And winged dreames (as gnat-swarms) fluttring, let
   Sad sleep, who faine his eies in rest would steep.
Why then at death doe weary mortals weep?
Sleep's but a shorter death, death's but a longer sleep.

7

And now the world, & dreames themselves were drown'd
In deadly sleep; the Labourer snorteth fast,
His brawny armes unbent, his limbs unbound,
As dead, forget all toyle to come, or past,
Onely sad Guilt, and troubled Greatnes crown'd
With heavy gold and care, no rest can tast.
   Goe then vaine man, goe pill the live and dead,
   Buy, sell, fawne, flatter, rise, then couch thy head
In proud, but dangerous gold: in silke, but restlesse bed.

8

When loe a sudden noyse breakes th' empty aire;
A dreadfull noyse, which every creature daunts,
Frights home the blood, shoots up the limber haire.
For through the silent heaven hells pursuivants
Cutting their way, command foule spirits repaire
With hast to Pluto, who their counsell wants.
   Their hoarse base-hornes like fenny Bittours sound;
   Th' earth shakes, dogs howle, & heaven it selfe astound
Shuts all his eies; the stars in clouds their candles drown'd.

9

Meane time Hels yron gates by fiends beneath
Are open flung; which fram'd with wondrous art
To every guilty soule yeelds entrance eath;
But never wight, but He, could thence depart,
Who dying once was death to endlesse death.
So where the livers channell to the heart
   Payes purple tribute, with their three-fork't mace
   Three Tritons stand, and speed his flowing race,
But stop the ebbing streame, if once it back would pace.

THE APOLLYONISTS

10

The Porter to th' infernall gate is Sin,
A shapelesse shape, a foule deformed thing,
Nor nothing, nor a substance: as those thin
And empty formes, which through the ayer fling
Their wandring shapes, at length they'r fastned in
The Chrystall sight. It serves, yet reignes as King:
  It lives, yet's death: it pleases, full of paine:
  Monster! ah who, who can thy beeing faigne?
Thou shapelesse shape, live death, paine pleasing, servile raigne.

11

Of that first woman, and th' old serpent bred,
By lust and custome nurst; whom when her mother
Saw so deform'd, how faine would she have fled
Her birth, and selfe? But she her damme would smother,
And all her brood, had not He rescued
Who was his mothers sire, his childrens brother;
  Eternitie, who yet was borne and dy'de:
  His owne Creatour, earths scorne, heavens pride,
Who th' Deitie inflesht, and mans flesh deifi'de.

12

Her former parts her mother seemes resemble,
Yet onely seemes to flesh and weaker sight;
For she with art and paint could fine dissemble
Her loathsome face: her back parts (blacke as night)
Like to her horride Sire would force to tremble
The boldest heart; to th' eye that meetes her right
  She seemes a lovely sweet, of beauty rare;
  But at the parting, he that shall compare,
Hell will more lovely deeme, the divel's selfe more faire.

13

Her rosie cheeke, quicke eye, her naked brest,
And whatsoe're loose fancie might entice,
She bare expos'd to sight, all lovely drest
In beauties livery, and quaint devise:
Thus she bewitches many a boy unblest,

PHINEAS FLETCHER

Who drench't in hell, dreames all of Paradise:
   Her brests his spheares, her armes his circling skie;
   Her pleasures heav'n, her love eternitie:
For her he longs to live, with her he longs to die.

14

But he, that gave a stone power to descry
'Twixt natures hid, and checke that mettals pride,
That dares aspire to golds faire puritie,
Hath left a touch-stone, erring eyes to guide,
Which cleares their sight, and strips hypocrisie.
They see, they loath, they curse her painted hide;
   Her, as a crawling carrion, they esteeme:
   Her worst of ills, and worse then that they deeme;
Yet know her worse, then they can think, or she can seem.

15

Close by her sat Despaire, sad ghastly Spright,
With staring lookes, unmoov'd, fast nayl'd to Sinne;
Her body all of earth, her soule of fright,
About her thousand deaths, but more within:
Pale, pined cheeks, black hayre, torne, rudely dight;
Short breath, long nayles, dull eyes, sharp-pointed chin:
   Light, life, heaven, earth, her selfe, and all shee fled.
   Fayne would she die, but could not: yet halfe dead,
A breathing corse she seem'd, wrap't up in living lead.

16

In th' entrance Sicknes, and faint Languour dwelt,
Who with sad grones tolle out their passing knell:
Late feare, fright, horrour, that already felt
The Torturers clawes, preventing death, and hell.
Within loud Greife, and roaring Pangs (that swelt
In sulphure flames) did weep, and houle, and yell.
   And thousand soules in endles dolours lie,
   Who burne, frie, hizze, and never cease to crie,
Oh that I ne're had liv'd, Oh that I once could die!

THE APOLLYONISTS

17

And now th' Infernal Powers through th' ayer driving,
For speed their leather pineons broad display;
Now at eternall Deaths wide gate arriving,
Sinne gives them passage; still they cut their way,
Till to the bottome of hells palace diving,
They enter Dis deepe Conclave: there they stay,
    Waiting the rest, and now they all are met,
    A full foule Senate, now they all are set,
The horride Court, big swol'ne with th' hideous Counsel swet.

18

The mid'st, but lowest (in hells heraldry
The deepest is the highest roome) in state
Sat Lordly Lucifer: his fiery eye,
Much swol'ne with pride, but more with rage, and hate,
As Censour, muster'd all his company;
Who round about with awefull silence sate.
    This doe, this let rebellious Spirits gaine,
    Change God for Satan, heaven's for hells Sov'raigne:
O let him serve in hell, who scornes in heaven to raigne!

19

Ah wretch, who with ambitious cares opprest,
Long'st still for future, feel'st no present good:
Despising to be better, would'st be best,
Good never; who wilt serve thy lusting mood,
Yet all command: not he, who rais'd his crest,
But pull'd it downe, hath high and firmely stood.
    Foole, serve thy towring lusts, grow still, still crave,
    Rule, raigne, this comfort from thy greatnes have,
Now at thy top, Thou art a great commanding slave.

20

Thus fell this Prince of darknes, once a bright
And glorious starre: he wilfull turn'd away
His borrowed globe from that eternall light:
Himselfe he sought, so lost himselfe: his ray
Vanish't to smoke, his morning sunk in night,

PHINEAS FLETCHER

And never more shall see the springing day:
 To be in heaven the second he disdaines:
 So now the first in hell, and flames he raignes,
Crown'd once with joy, and light: crown'd now with fire
(and paines.

21

As where the warlike Dane the scepter swayes,
They crowne Usurpers with a wreath of lead,
And with hot steele, while loud the Traitour brayes,
They melt, and drop it downe into his head.
Crown'd he would live, and crown'd he ends his dayes:
All so in heavens courts this Traitour sped.
 Who now (when he had overlook't his traine)
 Rising upon his throne, with bitter straine
Thus 'gan to whet their rage, & chide their frustrate paine.

22

See, see you Spirits (I know not whether more
Hated, or hating heaven) ah see the earth
Smiling in quiet peace, and plenteous store.
Men fearles live in ease, in love, and mirth:
Where armes did rage, the drumme, & canon rore,
Where hate, strife, envy raign'd, and meagre dearth;
 Now lutes, and viols charme the ravish't eare.
 Men plow with swords, horse heels their armors weare.
Ah shortly scarce they'l know what warre, & armors were.

23

Under their sprowting vines they sporting sit.
Th' old tell of evils past: youth laugh, and play,
And to their wanton heads sweet garlands fit,
Roses with lillies, myrtles weav'd with Bay:
The world's at rest: Erinnys, forc't to quit
Her strongest holds, from earth is driven away.
 Even Turks forget their Empire to encrease:
 Warres selfe is slaine, and whips of Furies cease.
Wee, wee our selves I feare, will shortly live in peace.

THE APOLLYONISTS

24

Meane time (I burne, I broyle, I burst with spight)
In midst of peace that sharpe two edged sword
Cuts through our darknes, cleaves the misty night,
Discovers all our snares; that sacred word
(Lo[ck']t up by Rome) breakes prison, spreads the light,
Speakes every tongue, paints, and points out the Lord,
   His birth, life, death, and crosse: our guilded Stocks,
   Our Laymens bookes, the boy, and woman mocks:
They laugh, they fleer, and say, Blocks teach, and worship
                                                        (Blocks.

25

Spring-tides of light divine the ayre suround,
And bring downe heaven to earth; deafe Ignoraunce,
Vext with the day, her head in hell hath dro[wn']d:
Fond Superstition, frighted with the glaunce
Of suddaine beames, in vaine hath crost her round.
Truth and Religion every where advaunce
   Their conqu'ring standards: Errour's lost and fled:
   Earth burnes in love to heaven: heaven yeelds her bed
To earth; and common growne, smiles to be ravished.

26

That little swimming Isle above the rest,
Spight of our spight, and all our plots, remaines
And growes in happines: but late our nest,
Where wee and Rome, and blood, and all our traines,
Monks, Nuns, dead, and live idols, safe did rest:
Now there (next th' Oath of God) that Wrastler raignes,
   Who fills the land and world with peace, his speare
   Is but a pen, with which he downe doth beare
Blind Ignoraunce, false gods, and superstitious feare.

27

There God hath fram'd another Paradise,
Fat Olives dropping peace, victorious palmes,
Nor in the midst, but every where doth rise
That hated tree of life, whose precious balmes
Cure every sinfull wound: give light to th' eyes,

PHINEAS FLETCHER

Unlock the eare, recover fainting qualmes.
   There richly growes what makes a people blest;
   A garden planted by himselfe and drest:
Where he himselfe doth walke, where he himselfe doth rest.

28

There every starre sheds his sweet influence,
And radiant beames: great, little, old, and new
Their glittering rayes, and frequent confluence
The milky path to Gods high palace strew:
Th' unwearied Pastors with steel'd confidence,
Conquer'd, and conquering fresh their fight renew.
   Our strongest holds that thundring ordinaunce
   Beats downe, and makes our proudest turrets daunce,
Yoking mens iron necks in his sweet governaunce.

29

Nor can th' old world content ambitious Light,
Virginia our soile, our seat, and throne,
(To which so long possession gives us right,
As long as hells) Virginia's selfe is gone:
That stormy Ile which th' Ile of Devills hight,
Peopled with faith, truth, grace, religion.
   What's next but hell? That now alone remaines,
   And that subdu'de, even here he rules and raignes,
And mortals gin to dreame of long, but endles paines.

30

While we (good harmeles creatures) sleep, or play,
Forget our former losse, and following paine:
Earth sweats for heaven, but hell keeps holy-day.
Shall we repent good soules? or shall we plaine?
Shall we groane, sigh, weep, mourne, for mercy pray?
Lay downe our spight, wash out our sinfull staine?
   May be hee'l yeeld, forget, and use us well,
   Forgive, joyne hands, restore us whence we fell:
May be hee'l yeeld us heaven, and fall himselfe to hell.

THE APOLLYONISTS

31

But me, oh never let me, Spirits, forget
That glorious day, when I your standard bore,
And scorning in the second place to sit,
With you assaulted heaven, his yoke forswore.
My dauntlesse heart yet longs to bleed, and swet
In such a fray: the more I burne, the more
   I hate: should he yet offer grace, and ease,
   If subject we our armes, and spight surcease,
Such offer should I hate, and scorne so base a peace.

32

Where are those spirits? Where that haughty rage,
That durst with me invade eternall light?
What? Are our hearts falne too? Droope we with age?
Can we yet fall from hell, and hellish spight?
Can smart our wrath, can griefe our hate asswage?
Dare we with heaven, and not with earth to fight?
   Your armes, allies, your selves as strong as ever,
   Your foes, their weapons, numbers weaker never.
For shame tread downe this earth: what wants but your
                                               (endeavour?

33

Now by your selves, and thunder-danted armes,
But never danted hate, I you implore,
Command, adjure, reinforce your fierce alarmes:
Kindle, I pray, who never prayed before,
Kindle your darts, treble repay our harmes.
Oh our short time, too short, stands at the dore,
   Double your rage: if now we doe not ply,
   We 'lone in hell, without due company,
And worse, without desert, without revenge shall ly.

34

He, Spirits, (ah that, that's our maine torment) He
Can feele no wounds, laughs at the sword, and dart,
Himselfe from griefe, from suff'ring wholly free:
His simple nature cannot tast of smart,
Yet in his members wee him grieved see;

PHINEAS FLETCHER

For, and in them, he suffers; where his heart
   Lies bare, and nak't, there dart your fiery steele,
   Cut, wound, burne, seare, if not the head, the heele.
Let him in every part some paine, and torment feele.

35

That light comes posting on, that cursed light,
When they as he, all glorious, all divine,
(Their flesh cloth'd with the sun, and much more bright,
Yet brighter spirits) shall in his image shine,
And see him as hee is: there no despight,
No force, no art their state can undermine.
   Full of unmeasur'd blisse, yet still receiving,
   Their soules still childing joy, yet still conceiving,
Delights beyond the wish, beyond quick thoughts perceiving.

36

But we fast pineon'd with darke firy chaines,
Shall suffer every ill, but doe no more,
The guilty spirit there feeles extreamest paines,
Yet feares worse then it feeles: and finding store
Of present deaths, deaths absence sore complaines:
Oceans of ills without or ebbe, or shore,
   A life that ever dies, a death that lives,
   And, worst of all, Gods absent presence gives
A thousand living woes, a thousand dying griefes.

37

But when he summes his time, and turnes his eye
First to the past, then future pangs, past dayes
(And every day's an age of misery)
In torment spent, by thousands downe he layes,
Future by millions, yet eternity
Growes nothing lesse, nor past to come allayes.
   Through every pang, and griefe he wild doth runne,
   And challenge coward death, doth nothing shunne,
That he may nothing be; does all to be undone.

THE APOLLYONISTS

38

O let our worke equall our wages, let
Our Judge fall short, and when his plagues are spent,
Owe more then he hath paid, live in our debt:
Let heaven want vengeance, hell want punishment
To give our dues: when wee with flames beset
Still dying live in endles languishment.
   This be our comfort, we did get and win
   The fires, and tortures we are whelmed in:
We have kept pace, outrun his justice with our sin.

39

And now you States of hell give your advise,
And to these ruines lend your helping hand.
This said, and ceas't; straight humming murmures rise:
Some chafe, some fret, some sad and thoughtfull stand,
Some chat, and some new stratagems devise,
And every one heavens stronger powers ban'd,
   And teare for madnesse their uncombed snakes,
   And every one his fiery weapon shakes,
And every one expects who first the answer makes.

40

So when the falling Sunne hangs o're the maine,
Ready to droppe into the Westerne wave,
By yellow Chame, where all the Muses raigne,
And with their towres his reedy head embrave;
The warlike Gnat their flutt'ring armies traine,
All have sharpe speares, and all shrill trumpets have:
   Their files they double, loud their cornets sound,
   Now march at length, their troopes now gather round:
The bankes, the broken noise, and turrets faire rebound.

CANTO II.

1

WHat care, what watch need guard that tot'ring State
    Which mighty foes besiege, false friends betray,
Where enemies strong, and subtile swol'ne with hate,
Catch all occasions; wake, watch night and day?
The towne divided, even the wall and gate
Proove traitours, and the Councill' selfe takes pay
    Of forraigne States, the Prince is overswai'd
    By underminers, puts off friendly aid,
His wit by will, his strength by weakenes over-laid?

2

Thus men: the never seene, quicke-seeing-fiends:
Feirce, craftie, strong; and world conspire our fall:
And we (worse foes) unto our selves false friends:
Our flesh, and sense a trait'rous gate, and wall:
The spirit, and flesh man in two factions rends:
The inward senses are corrupted all,
    The soule weake, wilfull, swai'd with flatteries,
    Seekes not his helpe, who works by contraries,
By folly makes him wise, strong by infirmities.

3

See drousie soule, thy foe ne're shuts his eyes,
See, carelesse soule, thy foe in councell sits:
Thou prayer restrain'st, thy sin for vengeance cries,
Thou laugh'st, vaine soule, while justice vengeance fits.
Wake by his light, with wisedomes selfe advise:
What rigorous Justice damnes, sweet Mercy quits.
    Watch, pray, he in one instant helps and heares:
    Let him not see thy sins, but through thy teares,
Let him not heare their cries, but through thy groning feares.

THE APOLLYONISTS

4

As when the angry winds with seas conspire,
The white-plum'd hilles marching in set array
Invade the earth, and seeme with rage on fire,
While waves with thundring drummes whet on the fray,
And blasts with whistling fifes new rage inspire:
Yet soone as breathles ayres their spight allay,
   A silent calme insues: the hilly maine
   Sinks in it selfe, and drummes unbrac't refraine
Their thundring noyse, while Seas sleep on the even plaine.

5

All so the raging storme of cursed fiends
Blowne up with sharp reproach, and bitter spight
First rose in loud uprore, then falling, ends,
And ebbes in silence: when a wily spright
To give an answere for the rest intends:
Once Proteus, now Equivocus he hight,
   Father of cheaters, spring of cunning lies,
   Of slie deceite, and refin'd perjuries,
That hardly hell it selfe can trust his forgeries.

6

To every shape his changing shape is drest,
Oft seemes a Lambe and bleates, a Wolfe and houles:
Now like a Dove appeares with candide brest,
Then like a Falcon, preyes on weaker foules:
A Badger neat, that flies his 'filed nest:
But most a Fox, with stinke his cabin foules:
   A Courtier, Priest, transform'd to thousand fashions,
   His matter fram'd of slight equivocations,
His very forme was form'd of mentall reservations.

7

And now more practicke growne with use and art,
Oft times in heavenly shapes he fooles the sight:
So that his schollers selves have learn't his part,
Though wormes, to glow in dark, like Angels bright.
To sinfull slime such glosse can they impart,

PHINEAS FLETCHER

That, like the virgine Mother, crown'd in light,
  They glitter faire in glorious purity,
  And rayes divine: meane time the cheated eye
Is finely mock't into an heavenly ecstasy.

8

Now is he Generall of those new stamp't Friers,
Which have their root in that lame souldier Saint,
Ignatius. Who takes his ominous name from *Strife, and Fires,
Themselves with idle vaunt that name attaint,
Which all the world adores: These Master lyers
With trueth, Abaddonists, with Jesus paint
  Their lying title. Fooles, who think with light
  To hide their filth, thus lie they naked quite:
That who loves Jesus most, most hates the Jesuite.

9

Soone as this Spirit (in hell Apollyon,
On earth Equivocus) stood singled out,
Their Speaker there, but here their Champion,
Whom lesser States, and all the vulgar rout
In dangerous times admire and gaze upon,
The silly Commons circle him about,
  And first with loud applause they usher in
  Their Oratour, then hushing all their din,
With silence they attend, and wooe him to begin.

10

Great Monarch, ayers, earths, hells Soveraigne,
True, ah too true you plaine, and we lament,
In vaine our labour, all our art's in vaine;
Our care, watch, darts, assaults are all mispent.
He, whose command we hate, detest, disdaine,
Works all our thoughts and workes to his intent:
  Our spight his pleasure makes, our ill his good,
  Light out of night he brings, peace out of blood:
What fell which he upheld? what stood which he withstood?

THE APOLLYONISTS

11

As when from mores some firie constellation
Drawes up wet cloudes with strong attractive ray,
The captiv'd seas forc't from their seat and nation,
Begin to mutinie, put out the day,
And pris'ning close the hot drie exhalation,
Threat earth, and heaven, and steale the Sunne away:
   Till th' angry Captive (fir'd with fetters cold)
   With thundring Cannons teares the limber mould,
And downe in fruitfull teares the broken vapour's roul'd.

12

So our rebellion, so our spightfull threat
All molten falls; he (which my heart disdaines)
Waters heavens plants with our hell-flaming heat,
Husband's his graces with our sinfull paines:
When most against him, for him most we sweat,
We in our Kingdome serve, he in it raignes:
   Oh blame us not, we strive, mine, wrastle, fight;
   He breakes our troopes: yet thus, we still delight,
Though all our spight's in vain, in vain to shew our spight.

13

Our fogs lie scatt'red by his piercing light,
Our subtilties his wisedome overswaies,
His gracious love weighs downe our ranck'rous spight,
His Word our sleights, his truth our lyes displayes,
Our ill confin'd, his goodnesse infinite,
Our greatest strength his weaknesse overlaies.
   He will, and oh he must, be Emperour,
   That heaven, and earth's unconquer'd at this houre,
Nor let him thanke, nor do you blame our wil, but pow'r.

14

Nay, earthly Gods that wont in luxury,
In maskes, and daliance spend their peacefull daies,
Or else invade their neighbours liberty,
And swimme through Christian blood to heathen praise,
Subdue our armes with peace; us bold defie,

Arm'd all with letters, crown'd with learned bayes:
　　With them whole swarmes of Muses take the field;
　　And by heavens aide enforce us way to yield;
The Goose lends them a speare, and every ragge a shield.

15

But are our hearts fal'ne too; shall wee repent,
Sue, pray, with teares wash out our sinfull spot?
Or can our rage with greife, and smart relent?
Shall wee lay downe our armes? Ah, feare us not;
Not such thou found'st us, when with thee we bent
Our armes 'gainst heaven, when scorning that faire lot
　　Of glorious blisse (when we might still have raign'd)
　　With him in borrowed light, and joyes unstain'd,
We hated subject crownes, and guiltlesse blisse disdain'd.

16

Nor are we changelings: finde, oh finde but one,
But one in all thy troopes, whose lofty pride
Begins to stoope with opposition:
But, as when stubborn winds with earth ralli'de
(Their Mother earth) she ayded by her sonne
Confronts the Seas, beates of the angry tide:
　　The more with curl'd-head waves, the furious maine
　　Renues his spite, and swells with high disdaine,
Oft broke, and chac't, as oft turnes, & makes head againe:

17

So rise we by our fall: that divine science
Planted belowe, grafted in humane stocke,
Heavens with frayle earth combines in strong alliance:
While he, their Lion, leads that sheepish flock,
Each sheepe, each lambe dares give us bold defiance:
But yet our forces broken 'gainst the rocke
　　We strongly reinforce, and every man
　　Though cannot what he will's, will's what he can,
And where wee cannot hurt, there we can curse, and banne.

THE APOLLYONISTS

18

See here in broken force, a heart unbroke,
Which neither hell can daunt, nor heaven appease:
See here a heart, which scornes that gentle yoke,
And with it life, and light, and peace, and ease:
A heart not cool'd, but fir'd with thundring stroke,
Which heaven it selfe, but conquer'd cannot please:
   To drawe one blessed soule from's heavenly Cell,
   Let me in thousand paines and tortures dwell:
Heaven without guilt to me is worse then guilty hell.

19

Feare then no change: such I, such are we all:
Flaming in vengeance, more then Stygian fire,
When hee shall leave his throne, and starry hall,
Forsake his deare-bought Saints, and Angells quire,
When he from heaven into our hell shall fall,
Our nature take, and for our life expire;
   Then we perhaps (as man) may waver light,
   Our hatred turne to peace, to love our spight,
Then heaven shall turne to hell, and day shall chaunge to night.

20

But if with forces new to take the feild
Thou long'st, looke here, we prest, and ready stand:
See all that power, and Wiles that hell can yeeld
Expect no watchword, but thy first command:
Which given, without or feare, or sword, or sheild
Wee'le fly in heaven's face, I and my band
   Will draw whole worlds, leave here no rome to dwell.
   Stale arts we scorne, our plots become black hell,
Which no heart will beleeve, nor any tongue dare tell.

21

Nor shall I need to spurre the lazy Monke,
Who never sweats but in his meale, or bed,
Whose forward paunch ushers his uselesse truncke,
He barrels darkenes in his empty head:
To eate, drinke, void what he hath eat and drunke,

PHINEAS FLETCHER

Then purge his reines; thus these Saints merited:
  They fast with holy fish, and flowing wine
Not common, but (which fits such Saints) *Divine:
Poore soules, they dare not soile their hands with precious mine!

* Hence called *Vinum Theologicum*.

22

While th' earth with night and mists was overswai'd,
And all the world in clouds was laid a steep,
Their sluggish trade did lend us friendly aid,
They rock't and hush't the world in deadly sleep,
Cloyst'red the Sunne, the Moone they overlaid,
And prison'd every starre in dungeon deep.
  And when the light put forth his morning ray,
    My famous Dominicke tooke the light away,
And let in seas of blood to quench the early day.

23

But oh, that recreant Frier, who long in night
Had slept, his oath to me his Captaine brake,
Uncloyst'red with himselfe the hated light;
Those piercing beames forc't drowsie earth awake,
Nor could we all resist: our flatt'rie, spight,
Arts, armes, his victorie more famous make.
  Down cloysters fall; the Monkes chac't from their sty
    Lie ope, and all their loathsome company;
Hypocrisie, rape, blood, theft, whooredome, Sodomy.

24

Those troupes I soone disband now useles quite;
And with new musters fill my companies;
And presse the crafty wrangling Jesuite:
Nor traine I him as Monks, his squinted eyes
Take in and view ascaunce the hatefull light:
So stores his head with shifts and subtilties.
  Thus being arm'd with arts, his turning braines
    All overturne. Oh with what easy paines
Light he confounds with light, and truth with truth distaines.

THE APOLLYONISTS

25

The world is rent in doubt: some gazing stay,
Few step aright, but most goe with the croud.
So when the golden Sun with sparkling ray
Imprints his stamp upon an adverse cloud,
The watry glasse so shines, that's hard to say
Which is the true, which is the falser proud.
   The silly people gape, and whisp'ring cry
     That some strange innovation is ny,
And fearefull wisard sings of parted tyranny.

26

These have I train'd to scorne their contraries,
Out-face the truth, out-stare the open light:
And what with seeming truths and cunning lies
Confute they cannot, with a scoffe to sleight.
Then after losse to crowe their victories,
And get by forging what they lost by fight.
   And now so well they ply them, that by heart
     They all have got my counterfeiting part,
That to my schollers I turne scholler in mine art.

27

Follow'd by these brave spirits, I nothing feare
To conquer earth, or heaven it selfe assayle,
To shake the starres, as thick from fixed spheare,
As when a rustick arme with stubborne flayle
Beates out his harvest from the swelling eare;
T' eclipse the Moone, and Sun himselfe injayle.
   Had all our army such another band,
     Nor earth, nor heaven could long unconquer'd stand:
But hell should heaven, and they, I feare, would hell command.

28

What Country, City, Towne, what family,
In which they have not some intelligence,
And party, some that love their company?
Courts, Councells, hearts of Kings find no defence,
No guard to barre them out: by flattery

PHINEAS FLETCHER

They worme and scrue into their conscience;
  Or with steel, poyson, dagges dislodge the sprite.
  If any quench or dampe this Orient light,
Or foile great Jesus name, it is the Jesuite.

29

When late our whore of Rome was disaray'd,
Strip't of her pall, and skarlet ornaments,
And all her hidden filth lay broad displayd,
Her putride pendant bagges, her mouth that sents
As this of hell, her hands with scabbes array'd,
Her pust'led skin with ulcer'd excrements;
  Her friends fall off; and those that lov'd her best,
  Grow sicke to think of such a stinking beast:
And her, and every limbe that touch't her, much detest.

30

Who help't us then? Who then her case did rue?
These, onely these their care, and art appli'de
To hide her shame with tires, and dressing new:
They blew her bagges, they blanch't her leprous hide,
And on her face a lovely picture drew.
But most the head they pranck't in all his pride
  With borrowed plumes, stolne from antiquitie:
  Him with blasphemous names they dignifie;
Him they enthrone, adore, they crowne, they deifie.

31

As when an image gnawne with wormes, hath lost
His beautie, forme, respect, and lofty place,
Some cunning hand new trimmes the rotten post,
Filles up the worme-holes, paints the soyled face
With choicest colours, spares no art, or cost
With precious robes the putride trunck to grace.
  Circles the head with golden beames, that shine
  Like rising Sun: the Vulgar low incline;
And give away their soules unto the block divine.

THE APOLLYONISTS

32
So doe these Dedale workmen plaster over,
And smooth that Stale with labour'd polishing;
So her defects with art they finely cover,
Cloth her, dresse, paint with curious colouring:
So every friend againe, and every lover
Returnes, and doates through their neate pandaring:
   They fill her cup, on knees drinke healths to th' whore;
   The drunken nations pledge it o're and o're;
So spue, and spuing fall, and falling rise no more.

33
Had not these troopes with their new forged armes
Strook in, even ayre, earth too, and all were lost:
Their fresh assaultes, and importune alarmes
Have truth repell'd, and her full conquest crost:
Or these, or none must recompence our harmes.
If they had fail'd wee must have sought a coast
   I'th' Moone (the Florentines new world) to dwell,
   And, as from heaven, from earth should now have fell
To hell confin'd, nor could we safe abide in hell.

34
Nor shall that little Isle (our envy, spight,
His paradise) escape: even there they long
Have shrowded close their heads from dang'rous light,
But now more free dare presse in open throng:
Nor then were idle, but with practicke slight
Crept into houses great: their sugred tongue
   Made easy way into the lapsed brest
   Of weaker sexe, where lust had built her nest,
There layd they Cuckoe eggs, and hatch't their brood unblest.

35
There sowe they traytrous seed with wicked hand
'Gainst God, and man; well thinks their silly sonne
To merit heaven by breaking Gods command,
To be a Patriot by rebellion.
And when his hopes are lost, his life and land,

And he, and wife, and child are all undone,
  Then calls for heaven and Angells, in step I,
  And waft him quick to hel; thus thousands die,
Yet still their children doat: so fine their forgerie.

36

But now that stormy season's layd, their spring,
And warmer Sunnes call them from wintry cell;
These better times will fruits much better bring,
Their labours soone will fill the barnes of hell
With plenteous store; serpents, if warm'd, will sting:
And even now they meet, and hisse, and swell.
  Thinke not of falling, in the name of all
  This dare I promise, and make good I shall,
While they thus firmely stand, wee cannot wholly fall.

37

And shall these mortals creep, fawne, flatter, ly,
Coyne into thousand arts their fruitfull braine,
Venter life, limbe, through earth, and water fly
To winne us Proselytes? Scorne ease, and paine,
To purchase grace in their whore-mistres eye?
Shall they spend, spill their dearest blood, to staine
  Romes Calendar, and paint their glorious name
  In hers, and our Saint-Rubrick? Get them fame, (shame?
Where Saints are fiends, gaine losse, grace disgrace, glory

38

And shall wee, (Spirits) shall we (whose life and death
Are both immortall) shall we, can we faile?
Great Prince o' th' lower world, in vaine we breath
Our spight in Councell; free us this our jayle:
Wee doe but loose our little time beneath;
All to their charge: why sit we here to waile?
  Kindle your darts, and rage; renew your fight:
  We are dismist: breake out upon the light,   (fright.
Fill th' earth with sin, and blood; heaven with stormes, and

THE APOLLYONISTS

39

With that the bold black Spirit invades the day,
And heav'n, and light, and Lord of both defies.
All hell run out, and sooty flagges display,
A foule deformed rout: heav'n shuts his eyes;
The starres looke pale, and early mornings ray
Layes downe her head againe, and dares not rise:
   A second night of Spirits the ayre possest;
   The wakefull cocke that late forsooke his nest,
Maz'd how he was deceav'd, flies to his roost, and rest.

40

So when the South (dipping his sable wings
In humid seas) sweeps with his dropping beard
The ayer, earth, and Ocean, downe he flings
The laden trees, the Plowmans hopes new-eard
Swimme on the playne: his lippes loud thunderings,
And flashing eyes make all the world afeard:
   Light with darke cloudes, waters with fires are met,
   The Sunne but now is rising, now is set,
And finds West-shades in East, and seas in ayers wet.

CANTO III.

1

False world how doest thou witch dimme reasons eies?
   I see thy painted face, thy changing fashion:
Thy treasures, honours all are vanities,
Thy comforts, pleasures, joyes all are vexation,
Thy words are lyes, thy oaths foule perjuries,
Thy wages, care, greife, begg'ry, death, damnation:
   All this I know: I know thou doest deceive me,
   Yet cannot as thou art, but seem'st, conceave thee:
I know I should, I must, yet oh I would not leave thee.

2

Looke as in dreames, where th' idle fancie playes,
One thinkes that fortune high his head advances:
Another spends in woe his weary dayes;
A third see[k]es sport in love, and courtly daunces;
This grones, and weeps, that chants his merry laies;
A sixt to finde some glitt'ring treasure chaunces:
   Soon as they wake, they see their thoughts were vaine,
   And quite forget, and mocke their idle braine,
This sighs, that laugh's to see how true false dreames can faine.

3

Such is the world, such lifes short acted play:
This base, and scorn'd; this high in great esteeming,
This poore, & patched seemes, this rich, and gay;
This sick, that strong: yet all is onely seeming:
Soone as their parts are done, all slip away;
So like, that waking, oft wee feare w'are dreaming,
   And dreaming hope we wake. Wake, watch mine eies:
   What can be in the world, but flatteries,   (lies?
Dreames, cheats, deceits, whose Prince is King of night and

THE APOLLYONISTS

4
Whose hellish troopes fill thee with sinne, and blood;
With envie, malice, mischiefs infinite:
Thus now that numerous, black, infernall brood
O're-spread thee round; th' earth struck with trembling fright
Felt their approach, and all-amazed stood,
So suddain got with child, & big with spight.
   The damned Spirits fly round, and spread their seede:
   Straight hate, pride, strife, warres, and seditions breed,
Get up, grow ripe: How soone prospers the vicious weed!

5
Soone in the North their hellish poyson shed,
Where seldome warres, dissention never cease:
Where Volga's streames are sail'd with horse and sled,
Pris'ning in Chrystal walls his frozen seas:
Where Tartar, Russe, the Pole, and prospering Swed
Nor know the sweet, nor heare the name of peace:
   Where sleeping Sunnes in winter quench their light,
   And never shut their eyes in Summer bright;
Where many moneths make up one onely day, and night:

6
There lie they cloyst'red in their wonted Cell:
The sacred nurseries of the Societie:
They finde them ope, swept, deck't: so there they dwell,
Teaching, and learning more and more impietie.
There blow their fires, and tine another hell,
There make their Magazine, with all varietie
   Of fiery darts; the Jesuites helpe their friends:
   And hard to say, which in their spightfull ends
More vexe the Christian world, the Jesuites, or the Fiends.

7
The Fiends finde matter, Jesuites forme; those bring
Into the mint fowle hearts, sear'd conscience,
Lust-wandring eyes, eares fil'd with whispering,
Feet swift to blood, hands gilt with great expence,
Millions of tongues made soft for hammering,

PHINEAS FLETCHER

And fit for every stampe, but truths defence:
   These (for Romes use, on Spanish anvile) frame
   The pliant matter; treasons hence diflame,
Lusts, lies, blood, thousand griefes set all the world on flame.

8

But none so fits the Polish Jesuite,
As Russia's change, where exil'd *Grecian Priest
Late sold his Patriarchal chaire, and right;
That now proud Mosko vants her lofty crest
Equall with Rome: Romes head full swolne with spight,
Scorning a fellow head, or Peer, but Christ,
  Straines all his wits, & friends; they worke, they plod
  With double yoke the Russian necks to load;
To crowne the Polish Prince their King, the Pope their God.

* Hierom Patriarch of the Greeke Church came unto Mosco in the yeare 1588. sold to Theodore Ivanovich Emperour of Russia his Patriarchal right; who presently installed into it the Metropolitane of Mosco.

9

The fiends, and times yeeld them a fit occasion
To further their designes: for late a *Beast
Of salvage breed, of straunge and monsterous fashion,
Before a Fox, an Asse behind, the rest
A ravenous Wolfe, with fierce, but slie invasion
Enters the Russian court, the Lyons nest,
  Worries the Lions selfe, and all his brood:
  And having gorg'd his mawe with royall blood, (food!
Would sleepe. Ah short the rest, that streames from such a

* Borrise Federowich brother to the Empresse of Russia, having by the simplicitie of that Emperour aspired to that kingdome, by murther of the chiefe Nobility, & extirpation of the royall seed; entred as subtily as he ruled cruelly, & died foolishly, killing himselfe whē his treasures were yet untoucht & great, & the chiefe City might have beene won to have stood to him.

10

Ah silly man, who dream'st, that honour stands
In ruling others, not thy selfe! Thy slaves
Serve thee, and thou thy slaves: in iron bands
Thy servile spirit prest with wild passions raves.
Base state, where but one Tyrant realmes commands:
Worse, where one single heart serves thousand knaves.
  Would'st thou live honoured? Clip ambitious wing,
  To reasons yoke thy furious passions bring.
Thrice noble is the man, who of himselfe is King.

THE APOLLYONISTS

11

With mimicke skill, they trayne a *caged beast,
And teach him play a royall Lyons part:
Then in the Lyons hide, and titles drest
They bring him forth: he Master in his art,
Soone winnes the Vulgar Russe, who hopes for rest
In chaunge; and if not ease, yet lesser smart:
   All hunt that monster, he soone melts his pride
   In abject feare; and life himselfe envi'de:
So whelp't a Fox, a Wolfe he liv'd, an Asse he di'de.

12

Proud of his easy crowne and straunge successe,
The [*]second beast (sprung of a baser brood)
Comes on the stage, and with great seemelinesse
Acts his first scenes; now strong 'gins chaunge his mood,
And melts in pleasure, lust, and wantonnesse:
Then swimmes in other, sinkes in his owne blood.
   With blood, and warres the ice and liquid snowes
   Are thaw'd; the earth a red sea overflowes.
Quarrells by falling rise, and strife by cutting growes.

13

Some fiends to Grece their hellish firebrands bring,
And wake the sleeping sparks of Turkish rage;
Where once the lovely Muses us'd to sing,
And chant th' Heroes of that golden age;
Where since more sacred Graces learn'd to string
That heav'nly lyre, and with their canzons sage
   Inspirit flesh, and quicken stinking graves,
   There (ah for pitty!) Muses now are slaves,
Graces are fled to heav'n, and hellish Mahomet raves.

14

But Lucifers proud band in prouder Spaine
Disperse their troopes: some with unquench't ambition
Inflame those Moorish Grandes, and fill their braine
With subtile plots; some learne of th' Inquisition
To finde new torments, and unused paines:

*Griskey Strepey a Mosique, & sometime Chorister at Precheste in Mosko, and from thence with an Embassadour passing into Polonia, and there cloystered, was taught by the Jesuites to play the King, and usurping the name of Demetrius (slaine by Borrise Federowich) under that mask with the Polonian forces, and by the revolt of the Russes was crowned Emperour.

*At his first entry the counterfeit Demetrius, wan the applause and good opinion of many, and very politickly behaved himsel[l]fe: but when he conceaved himselfe to be setled on the throne; he grew lascivious, and insolent, and bloody: and by a conspiracy was slaine, and his dead corps exposed to all shame and contempt.

PHINEAS FLETCHER

Some traine the Princes with their lewd tuition,
   That now of Kings they scorne to be the first,
   But onely: deep with Kingly dropsies pierc't
Their thirst drinkes kingdomes downe, their drinking fires
                                                     (their thirst.

15

Æquivocus, remembring well his taske,
And promise, enters Rome; there soone he eyes
Waters of life tunn'd up in stinking caske
Of deadly errours poyson'd truth with lies:
There that stale purple Whore in glorious maske
Of holy Mother Church he mumming spies,
   Dismounted from her seven headed beast,
   Inviting all with her bare painted breast,
They suck, steep, swell, and burst with that envenom'd feast.

16

Nor stayes, till now the stately Court appeares,
Where sits that Priest-King, all the Alls Soveraigne:
Three mitred crownes the proud Impostor weares,
For he in earth, in hell, in heav'n will raigne:
And in his hand two golden keyes he beares,
To open heav'n and hell, and shut againe.
   But late his keyes are marr'd, or lost; for hell
   He cannot shut, but opes, and enters well:
Nor heav'n can ope, but shut; nor heav'n will buy, but sell.

17

Say Muses, say; who now in those rich fields
Where silver Tibris swimmes in golden sands,
Who now, ye Muses, that great scepter wields,
Which once sway'd all the earth with servile bands?
Who now those Babel towres, once fallen, builds?
Say, say, how first it fell, how now it stands?
   How, and by what degrees that Citie sunk?
   Oh are those haughty spirits so basely shrunk?
Cesars to chaunge for Friers, a Monarch for a Monk?

THE APOLLYONISTS

18

Th' Assyrian Lyon deck't in golden hide, *Dan. 7. 4.*
Once grasp't the Nations in his Lordly paw:
But him the Persian silver Beare defi'd, *Dan. 7. 5.*
Tore, kill'd, and swallowed up with ravenous jaw;
Whom that Greeke Leopard no sooner spi'de, *Dan. 7. 6.*
But slue, devour'd, and fill'd his empty maw:
  But with his raven'd prey his bowells broke;
  So into foure divides his brasen yoke.
Stol'ne bits, thrust downe in hast, doe seldome feed, but choke.

19

Meane time in Tybris fen a dreadfull Beast *Dan. 7. 7.*
With monstrous breadth, and length seven hills o're-spreads:
And nurst with dayly spoyles and bloody Feast
Grew up to wondrous strength: with seven heads,
Arm'd all with iron teeth, he rends the rest,
And with proud feet to clay and morter treads.
  And now all earth subdu'de, high heav'n he braves,
  The head he kills, then 'gainst t[h]e body raves:
With Saintly flesh he swells, with bones his den he paves.

20

At length five heads were fall'ne; the sixt retir'd *Apoc. 17. 10.*
By absence yeelds an easy way of rising
To th' next, and last: who with ambition fir'd,
In humble weeds his haughty pride disguising,
By slow, sly growth unto the top aspir'd:
Unlike the rest he veiles his tyrannising
  With that Lambs head, & horns: both which he claimes; *Apoc. 13. 11.*
  Thence double raigne, within, without hee frames:
His head the Lamb, his tongue the Dragon loud proclames.

21

Those Fisher Swaynes, whome by full Jordans wave
The Seas great Soveraigne his art had taught,
To still loud stormes when windes and waters rave,
To sink their laden boats with heavenly fraught,
To free the fish with nets, with hookes to save:

PHINEAS FLETCHER

For while the fish they catch, themselves were caught:
   And as the scaly nation they invade,
     Were snar'd themselves. Ah much more blessed trade
That of free Fisher swaines were captive fishes made!

22

Long since those Fisher swains had chang'd their dwelling;
Their spirits (while bodies slept in honour'd toombes)
Heavens joyes enjoy, all excellence excelling;
And in their stead a crue of idle groomes
By night into the ship with ladders stealing,
Fearles succeed, and fill their empty roomes.
   The fishers trade they praise, the paynes deride:
   Their narrow bottomes strech they large & wide,
And make broad roomes for pomp, for luxury, and pride.

23

Some from their skiffs to crownes and scepters creep,
Heavens selfe for earth, and God for man rejecting:
Some snorting in their hulks supinely sleep,
Seasons in vaine recall'd, and winds neglecting:
Some nets, and hookes, and baits in poyson steep,
With deathfull drugges the guiltles seas infecting:
   The fish their life and death together drink;
   And dead pollute the seas with venom'd stink:
So downe to deepest hell, both fish and fishers sink.

24

While thus they swimme in ease, with plenty flowe,
Each losel gets a boat, and will to sea:
Some teach to work, but have no hands to rowe;
Some will be lights, but have no eyes to see;
Some will be guides, but have no feete to goe;
Some deafe, yet ears; some dumbe, yet tongues will bee;
   Some will bee seasoning salt, yet drown'd in gall:
   Dumbe, deafe, blinde, lame, and maime; yet fishers all,
Fit for no other use but 'store an Hospitall.

THE APOLLYONISTS

25

Mean time the Fisher, which by Tibers bankes
Rul'd leasser boates, casts to enlarge his See:
His ship (even then too great) with stollen plankes
Length'ning, he makes a monstrous Argosie;
And stretches wide the sides with out-growne flankes:
Peter, and Paul his badge, this' sword, that's key
  His feyned armes: with these he much prevailes,
  To him each fisher boy his bonnet veyles,
And as the Lord of seas adores with strooken sayles:

26

Nor could all Seas fill up his empty mawe;
For earth he thirsts; the earth invades, subdues:
And now all earthly Gods with servile awe
Are highly grac't to kisse his holy shooes:
Augustus selfe stoops to his soveraigne lawe,
And at his stirrop close to lacky sues:
  Then heavens scepter claymes, then hell and all.
  Strange turne of chaunges! To be lowe, and thrall   (fall.
Brings honour, honour strength, strength pride, and pride a

27

Upon the ruines of those marble towres,
Founded, and rays'd with skill, and great expence
Of aunceint Kings, great Lords, and Emperours,
He built his Babel up to heav'n, and thence
Thunders through all the world: On sandy floores
The ground-worke slightly floats, the walls to sense
  Seeme Porphyr faire, which blood of Martyrs taints;
  But was base lome, mixed with strawy Saints;
Daub'd with untemper'd lime, which glistering tinfoyle paints.

28

The Portall seemes (farre off) a lightsome frame;
But all the lights are false; the Chrystall glasse
Back't with a thick mud-wall beates off the flame,
Nor suffers any sparke of day to passe.
There sits dull Ignoraunce, a loathly dame,

PHINEAS FLETCHER

Two eyes, both blind; two eares, both deafe shee has;
  Yet quick of sense they to her selfe appeare.
  Oh who can hope to cure that eye, and eare,
Which being blind, & deafe, bragges best to see, & heare!

29

Close by her children two; of each side one,
A Sonne and Daughter sate: he Errour hight,
A crooked swaine; shee Superstition.
Him Hate of Truth begot in Stygian night;
Her Feare, and falsely call'd, Devotion;
And as in birth, so joyn'd in loose delight,
  They store the world with an incestuous breed,
  A bastard, foule, deform'd, but num'rous seed;
All monsters; who in parts, or growth, want, or exceed.

30

Her Sonne invites the wandring passengers
And calls aloud, Ho, every simple swaine
Come, buy crownes, scepters, miters, crosiers,
Buy thefts, blood, incests, oaths, buy all for gaine:
With gold buy out all Purgatory feares,
With gold buy heaven and heavens Soveraigne.
  Then through an hundred Labyrinths he leads
  The silly soule, and with vaine shadowes feeds:
The poore stray wretch admires old formes, and anticke deeds.

31

*Saint Fulbert sucked the brests of the blessed Virgine, so saith Bar[o]nius. Annal. 1028. n. 5.

*Dominicks books lay dry a whole night in a river. Antoninus, Sum.

The daughter leads him forth in Pilgrims guise
To visite holy shrines, the Lady Hales;
The Doves, and Gabriels plumes in purple dyes,
Cartloads of Crosse, and straunge-engendring nayles:
The simple man adores the sottish lyes:
Then with false wonders his frayle sense assayles,
  Saint *Fulbert nurst with milke of Virgine pure,
  Saint Dominicks* bookes like fish in rivers dure;
Saint Francis birds, & wounds; & Bellarmines breeches cure.

THE APOLLYONISTS

32

The Hall is vastly built for large dispence;
Where freely ushers loosest Libertie,
The waiters Lusts, the Caterer vaine Expence,
Steward of th' house wide panched Gluttonie;
Bed-makers ease, sloth, and soft wanton sense;
High Chamberlaine perfumed Lecherie:
  The outward Courtes with Wrong, and Bribery stink,
    That holy *Catherine smelt the loathsome sink
From French Avinions towers, to Tuscan Siens brinke.

* *This is affirmed by Antonine hist.*

33

The stately presence Princely spoyles adorne
Of vassal Kings: there sits the man of pride,
And with his dusty *feete (oh hellish scorne!)
Crownes and uncrownes men by God deifi'de.
*He is that seeing, and proud-speaking Horne,
Who stiles himselfe Spouse of that glorious Bride;
  The *Churches Head, and Monarch; Jesses rod;
    The precious corner stone; supreame Vice-God; (God.
The Light, the Sunne, the Rock, the Christ, the Lord our

* *Celestine 3 thus delt with Henry 6 Emperour.*
* *Dan. 7. 8.*
* *All these titles & many more are given to the Popes by their vassals, and by them accepted and justified.*

34

There stand the Pillars of the Papacie;
Stout Champions of Romes Almighty power,
Carv'd out as patterns to that holy See.
First was that Boniface, the cheifest flower
In Papal Paradise, who climb'd to bee
First universall Bishop-governour.
  Then he, that would be Pope and Emperour too:
    And close by them, that monstrous Prelate, who
Trampled great Fredericks necke with his proud durty shooe.

Boniface 3.

Boniface 8.

Alexander 3.

35

Above the rest stood famous Hildebrand,
The Father of our Popish chastitie:
Who forc't brave Henry with bare feet to stand,
And beg for entrance, and his amitie.
Finely the workman with his Dedal hand

PHINEAS FLETCHER

Had drawne disdaine sparkling in's fiery eie,
  His face all red with shame and angry scorne,
  To heare his sonne lament, his Empresse mourne,
While this chast Father makes poore Asto weare the horn.

36

Alexand. 6.   There stood Lucretia's Father, Husband, Brother,
  The monster Borgia, cas'd in lust and blood :
Paul 3.   And he that fil'd his child, and quell'd his Mother :
Pius 4.   He, that was borne, liv'd, died in lust : there stood
John 8, or rather Joan.   The female Pope, Romes shame, and many other
Kindled for hell on earth in lustfull flood.
  These Saints accurse the married chastity,
  A wife defiles : oh deep hypocrisy !
Yet use, reward, and praise twice burning Sodomy.

37

And with those fleshly stood the spirituall Bauds :
They choose, and frame a goodly stone, or stock,
Then trimme their puppet god with costly gauds.
Ah who can tell which is the verier block,
His god, or he ? Such lyes are godly frauds.
Some whips adore, the crosse, the seamelesse frock,
  Nayles, speare, reed, spunge ; some needing no partaker,
  Nor using any help, but of the Baker,   (Maker.
(Oh more then power divine !) make, chew, and voide their

38

By these were plac'd those dire incarnate fiends
Studied in that black art, and that alone :
Silvester 2 and many others.   One leagu'd himselfe to hell t' effect his ends,
In Romes Bee-hive to live the Soveraigne Drone :
Gregory 7.   Another musters all the Divels his friends
To pull his Lord out of his rightfull throne ;
  And worse then any fiend, with magicke rite
  He casts into the fire the Lord of light :
So sacrific'd his God to an infernall spright.

THE APOLLYONISTS

39

But who can summe this holy rablement?
This prais'd the Gospel as a gainfull tale;   *Leo 10.*
That questions heav'ns reward, hels punishment;
This for his dish in spight of God doth call;   *John 23,*
That heaven taints, infects the Sacrament;   *and 24.*
The bread, and seale of life perpetuall: *Henry*
   And pois'ning Christ, poisons with him his King; *Emperour was poysoned*
He life and death in one draught swallowing,   *in the Sacrament*
Wash't off his sinfull staines in that Lifes deadly spring. *given by a Preist, set on by Robert King of Naples, and Robert by Clement 5. Avent.*

CANTO IIII.

1

Looke as a goodly Pile, whose ayrie towres
   Thrust up their golden heads to th' azure sky,
But loosely leanes his weight on sandy floores:
Such is that mans estate, who looking high,
Grounds not his sinking trust on heavenly powres:
His tott'ring hopes no sooner live, but die.
   How can that frame be right, whose ground is wrong?
   Who stands upon his owne legges, stands not long:
For man's most weake in strength, in weaknes only strong.

2

Thus Rome (when drench't in seas of Martyrs blood,
And tost with stormes, yet rooted fast on Christ)
Deep grounded on that rocke most firmely stood:
But when, with pride and worldly pompe entic't
She sought her selfe, sunke in her rising flood.
So when of late that boasted Jesuite Priest   *Drury*
   Gath'red his flocke, and now the house 'gan swell,
   And every eare drew in the sugred spell,
Their house, and rising hopes, swole, burst, and head-long fell.

PHINEAS FLETCHER

3

Through this knowne entraunce past that subtile Spright:
There thundring Paul retir'd he sullen found,
Boyling his restles heart in envious spight,
Gall'd with old sores, and new Venetian wound:
His thoughtfull head lean'd downe his carefull weight
Upon a chayre, farre fetch't from Dodon ground.
   Thence without feare of errour they define;
   For there the Spirit his presence must confine. (divine!
Oh more then God, who makes his bread, blocks, chayres

4

But that true Spirit's want this false supplies:
He folds that Scorners chayre in's cloudy wings,
And paints, and gilds it fayre with colour'd lies.
But now from's damned head a snake he flings
Burning in flames: the subtile Serpent flies
To th' aymed marke, and fills with firy stings
   The Papal brest; his holy bosome swells
   With pride & rage; straight cals for books, lights, bells,
Frets, fumes, fomes, curses, chafes, and threatens thousand hells.

5

So when cold waters wall'd with brasen wreath
Are sieg'd with crackling flames, their common foe,
The angry seas 'gin fome and hotly breath,
Then swell, rise, rave, and still more furious grow:
Nor can be held; but, prest with fires beneath,
Tossing their waves breake out, and all o'reflow.
   In hast he calls a Senate; thither runne
   The blood-red Cardinalls, Friers white, and dunne,
And with, and 'bove the rest Ignatius' eldest sonne.

6

The conclave fills apace; now all are met:
Each knowes his stall, and takes his wonted place.
So downe they sit; and now they all are set:
Æquivocus, with his bat-wing'd embrace,
Clucks, broods his chickens, while they sadly treat;

THE APOLLYONISTS

Their eyes all met in th' holy Fathers face,
  There first foresee his speech: a dusky cloud
  Hangs on his brow; his eyes fierce lightnings shroud,
At length they heare it breake, and rore in thunders loud.

7

Thrice-glorious founders of Romes Hierarchy,
Whose towring thoughts and more then manly spirit
Beyond the spheares have ray'sd our Monarchy,
Nor earth, nor heaven can pay your boundlesse merit.
Oh let your soules above the loftiest sky
Your purchast crownes and scepters just inherit.
  Here in your pourtraits may you ever live;
  While wee (poore shadowes of your pictures) grieve
Our sloth should basely spend, what your high vertues give.

8

I blush to view you: see Priest-kings, oh see
Their lively shades our life as shades upbrayd:
See how his face sparkles in majesty,
Who that first stone of our vast Kingdome layd,   *Boniface* 3.
Spous'd the whole Church, and made the world his See:
With what brave anger is his cheek arrayd,
  Who Peters useles keyes in Tiber flings?
  How high he lookes that treades on Basilisks stings,   *Julius* 8.
And findes for's lordly foot no stool, but necks of Kings?   *Alexander* 3.

9

See where among the rest great Clement stands,   *Clement* 5.
Lifting his head 'bove heaven, who Angels cites
And bids them lowly stoop at his commands,
And waft tir'd soules to those eternall lights.
But what they wonne, we loose; Townes, Cities, Lands
Revolt: our Buls each petty Lamb-kin slights:
  We storme and thunder death, they laugh, and gren.
  How have we lost our selves? Oh where, and when (men.
Were we thus chang'd? Sure they were more, we lesse then

PHINEAS FLETCHER

10

Luther. Can that uncloist'red Frier with those light armes,
That sword and shield, which we mocke, scorne, defie,
Wake all the sleeping world with loud alarmes,
And ever conqu'ring live, then quiet die?
And live, and dead load us with losse and harmes?
A single simple Frier? And oh shall I,
 Christ, God on earth, so many losses beare
  With peace and patience? Who then Rome will feare?
Who then to th' Romane God his heart and hands will reare?

11

Belgia is wholy lost, and rather chuses
Warres, flame, and blood, then peace with Rome & Spain.
Fraunce halfe fal'ne off, all truce and parl' refuses:
Edicts, massacres, leagues, threats, all are vaine.
Their King with painted shew our hope abuses,
And beares our forced yoke with scorne, and paine.
 So Lyons (bound) stoop, crouch with fained awe,
  But (loos'd) their Keeper seize with Lordly paw,
Drag, rend, & with his flesh full gorge their greedy maw.

12

* Dandalus Duke of Venice was copeld by the Pope Clement the 5. to crouch under the table chained like a dogge, before he could obtain peace for the Venetians.

See where proud Dandal chain'd, some scraps expecting,
Lies cur-like under boord, and begs releife:
But now their Corno our three crownes neglecting
Censures our sacred Censures, scornes our Briefe.
Our English plots some adverse power detecting
Doubles their joy, trebles our shame and griefe.
 What have we reap't of all our paines and seed?
  Seditions, murthers, poysons, treasons breed
To us more spight and scorne; in them more hate & heed.

13

That fleet, which with the Moone for vastnesse stood,
Which all the earth, which all the sea admires,
Amaz'd to see on waves a Moone of wood,
Blest by our hands, frighted with suddaine fires
And Panicke feares, sunke in the gaping flood:

THE APOLLYONISTS

Some split, some yeeld, scarce one (that torne) retires.
  That long wish't houre, when Cynthia set i' th' maine,
  What hath it brought at length, what change, what gain?
One bright star fell, the Sun is ris'ne, and all his traine.

14

But Fates decree our fall: high swelling *names
Of Monarch, Spouse, Christ, God, breed much debate,
And heape disdaine, hate, envy, thousand blames:
And shall I yeeld to envy, feare their hate,
Lay downe my titles, quit my justest claimes?
Shall I, earths God, yeeld to uncertaine fate?
  Sure I were best with cap in hand to pray
  My sheepe be rul'd: I scorne that begging way;
*I will, I must command; they must, they shall obay.

15

Shall I, the worlds bright Sunne, heavens Oracle,
The onely tongue of Gods owne mouth, shall I,
Of men, of faith the Judge infallible,
The rule of good, bad, wrong, and equitie,
Shall I, Almighty, Rock invincible,
Stoop to my servants, beg authoritie?
  Rome is the worlds, I Romes Head: it shall raigne:
  Which to effect, I live, rule, this to gaine
Is here my heaven; to loose is hells tormenting paine.

16

So said, and ceas'd: while all the Priestly Round
In sullen greife, and stupide silence sat:
This bit his lip, that nayl'd his eye to th' ground,
Some cloud their flaming eyes with scarlet hat,
Some gnash't their spightfull teeth, some lowr'd, and frown'd:
Till (greife and care driven out by spight and hate)
  Soft murmurs first gan creep along the croud:
  At length they storm'd, and chaf't, & thundred loud,
And all sad vengeance swore, and all dire mischeife vow'd.

* *The Card. Giure made a motion in the holy office concerning the moderating the Popes titles. But the Pope would give no way to it: as beeing no greater then the authority of Peters successour did require.*

* *Paul 5 in all his conferences with the Venetians had that continually in his mouth I must be obeyed.* Hist. Inter. Ven. *It was the saying of Paul 5 that he was purposely set to maintaine the churches authoritie, and that hee would account it a part of his happines to dye for it.* Hist. Interd. Ven.

167

PHINEAS FLETCHER

17

So when a sable cloud with swelling sayle
Comes swimming through calme skies, the silent ayre
(While fierce winds sleepe in Æol's rocky jayle)
With spangled beames embroydred, glitters faire:
But soone 'gins lowre and grone; straight clatt'ring hayle
Fills all with noyse: Light hides his golden hayre;
   Earth with untimely winter's silvered.
   Then Loiol's eldest Sonne lifts up his head,
Whom all with great applause, and silence ushered.

18

Pope Innocent the 3 dreamed that the Lateran church at Rome was falling, but that Saint Dominick setting to his shoulders underpropt it, wherupon he confirmed his order.

Most holy Father, Priests, Kings Soveraigne,
Who equal'st th' highest, makest lesser Gods,
Though Dominick, and Loiola now sustaine
The Lateran Church, with age it stoopes, and noddes:
Nor have we cause to rest, or time to plaine:
Rebellious earth (with heaven it selfe to oddes)
   Conspires to ruine our high envi'de state:
   Yet may wee by those artes prolong our date,
Whereby wee stand; and if not chaunge, yet stay our fate.

19

When captaines strive a fort or towne to winne,
They lay their batt'ry to the weakest side;
Not where the wall, and guard stands thicke, but thinne:
So that wise Serpent his assault appli'de,
And with the weaker vessell would beginne:
He first the woman with distrust and pride,
   Then shee the man subdues with flatt'ring lies;
   So in one battaile gets two victories:
Our foe will teach us fight, our fall will teach us rise.

20

Bellarmine. Our Cheife who every slight and engine knowes,
While on th' old troupes he spent his restles paines,
With equall armes assaulting equall foes,
What hath he got, or wee? What fruite, what gaines
Ensu'de? we beare the losse, and he the blowes:

THE APOLLYONISTS

And while each part their wit, and learning straines,
  The breach repaires, and (foil'd) new force assumes:
  Their hard encounters, and hot angry fumes
Strike out the sparkling fire, which lights them, us consumes.

21

In stead of heavy armes hence use we slight:
Trade we with those, which train'd in ignorance
Have small acquaintance with that heavenly light;
Those who disgrac't by some misgovernance
(Their owne, or others) swell with griefe or spight.
But nothing more our Kingdome must advance,
  Or further our designes, then to comply
  With that weake sexe, and by fine forgerie
To worme in womens hearts, chiefly the rich and high.

22

Nor let the stronger scorne these weaker powres;
The labour's lesse with them, the harvest more:
They easier yeeld, and win; so fewer houres
Are spent: for women sooner drinke our lore,
Men sooner sippe it from their lippes, then ours:
Sweetly they learne, and sweetly teach: with store
  Of teares, smiles, kisses, and ten thousand arts
  They lay close batt'ry to mens frayler parts:
So finely steale themselves, and us into their hearts.

23

That strongest Champion, who with naked hands
A Lyon tore, who all unarm'd and bound
Heap't mounts of armed foes on bloody sands;
By womans art, without or force or wound
Subdu'de, now in a mill blind grinding stands.
That Sunne of wisedome, which the Preacher crown'd
  Great King of arts, bewitch't with womens smiles,
  Fell deepe in seas of folly by their wiles.
Wit, strength, and grace it selfe yeeld to their flatt'ring guiles.

PHINEAS FLETCHER

24

This be our skirmish: for the maine, release
The Spanish forces, free strong Belgia
From feare of warre, let armes and armies cease.
What got our Alva, John of Austria?
Our Captaine, Guile; our weapons ease, and peace:
These more prevaile then Parma, Spinola.
    The Dutch shall yeeld us armes, and men; there dwell
    Arminians, who from heaven halfe way fell: (hell.
A doubtfull sect, which hang 'tween truth, lies, heaven and

25

These Epicens have sowne their subtile brayne
With thorny difference, and neat illusion:
Proud, fierce, the adverse part they much disdaine.
These must be handled soft with fine collusion,
For Calvins hate to side with Rome and Spaine,
To worke their owne, and their owne-homes confusion.
    And by large summes, more hopes, wee must bring in
    Wise Barnevelt to lay our plotted gin:
So where the Lyon fayles, the Fox shall eas'ly win.

26

The flowres of Fraunce, those faire delicious flowres,
Which late are imp't in stemme of proud Navar,
With ease wee may transferre to Castile bowres.
Feare not that sleeping Lyon: this I dare,
And will make good spight of all envious powres,
When that great bough most threats the neighb'ring ayre,
    Then shall he fall: when now his tho[u]ghts worke high,
    And in their pitch their towring p[r]ojects fly,
Then shall he stoop; his hopes shall droop, and drop, & dy.

27

Wee have not yet forgot the shamefull day,
When forc't from Fraunce and our new holds to fly
(Hooted, and chac't as owles) we ran away.
That Pillar of our lasting infamy
Though raz'd, yet in our minds doth freshly stay.

THE APOLLYONISTS

Hence love wee that great King so heartily,
  That but his heart nought can our hearts content:
  His bleeding heart from crazy body rent,
Shrin'd in bright gold shall stand our Jesuite monument.

28

This be our taske: the aged truncke wee'l lop,
And force the sprigges forget their former kind:
Wee'l graft the tender twigges on Spanish top,
And with fast knots Fraunce unto Spaine wee'l bind,
With crosse, and double knotts: wee'l still, and drop
The Romane sap into their empty mind:
  Wee'l hold their heart, wee'l porter at their eare,
  The head, the feet, the hands wee'l wholy steare:
That at our nod the head the heart it selfe shall teare.

29

All this a Prologue to our Tragedy:
My head's in travaile of an hideous
And fearfull birth; such as may fright the sky,
Turne back the Sun: helpe, helpe Ignatius.
And in this act proove thy new Deity.
I have a plot worthy of Rome and us,
  Which with amazement heaven, and earth shall fill:
  Nor care I whether right, wrong, good, or ill:
Church-profit is our law, our onely rule thy will.

30

That blessed Isle, so often curst in vaine,
Triumphing in our losse and idle spight,
Of force shall shortly stoop to Rome and Spayne:
I'le take a way ne're knowne to man or spright.
To kill a King is stale, and I disdaine:
That fits a Secular, not a Jesuite.
  Kings, Nobles, Clergy, Commons high and low,
  The Flowre of England in one houre I'le mow,
And head all th' Isle with one unseen, unfenced blow.

PHINEAS FLETCHER

31

A goodly frame, rays'd high with carved stones,
Leaning his lofty head on marble stands
Close by that Temple, where the honour'd bones
Of Britaine Kings and many Princely Grands
Adorned rest with golden scutcheons:
Garnish't with curious worke of Dedal hands.
  Low at his base the swelling Thamis falls,
  And sliding downe along those stately halls,
Doth that chiefe Citie wash, and fence with liquid walls.

32

Here all the States in full assembly meet,
And every order rank't in fit array,
Cloth'd with rich robes fill up the crowded street.
Next 'fore the King his Heier leades the way,
Glitt'ring with gemmes, and royall Coronet:
So golden Phosphor ushers in the day.
  And all the while the trumpets triumphs sound,
  And all the while the peoples votes resound: (ground.
Their shoutes and tramplings shake the ayre and dauncing

33

There in Astrea's ballaunce doe they weigh
The right and wrong, reward and punishment;
And rigour with soft equitie allay,
Curbe lawles lust, and stablish government;
There Rome it selfe, and us they dare affray
With bloody lawes, and threatnings violent:
  Hence all our suff'rings, *torments exquisite,
  Varied in thousand formes, appli'de to fright
The harmeles yet (alas!) and spotles Jesuite.

* *The printed lies concerning the torments of their Romane Martyrs which I sawe in the study of that learned Knight Sir Thomas Hutchinson priviledged by the Pope are for their monstrous impudency incredible.*

34

But Cellars large, and cavernes vaulted deep
With bending arches borne, and columnes strong
Under that stately building slyly creep:
Here Bacchus lyes, conceal'd from Juno's wrong,
Whom those cold vaults from hot-breath'd ayers keep.

THE APOLLYONISTS

In place of these wee'l other barrels throng,
  Stuf't with those firy sands, and black dry mould,
  Which from blue Phlegetons shores that Frier bold
Stole with dire hand, and yet hells force and colour hold.

35

And when with numbers just the house gins swell,
And every state hath fill'd his station,
When now the King mounted on lofty sell,
With honyed speech and comb'd oration
Charm's every eare, midst of that sugred spell
I'le teare the walls, blow up the nation,
  Bullet to heaven the stones with thunders loud,
  Equall to th' earth the courts, and turrets proud,
And fire the shaking towne, & quench't with royall blood.

36

Oh how my dauncing heart leapes in my breast
But to fore-thinke that noble tragedie!
I thirst, I long for that blood-royall feast.
See where their lawes, see, Holy Father, see
Where lawes and Makers, and above the rest
Kings marshal'd in due place through th' ayer flee:
  There goes the heart, there th' head, there sindged bones:
  Heark, Father, heark; hear'st not those musicke tones?
Some rore, some houle, some shriek; earth, hell, and ayer grones.

37

Thus sang, and downe he sat; while all the Quire
Attune their ecchoing voices to his layes:
Some Jesuite Pietie, and zealous fire,
Some his deepe reaching wit, and judgement praise:
And all the plot commend, and all admire,
But most great Paul himselfe: a while he stayes,
  Then suddaine rising, with embraces long
  He hugges his sonne, while yet the passion strong
Wanting due vent, makes teares his words, and eyes his tongue.

PHINEAS FLETCHER

38

At length the heart too full his joy dispers't,
Which mounting on the tongue, thus overflowes:
You Romane Saints, to whose deare reliques herst
In golden shrines every true Catholike bowes,
And thou of lesser gods the best and first,
Great English Thomas, ushering our vowes,
   Who giv'st heaven by thy blood, and precious merit,
   I see we still your love and helpe inherit,
Who in our need rayse up so true a Romane spirit.

Thomas Becket.

39

What meed (my Sonne) can Christ, or he above,
Or I beneath, to thy deservings weigh?
What heaven can recompence thy pious love?
In Lateran Church thy statue crown'd with bay
In gold shall mounted stand next highest Jove:
To thee wee'l humbly kneele, and vowe, and pray:
   Haile Romes great Patron, ease our restles cares,
   Possesse thy heaven, and prosper our affayres,
Even now inure thine eare to our religious prayers.

40

So up they rose as full of hope, as spight,
And every one his charge with care applies.
Equivocus with heart, and pinions light
Downe posting to th' Infernall shadowes flies;
Fills them with joyes, such joyes as Sonnes of night
Enjoy, such as from sinne and mischiefe rise.
   With all they envy, greive, and inly grone
   To see themselves out-sinn'd: and every one
Wish't he the Jesuit were, and that dire plot his owne.

CANTO V.

1

LOoke as a wayward child would something have,
　Yet flings away, wralls, spurn's, his Nurse abuses:
So froward man, what most his longings crave,
(Likenes to God) profer'd by God refuses:
But will be rather sinnes base drudge and slave.
The shade by Satan promis'd greed'ly chuses,
　　And with it death and hell. Oh wretched state,
　　Where not the eyes, but feete direct the gate!
So misse what most we wish, and have what most we hate.

2

Thus will this man of sinne be like to Christ,
A King, yet not in heaven, but earth that raignes;
That murthers, saves not Christians; th' highest Preist,
Yet not to wait his course, (that he disdaines)
But to advaunce aloft his mitred crest;
That Christ himselfe may wait upon his traynes.
　　Straunge Priest, oft heaven he sells, but never buyes:
　　Straunge Doctor, hating truth, enforcing lyes:
Thus Satan is indeed, and Christ by contraryes.

3

And such his Ministers all glist'ring bright
In night and shades, and yet but rotten wood,
And fleshly Devils: such this Jesuite,
Who (Loiol's Ensigne) thirsts for English blood.
He culs choice soules (soules vow'd to th' Prince of night,
And Priest of Rome) sweares them (an English brood,
　　But hatch't in Rome for Spaine) close to conceale,
　　And execute what he should then reveale:
Binds them to hell in sin, & makes heavens Lord the seale.

4

Now are they met; this armed with a spade,
That with a mattocke, voide of shame and feare:
The earth (their Grandame Earth) they fierce invade,
And all her bowels search, and rent, and teare,
Then by her ruines flesh't, much bolder made,
They ply their worke; and now neere hell, they heare
    Soft voices, murmurs, doubtfull whisperings:
    The fearfull conscience prick't with guilty stings,
A thousand hellish formes into their fancy brings.

5

This like a statue stands; cold fright congeales
His marble limbes; to th' earth another falling,
Creeping behind a barrell softly steales:
A third into an empty hogshead cralling,
Locks up his eyes, drawes in his stragling heeles:
A fourth, in vaine for succour loudly calling,
    Flies through the aire as swift as gliding starre;
    Pale, ghastly, like infernall sprites afarre
Each to his fellow seemes: and so, or worse they are.

6

So when in sleep's soft grave dead senses rest,
An earthly vapour clamb'ring up the braine
Brings in a meagre ghost, whose launched brest
Showres downe his naked corps a bloody raine:
A dull-blue-burning torch about his crest
He ghastly waves; halfe dead with frightfull paine
    The leaden foot faine would, but cannot fly;
    The gaping mouth faine would, but cannot cry:
And now awake still dreames, nor trusts his open eye:

7

At length those streames of life, which ebbing low
Were all retir'd into the frighted heart,
Backe to their wonted chanels gan to flow:
So peeping out, yet trembling every part,
And list'ning now with better heed, they know

THE APOLLYONISTS

Those next adjoyning roomes hollow'd by art
  To lie for cellerage: which glad they hire,
  And cramme with powder, and unkindled fire:
Slacke aged Time with plaints and praires they daily tire.

8

Slow Time, which every houre grow'st old and young,
Which every minute dy'st, and liv'st againe;
Which mak'st the strong man weak, the weak man strong:
Sad time which fly'st in joy, but creep'st in paine,
Thy steppes uneven are still too short or long:
Devouring Time, who bear'st a fruitfull traine,
  And eat'st what er'e thou bear'st, why dost not flee,
  Why do'st not post to view a Tragedie,
Which never time yet saw, which never time shall see?

9

Among them all none so impatient
Of stay, as firy Faux, whose grisly feature
Adorn'd with colours of hells regiment
(Soot black, and fiery red) betrayd his nature.
His frighted Mother, when her time shee went,
Oft dream't she bore a straunge, & monstrous creature,
  A brand of hell sweltring in fire and smoke,
  Who all, and's Mother's selfe would burne and choke:
So dream't she in her sleep, so found she when she woke.

10

Rome was his Nurse, and Spaine his Tutour; she
With wolvish milk flesh't him in deadly lyes,
In hate of Truth, and stubborn errour: he
Fats him with humane blood, inures his eyes
Dash't braines, torne guts, and trembling hearts to see,
And tun'de his eare with grones and shrieking cryes.
  Thus nurst, bred, growne a Canniball, now prest
  To be the leader of this troup, he blest
His bloody maw with thought of such a royall feast.

PHINEAS FLETCHER

11

Meane time the Eye, which needs no light to see,
That wakefull Eye, which never winks or sleepes,
That purest Eye, which hates iniquitie,
That carefull Eye, which safe his Israel keepes,
From which no word, or thought can hidden bee,
Look's from his heaven, and piercing through the deepes,
    With hate, and scorne viewes the dire Jesuite
    Weary his hand, and quintessentiall wit,
To weave himselfe a snare, and dig himselfe a pit.

12

That Mounting Eagle, which beneath his throne
(His Saphire throne) fixed on Chrystall base,
Broadly dispreds his heaven-wide pineon,
On whome, when sinfull earth he strikes with 'maze,
He wide displayes his black pavilion,
And thundring, fires high towres with flashing blaze:
    Darke waters draw their sable curtaines o're him,
    With flaming wings the burning Angels shore him,
The cloudes, & guilty heavens for feare fly fast before him:

13

That mounting Eagle forth he suddaine calls,
Fly, winged Herald, to that Citie fly,
Whose towres my love, truth, wisedome builds and walls:
There to the Councell this foule plot descry:
And while thy doubtfull writ their wit appalls,
That great Peace-makers sense Ile open, I
    Will cleere his mind, and plaine those ridling folds.
    So said, so done: no place or time with-holds
His instant course, the towne he thinks, he sees, and holds.

14

There in another shape to that wise Peer
(That wisest Peer) he gives a darksome spell:
He was the states Treasure, and Treasurer,
Spaines feare, but Englands earthly oracle;
He Patron to my Mother Cambridge, where

THE APOLLYONISTS

Thousand sweet Muses, thousand Graces dwell:
But neither hee, nor humane wit could find
The riddles sense, till that learn'd royall mind,
Lighted from heaven, soone the knot, and plot untwin'd.

15

And now the fatall Morne approached neare:
The Sunne, and every starre had quench't their light,
Loathing so black a deed: the Articke Beare
Enjoyn'd to stay, trembling at such a sight,
Though drench't in ayrie seas, yet wink't for feare.
But hellish Faux laught at blinde heavens affright.
   What? Such a deed not seen? In vaine (saith he)
   You drowne your lights; if heaven envious be,
I'le bring hell fires for light, that all the world may see.

16

So entring in, reviewes th' infernall mines;
Marshals his casks anew, and ord'ring right
The tragicke Scene, his hellish worke refines:
And now return'd, booted, and drest for flight,
A watchfull Swaine the Miner undermines,
Holds, binds, brings out the Plot to view the light;
   The world amaz'd, hel yawn'd, earth gap't, heaven star'd,
   Rome howl'd to see long hopes so sudden mar'd:
The net was set, the fowle escap't, the fowler snar'd.

17

Oh thou great Shepheard, Earths, Heavens Soveraigne,
Whom we thy pasture-sheep admire, adore;
See all thy flocks prostrate on Britaine plaine,
Pluck't from the slaughter; fill their mouthes with store
Of incens't praise: oh see, see every swaine
'Maz'd with thy workes; much 'maz'd, but ravish't more:
   Powre out their hearts thy glorious name to raise;
   Fire thou our zealous lippes with thankfull laies;
Make this sav'd Isle to burne in love, to smoke in praise.

18

Teach me thy groome, here dull'd in fenny mire,
In these sweet layes, oh teach me beare a part:
Oh thou dread Spirit shed thy heavenly fire,
Thy holy flame into this frozen heart:
Teach thou my creeping Muse to heaven aspire,
Learne my rude brest, learne me that sacred art,
   Which once thou taught'st thy Israels shepheard-King:
   O raise my soft veine to high thundering;
Tune thou my lofty song, thy glory would I sing.

19

Thou liv'dst before, beyond, without all time;
Art held in none, yet fillest every place:
Ah, how (alas!) how then shall mortall slime
With sinfull eyes view that eternall space,
Or comprehend thy name in measur'd rime?
To see forth-right the eie was set i' th' face,
   Hence, infinite to come I wel descry,
   Past infinite no creature sees with eie:
Onely th' Eternall's selfe measures eternitie.

20

And yet by thee, to thee all live and move;
Thou without place or time giv'st times and places:
The heavens (thy throne) thou liftest all above,
Which folded in their mixt, but pure embraces
Teach us in their conjunctions chastest love,
Next to the Earth the Moone performes her races;
   Then Mercury; beyond, the Phosphor bright:
   These with their friendly heat, and kindly might,
Warme pallid Cynthia's cold, and draine her watry light.

21

Farre thou remoov'st slow Saturn's frosty drythe,
And thaw'st his yce with Mars his flaming ire:
Betwixt them Jove by thy appointment fly'th;
Who part's, and temper's well his Sonne and Sire;
His moist flames dull the edge of Saturnes sithe,

THE APOLLYONISTS

And ayry moisture softens Mars his fire.
  The Heart of heaven midst of heavens bodie rides,
  From whose full sea of light and springing tides
The lesser streames of light fill up their empty sides.

22

The Virgin Earth, all in green-silken weed
(Embroyder'd fayre with thousand flowres) arrayd:
Whose wombe untill'd knew yet nor plough, nor seed,
Nor midwifry of man, nor heavens ayd,
Amaz'd to see her num'rous Virgin breed,
Her fruit even fruitfull, yet her selfe a mayd:
  The earth of all the low'st, yet middle lies;
  Nor sinks, though loosely hang'd in liquid skies:
For rising were her fall; and falling were her rise.

23

Next Earth the Sea a testy neighbour raves,
Which casting mounts, and many a churlish hill,
Discharges 'gainst her walles his thundring waves,
Which all the shores with noyse and tumult fill:
But all in vaine; thou beat'st downe all his braves;
When thee he heares commanding, Peace, be still,
  Downe straight he lowly falls, disbands his traynes,
  Sinks in himselfe, and all his mountaines playnes,
Soft peace in all the shores, and quiet stillnes raygnes.

24

Thou mad'st the circling ayre aloft to fly,
And all this Round infold at thy command;
So thinne, it never could be seen with eye,
So grosse, it may be felt with every hand.
Next to the horned Moon and neighbour sky,
The fire thou highest bad'st, but farthest stand.
  Straungely thou temper'st their adverse affection:
  Though still they hate and fight, by thy direction
Their strife maintaines their owne, and all the worlds perfection.

PHINEAS FLETCHER

25

For Earth's cold arme cold Winter friendly holds;
But with his dry the others wet defies:
The Ayer's warmth detests the Water's colds;
But both a common moisture joyntly ties:
Warme Ayre with mutuall love hot Fire infolds;
As moist, his drythe abhorres: drythe Earth allies
   To Fire, but heats with cold new warres addresse:
   Thus by their peacefull fight, and fighting peace
All creatures grow, and dye, and dying still increase.

26

Above them all thou sit'st, who gav'st all being,
All every where, in all, and over all:
Thou their great Umpire, all their strife agreeing,
Bend'st [t]heir stiffe natures to thy soveraigne call:
Thine eye their law: their steppes by overseeing
Thou overrul'st, and keep'st from slipp'ry fall.
   Oh if thy steady hand should not maintaine
   What first it made, all straight would fall againe,
And nothing of this All, save nothing would remaine.

27

Thou bid'st the Sunne piece out the ling'ring day,
Glitt'ring in golden fleece: The lovely Spring
Comes dauncing on; the Primrose strewes her way,
And satten Violet: Lambs wantoning
Bound o're the hillocks in their sportfull play:
The wood-musicians chant and cheerely sing;
   The World seemes new, yet old by youths accruing.
   Ah wretched men, so wretched world pursuing,
Which still growes worse with age, and older by renuing!

28

At thy command th' Earth travailes of her fruit;
The Sunne yeelds longer labour, shorter sleep;
Out-runnes the Lyon in his hot pursuit;
Then of the golden Crab learnes backe to creep:
Thou Autumne bid'st (drest in straw-yellow suit)

THE APOLLYONISTS

To presse, tunne, hide his grapes in cellars deep:
  Thou cloth'st the Earth with freez in stead of grasse,
  While keen-breath'd winter steeles her furrow'd face,
And vials rivers up, and seas in Chrystall glasse.

29

What, but thy love and thou, which feele no change?
Seas fill, and want: their waters fall, and grow;
The windy aire each houre can wildly range;
Earth lives, and dies; heavens lights can ebbe, and flow:
Thy Spowse her selfe, while yet a Pilgrim strange,
Treading this weary world (like Cynthia's bow)
  Now full of glorious beames, and sparkling light;
  Then soone oppos'd, eclips't with earthly spight
Seemes drown'd in sable clouds, buried in endles night.

30

See, Lord, ah see thy rancorous enemies
Blowne up with envious spight, but more with hate,
Like boisterous windes, and Seas high-working, rise:
So earthly fires, wrapt up in watry night,
With dire approach invade the glistring skies.
And bid the Sunne put out his sparkling light;
  See Lord, unles thy right hand even steares
  Oh if thou anchour not these threatning feares,
Thy Ark will sayle as deepe in blood, as now in teares.

31

That cursed Beast, (which with thy Princely hornes,
With all thy stiles, and high prerogatives
His carrion cor's and Serpents head adornes)
His croaking Frogges to every quarter drives:
See how the key of that deep pit he tournes,
And cluck's his Locusts from their smoky hives:
  See how they rise, and with their numerous swarmes
  Filling the world with fogges, and fierce alarmes,
Bury the earth with bloodles corps, and bloody armes.

PHINEAS FLETCHER

32

The bastard Sonne of that old Dragon (red
With blood of Saints) and all his petty states;
That triple monster, Geryon, who bred,
Nurs't, flesh't in blood thy servants deadly hates,
And that seduced Prince who hath his head
Eyes, eares, and tongue all in the Jesuite pates;
   All these, and hundred Kings, and nations, drunk
   With whorish Cup of that dire witch and punk,
Have sworne to see thy Church in death for ever sunk.

33

Now from those hel-hounds turne thy glorious eyes;
See, see thy fainting Spouse swimme, sinke in teares:
Heare Lord, oh heare her grones, and shrieking cries:
Those eyes long wait for thee: Lord to thine eares
She brings heart, lips, a Turtle sacrifice.
Thy cursed foe that Pro-Christ trophies reares:
   How long (just Lord) how long wilt thou delay
   That drunken whore with blood and fire to pay? (stay?
Thy Saints, thy truth, thy name's blasphem'd; how canst thou

34

Revel. 19. 11.
12. 13. 14.
Revel. 14. 20.

Oh is not this the time, when mounted high
Upon thy Pegasus of heavenly breed,
With bloody armes, white armies, flaming eye,
Thou vow'st in blood to swimme thy snowy steed;
And staine thy bridle with a purple dye?
This, this thy time; come then, oh come with speed,
   Such as thy Israel saw thee, when the maine
   Pil'd up his waves on heapes; the liquid plaine
Ran up, and with his hill safe wall'd that wandring traine.

35

Such as we saw thee late, when spanish braves
(Preventing fight with printed victorie)
Full fraught with brands, whips, gyves for English slaves,
Blest by their Lord God Pope, thine enemie,
Turn'd seas to woods; thou arm'd with fires, winds, waves,

THE APOLLYONISTS

Fround'st on their pride: they feare, they faint, they fly:
  Some sink in drinking seas, or drunken sand,
  Some yeeld, some dash on rocks; the Spanish Grand
Banquets the fish in seas, or foules, and dogs on land.

36

Oh when wilt thou unlock the seeled eyes
Of those ten hornes, and Kings, which with the Beast   *Revel.* 17. 12. 13. 16.
(Yet by thy hand) 'gan first to swell and rise?
How long shall they (charm'd with her drunken feast)
Give her their crownes? Bewitch't with painted lies,
They dreame thy spirit breathes from her sug'red breast,
  Thy Sun burnes with her eye-reflected beames,
  From her life, light, all grace, and glory streames.
Wake these enchaunted sleepes, shake out these hellish dreames.

37

Wake lesser Gods, you sacred Deputies
Of heavens King, awake: see, see the light
Bares that foule whore, dispells her sorceries,
Blanch't skin, dead lippes, sowre breath, splay foot, owl-sight.
Ah can you dote on such deformities?
While you will serve in crownes, and beg your right,
  Pray, give, fill up her never fill'd desire,
  You her white Sonnes: else knives, dags, death your hire.
Scorne this base yoke; strip, eat, and burne her flesh in fire. *Revel.* 17. 16.

38

But thou, Greate Prince, in whose successfull raigne,
Thy Britanes 'gin renue their Martiall fame,
Our Soveraigne Lord, our joy more Soveraigne,
Our onely Charles, under whose ominous name
Rome wounded first, still pines in ling'ring paine;
Thou who hast seen, and loath'd Romes whorish shame,
  Rouse those brave Sparkes, which in thy bosome swell,
  Cast downe this second Lucifer to hell:
So shalt thou all thy Sires, so shalt' thy selfe excell.

PHINEAS FLETCHER

39

'Tis not in vaine, that Christ hath girt thy head
With three fayre peacefull Crownes: 'tis not in vaine,
That in thy Realmes such spirits are dayly bred,
Which thirst, and long to tug with Rome, and Spayne:
Thy royall Sire to Kings this lecture red;
This, this deserv'd his pen, and learned veine:
   Here, noble Charles, enter thy chevalrie;
   The Eagle scornes at lesser game to flie;
Onely this warre's a match worthy thy Realmes, & Thee.

40

Ah happy man, that lives to see that day!
Ah happy man, who in that warre shall bleed!
Happy who beares the standard in that fray!
Happy who quells that rising Babel seed!
Thrice happy who that whore shall doubly pay!
This (royall Charles) this be thy happy meed.
   Mayst thou that triple diademe trample downe,
   This shall thy name in earth, and heaven renowne,
And adde to these three here there a thrice triple crowne.

FINIS.

SICELIDES
A PISCATORY.

As it hath beene Acted in Kings Colledge, in Cambridge.

LONDON,

Printed by *I. N.* for *William Sheares*, and are to be sold at his shoppe, at the great South doore of St. *Pauls Church*, 1631.

Dramatis Personæ.

Perindus, A Fisher, sonne to *Tyrinthus,* in love with *Glaucilla.*
Armillus, A Shepheard, and acquainted with *Perindus.*
Thalander, A Fisher, sonne to *Glaucus* [and *Circe*], in love with *Olinda,* disguised and called *Atyches.*
Alcippus, A Fisher.
Pas, A Fisher, in love with *Cosma.*
Fredocaldo, An old Fisher, in love with *Cosma.*
Olinda, Sister to *Perindus.*
Glaucilla, Sister to *Thalander.*
Cosma, A light Nymph of *Messena.*
Cancrone,} Two foolish Fishers, servants to old *Tyrinthus.*
Scrocca,
Tyrinthus, Father to *Perindus* and *Olinda.*
Conchylio, *Cosmaes* page.
Rymbombo, Cyclops.
Dicæus, *Neptunes* chiefe Priest.
Nomicus, An inferior Priest.
Glaucus,} *Muti.*
Circe,
Gryphus, *Tyrinthus* his man.
Cuma, *Perindus* his boy.
Executioners.
Chorus, of {Priests.
 Fishers.

PROLOGUS CHAMUS.

BEgin, *thou royall Muse, Envie nere uses,*
   To dwell in gentle Courts, or sacred Muses:
To begge of them, [w]hat common courtesie
Must grant; were to condemne both them, and thee:
Thy Came assures thee, they will all agree,
Gently to beare their Actors infancy;
Infants oft please; the choycest Poet[s] song,
Breeds lesse delight then th' infants prattling tongue.
Then let me here intreate your minds to see,
In this our England, *fruitfull* Sicely,
Their two twinne Iles; so like in soyle and frame,
That as two twinnes they'r but another same.
But this they begge, which you may graunt with ease:
That all these paines to pleasure you, may please.

SICELIDES.

Act. 1.   *Scen.* 1.

Enter PERINDUS, ARMILLUS, CUMA.

Perindus.

CUma! beare home our spoyles, and conquering weapons,
 And trusse them on a wreath as our just trophie:
And when *Cancrone* [comes], returne to mee. *Exit Cuma*
Thus: if but thus: yet thus my state is better,
While lesser cares do laugh and mocke the greater;
This change is best when changing I frequent,
Even now that moyst, now this drie element,
When with this scepter, setting on the Land,
The scalie footlesse people I command:
When riding on my wooden horse, I see
The Earth that never mooves, remoove from me.
And why my friend doth not this guise beseeme me?
In this I am not wretchlesse as you deeme me.
   Ar. Not that I censure, but demande the cause,
Why being borne, and bred, in shepheards lawes;
You have our Hills, and Downes, and Groves forsaken,
And to these Sands, and Waves your selfe betaken.
   Per. Shepheard or fisher, I am still the same,
I am a sea guest not for gaine, but game.
   Ar. A gamesome life? thus with unarmed armes
To fight gainst windes, and winters sharpe alarmes,
And paddle in chill *Neptuns* Icie lappe?
But if in fishing any ple[as]ure be,

PHINEAS FLETCHER

In Shepheards life there is much more say we.
    Per. Yet Fishers life with me doth mo[re] consort,
This sporting serves to moralize my sport:
Viewing the stormes, and troublesome waves; I finde
Some thing in nature rest-lesse as my minde:
Each captive fish tels me that in deaths snare,
My heart is not the onely prisoner.
Walke [I] along the shore——
    [*Ar.*] Oft there he walkes
Oft there with me or with the waves hee talkes.
    Per. There in the tide I see fleete fortunes changing,
And state of man, weake state: that's never standing:
But rises still, or fals all as the maine,
That ebs to flow, or flowes to ebbe againe.
Yet fortune I accuse thee not for ra[n]ging,
Let others plaine, I never felt the[e] changing,
B[a]d wast thou at the first, and so art still,
Before I knew what's good, I knew the ill:
And since of all my goods thou first bereav'st me,
I neere expected good, thou neere deceivd'st me;
Therefore although [the] Oracle from whence
I late ariv'd, would feede vaine confidence;
Yet since so sure assurance thou doest give mee,
Still of the two fortune I must beleeve thee.
    Ar. Vaine feare when th' Oracle doth promise good;
The heavens decrees by chance weere neere withstood.
You feare without a cause, oft cause-lesse fright,
Is th' onely cause that makes that on us light
Which most wee feare, ever a jealous eye
Makes enemies by fearing e[nm]ity.
    Per. What fearefull tempest doe the waves foretell,
When seas without a storme to mountaynes swell.
    Ar. Ill is invited when it is suspected
And griefe already come where he's expected.
    Per. The greatest evills oft are where the[y] shew not,
I feare the more, because my feare I know not.
Musicke! how sad it sounds; my damped heart
Tells me in these sad straines I beare a part:
I wrong thee fate, or else thou now doest straine thee
W[ith] some unused wel[c]ome t' entertaine me.

SICELIDES

Act. 1. Scen. 2.

Enter Dicæus Neptunes *Priest following* Olinda, *led by two Nymphes* Cosma *and* Glaucilla, *before and after a Chorus of Fishers and Priests singing.*

Song.
    Go go thy countries joy and jewell,
    The seas and rockes were ever cruell;
    Men then may pitty thee in vaine,
    But not helpe nor ease thy payne.
    Take then these t[e]ares th[y] la[t]est due,
    For ever now alasse adiew.

  Olin. Glaucus; to thee I frendlesse maide,
In these last gifts my vowes have payd:
These once *Olindas*, now are thine,
This net, and hooke, this rod, and line:
Thou knowst, why here my sports I give thee,
Hence came my joyes, and here they leave me.
  Gla. Olinda, if that smiles were proofes of sorrow,
Sure I should thinke thee full of woe, and sadnesse,
But in so heaped griefe, when every eye
Yeilds tribute to so great a misery,
Thou only smilst, why every teare thou seest,
Is paid to thee—.
  Olin. The lesse I need to pay:
Gl[au]cilla I cannot mourne, when I am married.
  Gla. Married? now heaven defend me, if this be marriage.
So to be gript in pawes of such a monster,
And bedded in his bowells———
  Cos. Olinda I should weepe,
And spend the short'nd breath that fate affords me,
In cursing fate which makes my breath so short.
  Olin. Peace peace my *Cosma*, thou wouldst have me mad
With reason!
  Cos. No: reason is never sencelesse.
  Olin. Thinkst thou me sencelesse friend?

Gla. Dost not thou prove it?
Olin. Why my *Glaucilla* I see thy drowned eyes,
I feele thy kinde imbracements, and which thou seest not,
Nor feelst, I feele and see, more mirth and joy
Spring in my heart, then if I now were leading
To the best bed that *Sicely* affords me.
Glaucilla if there were but fit occasion
That I might shew thee this tormented heart,
It would affright thee friend to heare me tell
How many deaths live in so narrow Hell.
Dicæ. We stay too long; goe on: these idle teares
Quench not her griefe, but adde new kindled feares.
Olin. *Dicæus*; no feare within this brest is lying.
Who living dies, feares not to live by dying.
      Exeunt ad rupem rufam, manent reliqui.

Act. 1. Scen. 3.

Enter Perindus, Armillus.

Ar. Saw you the troope which past along here?
Per. Yes.
Ar. Who is it ledde with such a mournfull show?
Per. My sister.
Ar. Who the faire *Olinda*?
Per. Yes.
Ar. And doe you know the end and purpose?
Per. No.
Ar. Nothing but no and yes? fie fie *Perindus*!
Your too much passion shewes you want affection;
Your sister in such sort convey'd, and you
So carelesse of her griefe? it much misseemes you
Why learne you not the cause?
Per. Thou counsailst well,
Griefe weary of it selfe, all sence depriving,
Felt neyther sence, nor griefe, by overgrieving.   *Enter*
But see my *Atyches*: what different passions   *Atyches.*
Strive in his doubtfull face, pitty would weepe,
And danger faine would rocke high thoughts a sleepe,

SICELIDES

Whiles resolution chides the daring [t]eare,
And courage makes poore feare afrade to feare.
  Atych. Thou God that rulst the sunnes bright flaming cart
If thou my grand-sire art, as sure thou art
For in my breast I feele thy powe[r] divine,
Firing my soule, which tels mee I am thine:
Direct my hand and guide this poynted dart,
That it may peirce, and rive the monsters heart.
  Per. Atyches.
  Atych. Ah *Perindus* this lucklesse howre
Bids thee unwelcome fly and never more,
Never approach to view this deadly shore.
  Per. Why whats the newes?
  Atych. Thy sister the [*Olinda* fayre] must die.
  Ar. So must we all.
  Atych. But none of all as she.
  Per. Canst tell the cause and manner?
  Atych. Yes; and till the sunne
Twixt noone and night his middle race shall runne,
The rites will not be finisht; 'tis briefly thus.
Thou knowst by Neptunes temple close the[re] growes
A sacred garden, where every flowe[r] blowe[s]:
Here blushing roses, there the Lillies white,
Here Hyacinth, and there Narcissus bright:
And underneath, the creeping violets show:
That sweetnes oft delights to dwell below:
Vaulted above with thousand fragrant trees,
And under p[av']d with shamefast Strawberies,
Which creeping lowe doe sweetely blushing tell,
That fairest pleasantst fruits, doe humblest dwell.
Breifly a little Heaven on Earth it seemes:
Where every sweete and pleasure fully streames.
  Ar. Fisher thou now describ'st some paradice,
Can any ill from so much good arise?
  Atych. Henbane and roses in o[ne] garden growe,
Ah that from fruits so sweete, such gall should flowe!
Here faire Olinda, with her [N]ymphs arrives,
And time away, time to fast posting drives,
While [M]ago that deformed enchanter, ranging
Along these trees, his shape and habit changing

PHINEAS FLETCHER

Seem'd then Glaucilla, such his sta[r]like eyes,
Such haire, such lipps, such cheekes, such rosie dies,
So like Glaucillas selfe that had shee spide him,
More would shee doubt her selfe, the more shee eyd him.
    Ar. Can art forge nature with so true a lie?
    Atych. The falsest coine is fairest to the eie,
Singling thy sister forth, they chance to see,
The sacred graft of that He[s]perian tree,
Whose golden apples much the eye delighting,
Would tempt the hands: the longing tast inviting:
And now the subtill witch spies fit occasion,
And with fi[n]e speech and oaths, and soft perswation,
So wor[k]s he[r] mind; that shee ([ah] little guessing,
What monster lay under that fain[e]d dressing)
Puls of th' unhappie fruit; straight downe shee falls,
And thrice a thundring voice *Dicæus* calls;
The preist knew what the fearefull voice portended,
And faire *Olinda* halfe dead apprehended:
And to the temple beares her, there reserving
Till the third day with death payes her deserving.
So *Neptune* bids, that who shall touch the tree
With hands profane, shall by *Malorcha* die;
Malorcha bread in seas, yet seas do dread him,
As much more monstrous then the seas that bred him.
    Per. Ah my *Olinda* who can pitty thee
That wouldst not pitty th' excellent *Thalander*?
'Tis just yee seas: well doth impartiall fate
With monstrous death punish thy monstrous hate.
[But] whither art thou now thus armed going?
    Atych. Downe to the fatall rocke I goe to see
And act a part in this foule Tragedy.
    Per. Why canst thou hope such losses to repayre?
    Atych. Who nothing hopes yet nothing ought despaire.
    Per. What 'tis impossible? ah cease to prove?
    Atych. What ever was impossib[l]e to love?
    Per. 'Tis certaine [death]; thou adst thy death to hers.
    Atych. Unworthy love that life ['f]or[e] love prefers.
    Per. What good canst do when thou canst not restore her?
    Atych. To live with her or else to die before her.
    Per. 'Tis fate that in this monster bids engrave her.

SICELIDES

Atych. And 'tis my fate to die with her or save her.
Per. In vaine to fight against all conquering *Jove*.
Atych. But in my hand shall fight *Jove* conquering love.
Per. Atyches why shouldst thou thus betray thy selfe?
She [i]s my sister, and as deare to me
As ever was a sister to a brother:
Had fate felt any hope, my willing hand
Should be as prest to give her ayd as any.
Were not the fight gainst heaven I might adventure,
But here I needs must leave her, though a brother;
She never loved [th]ee.
   Atych. I lov'd her ever.
   Per. More shouldest thou hate her now.
   Atych. Can Seas or Rivers stand, can Rocks remoove?
Could they? yet could I never cease to love:
Perindus, if now I see thee last, farewell:
Within thy breast all jo[y] and quiet dwell.
Adiew: *Olinda* now to thee I flye
For thee I liv'd, for thee i'le gladly die.
                           Exit Atyches.
   Per. Goe choycest spirit: the heavenly love regard thee,
And for thy love, with life, and love reward thee.

Act. 1. *Scen.* 4.

Enter *Perindus, Armillus.*

   Ar. Perindus thou knowst how late was my arrivall,
And short abode in this your *Sicely*,
And how delighted with these accidents
So strange and rare, I have decreed to make
Some longer stay, but since I saw this *Atyches*
His love more strong then death, a resolution
Beyond humanity, I much desir'd
To know him, what he is, and what his country
That breeds such minds: let me intreate you then
At large to give me all this [perfect] story.
Somewhat t'will eas[e] your griefe, just are his paines
That sorrow with more sorrow entertaines.

PHINEAS FLETCHER

Per. It will be tedious, and my heavy minde
Fit words for such a tale can never finde:
Yet I'le unfold it all, that you may see
How beautious love showes [cloath'd] in [constancy]:
Who hath not heard of *Glaucus* [haplesse love]?
Whilst fairest *Scylla* baths, him love inspires;
At once herselfe she cooles and him she fires.
A sea god burnt in flames, and flames most please him,
Glaucus findes neither waves nor hearbes to ease him;
Cold were his [seas] more cold her coy disdaine:
Yet none of boeth could quench loves scorching flame:
Till Circe whom scornd love to madnes moves
Quenches at once her beautie and his loves.
There stands shee now a proofe of jealous spite
As full of horror now as then delight.
    [*Ar.*] The fruite of jealousie is ever curst,
But when tis grafted in a crab tis worst.
Bad in a man, but monstrous in a woman,
And which the greater monster hard to know
Then jelous Circe, or loath'd *Scylla* now.
    [*Per.*] After when time had easd his greife for *Scylla*,
Circe with charmes, and prayers and gifts had wone him,
Her love shee reapt in that high rocky frame,
Which ever since hath borne faire Circes name:
The Moone her fainting light 10 times had fed,
And 10 times more her globe had emptied:
When two fayre twins she brought, whose beauteous shine,
Did plainly prove their parents were divine.
The male *Thalander*, the female calld *Glaucilla*,
And now to youth arriv'd so faire they are
That with them but themselves who may compare?
All else excelling; each as faire as other
Thus best compard the sister with the brother.
    Ar. So lively to the eare thy speeches show them,
That I must halfe affect before I know them.
    Per. Vaine words that thinke to blase so great perfection,
Their perfectnes more proves words imperfection.
But if these words some little sparkle[s] move,
How would their sight inflame thy soule with love?
Scarce did his haire betray his blooming yeares,

SICELIDES

When with his budding youth his love appeares,
My selfe and sister equally he loves,
And as on those two poles heaven ever moves
So on us two his soule still fixt, still loving
Was ever constant, by his constant moving:
Yet never knew wee which was most respected,
Both equally and both he most affected.
In mee his worthy love with just reflexion,
Kindled an equall and a like affection,
But shee my sister most ungratefull maide,
With hate, ah hatefull vice, his love repaide.
 Ar. Ce[as']t he not then to love? this sure wee hold
That love not backe reflected soone grows cold.
 Per. No though all spite within her bosome sweld,
Spite of her spite his love her hate exceld;
At length to shew how much he was neglected,
His rivall ugly rivall shee affected:
Such rivall could I wish whose foule distortion,
Would make seeme excellent a meane proportion,
For *Mago* (thus his hated rivall's nam'd)
All blacke and foule, most strang[e] and ugly fram'd,
Begot by *Saturne*, on a sea-borne witch,
Resembling both, his haires like threeds of pitch,
Distorted feete, and eyes suncke in his head:
His face dead pale, and seem'd but mooving lead,
Yet worse within, for in his heart to dwell
His mothers furies [le]ave their darkest hell.
Yet when *Thalander* woo'd her, shee neglects him,
And when this monster flatterd shee respects him.
 Ar. I[s't] possible? troth Sir but that I feare mee,
If I should speake, some women should ore:heare mee:
Meethinks I now could raile on all their kinds,
But who can sound the depth of womens minds?
 Per. Shortly to come to th' height of all their wrong,
So could this *Mago* fill his smoothest tongue,
That shee *Thalander* banisht from her sight,
Never to see her more his sole delight:
And he to none his hidden greife i[m]parted,
But full of loving duty straight departed.
Leaving our groves in woods he grows a ranger,
To all but beasts and sencelesse trees a stranger.

PHINEAS FLETCHER

Thus in a desert like his love forsaken
When nothing but cold death his flames could slacken
Atyches spyed him, but so griefe had pin'd him,
That when he saw him plaine, he could not find him.
And so had sorrow all his graces reft
That in him, of him nothing now was left
Onely his love; [which with] his latest breath
He power'd into his eares, so slept in death.
The rest when better leisure time affords:
This lucklesse day askes rather teares then words.   *Exeunt.*

CHORUS.

Who neere saw death, may death commend,
Call it joyes Prologue troubles end:
The pleasing sleepe that quiet rockes him,
Where neither care; nor fancy mockes him.
But who in neerer space do[e] eye him,
Next to hell, as hell defye him:
No state, no age, no sexe can move him,
No beggars prey, no Kings reproove him:
In mid'st of mirth, and loves alarmes,
He puls the Bride from Bridegroomes arms:
The beaut[e]ous Virgin he contemnes,
The guilty with the just condemns.
All weare his cloth and none denyes,
Dres't in fresh colour'd liveries.
Kings lowe as beggars lie in graves,
Nobles as base, the free as slaves,
Bles't who on vertues life relying,
Dies to vice, thus lives by dying.
But fond that making life thy treasure,
Surfetst in joy, art drunke in pleasure.
Sweetes do make the sower more tart;
And pleasure sharp's deaths keenest dart.
Deaths thought is death to those that live,
In living joyes, and never grieve.
   Happelesse that happie art and knowst no teares:
   Who ever lives in pleasure, lives in feares.   *Exit.*
      Finis Actus Primi.

SICELIDES

Act. 2.   *Scen.* 1.

Enter Conchylio solus.

I Have been studying, what bold hardie foole
Invented fishers art, that tir'd with safety,
Would needs go play with waves, winds, death and hell;
The summe of fishers life is quickly found,
To sweate, freeze, watch, fast, toyle, be starvd or drownd.
Well had my Mistris found no better trade,
I would ere this have left these dabling deities,
But she while other fishers fish on the seas,
Sends me a fishing on the Land for flesh:
No game arrives amisse unto her net,
For shees not borne among the cliffs and rockes,
But from *Messena* comes to sport herselfe
And fish for fooles along these craggie shores;
I tooke her for a Nymph, but shees a woman,
A very woman, loveth all she sees,
This for his sprightly wit, and that for Musicke,
Him cause hee's faire, another for his blacknesse,
Some for their bashfulnes, more for their boldnesse,
The wiseman for his silence, the foole for his bibble babble;
And now she longs in haste for another fat cods-head,
A good fat so[p], and I must snare one for her.
She has (let me see I have the tallie)
Some hundred lovers, yet still desires another:
The first that passeth all the rest in love
Is called *Pas*: Hah know you your cue so well?
                                      Enter Pas.

He is a *malum collum*, alas poore foole;
He would engrosse my Mistris to himselfe;
He would have her all alone, let her alone for that;
And for that it will not be, he raves and sweares
And chides and fights, but what neede I describe him?
Hee'l doe't himselfe, come, [come,] begin, begin.

PHINEAS FLETCHER

Act. 2. *Scen.* 2.

Pas, Conchylio.

Pas. Who sowes the se[a], or plowes the easy shore?
Yet I, fond I, more fond, and sencelesse more:
Who strives in nets to prison in the winde?
Yet I in love a woman thought to bind:
Fond, too fond thoughts, that thought in love to tie
One more inconstant then inconstancy:
Looke as it is with some true Aprill day,
The sunne his glorious beames doth fayre display,
And straight a clowd breakes into fluent showres,
Then shines and raines, and cleares and straight it lowres:
And twenty changinges in one houre do prove,
So, and more changing is a womans love.
Fond then my thoughts, that thought a thing so vaine,
Fond love, to love what could not love againe.
Fond hopes, that anchor on so false a ground,
Fond thoughts that fir'd with love, in hope thus drownd:
Fond thoughts, fond hope, fond heart, but fondest I,
To graspe the winde, and love inconstancy.
Ah *Cosma, Cosma.*

Exit.

Con. Ah *Pas,* asse, passing asse; hah, ha, he:
Fond thoughts, fond hope, fond heart, but fondest I,
To graspe the winde, and love inconstancy; ha, ha, he,
This foole would have I know not what, the sea
To stand still like a pond, the Moone never to change,
A woman true to one, hee knowes not what:
She that to one all her affections brings
Cages herselfe and pinions *Cupids* wings.
Let's see whose the second; O the second
Is an old dotard who though now foure-score,
Yet nature having [left some] few hot embers
Rack't up in cold ashes, thinkes himselfe
All fire and flame, and therefore like the dwarfes
Who, though neere so old, yet still consort with boyes,

SICELIDES

So he among the freshest youth[s] in dancing,
In songs and sporting, spends his fadish time.
When snow on's head, show[r]es in his eye,
With winter lookes gives summer words the lye.
His name is *Fredocaldo*; he knowes his name,   *Enter*
No sooner cald but com[e]! what i[s't] he reads? *Fredocaldo.*
Upon my life some sonnet, Ile stand and heare.

Act. 2. *Scen.* 3.

Fredocaldo, Conchylio.

Fre.   I[*f*] *I am silver white, so is thy cheeke,*
           Yet who for whitenes will condemne it?
        If wrinkled, of[t] thy forehead is not sleeke,
           Yet who for frowning dare contemne it?
Boys full of folly, youth of rage,
Both but a journey to old age.
        I am not yet fayre Nymph to old to love,
           And yet woemen love old lovers:
        Nor yet to wa[ver]ing light, as false to prove,
           Youth a foule inside fairely covers.
Yet when my light is in the waine
Thy sunnes renew my spring againe.

Pretty very pretty, why yet I see
My braine is still as fresh as in my youth.
And quicke invention springs as currantly
As in the greenest head: this little disticke
I made this morne, to send unto my love.
See, here's a legge how full, how little waining,
My [nimble] limbs are still accompanied
With their kind fellow heate, no shaking palsie
Nor cramp has tane possession, my swift bloud streames
Runs quicke and speedie, through their burning channells.
Pish I am young, he is not antient
That hath a silver badge of hoarie haires

PHINEAS FLETCHER

But he that in sweete love is dead and cold:
So old men oft are young, and young men old.
I'le take my farewell of this prettie verse,
It is a [very] prettie verse, I'le reade it againe: *Conchylio throws*
If I am silver white and—O ho my spectacles. *downe his*
Ah naughtie boy, alas my spectacles. *spectacles.*
  Con. Ha ha he, your eyes *Fredocaldo* take up your eyes,
  Fre. Ah naughtie boy, alas my spectacles. (hah, ha, he.
Whether is he gone? O if I finde him.
  Con. Find mee without eyes? hah, ha, he.
  Fre. O my verses my verses. *Snatches his verses.*
  Con. A verie prettie verse: how fresh a braine that made it.
If I am silver white and—
Nay if you'l trie your [nimble] limbs come on.
                    Exit Fredocaldo. Enter Perindus.
Farewell frost: how? *Perindus:* oh how fitly
After warme winter comes a chill could summer.
This youth in all things is that old mans contrarie,
This a cold *May*, that a hot Januarie:
All my [M^rs] art cannot blowe up one sparkle;
If I should stay hee'd blast mee, adue sol in *Pis[c]es*,
Farewell good *Caldofredo*, I must after *Fredocaldo*.
                                      Exit.

Act. 2. Scen. 4.

Enter Perindus, Alcippus.

  Per. Bles't is that fisher swane that sancke i'th flood
Hee's food for them whom he would make his food.
But I most wretched, who so many yeares
Liv['d] safe in waters to be drownd in feares.
In f[ea]re and sorrow like *Titius* is my life
A coverd table furnisht still for griefe.
Hell love your paines, for all poore soules can prove
Is felt and spoke but thus c[u]relesse I love.

Enter Alcippus.

  Alcip. *Phœbus* write thou this glorious victory
And grave it on thy shining axel-tree

SICELIDES

That all may see a fisher hath done more
Then any age hereafter or before.
  Per. *Alcippus* what newes? me thinks I plaine descry
Joy mixt with wonder in thy doubtfull eye.
  Alcip. *Perindus* most happy have I found thee here.
  Per. I[s']t good? ah tell me, yet my grounded feare
Pleads hope impossible.
  Alcip. Were you away
To the Ecco I had told it, as griefe, so joy
Prest downe is burthensome, for now I see
Joy is no joy if bard from company.
Olinda by the Priests enchained-fast
Unto the fatall rocke downe to the wast
Was naked left, which thus was better dreast:
Beauty when most uncloth'd is clothed best:
And now the Priest all rites had finished
And those last words and hidden verses sayd:
Then thus he loud proclaimes, who dare adventure
Against this monstrous beast, now let him enter
And if he conquer by his bold endeavour
This goodly maid shall bee his prize forever
Straight was the monster loos'd, whose ugly sight
Strooke every trembling heart with cold affright
Some sweate, some freeze, some shreike, some silent weare,
The eye durst neyther winke nor see for feare:
Heaven hid his light, the fearefull sunne did shrowd
His glorious eye under a jetty cloud.
  Per. Saw'st thou the Orke?
  Alcip. Yes, and my panting heart
To thinke I saw it in my brest doth start.
  Per. Can'st thou describe it?
  Alcip. Never tongue can tell
What to it selfe no thought can pourtray well.
More bigge then monstrous *Python*, whom men faine
By *Phœbus* first was bred, by *Phœbus* slaine.
His teeth thicke rankt in many a double band
Like to an armed battell ready stand;
His eyes sunke in's head, more fearefull stood
Like bloodie flame or like to flaming blood;
Not any eare upon his head appeares,

PHINEAS FLETCHER

No plaint nor prayer, no threat nor charme he [h]eares,
In sea and land he lives and takes from both
Each monsters part which most we feare and loath;
Soone as he felt him loose, he shakes his crest
And hungry posteth to his ready feast,
And as through seas his oares a passage teare
The thronging waves fly fast, and roare for feare.
  Per. Me thinks I see him and th' unhappy lover
Strook through with fright.
  Alcip. In all their shreiks he smiles,
Stretching his armes, to fight himselfe composes,
And nothing fear'd his body enterposes:
Shaking a dart the monster he defies
Who scorning such a foe to's banquet flyes:
But he with certaine aime his Javelin drives
Which as the sender bad at's eye arrives;
And fixt in's hollow sight, deepe drenched stood
Quenching the bloody fire with fiery blood.
The wounded monster lowdly gins to yell,
If Hell doe speake such is the voyce of Hell,
And to revenge his hurt he flies apace.
The other dart met him i'th' middle race,
And as along he blindly fast doth post
His way and t[o]ther eye together lost:
Thus blinde he quickly dies, and being dead
Leaves to his foe his spoiles, his pawes, his head.
  Per. Hercules thy twelve works with this one conferd
This one before thy twelve might be preferd.
  Alcip. Perindus then mightst thou have seene how love
Is not more bold then fearefull, he that strove
And conquered such a monster with a dart
To her faire eyes yeelds up his [conquered] heart:
Ah hadst thou seene how fearefull modestie
Joynd with chast love did chide the hungry eye
Which having long abstaind and long time fasted
Some of those dainties now would faine have tasted.
Ah ha[d]st thou seene wh[en] such fit time he got
How love to much remembring love forgot;
How th' eye which such a monster did outface
Durst not looke up upon her eie to gaze;

SICELIDES

How th' hand which such a bould fight undertooke
When her it toucht as with a palsie shooke.
As all that saw it thou wouldst soone have sayd
That never liv'd so fortunate a maid.
Most happy such a danger to recover
More happy farre by having such a lover.
And harke the Fishers home the victor bringing
Chant lowd his conquest, his due praises singing.

Act. 2. Scen. 5.

Enter in triumph with Chorus of Fishers and Priests singing Atyches crownd leading Olinda, following Glaucilla and Cosma.

Song.

    Olinda if thou yeeld not now
    The Orke lesse monstrous was then thou;
    No monster to the eye more hatefull
    Then beauty to desert ungratefull.
      Yeeld then thy heart and hand
      And sing along this sand
    Love rule heaven, sea, and land.

Per. *Atyches* how farest thou? O let these armes inlace thee
Methinks I hold halfe heaven when I imbrace thee.
Atych. Will *Perindus* goe with us to the temple?
Per. Most willingly and when thou once art there
Then 'tis a temple I may justly sweare.
                              Exeunt omnes.

Act. 2. Scen. 6.

Enter Cancrone and Scrocca with their boate from fishing.

Scr. Yet more larboord! hol[d] up against that wave! now
Can. I thinke we are upon the shallow.   (starboord!
Scr. Hold in *Cancrone*, I smell the shore.
                                    Cancrone fals in.

Can. Nay by your leave 'twas I that smelt it, for I am sure my nose kist it.

Scr. Take hold of the stretcher, and then fasten the rope.

Can. A rope stretch all such bottle-head botemen, had it been my lot to have bene Master at sea as 'tis yours, wee had neere taken such a journey in such a fly-boate, such a sowseare, such an egge-shell.

Scro. Come helpe to lave her.

Can. Its a true shee bo[a]te I warrant, shee leakes brackish all the yeare long.

Scr. Will you come Sir? you are yet in my jurisdiction on the water.

Can. Will you scale the fish sir, will you bring forth the nets sir, will you spread them upon the rocks sir? you are at my demand Sir upon the land, wee'l be knowne in our place: (*Scrocca drinks*) is that your laving?

Scro. Ah ha this is something fresher then *Neptuns* salt potion, seest not what a pickle I am in? but O those *Scyllaes* bandogs! (*bough wough*) [how] our boate bepist her selfe for feare.

Can. I and thou thy selfe for companie; faith wee were almost in *Thetis* powdring tub, but now *Scrocca* lets off with our liquor: *Sirrah* [heer's] halfe [this to] blew-beard *Neptune*, but he gets not one drop on't.

Scr. I and withall remember the roaring boy *Boreas* (*puff puff*): hold: you beare your poope too high *Cancrone*, y'ad neede goe pumpe.

Can. So mee thinks my braine is somewhat warmer now my wi[t]t gear's on.

> Let Neptune rage and roare and fome
> For now *Cancrone's* safe at home.

Scr. How now *Cancrone*! what? poefied?

Can. Why *Scrocca* is it such a matter for a waterman to be a poet now a daies?

Scro. I but I wonder that in all thy Poems thou never madst an Epitaph for thy grandsire that was eaten up by the Cyclops.

Can. Ah *Scrocca* I prethee doe not ming my grand-sire, thou'lt spoile my poetry presently; those hungry side slops; they eate him up crust and crum, and then kild him too and that which grieues me most: hee never sent mee word who it was that bit of's head, yet fayth, one draught more and have at him.

Hee drinkes.

Scr. Nay if one draught will serve, he shall never starve for an Epitaph.

Can. So: it's comming I have it *Scrocca.*

> Here lies Cancrones grandsire, who sans boate,
> Sa[ns] winde, sans seas saild downe the Cyclops throate.

Scr. Here lies? Why will you grave an Epitaph on the Cyclops belly? I'me sure hee lies yonder.

Can. Masse thou sayst true, but all our late writers begin so.

Scr. Well sir will you walke home and warme your poeticall vaine at the kitchin fire?

Can. Yes I care not if I doe, for I shall nere be well till I have got the chimney corner over my head.

> Farewell ye rockes and seas, I thinke yee'l shew it
> That Sicelie affords a water-Poet.

Act. 2. Scen. 7.

Enter Conchylio solus.

Hah, ha, he; I have laught my selfe weary: i[s']t possible
That fire and frost should thus keepe house together?
Sure age did much mistake him, when it set
His snowie badge on his blew riveld chin.
Were not his faces furrowes fild with snow,
His hams unstrung, his head so straightly bound,
His eyes so rainy, and his skinne so drie,
He were a pretty youth.

PHINEAS FLETCHER

Act. 2. Scen. 8.

Enter Cancrone and Scrocca.

Con. What old acquaintance? lie by Mistris a little; I'le fish a while, I may chaunce to catch a Cods-head; Ile stand and heare them.

S[c]r. Did not I tell you we were wrong sir?

Can. Me thought, we were at land vile soone.

S[c]r. I prethee on which hand was the cape of Peloro, when wee left Syllaes bandogs?

Can. That did belong to thy water office to marke, but sure it stood straight before a little o'th' on[e] side, right upon the left and then it left the right, and turned west by East, and then stood still North, North, by South.

Con. Well bould woodcocke without a bias.

Scr. Come looke about you to your land office. I'le hold a ped of oysters the rocke stands on yonder side; looke this way: I prethee is not this Circe's rocke?

Can. I like thy reasons wondrous well: it is her rocke and her distaffe too.

Con. I'le spine some thred out of this distaffe.

Scr. Then I sweare by Circes jugling box wee [are] come in o' th' wrong side.

Can. Looke into my poll, canst thou not perceive by the colour of my braines that I have unlac't her knavery? thou knowst Circ[e] is a plaguie witch.

Scr. I, she did translate a good father of mine into an hogge.

Can. She with her whisking white wand, has given this rocke a box ō the eare, & set it [on] the other side of the country.

Scr. I care not where Circ[e] dwells, but I am sure we dwell on this side, and wee have pusht in the cleane contrary way, and wat you what, wee have leapt through Hell-mouth: O strange how— *he falls downe and cries.*

SICELIDES

Can. O the Orke the huge huntie, puntie.
Scr. Up Cancrone I tell thee wee have scap't him.
Can. I tell thee *Scrocca* wee have not scap't him, he has eate us up.
Con. These fishers are new returnd from fishing, and know not that Atyches has slaine the Orke, I'le Orke them.
Can. Ah *Scrocca* I would this Orke were in *Neptunes* bellie, that will suffer such a worme to live in his dominions, I am a very macherell if the very name be not worse to mee then three nights cold fishing.
S[c]r. Mee thinks I am colder too then I was before.
Con. Let mee strike then before the iron be key cold. What hardie fishers dare approch this shore
Untrod by men this twenty years and more?
Can. Good now *Conchylio* doe not [tell] the [O]rke.
Scr. Wee did [not] eate the golden apples; wee.
Con. What old *Cancrone*? I am sorrie for your chance. The best that I advise you is that you returne round about the Cape presently before the O[r]ke smell you (if he were within twelve score he might wind them, foh.)
Can. Nay I shall be devourd.
Con. Plucke out a good heart man.
Can. If I could doe so I might save the Orke a labour; that will be done to my hand; I know I shall be devourd.
Con. Why man?
Can. Why my grandsire was deflourd, and they say deflouring goes in a blood.
Con. If I ridde you both of this feare will you worship mee?
Can. O worshipfull water-wight.
Scr. O *Neptunes* father.
Can. O *Glaucus* Mother.
Con. Why then thus; my deities oracle gives you answer thus:
When 2 famous fishers fall upon this sand   (by land.
Let them for feare of mightie Orke, leave seas, saile home
I have not pincht them for measure, I have given them Oracle up to the elbowes.
Can. Saile, ther's your office *Scrocca*, you must goe.
Scr. By land, there's your office, goe you.
Con. What, can you not expound?

Dragge up your bote and home-ward crosse this shore.
Can. Wee are all made; I understood you sir, but I did not know your meaning.
Scr. Pull you the bote at nose, i'le lift at the arse.
Can. Manners Jacke this is a land voyage, I am master.
Con. Hoh; roh; droh; *Horka, Corca, Suga ponto*; the monster coms, downe under the boate, turne it over: Ile helpe. Retire thou sacred monster (creepe on). These sweet soules are no food for thee (on on): 'tis time these soules were spent, they begin to stink; retire thou great god *Neptunes* scourg. } *they cover themselves over with their [boate] for feare of the Orke & creep[e] over the stage.*

    Retire I say while this twinne tortoise passes
    And dare not once to touch these fish flesh asses.

Hah, ha, he, farewell good tortoise, what good foutch? Haddocke Flare and Cod? you shall walke with me, Ile be your Orke: yet ile carry the Cod to my mistris *Cosma*, I know she loves it well: let *Conchilio* be turn'd into an Oyster if hee would not play the Orke every day for such sport, it shall go hard but ile [meete] with my friend *Cancrone* yet once againe.
                                             Exit.

CHORUS.

    Happy happie Fishers swaine[s]
      If that yee knew your happines;
    Your sport tasts sweeter by your paines,
      Sure hope your labour relishes;
    Your net your living, when you eate
    Labour finds appetite and meat.

When the seas and tempest roare
    You eyther sleepe or pipe or play,
And dance along the golden shore:
    Thus you spend the night and day;
Shrill windes a pipe, hoarse seas a taber
To fit your sports or ease your labour.

SICELIDES

First ah first the holy Muse
   Rap't my soules most happy eyes,
Who in those holy groves doe use
And learne those sacred misteries,
The yeares and months, old age and birth,
The palsies of the trembling earth.

The flowing of the sea and Moone
   And ebbe of both, and how the tides
Sinke in themselves and backward run.
How palled Cynthia closely slides,
Stealing her brother from our sight,
So robs herselfe and him of light.

But if cold natures frozen parts,
   My dull slow heart and cloudie braine,
Cannot reach those heavenly [ar]ts,
Next happie is the fishers paine
Whose lo[w] roofes peace doe safely hide
And shut out fortune, want and pride.

There shall I quiet fearelesse raigne,
   My boyes my subjects taught submission,
[A b]o[a]t my court, my sonnes my traine,
Nets my purvaiors of provision,
The steere my septer, pipe musition,
Labour my Phisicke, no Phisitian.

So shall I laugh the angry seas and skie:
Thus singing may I live, and singing die.

Act. 3. Scen. 1.

Enter Perindus.

WHen *Atyches* with better sight I eye,
   Some powre me thinks beyond humanity,
Some heavenly power within his bosome lyes
And plainely looks through th' windowes of his eyes.
Thalander, if that soules departed rest
In other men, thou livest in his brest,
He is more then he seemes, or else—but see! *Enter Glaucilla.*

PHINEAS FLETCHER

My love, my hate, my joy, my miserie.
  Glau. Perindus, whither turnst thou? if thy wandring love
My love eschew, yet nothing canst thou see
Why thou shouldst flye me, I am no monster, friend,
That seekes thy spoyle: looke on me, I am shee
To whom th' hast vowd all fayth and loyalty,
Whom thou with vowes and prayers and oathes hast ply'd
And praying wept, and weeping beene deny'd,
And dy'd in the denyall, I am she
Whom by my brothers importunity,
Thalanders meanes, thou want'st, who still persever:
Though thou art chang'd, I loving love for ever.
Tell me am I altered in minde or bodies frame?
What then I was am I not still the same?
  Per. Yes, yes, thou art the same both then and now
As faire, more faire then heavens clearest brow.
  Glau. What have I now deserved?
  Per. In heaven to dwell:
The purest starre deserves not heaven so well.
  Glau. Perindus, I am the same, ah I am she
I was at first, but thou, thou art not hee
Which once thou wast.
  Per. True, ah too true:
Then was I happy being so distressed,
And now most miserable by being blessed.
  Glau. Tell me what thus hath chang'd thy former love,
Which once thou sworst nor heaven nor hell could move:
How hath this scorne and hate stolne in thy heart
And on a Commick stage, hast learnt the art
To play a tyrant, and a foule deceiver?
To promise mercy, and performe it never?
To looke more sweete, maskt in thy lookes disguise,
Then mercies selfe, or pitties gracious eyes.
  Per. Fa, la, la, fa, la, la, lah.
  Glau. Ah me most miserable.
  Per. Ah me mo[re] miserable.
  Glau. Wretched *Glaucilla*, where hast thou set thy love!
Thy plaints his joy, thy teares his laughter move,
Sencelesse of these he sings at thy lamenting,
And laughs [and dances] at thy hearts tormenting.

SICELIDES

Wretched *Glaucilla*.
  Per. More wretched *Perindus*,
Where by refusing life, thou diest for whom
Thou livest, in whom thou drawst thy joy and breath,
And to accept thy life is more then death.
  Glau. *Perindus*.
  Per. Fa, la, la, fa, la, la, lah.

Exit Perindus.

Act. 3. *Scen.* 2.

Glaucilla sola.

Haplesse and fond, too fond and haplesse maide,
Whose hate with love, whose love with hate is payd,
Or learne to hate where thou hast hatred prov'd,
Or learne to love againe, where thou art lov'd ;
Thy love gets scorne: doe not so dearely earne it,
At least learne by forgetting to unlearne it.
Ah fond and haplesse maide, but much more fond
Canst thou unlearne the lesson thou has cond?
Since then thy fixed love will leave thee never,
He hates thy love, leave thou his hate forever,
And though his yce might quench thy loves desiring
Live in his love and die in his admiring.
Olinda so late abroad?   *Enter Olinda.*
The sunne is now at rest, heavens winking eyes
All drowsie seeme, love onely rest denies:
But thou art free as aire, what is the reason?
What glasse is this?
  Olin. Prethee *Glaucilla*
Doe not thus search my soules deepe ranckling wound
Which thou canst never helpe when thou hast found.
  Glau. Thy soule was wont to lodge within mine eare,
And ever was it safely harboured there:
My eare is not accquainted with my tongue
That eyther tongue or eare should doe thee wrong.
Yet doe not tell me, I'le [tell] thee, I spie
Thy burning feaver i[n] thy teltale eye.

PHINEAS FLETCHER

Thou lovst, deny it not, thou lovst *Olinda*.
In vaine a chest to locke up flames we seeke
Which now with purple fires thy blushing cheek[e].
    Olin. Th'art such a mistris in th[is] loving art
That all in vaine I hide my love sicke heart
And yet as vaine to open't now tis hid.
    Glau. Why so loves hee another?
    Olin. I would he did.
    Glau. Strange wish in love, much rather had I die.
Is he then perisht?
    Olin. Yes and with him I.
    Glau. I prethee tell me all, doe not conceale it,
Ile mourne with thee if that I cannot heale it.
    Olin. Heare then and who so ere maiyst be a bride
Learne this of me to hate thy maiden pride.
Atyches thou knowest?
    Glau. Thy champion?
    Olin. The same.
Almost a yeare since he came to this towne
When finding mee fishing along the shore
Silent he angles by mee, till at length
Seeing mee take a star fish, and fling't away
He straight demands why I refus'd that pray:
The cause I said was hate, he thus replied:
Alas poore fish how wretch'ed is your fate
When you are kild for love sav'd but for hate;
Yet then that fish much worse the fisher swaine
Who for his love by hate is causeles slaine.
    Glau. Yet happier he that's slaine by loves defying
Then she in [h]ate that lives yet ever dying.
    Olin. But soone as love he nam'd, I straight was parting.
He holding mee thus speaks; stay *Nymph* and heare
I bring thee newes which well deserves thine eare.
He which most loves thee and thou hatest most
Thalander (at his name my guiltie heart
Ashamed of itselfe did in me start);
He thus went on: *Thalander's* dead, and dying
By oath and all his love swore me to see thee
With these few words: *Thalander* quite forsaken
Would send to thee what thou from him hast taken

SICELIDES

All life and health, and ne're his love remooving
Wishes thee a freind more happie and as loving.
And with this prayer these legacies he sends thee,
This pipe his mother *Circes* gift, to bind
With this soft whistle the loud whistling wind;
And with this pipe he left this precious ring
Whose vertues cuers a venemous tooth or sting.
　Glau. Thalander were wee nothing like the other
Only thy love would prove thou art my brother.
Did not this move thee?
　Olin. *Glaucilla* why should I lie?
I tooke them as spoiles from a slaine enemie,
And for these gifts (sayes he) his last demand
Was this, [by me] that [hee] might kisse thy hand:
The last, the only gift thou canst impart
To such, so loving, and now dying heart!
I grant; [h]e gone, upon the Ring I spie
A Rubie cut most artificially,
Wherein was fram'd a youth in fire consuming,
And round within it as the Ring I turne,
I found these words, Alive or dead, I burne.
　Glau. These words well fitt his heart, so you, so I,
Thalander living loves, and loving dies.
　Olin. But oh those fained flames, such strange desires,
Such true, such lasting, never-quenched fires
Have kindled in my brest, that all the Art
Of *Triphons* selfe cannot allay my smart:
Ah *Glaucilla*, the scornefull proud *Olinda*;
Which at so sweete a love a mockery made,
Who scornd the true *Thalander*, loves his shade;
Whose thousand graces living could not turne mee,
His ashes now hee's dead to ashes burne mee.
　Glau. If thus you love him, how canst thou allow
Thy love to *Atyches*! late didst thou vowe
In *Neptunes* temple to be his for ever.
　Olin. My hand he married there, my heart ah never.
Glaucilla, I love him for his love to mee,
For such his venture, for such his victorie,
But most, because in love he is my rivall,
Because hee's like and love[s] my Love *Thalander*.

Ah, if my life will please him, let him take it,
He gave it mee and I would faine forsake it.
Had it beene mine to give, my wretched heart,
Not worth his dangerous fight, I would impart:
But that is thine, *Thalander* thine for ever,
With [th]ee tis buried and arise shall never.
  [*Glau.*] And wherefore serves this glasse?
  Olin. This is a dessamour *Cosma* lately gave mee.
  Glau. Olinda, knowst not yet the treachery
Of *Cosma,* she thy greatest enemy?
Prethee let me see't: shouldst thou this liquor prove,
I tell thee, friend, 'twill quench thy life and love.
But so Ile temper't, it shall better please thee,
And after few spent houres shall ever ease thee.
  Olin. Tis beyond art, who there can give reliefe.
Where patients hate the cure, more then the griefe?
  Glau. Yes, by my art, before th'art 12 houres older,
Ile ease thy heart, though never make it colder.   *Exeunt.*

Act. 3. *Scen.* 3.

Enter Conchilio.

  Con. Glaucilla and *Olinda?* I mar['l]e what mettle,
What leaden earth and water nature put
Into these Nymphes, as cold, as dull, as frozen
As the hard rockes they dwell on! But my Mistris
Shee's all quicksilver, never still, still moving,
Now is she with some shepheard or some fisher,
And here she sets me to entertaine all commers:
This is the houre her Lovers use to muster.
But who should this be? ist you, old boy?   *Enter Fredocaldo.*
Old ten i'th hundred, are you the captaine? boh!
  Fred. Beshrew your heart, you are a very naughty boy,
I shake every joynt of me.
  Con. No shaking palsey, nor crampe has tane possession
Of your nimble limbes: ha, ha, he.
  Fred. Boy, where's thy Mistris?
  Con. Where she would bee.
  Fred. Where's that?

SICELIDES

Con. Where you would bee.
Fred. What, in her bed?
Con. Ah old goate, doe I smell you? ye[s] in her bed.
Fred. May not I speake a word or two with her?
Con. What a fool tis? thou hast spoken twice 2 allreadie.
Fred. I but I would speake them in her eare.
Con. I know your errand but I preethee tell mee
Fredocaldoe how [is it] possible
That all the bellowes in loves fathers shoppe
Should kindle any fire in such a frost?
    Fred. Thou knowst not what is love, I tell thee boy
I love faire *Cosma* more then all her lovers.
    Con. Now in my conscience he says true, this old wood
Makes a brighter fire then the greenest ever.
    Fred. Conchylio th'art deceiv'd, hast [thou] not scene
That [often] *May* the lust of all the yeare
Nipt with the hoarie frost grows cold and chare?
And oft *October* though the yeares declining
With many daintie flowers is fairely shining;
For as the flaming sunne puts out the fire
So may the heate of love quench loves desir[e].
    Con. Could this dotard doe as well as speake, he might—
    Fred. I tell thee boy, when I was young—
    Con. That was at the siedge of *Troy*: now shall wee have
more tales then ever poets made. But what will you give
mee *Fredocaldoe* if I helpe thee in the rockie cave, neere to
the mirtle grove, to speake with *Cosma* all alone?
    Fred. If thou'l doe it, Ile give thee as faire an otter tamd
for fishing as ever was in *Sicely*.
    Con. Your hand on that: Ah old *Saturne* cold and dry!
well Ile doe't.
    Fred. But when *Conchylio* when?
    Con. Within this houre expect her.
    Fred. Wilt thou be sure?
    Con. Why did I ever deceive you?
    Fred. Never never.
    Con. Beleeve mee *Fredocaldoe* I say beleeve mee then.
    Fred. Farewell; I'le keepe my promise.
    Con. Faile not within this houre: *Exit Fredocaldoe.*
I know not what this old man's like, unlesse

PHINEAS FLETCHER

Our hill of *Sicely* the flaming *Ætna*:
Whose parche[d] bowells still in fire consuming
Fils all the val[e] with flame and pitchy fuming.
Yet on his top congealed snow doth lye
As if there were not fire nor *Phœbus* nie.
Why should we count this strange? when even so
This old mans heart's all fire, his head all snow?
But what fresh souldier's this?   *Enter Armillus.*
   Ar. My pretty wagge?
   Con. Sure you doe mistake me, sir, I am anothers.
   Ar. Thou dost mistake mee, boy, I know well whose thou art.
   Con. I doubt you doe not.
   Ar. Th'art faire *Cosmaes* boy.
   Con. My mother told me [noe].
   Ar. Th'art a very wagge, take this, my boy.
   Con. True sir, now I am yours indeede; what! yellow? yours to command: what would you with me?
   Ar. Seest thou?
   Con. Yes I see very well.
   Ar. Thou art too quicke: I prethee let me see thy Mistris.
   Con. Troth, sir, you cannot, shee's taken up with other business, or rather taken downe; yet i'le trie sir.   *Exit.*
   Ar. Oft have I marvaild how the erring eye,
Which of his proper object cannot lye,
In other subject[s], failes so in his duty
When hee's to judge of's chiefest object beauty.
None takes the night for day, the day for night.
The Lillies seeme alike to every sight:
Yet when we partiall judge of beauties graces,
Which are but colours plac't in womens faces,
The eye seemes never sure; the selfesame show
And face, this thinkes a swanne, and that a crow.
But sure our minds with strong affections tainted,
Looke through our eyes as through a glasse that's painted.
So when we view our loves, we never see
What th'are, but what we faine would have them be.
Thus *Atyches*, *Perindus* thus affecting
These *Nymphs,* make them seem worthiest their respecting,

SICELIDES

And thus to lov[e] their beauties never move them:
But therefore beautious seeme because they love them.
Methinks this *Cosma* farre them both excels,
In whose high forehead love commanding dwels.
I like not this same too much modestie;
Commend the Senate for their gravity.
The wanton *Nymph* doth more delight me farre,
The[se] modest *Nymphs* doe more seeme chaste then are,
Women are all alike, the difference this,
That seemes and is not, that both seemes and is.
Or if some are not, as they call it, ill,   *Enter Conchylio.*
They want the power and meanes, but not the will.
  Con. My Mistris as yet is so overlayd with sport or busines, she cannot speake with you: may not I know your errand?
  Ar. My errand boy is love.
  Con. Love (um) tis light enough, I shall carry it away: 'tis so short I shall remember it; but troth sir, another golden star this starlesse night dropt in my hand, may chance to give light to make my Mistris shine in your armes.
  Ar. Hold thee boy, hold thee: will that content thee?
  Con. Sir doe you know the myrtle grove?
  Ar. Yes well.
  Con. Your star will conduct [her] thither straight, within this houre shee'l meete you there.
  Ar. How canst thou assure it?
  Con. Trust mee I'le procure it;
Else never more let me see golden stars.
  Ar. I'le try thee boy, 'tis but one mis-spent houre,
If thou performe thy promise good *Conchylio,*
Many such glittering nights shall shine on thee.
  Con. If? make no question sir.
  Ar. Farewell.
  Con. Adiew.   *Exit.*
This strange new bird, this goose with golden eggs
Must with some graine of hope bee cherished,
And yet not fedde too fat; now for my Crab,
Here's his twin, if heavens signes are right.   *Enter Scrocca.*
Next to the crab, the twin must come in sight,
I'le out and seeke him.

PHINEAS FLETCHER

Act. 3. Scen. 4.

Scrocca, Cancrone.

Scr. Saile home by land quotha? well, I'le have that saddle boate hung up for a monument in the temple of Odoxcom[bria], hard by the everlasting shooes; and now to see the ill lucke on't, never more neede of fish, a bounsing feast toward[s], [a n]umber of guests, not a whiting, not a haddock, not a cod-mop in the house: and in stead of catching fish, wee must goe fish for our nets, *Cancrone*, come along, along, along: the Orke's dead and buried, the Orke's dead and buried.

Can. I but does not his ghost walke thereabout? *within.*
On afore, I'le follow hintly fintly, by the hobnailes of *Neptune*[s] horse-shooes—

Scr. Nay if you sweare, we shall catch no fish, what *Cancrone*, sneake you still? whoop, we shall fish fairely if your [sea a]rmore be off: *Enter Cancrone butning his coate.*
How now, what all in white?

Can. Seest not I am busified? doest thou thinke a man can button his coate and talke all at once?

Scr. My prettie sea-cob, why I preethee why in thy white?

Can. Ino triumph! Ino triumph! [I] tell thee this is my triumphing sute, did not wee vanquish the Orke?

Scr. I hope so too: but all our fellow fishers say t'was *Atyches*.

Can. [True,] *Atyches* kild him alive, and wee kild him dead.

Scr. I preethee on with thy gaberdine againe.

Can. My old scaly slimie gaberdine? why, if I should fish in that, every finne would smell mee.

Scr. Well, our nets are not above ground, what shall wee doe?

Can. Why then Sir, you must goe seeke them under ground.

Scr. Well Sir, you'l follow.   *Exit.*

Can. Muddie *Scrocca*, canst thou not perceive *Cancrones* inside by his new out-side? my old Orke apparell, my pitch patch poledavies had no good perfume for a sweete lover, as I now must bee: but why a lover? because I meane to kill the

SICELIDES

next *Orke* hand to hand; for my masters sisters sweetheart *Ataches*, because a lover, therefore an *Orkekiller*.

Enter Conchylio.

Con. What? old crab tortoise? has the Orke made you cast your shell?

Can. Fish mee no fishing: I'me all for flesh.

Con. Th[is] lob hath learnt that [lov]ers keepe no lent.

Can. Therfore thou blue-beard *Neptune*, and thou triumphing *Triton*, and thou watchet jacket *Glaucus, Daucus, Maucus*, and all the rest of the salt fish gods, I denounce you all, and for your formable farewell, I doe here reach forth to your dropping driveling deities my love warme hand to kisse.

So, have you done? Fie flapmouth   [*Conchylio* spits ins hand.
Triton, thou beslaverest mee.

Con. O doutie love[r]! heres more game for my mistresses net, or rather for mine.

Can. Nothing but *Venus* smocke or *Cupids* wing shall wipe it dry; surmount thy wagging wanton wing to mee, god *Cupid*.

Con. Are you there? I Orkt you once, and now Ile fit you [w^th] a *Cupid*.   *Exit Conchyl.*

Can. Mee thinks I am growne very eloquent alreadie; thanks sweete love; O now for my master *Perindus*, he has a fine crosse cut with's armes, and yet that Orke-catcher *Ataches* has a pesslence carriage on's pate: the *Nymphs* beleare him par[louslie]: so, so, so.

> Now Cupid doe I come to thee,
> To thee, upon my bare-head knee:
> Knee never bare-head yet before,
> Before it begged at thy doore.

Enter Scrocca, with his nets.

Scr. What? devout *Cancrone* knocking at *Cupids* doore?

Can. Ah *Scrocca*, thou hast corrupted the goodest verse! I was making my supplantation to *Trustie Triton* for good lucke, and see if he have not heard mee: our nets are returnd.

Scr. He might well heare thee for this once: for thou doest not trouble him often. But if I had not lookt to them better then he had, wee might have gone whistle for them: come *Cancrone*, will you goe?

Can. Yes I warrant you, I'le peradventure my person in a Cocke-boate.

Scr. Why then wee'l take the gallie foist.

Can. Goe foist if you will, the burnt child dreads the water, and good men are scantie, make much of one, *Cancrone.*

Scr. Well, if you come, you shall have us at the red roc[k]e.

Can. Yes, I'le fish on land for mermaids.   *Exit.*
This dog-fish had almost put mee out of my love-lesson. Now to thee againe, *courteous Cupid.*

> *All sunke and soust in soppy love,*
> *Cupid for thy mothers dove*
> *Helpe.*

Enter Conchylio in Cupids habitt.

Con. All haile, *Cancrone,*
According to thy wish I here am present
Great King of hearts, Duke of desires, Lord of love,
Whom mortals gentle *Cupid* doe ycleape.

Can. Beest thou *Cupid*? thou art vile like our *Conchylio.*

Con. True, *Cancrone,*
And lest the beames of my bright deitie
Should with their lustre wound those infant eyes,
I have vouchsaf't in this forme to appeare,
Lo, thy *Conchylio* and thy *Cupid* here :
What wouldst thou with mee?

Can. I have a suite to your godship.

Con. So it be not your Orke-suite I embrace it:
Say on, my darling.

Can. I am in love as they say, but I cannot tell whom to be in love withall.

Con. Here are *Nymphs* enow, *Urina, Olinda, Lilla, Glaucilla, Bobadilla.*

Can. Mee thinks that *Boberdil* sounds like a fine play-fellow for mee.

Con. No, I'le tell thee one, her [verie] name shall make thy mouth water.

Can. Make water in my mouth? thats *Urina,* I'le none of her, shee's too high coloured.

Con. No, tis *Cosma,* the fishers flame, the shepheards hope, whose beautie Pas admires.

SICELIDES

Can. I, but will you throw forth a good word for mee?
Con. I tell thee I'le make her all to belove thee, shee shall not rest till shee meete thee here; but first I must arme thee with some magicke charmes.
Can. What be they? my chops would faine be champing them.
Con. First you must anagramatize her name, then sympathize your owne.
Can. Tize, zize, thize. I shall ne're hit that.
Con. For an anagram I'le fit you: *Cosma* a smocke.
Can. Prettie.
Con. For the sympathie of your owne name [no more] but thus, your name *Cancrone* bids you counterfeite the countercreeping crab; and goe backward to her.
Can. Doe I looke like a crab? I had rather goe forward to a *Nymph*.
Con. Thirdly, because every fisher is borne under Pisces, therefore the signe is in the foote with you: you must come therefore with one foote bare.
Can. I but shall I not catch cold and cough and spoile my part?
Con. It must be the right foote: and then seest thou this mirtle tree? all my arrowes are made of the wood of it, thou must in her sight get up and gather the highest bough of it.
Can. I but what shall I doe with the bough?
Con. O the bough? why, setting thus a prettie while, you must wrappe a cockle garland about it, and then when the poore lasse melts and consumes with thy love—
Can. Then I'le throw it at her, & come downe to her, shall I not?
Con. Excellent well, I see thou art inspir'd.
Can. Nay I can take it, if you put it to mee.
Con. But the just nicke when thou must throw it is, when she says I die, I cry, I lie.
Can. I die, I cry, I lye, I would have her lie, but not die, but will you make her come indeede?
Con. I and in her best clothes too.
Can. Nay 'tis no such matter for clothes, but what must I say? I had almost forgot it.

Con. Nothing but a short charme, which I'le teach you as we goe; on afore, I'le follow you.
Can. Let me see: backward?
Con. Blockhead.
Can. Barelegge?
Con. Beetlepate.
Can. Cockleshell?
Con. Coxecombe.
Can. Boughs?
Con. Bussard.
Can. The towne's ours. Ino triumph, Ino triumph.
Con. I'le coole my hot lover, he shall sit on a perch for a stale, now must I be uncupidate, & shortly appeare here Cosmafied, it shall be hard but with the same limetwig I'le catch a bigger bird then this.

> *First I will serve my selfe, my mistris after;*
> *My baite is seeming love, my prey true laughter.*

Act. 3. Scen. 5.

Enter Pas solus.

What art, strength, wit, can tame a fish or flye?
The least of creatures us'd to liberty,
With losse of life shake off base captive chaines,
And with restraint [of food] all life disdaines.
But I, ah foole, yeld up my selfe a slave,
And what they shunne by death, doe basely crave:
My griefe more then my folly, who deplore
That which all others use to wish before:
My love loves too too much too many,
For while she liketh all, she loves not any.
Love, let my prayers yet thus farre onely move thee,
Let me her falsly, or she truely love me.   *Enter Cosma.*
See where she comes; [o] that so bright a sunne
Should have no spheare, no certaine race to runne:
I'le stand and over-heare her.

SICELIDES

Cos. I can but smile to thinke how foolish wise
Those women are, that chuse their loves for wisedome.
Wisedome in men's a golden chaine to tie
Poore women in a glorious slavery.   (women.
   Pas. Hark Heavens! O monstrous! harke: O women,
   Cos. Fond men, that blame the love that ever ranges.
To foule and sluttish love, that never changes!
The Muses love by course to change their meeter,
Love is like linnen often chang'd, the sweeter.
   Pas. Thus these neate creatures, dead with love and all,
By shunning beastlines, make it beastiall.
   Cos. Our beauty is our good, the cause of love:
Fond that their good to th' best will not improve;
What Husbandman neglects his time of sowing?
What fisher loseth winds, now fairely blowing?
Beauty our good: ah good, [too] short and brittle,
A little little good, for time as little,
How easie doest thou slide, and passe away?
Unborne, full growne, and buried in a day.
Thy spring is short, and if thou now refuse it,
Tis gone, when faine thou wouldst, thou shalt not use it.
The time and every minute daily spends thee.
Spend thou the time, while time fit leisure lends thee.
   Pas. Does she not blush? hark, women, heres your
Maids, [if] you want a Mistris; heres a teacher.   (preacher,
   Cos. Now since *Conchylio* spake of this *Armillus*,
My new found lover, I halfe long to try him:
[If he bee as hee seems, I'le not denye him.]
Too cruell she that makes her hearts contenting,
To see a heart languish in loves tormenting.
What though i'th' night we live most wantonly?
I' th' morne with clothes we put on modestie.
Thus though [I] sport, and wanton all the night
Next sunne ile act a part of feare and fright.   (creatures.
   Pas. Modestie? marry guipp: these are your modest
   Cos. Long have I hated *Olinda*, and *Glaucilla*,
And one of them by this hath drunke her last,
The next shall follow ere the next day's past.
The ginne is layd, and if it hit aright,
This is her last, this her eternall night.

Perindus long I [have lov'd,] who ever scorn'd mee,
Because he loves *Glaucilla*; I know hee'l grieve:
But when the tempest once is overblowne,
Hoyst up all sailes; the prize is sure mine owne.
Ill for a woman is that woman plac't,
Who like old *Janus*, is not double fac't.
Now to *Armillus* who sure expects me.
How darke the night? more fit for Lovers play.
The darkest night is lovers brightest day.   *Exit Cosma.*
    Pas. Well Mistris *Jana* with your double face,
I thinke I shall outface you by and by.
Ile fit you for a face i'fayth, I could be mad now.
Well, since you are sportive, i'le make one i'th play;
You have a foole already, i'le act a Devill;
And since you needes must to a new consort,
Ile beare a part, and make or marre the sport.
Enter Perindus.

Act. 3.   *Scen.* 6.

Perindus. Pas.

    Per. Atyches?
    Pas. No: *Pas.*
    Per. If thou seest *Atyches*, send him hither friend;   *Exit*
Of all the plagues that torture soules in hell,   *Pas.*
Tantale, thy punishment doth most excell.
For present goods, thy evill most expresse,
Making thee unhappy in thy happinesse.
Such are my paines: my blessednes torments mee,
I see, and [not] enjoy what mo[st cont]ents me.
My life then love, I rather would forsake,
Yet for my life, my love I dare not take.
Glaucilla, couldst thou see this wretched brest,
What torments in it never resting rest,
Whom now thou thinkst the cause of all thy greeving,
Then thou wouldst judge the wretchedst creature living.
She's here.   *Enter Glaucilla.*

SICELIDES

Glau. *Perindus,* whither goest thou? the day's enough
To shew thy scorne, the night was made for rest.
For shame if not for love, let night relieve me:
Take not that from mee, which thou wilt not give me.
Knowst thou this place? even here thou first didst vow,
Which I beleev['d], and still me thinkes even now
Cannot unbeleev't, that when thy constant heart,
From his first onely vowed love should start,
These waving seas should stand, [t]hose rocks remove.
   Per. Fa, la, la, fa, la, la, lah.
   Glau. O dancing levity, you steady rocks,
Still stand you still? his fayth he lightly mocks.
Yee fleeting waves, why doe you never stand?
His [love, his words], his oathes, are writ in sand.
In rocks and seas I finde more sense and loving,
The rock[s] lesse hard then he, the sea[s] lesse moving.
   Per. Didst never see the rockes in sayling move?
   Glau. Not move, but seeme to move.
   Per. My picture right.
   Glau. What says *Perindus*?
   Per. Ha, ha, he, how scurvily griefe laughs!
   Glau. Perindus, by all the vowes I here conjure thee,
The vow[s] that on thy soule thou didst assure me,
Tell me why thus my love thou false refusest?
Why me thy fayth thy selfe thou thus [abusest]?
   Per. Ay me.
   Glau. How fares my love?
   Per. Ah *Glaucilla.*
   Glau. I know thou canst not hate me.
   Per. I cannot hate, but laugh, and dance and sport,
This is not hate, *Glaucilla,* 'tis not hate.
   Glau. Canst thou *Perindus* thus delude me?
I've liv'd enough, farewell: thou last hast viewd mee.
   Per. Glaucilla?
   Glau. How canst thou speake that hated name?
   Per. Stay.
   Glau. To be mockt?
   Per. Stay, i'le tell thee all.
   Glau. Me thinks this forced mirth does not beseeme thee:
Sure 'tis not thine, it comes not from thy heart.

PHINEAS FLETCHER

Per. Glaucilla, call backe thy wish, seeke not to know
Thine or my death, thou winst thine overthrow.
  Glau. Thy griefe is common, I have my part in thine:
Take not that from me which is justly mine.
  Per. If I had any joy, it were thine owne,
But grant me to be wretched all alone.
  Glau. Now all thy griefe is mine, but it unhiding,
Halfe thou wilt take away, by halfe dividing.
  Per. Thou seekst my love, it is my love to hide it,
And I shall shew more hate, when I divide it.
  Glau. Thy love thus hid, to me [all] hatred proves,
Unhide thy hate, this hate will shew it loves.
  Per. Glaucilla, while my griefes untouched rest,
My better part s[l]ee[p]es quiet in [m]y brest.
  Glau. So thou art well, but still my better part,
Perindus, sinkes all loaden with his smart:
So thou my finger cu[r]'st, and woundst my heart.
  Per. Since then thou wilt not give me leave to hide it,
Briefely 'tis thus: when thou thy love hadst vowd me
Most sure, but yet no certaine time allowd me;
My marriage day as all my good desiring,
To *Proteus* Cell I went, the time enquiring,
There heard these words, the cause of all my sadnes,
The cause of all my seeming hate and gladnesse.
Thus went th' Oracle.

> *The day, that thou with griefe so long forbearest,*
> *Shall bring thee what thou wishest most and fearest.*
> *Thy sisters grave shall bee her marriage bed,*
> *In one selfe day twice dying, and once dead.*
> *Thy friend, whom thou didst ever dearest choose,*
> *In loosing thou shalt finde, in finding loose.*
> *And briefly to conclude the worst at last,*
> *Thou, or thy Love shall from a rocke be cast.*

Glaucilla, had thy love but with my life beene priz'd,
My life t'enjoy thy love I had despis'd.
But since it may be thine, thy life[s] destroying,
Shall nere bee given for my loves enjoying:
Much rather, let me live in fires tormenting,
Then with such purchase buy my hearts contenting.

SICELIDES

Glau. Then love's the cause of all thy seeming hate,
What hast thou seene in me, that I should seeme,
My life more then thy love, or mine esteeme?
Perindus thy hate hath cost me often dying,
So hast thou given mee death, by death denying:
For th' Oracle, with death I am contented,
And will not feare, what cannot be prevented.
   Per. Yet though such mischiefe *Proteus* did divine,
Much better sped I at [th]y fathers shrine:
Comming to Delphos, where the Pythian maid
Told me my wishes should be fully paid
And that within few dayes I should arrive
Through many bitter stormes, into the hive.
   Glau. Why doubtst thou then? adiew love till to morrow,
Next rising sunne shall to thee ease thy sorrow.
   Per. Maist thou prove true, or if heaven bad decree
The good be thine, light all the bad on me.
   Glau. Farewell.   *Exit.*
   [*Per.*] Thou givest *Glaucilla* what thou wishest good rest.
This victory my minde hath whole possest,
And from my eyes shuts out all sleepe and rest:
If I but slumber, streight my fancie dreames,
This *Atyches* is much more then he seemes:
Comming to his couch, I found his emptie bed
As yet untoucht, himselfe from sleepe is fled.
But soft, whom have wee here?   *Enter Atyches.*
   Atych. The Oxe now feeles no yoke, all labour sleepes,
The soule unbent, this as her play-time keepes,
And sports it selfe in fancies winding streames,
Bathing his thoughts in thousand winged dreames.
The fisher tyr'd with labour, snorteth fast,
And never thinks of paines to come or past,
Only love waking rest and sleepe despises,
Sets later then the sunne, and sooner rises.
With him the day as night, the night as day,
All care, no rest, all worke, no holy-day.
How different from love is lovers guise!
He never opes, they never shut their eyes.
   Per. Ha: this is he, I'le stand and overheare him.
   Atych. So: I am alone, ther's none but I,

PHINEAS FLETCHER

My griefe, my love, my wonted company,
And which best fits a grieved lovers sprite,
The silent stars and solitarie night.
Tell mee heavens sentinels that compasse round
This ball of earth, on earth was [e]ver found
A love like mine, so long, so truly serv'd,
Whose wage is hate, have all my paines deserv'd
Contempt? mine and her fo[es] shee deare affected:
The more I lov'd, the more I was neglected.
Since thou canst love where thou hast hatred prov'd,
Olinda, how canst thou hate where thou art lov'd?
Thy body is mine by conquest, but I find,
Thy bodie is not alwayes with thy mind.
Give both or none, or if but one, o'th'two
Give mee thy mind, and let thy bodie goe.
If this without thy minde I only have,
What giv'st thou more to me then to thy grave?
Proove mee, my deare, what canst thou hate in mee?
Unlesse my love, my love still bent on thee?
My name's *Thalander*, perhaps it doth displease thee,
I will refuse my name, if that may ease thee.
Thalander to exile wee'l still confine,
And i'le be *Atyches*, so I bee thine.
 Per. *Thalander*? i[s']t possible? I oft suspected.
How he is altered! not himselfe! i[s']t possible?
 Aty. Yet what thou hat'st, thy brother loves as well.
Tell me, my dearest love, what have I done?
What has *Thalander* done? ah tell mee.
 Per. More
Then thousand such as she can nere restore,
Thalander; start not; how have my eyes deceiv'd me?
Ah, let me blesse my armes with thy embraces.
My deare, *Thalander*, my only life, my heart,
My soule, O of my soule the better part.
I[s']t thee I hold; I scarce dare trust mine eyes,
Which thus deceiv'd mee by their former lies.
 Aty. Thou welcomst miserie while thine armes infold mee.
 Per. I am the blessedst man that lives to hold thee.
My heart doth dance to finde thee.
 Aty. Ah *Perindus*,

SICELIDES

When least thou thinkst, thou art deceived most,
My selfe, my love, my labour I have lost;
[That thou hast found mee then how canst thou prove]
When I have lost my selfe, to finde my love?
  Per. In losing of thy [selfe, thy love] th'ast found;
She loves thee friend most dearely, [all the ground
Of all her frownes to thee, of all thy smart
Is 'cause shee thinks thou art not who thou art.
  Aty. If this be true? if this be possible?
  Per. Thalander, heere I sweare
By all thy love, shee holds thy love most deare.]
And though she thought thy love would be her death,
Yet for and in thy love, shee'd lose her breath,
And nothing else should grieve her in the end
She had [but] one life for such a love to spend.
  Aty. Doe not deceive me.
  Per. Why shouldst thou mistrust me?
  Aty. Perindus, my joy, by too much joy enjoying,
I feele not halfe my joy, by over-joying.
  Per. Her selfe shall speake it. Come, let's goe.
  Aty. 'Tis night!
  Per. Shee'l thinke it day, when thou art in her sight.
  Aty. Lead me, for yet my mind, too much affected
To have it so, makes truth it selfe suspected.
                                        Exeunt.

CHORUS.

*Love is the fire, damme, nurse, and seede
Of all that aire, earth, waters breede.
All these earth, water, aire, fire,
Though contraries, in love conspire.
Fond painters: love is not a lad,
With bow, and shafts, and feathers clad;
As he is fancied in the braine
Of some loose loving idle swaine,
Much sooner is he felt then seene,
His substance subtile, slight and thinne,
Oft leapes hee from the glancing eyes,
Oft in some smooth mount he lyes,*

Soonest he winnes, the fastest flyes:
Oft lurkes he twixt the ruddy lips,
Thence while the heart his Nectar sips,
Downe to the soule the poyson slips,
Oft in a voyce creeps downe the eare,
Oft hides his darts in golden haire,
Oft blushing cheeks do light his fire[s],
Oft in a smooth soft [s]kinne retires,
Often in smiles, often in teares;
His flaming heate in water beares,
When nothing else kindles desire,
Even vertues selfe shall blow the fire:
Love with thousand darts abounds,
Surest and deepest vertue wounds,
Oft himselfe becomes a dart,
And love with love, doth love impart.
Thou painfull pleasure, pleasing paine,
Thou gainefull l[oss]e, thou losing gaine:
Thou bitter sweete, easing disease,
How doest thou by displeasing please?
How doest thou thus bewitch the heart?
To love in hate, to joy in smart.
To thinke it selfe most bound, when free,
And freest in his slavery.
Every creature is thy debter,
None but loves, some worse, some better:
Onely in love, they happy proove,
Who love what most deserves their love.

Act. 4. Scen. 1.

Enter Perindus and Thalander.

Per. BE patient.
    Aty. Yes, I am patient,
And suffer all, [till] all heavens ills are spent.
  Per. You give your selfe to griefe.
  Aty. Sencelesse and mad.
Who in much griefe, is not extremely sad?

SICELIDES

 Per. Alas sir, she was mortall, and must die.
 Aty. True, true, and could the fates no time espie
But this? to me she never liv'd till now,
And now *Perindus*? now! oh——
 Per. She was my sister!
 Aty. Alas, thy sister!
She was my life, my soule, she was my love,
She was—words know not what she was to me:
She was—thou most accursed word of was.
 Per. Be comforted.   (Iesse
 Tha. Perindus, the very name of comfort, is most comfort-
Comfort, joy, hope, liv'd in her cheerfull smiling,
And now must die, or live in far exiling.
Comfort, joy, hope, for ever I deny you,
And would not name you now but to defie you.
 Per. Sir, with more patience you have often borne
Far greater evils.
 Tha. Perindus, doe not say so,
If thou yet love me, prethee doe not say so:
Was ever ill as this? hels breviary,
All torment in this narrow space is layd,
The worst of [i]ll[s], in these two words are sayd:
Olinda dead? dead! whither doest thou lead mee?
Why, I can goe alone, alone can finde
The way I seeke, I see it best when blinde.
I prethee leave me.
 Per. Thalander, I'le not leave thee,
Should heaven with thunder strike these arms that claspe thee,
My dying hands should but more firmely graspe thee.
 Tha. Thou violat'st thy love in thy mistaking,
And cleane forsak'st thy friend, in not forsaking.
Olinda: I cannot come, they heere enchaine me.
But neyther can, nor shall they here detaine me.
I'th' meane time, all the honour I can give thee,
Is but a grave, that sacred rocke, the place
Of my conception, and my buriall:
Since *Hymen* will not, death shall make thee mine,
If not my marriage, my death-bed shall be thine.
              Exeunt.

PHINEAS FLETCHER

Act. 4. Scen. 2.

Enter Rimbombo.

Farewell yee mountaines, and thou burning *Ætna*,
If yet I doe not beare thee in my brest,
And am my selfe, a living walking *Ætna*,
The Nymphs that on you dwell, are too [too] coy,
Too coy and proud, more fierce then robbed tygre[s]
More deafe then seas, and more inflexible
Then a growne O[a]ke, false, flattering, cruell, craftie,
And which most grieves me, when I would embrace them,
Swifter then chased Deere, or dogs that chase them,
You heavens, what have we poore men deserved,
That you should frame a woman, I and make her
So comely and so needefull? why should you cloath them
With [such a pleasing] shape? why should you place
Gold in their haire, allurement in their face?
And that which most may vex us, you impart
Fire [to] their burning eyes, yce to their heart.
Why sweeten you their tongues with sugred charmes
And force men love, and need their greatest harmes?
And most of all, why doe you make them fleete?
Minds as the windes, and wings upon their feete?
Of hundred women that I know, [but one,]
But one [of all] deserves to be a woman.
Whom better heavens have not made more faire,
Then courteous, loving, kinde, and debonaire:
She, when she usd our Mountaines, oft would stay,
And heare me speake, and vow, and sweare, and pray.
Here I have learnt, she haunts along these shores:
Within these rockie clifts i'le hide my selfe,
Till fit occasion, if shee have chang'd her minde,
Then safely may I curse all women-kinde.   *Exit.*

SICELIDES

Act. 4. Scen. 3.

Enter Armillus.

Love, without thee, all life is tedious,
Without thee, there's no sweete, no joy, no life;
Thou first gav'st life, and still with new succession,
Continuest what thou gav'st, with sweet inticements,
Taming the strongest rebellion, thy weapons women,
Whom thou so fram'st, that proudest men are glad,
Beaten with them, gently to kisse the rod.
Eyther my weighty passions pull too fast
The wheele of time, or else the houre is past:
But this is she, or I mistake it.

Enter Cosma.

Cos. Women that to one man their passions bind,
As this man alters, so alters still their mind:
Thus ever change they, as those changing faires,
And with their lovers still their love impaires:
But I, when once my lovers change their graces,
Affect the same, though now in other faces:
Thus now my mind is firme, and constant prov'd,
Seeing I ever love, what first I lov'd.
Who blames the speedy heaven, for ever ranging?
Love's fiery, winged, light, and therfore changing.
  Ar. True, fairest Nymph, Love is a fire still burning,
And if not slak't, the heart to ashes turning.
  Cos. If I could scold, sir you might [well] be chidden,
For comming to my thoughts before y'are bidden.
  Ar. Blame me not (Sweet) thy words do fanne thy fires,
And coole the flames which thy faire eye inspires.
  Cos. The fire so lately applied, so lately fram'd?
Me thinks, greene wood should not be yet inflam'd.
  Ar. Loves flame is not like earths, but heavens fire,
Like lightning, with a flash it lights desire.
  Cos. I love not lightning: lightning love that flashes
Before't be all on fire, will be all ashes.

Ar. Gather the fruite then while 'tis yet unblasted.
Cos. I[s']t worth the gathering? is it pleasing tasted?
Ar. Take say of this. *kisses her.*
Monster?

Enter Pas offering to kisse on the other side, disguised like a fury.

Cos. Helpe ho.
Exeunt Armil. Cos. severall waies.

Act. 4. Scen. 4.

Pas. Fredocaldo.

Pas. The Doe was almost strooke, 'twas time I came,
For once I'le be a keeper of the game.
I see 'tis Owle-light, *Minervaes* waggoner,   *Enter*
My old rivall, who this twenty yeeres   *Fred.*
Saw nothing but what shin'd through glasse windowes;
What comes he for? I'le stay a while and watch him.
  Fred. Most happy age that shall be crown'd with love
Of thy love, *Cosma*: I am not as I seeme,
Farewell old age, I now am young againe
And feele not ages, but a lovers paine,
In love I dare adventure with the best,
Old beaten souldiers are the worthiest:
If all my rivalls heard [mee] I could dare them,
If furies should out-front me, I'de out-stare them. *Pas runs*
                                                upon him, hee
      Enter Conchylio in his Mistresses   *falls and lyes.*
                apparell.   *Exit Pas.*
  Con. How well my Mistris *Cosmaes* clothes do fit me?
What pitty 'twas, I was not made a woman?
I thinke I should have made a pretty Nymph: ha?
I could have beene a[s] pittifull [a] creature,
And yet perhaps, a good unhappy wench.
Cosma by this hath met with her *Armillus*,
And sports her selfe: could I meete *Fredocaldo*,
I should have sport enough: *She stumbles at Fred.*
What *Fredocaldo* dead? courage, man.

SICELIDES

Fred. I had a fearefull dreame, and scarce am waken.
Con. Come shake off dreames, sleepe is not fit for lovers,
Wee'l to the rocky cave.
Fred. My sunne? my fire?
Con. But *Fredocaldo*, can you thinke that fire
Can love cold water, the sunne can frost desire?
Fred. I tell thee fairest *Cosma*, those faire eyes
Bring backe my spring, [and me two enimies.]
Wrong not thy selfe, deare love, so faire a day
Cannot but make mid-winter turne to May.
Cold rhewms I feele not, no frost's lockt in this chest,
Thy love begets a summer in my brest.
Con. Fie *Fredocaldo*: not in the open aire.
Exeunt.

Act. 4. Scen. 5.

Armillus. Cosma.

Ar. What furies haunt this grove? is not this *Cosma*?
Yes: here again she comes. Most blessed heavens,
Enter Cosma.
I see that yee are more gracious then Hell's spightfull.
Cosma?
Cos. Armillus.
Ar. My love.
Cos. Sure thou hast done some cruell murder,
And the unexpiate ghost thus haunts thee.
Ar. I never thought it, *Cosma*:
Rather some power of these woods, too envious
Of my good hap, and jealous of thy favor,
Thus crosses our desires: but if againe
He chance to interpose his horrid face,
I'le rather dye, then leave thy wisht embrace.   *Enter Pas*
All hell and furies haunt us.   *Exit Ar.*   *disguised.*
Pas. Well overtaken, Nimph, start not, you are sure,
See I am your familiar.
Cos. Beshrew your heart
For thus affrighting me.
Pas. Doe you not blush
To cast your love upon a man, whose love

Is as himselfe an alien? to thine owne
Thou mak'st thee strange, familiar to unknowne.
    Cos. Pish, thou art foolish, did I ever binde thee
[Only to me]? why shouldst thou then confine me
To thy sole passion? so oft before
You men have chang'd, that you can change no more:
From bad to worse, from worse, to worst of all:
There lie you now, and can no lower fall:
And as you wisht that we should never rove,
We pray as fast, that you at length could move.
Cease then for shame to raile at womens ranging:
When men begin, women will leave their changing.
Farewell.
    Pas. Nay soft, I am [a] dog well bitten,
And will not part so easily with my prey,
I have not tasted venison many a day.
    Cos. I cannot well deny thee, 'tis thy right:
Thou well hast purchast it, this be thy [n]ight.
                                              Exeunt.

Act. 4. *Scen.* 6.

Conchilio.

   Con. Ha, ha, he:
This old dry stubble, how it crackes i'th' burning!
Alas poore saplesse oake: 'tis time 'twere down,
I stayd till he was ready, all unready,
But when he 'gan to put on his spectacles,
Away slipt I: hee'l doe my mistris little hurt.
Spectacles! hah, ha, he!
Now for my loving Lobster, this is his time;
And if the *Cyclops* too doe keepe his promise,
O what a rare compound of mirth I'le make,
While the one with sh[a]me, the other with feare I'le take!
The fish comes alreadie to the net. *Enter Cancrone, going backe-*
   Can. To all I speake, but I tell no man,   *ward upon her.*
Whether I love *Nymph* or woman.   *He lookes over his*
   Con. Tell not mee, but tell the rocks,   *shoulders.*
Not words must disciple you but knocks.
I am out of your debt for a rime.

SICELIDES

Can. I thinke shee knew my cue, the charme begins to worke already.

Con. I know not how this fishers hooke hath caught mee; I eve[n] for his rudenesse love him: 'tis the badge of innocencie.

Can. Somewhat rude if you will, but innocent in your face.

Con. O those glearing eyes that dart the beames, The beames that drown[e] my heart with fierie streames.

Can. Now to *Cupids* arrowe tree, and she sinks downe-right condoling; *Cosma*, I have pitty on thee, but it beseemes a man of my confession, to have a negligent care of his good reparation abroad in the world and else-where; I would be loth to be seene in my love-worke, i'le mount the tree and scry the coast.

He goes up the tree.

Con. Stay not, but come againe thy selfe, sweete heart, to receive me.

Can. O ho, here's bundance of people, bundance a lookers on, I dare not love thee before them all, wee'l into the myrtle grove present[ly].

Con. Quickly returne, my love, returne *Cancrone* my dearest.

Can. Stand forth *Cosma*, and say on till thou come to that, I cry, I dye, I lye.

Con. I spie him now approaching.   *Enter Rimbombo.*
What though he be all r[u]gge[d] in his limbs?
What though his gesture taste of violence?
We Nymphes, they say, like not such wooers worst.

Rim. Thou speakest of thy *Rimbombo*, [now I find]
That myrtle groves which love the winding shores,
Deserve to bee to *Venus* consecrate,
As faster friends to lovers, then the woods
And caves of all the Mounts of *Sicily*,
Whose Nymphs do coyly shunne and mocke our troopes.

Con. You come somewhat before your time, *Rimbombo*,
And yet in love prevention is no crime:
Lovers may come before, not out of time.
And truly I wish, y'had come a little sooner.
Even now a mongrell crabbed fisher swaine
Laid siege to this unconquer[able] fort.

Rim. What wight of bravest blood by sea and land
Dares share with mee in *Cosmaes* love?
By *Polypheme* my sea-bred [s]ire I vow,
The sand on which he treads, is not so small,

As shall this pestell make his pounded bones.
   Con. Nay now he treadeth not upon these sands,
But is fled up to the hills, and shortly thence
Will of himselfe come tumbling downe to mee.
   Rim. I would he durst: I never yet but once
Did tast of fishers blood, tis jollie sweete:
Come fisher, this way or that way
I am for you at both weapons, club or teeth:
Let's to the grove, see, every mirtle tree
Bids warre to fishers peace, and joy to mee.
Why weepes my *Cosma*?
Sweete, feare not that which thou desirest.
   Con. Sweete *Cyclops*, meanst thou to ravish mee?
   Rim. O heavens thine owne appointed time and place,
Thine owne sweete *Cyclops*, and can ravishment?—
   Con. Why this [then] know; wee *Nymphs* that long live chast,
And weare our girdle of virginity——
But lo, *Diana* stops my tongue, shee bends
Her deadly bow, I dare not.
   Rim. Speake on,
Here's none but trees, and thy trustie true *Rimbombo*.
   Con. By that bright flame which like one only sunne
Gives day [to th'] spheare of thy majesticke face,
I thee adjure, that thou disclose to none
This sacred mysterie.
   Rim. Not to my mother: no not in my dreame:
Say on.
   Con. Wee neither yeeld, nor take in love delight,
Untill our girdle first be once unplight
By lovers hands, and then about his wast,
By our owne hands the same be tied fast.
Now all is out.
   Rim. A pretty piece of work, my hands do their office nimbly;
I have unfettered thee, come put this sweete yoke on mee.
   Con. Nay turne about, it must be tied contrarie to other
girdles, just behind. Stand neerer to mee, yet neere[r].
   Rim. As close as thou wilt, *Cosma*; I would your filthy
fisher saw us now, 't would make his teeth water.
   Con. Hang him stinking Lobster, he daires not look upon
any of thy kinne: his haddocke eyes would start out of his
head, if he should see but one haire of *Rimbomboes* head.

SICELIDES

Rim. How long wilt thou be tying mee?

Con. The more knots I tie, the faster will my love be to you: but you'l be prating of this secret, when you come home among your mounting *Nymphs*.

Rim. If I doe, then geld mee: hast thou done?

Con. I have but three knots to tie: they are all true [lovers] knots.

Rim. When thou hast done, preethee come kisse me, *Cosma*, I see thou art a pure virgin, thou never didst this office before, [that] thou art no quicker at it. What *Cosma*? what? no *Cosma*! what a woodden wench? here's a true love knot with a witnes. O faithlesse *Cosma*! O witlesse *Rimbombo*! O *Nymph[s]*! O fishers! O shepheards! O Satyrs! O *Cyclops*! *Conchylio steales away, leaving him bound to the tree where Canc.ne is.*

Enter Conchylio againe.

Con. Ha, ha, ha: O love! O wit! O tree! O girdle! O platter face! O oyster ey[e]!

Rim. Thou bitch, thou witch, thou spawne of a mermaid.

Con. Thou Ætna, thou Chaos, thou Hell: nay tugge and tugge, my virginitie is tough and strong enough: O for some *Nymphs* fishers or shepheards to baite this *Orke*. I'le out and call in some bandog[s]: so ho, so ho, ho, ho.   *Exit.*

Rim. The knots are so many, the girdle so strong, and the tree stands so fast. O anger! O shame! here shee'll bring in all the country to laugh mee to death, hide yet thy face with some of these lower boughs.

Enter Conchylio.

Con. So ho, so ho: O dogged fortune! not one *Nymph* to be found, not one feate fisher! not one: but that feating fisher that is readie to wing his sea [s]oken net on the *Cyclops* blockhead.

Rim. Away thou monstrous woman, oh, oh.

Can. Away thou monstrous ma[n], ah ha hey.

Rim. How now! what's that? what, have I another witnes of my folly? what gobbet of mans flesh grows upon this tree?

Con. Ile have a graft of this mirtle tree, it beares fine love wormes, on the stocke, a maggot wou'd up in a Cobweb, on the bough a barnacle, which ere long will fall and turne to a goose: now *Cupids* gosling, now on your bare-head knee, goe begge at *Cupids* doore.

Can. Ah cursed *Cupid*, i'le no more of thy service, I had rather fight with nine Orkes, ha, hei, au.

Rim. Come downe thou fished bit; my mouth shall catch thee. Gentle *Cosma,* i'le forgive thee all, & love thee yet, if thou wilt helpe to reach my walking sticke; i'le make my young Orke-ketcher beleeve he shall bee his grandsires heire.

Con. Your staffe? marry and shalt, it's a pretty pole to bang those boughes withall, and when thou doest it, doe but gape, and that rotten plumme will fall into thy mouth.

Can. Nay, I kn[e]w of old I should be devoured.

Con. Thy staffe, *Rimbombo,* is not for a weak Nymph to lift.

Rim. Yet a little more to this hand: Oh oh, my shoulder's thunderstrook! O coward *Jove,* to strike me on the backe, but wast our fisher lubber? is he escap't our hands?

Con. Why *Cancrone,* rise, i'le helpe thee.

Can. Good *Charon* carry me over gently, my bones are sore, and your boate side so hard.

Con. Give me thy hand, i'le waft thee.

Can. I tell thee *Charon,* I have nothing to give thee for ferriage, i'le helpe to row, I have beene a poore fisher while I liv'd.

Rim. I would I were there too, but that I should sinke *Charons* boate with a tree at my backe.

Con. Why valorous *Cancrone,* view thy selfe and mee thy capt[ain]e *Cosma,* we are conquerours, behold our enemies in fetters fast bound.

Can. Am I alive indeede? me thought this legge hung out of *Charons* boate i'th' water, did I tie the Orke there; Come captain, let's goe triumphing to the temple.

Con. Nay, the Ork's dead and buried, this is the second fatall fo[e] the *Cyclops.*

Can. Is he safe? i'le make side-slops on him. I lay studying how to deale with him upon equall tearmes: come if thou darest, thou sea-bred brat of *Polyphemes* sire, you that would licke your lips at sweete fishers blood! sweete fishers blood! marke that *Cosma*: I hope you thinke so too.

Rim. Sweete fisher, I will turne thy netmaker if thou wilt undoe me.

Can. No, it shall nere be said that I was the undoing of any man by net-making, and besides, I have forsworne the muddie trade.

SICELIDES

Con. *Cancrone*, wher's thy spirit? this is [he] that pocketted up thy grandsire in his wide intrailes.

Can. Me thought, when I was on the tree, his breath smelt of fish, my stomacke even foam'd at him. Now then, sir *Bompelo*, as that Orke mouth of thine did crumme thy porridge with my grandsires braines, and then gave him his deaths wound too, so will I first mince out thy scald-pate bones, and give thy flesh [to fishers] boy[s] for haddocks meate, & then, O then I will geld thee, that thou never shalt run rutting after the Nymphs. How lik'st thou this?

Rim. Shame and scorne make me silent.

Con. Nay, I will tell thee fitter vengeance, use him, as sage *Ulysses* did his father *Polypheme*.

Can. That same *Foolishes* had a pole-cat head, I meane to mitigate him: [it] was something, as it ware about branding a huge stone in a cave, in a goate skinne with *Polypheme*, when the fire-brand was asleepe.

Con. I, I, in the cave he branded out *Polyphemes* eye, when he was asleepe, and you must imitate him: here take his owne staffe, and make it an extinguisher for that glazing lampe.

Rim. This sport I like worst of all: helpe, gods of the woods.

Can. I'le blow the coale while you take your aime, but will your farginity hold him fast?

Con. I warrant you it has been tried, come be thou my rest, i'le tilt on thy shoulders.

Can. Raunt tara, raunt taunt: & I shall make you stumble, let me come hindermost. *Cancrone fals, and his dagger from him in the Cyclops reach.*

Con. O your Whineyeard, the enemy hath seazd on't.

Can. 'Tis no matter, hee'l hardly make it fly out of the Eele-skinne, it hath seene no sunne this five quarters of a yeere I am sure.

Con. I hope the salt breath of the sea hath seald it up.

Can. O *Cosma*, 'tis out, let us out too.

Con. O *Cancrone*, loe thy *Cosma*, *Cupid*, and *Conchilio*. *Cyclops*, blame not this my supposed sexe, No Nymph, but lad hath caught thee in this snare. *Exit*.

Rim. The greater shame, and fouler scorne to me. Up to the hill, *Rimbombo*, flye this shore, And never deale with fisher-Nymph-lad more. *Exit*.

245

PHINEAS FLETCHER

CHORUS.

This his wives quicke fate lamenting,
Orp[he]us sate his soule tormenting:
While the speedy wood came running,
And rivers stood to heare his cunning:
The hares ran with the dogs along,
Not from the dogs, but to his song:
But when all his verses turning,
Onely fram'd his poore hearts burning:
Of the higher powers complaining,
Downe he went to hell disdaining:
There his silver Lute-strings hitting,
And his potent verses fitting:
All the sweets that ere he tooke
From his sacred mothers brooke:
What his double sorrow gives him,
And love that doubly double grieves him:
There he spends to moove deafe hell,
Charming Devils with his spell:
And with sweetest asking leave
Does the Lord of ghosts deceave.
C[h]aron amaz'd his boate foreslowes,
While the boate, the sculler rowes,
And of it selfe to th' shoare doth floate,
Tripping on the dancing moate.
The threeheaded Porter preast to heare,
Prickt up his thrice double eare,
The Furies, plagues for Guilt up-heaping,
Now as guilty, fell a weeping:
Ixion, though his wheele stood still,
Still was wrapt with Musickes skill.
Tantale might have eaten now,
The fruite as still as was the bough,
But he foole no [hu]nger fearing,
Starv'd his tast to feede his hearing.

SICELIDES

Thus since love hath wonne the field,
Heaven and Hell, to Earth must yeeld,
Blest soule that dyest in loves sweete sound,
That lost in love in love art found.
If but a true-loves joy thou once doe prove,
Thou wilt not love to live, unlesse thou live to love.

Act. 5. *Scen.* 1.

Enter Alcippus and Thalander with a torch.

Tha. TEll me, *Alcippus*, is it day or night? (light.
    Al. The light you beare, shews you there is no
Tha. This is none: light was light [but] in her eyes,
In them it liv'd, put out with them it dies.
The sunne is quench't.
    Al. Yet soone will shine againe.
    Tha. Not possible! heavens light will ever plaine.
When her two living stars can sinke and die,
How can the sunne dreame immortality?
    Al. Sir, if your [love] to mee, or mine to you,
Might give me priviledge, I faine would tell you,
That this too fixed love seemes rather doting.
    Tha. [Tell me] *Alcippus*, didst thou ever love?
    Al. I thinke sir never.
    Tha. I thinke so too, nor canst know what love is.
    Al. Yet this I know, love still is of the fairest,
Fond then the love, that loves the withered,
But madnesse seemes to dote upon the dead.
    Tha. True, true, *Alcippus*, love is of the fairest,
And therefore never tyed unto the body:
Which if compared unto the mindes faire graces,
Seemes like the blocke that *Lunaes* face defaces;
But grounded on the mind, whose vertuous parts.
And living beauties are loves surest darts;
Which makes me now as freely love as ever:
Her vertue and my love decayeth never.
Seest thou this rocke, *Alcippus*? tis a temple,

PHINEAS FLETCHER

Olindaes temple! 'tis a sacred shrine,
Where vertue, beauty, and what ere['s] divine,
Are to be worshipt, prethee friend now leave me,
Here is an Altar, [and] I must sacrifice.
    Al. If you will leave your griefe.
    Tha. I will, I will:
Indeede I will; leave me: griefs ebbe growes lowe,
When private [t]ear[e]s th' eye-bankes overflow.
    Al. I will retire, not leave him: well I feare,
When two such flood-streams meet, love and despaire.
    Tha. Thou blessed Altar, take these worthlesse offrings,
The[se] corral's once more drown'd in brine of sorrow,
These pearly shells, which dayly shall bee fild
With my hearts water, through my eyes distild.
You corralls, whose fresh beauties are a shadow
Of her sweete blushes, tell her living graces,
Though now as you pluckt from their native places,
Are yet as you from your first seate remov'd,
Here fresher shining then when first I lov'd.
Thou rocke, that in thy blest armes doest infold her,
Witnes my heart as firme as you do[th] hold her.
And now goodnight thou set sunne beauties, never,
[Ah] never more to be seene, goodnight for ever.
Thou silver forehead and thou golden haire,
My best, my onely treasure when you were:
You snowy plaines, and you faire modest dies,
[You living stars wch fooles wee called eyes]
[Once] living stars, but now two quenched lights,
Whose fall, heavens stars with feared ruine frights:
You eyebrowes, which like Rainbowes two appeare;
A miracle, Rainebowes on skie so cleare:
And all you unseene beauties softly rest,
Sleepe, quiet sleepe you in this stony chest.
I cannot long, I will not long be from you,
Shortly i'le come and in this rockie bed
Slumber with my *Olinda*, with *Olinda*
I'le sleepe my fill, meane time as neere as may be,
Here rest mine eyes, rest close by your *Olinda*.
                          He lies downe by the rocke.
Harke, harke; *Arion*, thou choice *Musician*,
Sing mee a note that may awake pale death,

SICELIDES

Such as may move deafe Hell, and Stygian *Jove*,
Such as once *Orpheus*——O I am idle, idle:
Sleep, sleep, mine eyes, this short releasement take you,
Sleepe, sleepe for ever; never more awake you.
Her face your object never more shall be,
Sleepe then, vaine eyes, why should you wish to see?

Act. 5. *Scen.* 2.

*The Rocke opens: Enter Olinda led by Glaucus and Circe:
they retire leaving Olinda.*

Song.

 Olin. Thou worthiest daughter of the greatest light,
Most powerfull *Circe*, and tho[u] honour'd *Glaucus*,
What dutie a poore fisher maid may give you,
In thankes, and vowes, and holy offerings,
Shall still be ready at your sacred altars.
Thalander, now to thee, what sacrifice?
What offerings may appease thy wronged love?
What have I but my selfe? ah worthlesse prize
Of such, so tryed, and so unmov'd a faith.
Ah, could I spend my body, weare my soule,
And then resume another soule and body,
And then consume that soule and body for thee,
All would not pay the use of halfe my debt.
How pale he lookes, how strangely alter'd!
Is he not dead? no, no, his pulse is quicke,
His heart is strong, and rising, in his heate,
Threatens with strokes, my churlish hand to beate:
Nature, how couldst in one so firmely tie
Perpetuall motion to fixt constancy?
How can this wonder fall in Notion,
A heart unmov'd, yet still in motion!
Alas he weepes, I hope his griefe and feares
Swimme fast away in those sad streaming teares.
Th'ast mourn'd enough, more justly may I weepe,
Leave me thy teares, rest thou and sweetely sleepe.

PHINEAS FLETCHER

Thalander starts up.

Tha. *Morpheus*, one more such dreame shall buy me.
Where, where art, *Olinda*? whither, whither flyest thou?
  Olin. Nay whither flies *Thalander*? here's *Olinda*:
Tell mee why wak'd the substance thou eschewest,
Whose shadowe in a dreame thou gladly viewest.
  Tha. Thou fairest shadow of a *Nymph* more faire,
Death yet I see cannot thy light impaire.
  Olin. Thou dreamest still *Thalander*!
  Tha. Ah too too true;
For such a sight wake shall I never viewe.
  Olin. I live.
  Tha. Would I were dead on that condition.
  Olin. So would not I: beleeve me friend, I live.
  Tha. Could I beleeve it [*Olinda*], I were happie.
  Olin. If mee thou wilt not, trust thy sence, thy eyes.
  Tha. They saw thee dead, how shall I trust my eie,
Which either now or then did vowch a lie?
  Olin. Credit thy touch.
  Tha. Then like a dreame thou'lt flie.
  Olin. Thou flyest, thou art the shadow love not I:
Thalander, take this [hand], tis thine for ever,
Nothing but death, nor death this knot shall sever.

Enter Alcippus.

Al. How['s] this! have you [learnt your] mother *Circes* art
To raise the dead? wonder? [I] thinke shee lives.
  Olin. What says *Thalander*? does he yet beleeve mee?
  Tha. If thou art dead, faire hand, how doest revive mee?
  Olin. *Thalander*, heart and hand had now beene cold
But for *Glaucilla*; she preventing *Cosma*,
Temper'd the poysonous viall, changing death
For sleepe, so gave mee life, [&] thee [thy] love.
  Tha. *Alcippus*, art thou there? thou art my freind
I prethee tell mee true, true *Alcippus*!
Doest thou not see *Olinda*?
  Al. I see her in your hand.
  Tha. Art sure tis she? tell me, are wee alive?
Art sure we wake? are we not both mistaken?

SICELIDES

If now I sleepe, O let me never waken.
  Al. If you would surely know, trie if shee breathe.
  Tha. Thy hand lives: doe thy lips live too *Olinda*?
Alcippus, shee lives, [shee lives] and breathes, *Alcippus*:
And with that sugred brea[th] my heart [ha]th fir'd,
And life and love with thousand joyes inspir'd.
Ah my *Olinda*.
  Olind. My deare, my deare *Thalander*.
  Tha. Ist possible thou liv'st? ist sure I hold thee?
These happy armes shall never more unfold thee.
  Olin. Tell mee, my love, canst thou such wrongs forgive
  Tha. My joy, my soule.   (mee?
  Olin. I never more will grieve [thee].
Canst thou forget my hate, my former blindnes?
If not, boldly revenge my rash unkindnes.
Pierce this vile heart my soules ungratefull center,
Pierce with thy dart where loves dart could not enter.
  Tha. For thy defence my hand shall still attend thee,
My hand and heart, but never to offend thee:
The only penance that I enjoyne thee ever,
Is that wee live and love and joy together.
Thinke not my hand will sacriledge commit,
To breake this temple where all Graces sit.
  Olin. True, true my love, tis vow'd a temple now,
Where ever shall be worshipt love and thou.
  Al. You happie paire, since *Cosma*'s spight's defeated,
And *Mago*[*es*] charmes, and death by love is cheated,
Why stand you here? tis time from hence to move:
This was the bedde of death, and not of love.
Death hath his part of night, love challengeth
The rest, love claimes the night as well as death.
  Tha. What sayes my love?
  Olin. W[th] my *Thalander* ever,
With thee to life or death, but from thee never.   *Exeunt.*
  Al. This halfe perswades mee to become a lover.
Where better could her love then here have neasted?
Or he his thoughts more daintily have feasted?
                                    Manet Alcippus.

PHINEAS FLETCHER

Act. 5. Scen. 3.

Enter Tyrinthus and Gryphus.

Tyr. Knowst thou *Perindus* [f]is[h]er, or *Olinda*?
Al. I know them both sir.
Tyr. Live they yet and breathe?
Al. They live and now most happy. *Exit Alcippus.*
Tyr. Thou mak'st me happy, in thy happy newes.
All thankes yee heavenly powers, when I forget
Your goodnesse in my childrens life and safety,
Let heaven forget both me and mine for ever.
Gryphus, backe to our shippe, and fetch mee thence
The vestments vowd to Neptune, and the chest,
Wherein I lockt my other offerings. *Exit Gryphus.*
This rocke my heart prefers before a palace.
Fond men that have enough yet seeke for more,
I thought by traffique to encrease my store,
And striving to augment this carefull pelfe,
I lost my goods, my liberty, my selfe:
Taken by *Persians* on the *Græcian* seas,
So I my captaine and the King did please,
Soone was I loosed from my slavish band,
And straight preferd to have a large command,
There have I now consum'd these thrice five summers,
There might I have liv'd long in wealth and honour,
But ah thou little home, how in thy want
The world so spacious, yet seemes too too scant!
At my departure hence I left two infants,
Perindus and *Olinda*, the boy some eyght,
The girle but two yeeres old, their mother dead,
Who giving life t[o] th' girle, so tooke her death,
And left her owne, to give her infant breath.
Great *Jove* and *Neptune*, I will keepe my vowes,
Seeing my children live, two chosen bulls,
With mirtle crownd, and Oake leaves laid with gold,
Shall fall upon your altars.

SICELIDES

Enter Pas.

Pas. You sacred vertues, truth and spotlesse fayth,
Where will you live, if not in such a Nymph?
Whose brest will you now seeke? what mansion?
  Tyr. My trembling heart doth some great ill divine,
And tels me, every griefe and feare is mine.
  Pas. Where now can unsuspected friendship rest,
If treachery possesse so faire a brest?
  Tyr. Fishe[r] what newes?
  Pas. Sir, little as concernes you.
  Tyr. Pray heavens it doe not.
  Pas. Your habit speakes a stranger,
And yet me thinkes, I somewh[ere] else have seene,
Some lineaments of that face: are you *Tyrinthus*?
  Tyr. The same.
  Pas. O cruell heavens! could you finde
No other time, to give him backe his country?
If thus you give, happy whom you deny,
The greater good, the greater injury:
Thy onely daughter—
  Tyr. Is dead.   *Tyrinthus falls.*
  Pas. I should have sayd so. Alas, he falls.
Tyrinthus, what, one blow thus strike thee
Under fortunes feete? How loth his life returnes!
  Tyr. How well I had forgot my griefe,
And found my rest, with losse of restlesse life!
Thou much hast wrong'd me, fisher, 'tis no love,
Death from his just possession to remove:
Heavens, ye have thankes for both, yet one you slue,
Give backe halfe of m[y] thankes, take but your due:
I owe you nothing for *Olinda*, nothing.
Ah poore *Olinda*: I shall never more,
Never more see thee: thy father must lament thee,
Thy father, who in death should long prevent thee,
How long since died shee?
  Pas. With the last sunne she fell.
  Tyr. Sure heavens, ye mocke me: alas, what victory?
What triumph in an old mans misery?
When you have wonne, what conquest, that you slue

A wretch that hate[s] his life as much as you?
   Pas. Sir, you forget your selfe: to warre with heaven,
Is no lesse fond, then dangerous.
   Tyr. Tell me fisher, have you a child?
   Pas. No sir.
   Tyr. No marvell then
Thou blam'st my griefe, of which thou hast no sence:
First lose a child, then blame my patience.
   Pas. If thou be griev'd, this is no way to ease it,
Sooner we anger heaven, then thus appease it.
   Tyr. But when the heart such weight of sorrow beares,
It speakes from what it feeles, [not] what it feares.
Died she [by naturall], or by violent meanes?
   Pas. Nature refus['d] an office so unnaturall.
   Tyr. Hard fate, most fitly were you women made:
Since fate unmercifull, unmoved stands,
Well was lifes distaffe put in womens hands.
Kild by a man?
   Pas. No man was so un[manly].
   Tyr. A woman!
   Pas. Yes.
   Tyr. Fit instrument of women:
What was the weapon?
   Pas. The cowards weapon, poyson.
   Tyr. Canst tell the murderers name?
   Pas. Her name *Glaucilla*:
A Nymph thought absolute, though now infected,
That heaven it selfe might sooner bee suspected.
   Tyr. Tell me the circumstance.
   Pas. 'Twill but more grieve you.
   Tyr. True, but 'tis pitty in unhelpt distresse,
Condemned soules with all the weight to presse.
   Pas. *Olinda* this last night complain'd to *Cosma*,
(A Nymph which lately came from faire *Messena*)
That this *Glaucillaes* powerfull charmes had fir'd her,
And with *Thalanders* love now dead, inspir'd her
With such a feeling griefe, her griefe lamenting,
That she, to helpe so desperate love consenting,
Gave her a water which she oft did prove,
Would eyther quench or ease the paines of love,

SICELIDES

Which *Cosma* swore, the other nere denyed.
Glaucilla chang'd, *Olinda* dranke and dyed.
Dicæus hearing this—
   Tyr. Lives then *Dicæus*?
   Pas. As well and just as ever.
   Tyr. His life doth somewhat mend
My childs sad death, after a child, a friend.
   Pas. Dicæus by this evidence condemnes her
By [t]h' law, from that high rocke to fall, and she
With smiling welcom'd death, and quietly
Steal'd to the rocke from whence shee must be cast.
Wonder so heavie guilt should flye so fast!
She led her leaders to that deepe descending,
The guilty drawes the guiltlesse to their ending:
And thus I left them, and with her just *Dicæus*,
To see her execution, who goes not from her,
Till from the rocke, in seas she leave her breath,
Die must she as she kild, water her crime and death.
   Tyr. Ah [my *Olinda*!] had I seene thee yet
And clos'd thine eyes, alas my poore *Olinda*!
   Pas. This griefe is vaine and can no more revive her,
You lose your teares.
   Tyr. When that I hold most deare
Is ever lost, poore losse to lose a teare.   [you,
   Pas. Your sonne st[ill l]ives, the good which heav'n bereaves
You quickly see, but see not what it leaves you.
   Tyr. Art sure he lives?
   Pas. Two houres since, sad I left him,
But safe.
   Tyr. What chances happen in an houre?
By this he may be dead and buried.
But yet *Perindus*, if thou living be,
My halfe joy lives, my halfe joy dies in thee.

Act. 5. *Scen.* [4].

Enter *Cancrone* and *Scrocca* bound: *Nomicus* the Priest.

   Can. Ah *Scrocca*, thou hast often heard me say, it would be my lucke to be devoured; and to tell thee true, I ever fear'd those *Cyclops* most; I never had any minde to them.

Scr. Why *Cancrone*, this is the slavery on't, had wee beene Master fishers, we should never have beene troubled to climbe up these Mountaines, wee [should have] beene cast to our old acquaintance the fish.

Tyr. Fisher, knowst thou these men?

Pas. I know the men, but not their meaning.

Can. That would never have angred me, thou knowst wee have fed upon fish this many yeere, and for us to have made them one merry meale, had beene but the signe of a thankefull nature, but ah those C[y]clops, clops, clops. *Scrocca*, I cannot digest them.

Scr. I feare they will 'gest us well enough.

Can. And yet I care not much if I were sure to bee eaten up by that *Cyclops* that ate up my grandsire, for then I might have some hope to see the good old man once againe before I die.

Scr. I care not whose hands I fall into, I'me sure hee shall have no sweete bitte of mee now; nothing grieves mee, but that having done but one good deede in all my life, I must die for that.

Nom. Thou foolish fisher, thinkst it good to stop
The course of justice, and breake her sword, the Law?
By Law thou liv'st: hee justly death deserves,
Who that destroyes, which him and his preserves.

Tyr. Are not these my old men, *Scrocca* and *Cancrone*?

Scr. Well sir, you may say what you will, but if wee live by the Law, how commeth it to passe, that we must die by the Law?

Can. Mee thinks I see how busie [that] *Rimronce* will bee about me: he surely will be upon my backe, for my being upon his, a while a goe.

Scr. Nay *Cancrone*, thou diest for saving thy master too.

Tyr. Ay me, my sonne?

Can. I have no minde to climbe these Mountaines, I begin to bee short-winded already, I shall never hold out; had I thought it would have come to this, I would have bene vilely tempted to ha let my Master drowne quickly.

Scr. What, man? thou could'st never have done thy Master better service then to dye for him, nay, if *Perindus* live, I care not.

Tyr. Perindus? I can hold no longer, friend, who is thy Master? why art thou manacled?

SICELIDES

Scr. Mantled hither! marry this Priest hath mantled us for saving our Master *Perindus*.
Tyr. Ay me, my sonne.
Can. Uds fish, old Master, where have you beene this 20 yeeres and more?
Nom. *Tyrinthus*! at such a time! sir, your arrivall
Is eyther very happy, or else most haplesse,
Eyther to see, or else prevent a danger.
Tyr. Priest, how is my *Perindus*?
Nom. Doom'd to die.
Tyr. What is the cause?
Nom. His will.
Tyr. Who could perswade him?
Nom. She who most strove to hinder and disswade him.
Tyr. What had he done?
Nom. That which deserves all life and love.
Tyr. How fine the heavens powers can sorrowes frame!
The fates will play, and make my woe their game.
Where is he?
Can. Safe enough I warrant you, get's leave of the Priest, master, and wee'l goe fetch him.
Scr. We caught him out of the water.
Can. O, he had supt a bundance of salt porridge!
Scr. And brought him to the shippe where the mariners keepe him.
Tyr. Why stand I idle here! [To] the shore i'le fly,
And eyther with him live, or for him die.
Can. Master, master, master.   *Exit Tyrinthus.*
Pas. Ile follow him: nature can doe no lesse
Then eyther helpe, or pitty such distresse.   *Exit Pas.*
Can. Nay if you goe too, then farewell all,
Farewell ye rockes, farewell to thee O love,
You lovely rockes, you hard and rocky love.
Nay I shall turne swa[n]ne presently and sing my finall song.
Nom. I marvell what it is that stayes *Dicæus*.
Can. Marry let him stay till I send for him, the *Cyclops* shall want their breakefast this month.
Nom. Here I must stay for him.

PHINEAS FLETCHER

Act. 5. Scen. 5.

Enter Cosma.

Cos. Faine would I know how my ginne thrives and prospers. *Olinda*['s] fast, and by my disamour
Hath quencht her love with death: if now *Glaucilla*
Be taken in that snare, then am I cunning:
Well may I prove a fisher, who have tooke
T[w]o maides so soone with one selfe baite and hooke.
Is not that *Nomicus*? I shall learne of him.
Nomicus?

Nom. Who *Cosma?*
Cos. Why are these fishers bound?
Can. For you.
Cos. For mee?
Can. I for you, had not you cus'd *Glaucilla,* shee had not bene condemnd: if shee had not beene condemnd, *Perindus* would not have died for her: if he would not have died for her, he had not fallen from the rocke: had he not fallen from the rocke, we had not sav'd him: if wee had not sav'd him, wee had not beene bound: were wee not bound, wee would showe a faire payre of heeles.
Cos. What talks this foole? *Perindus* falne from the rocke!
Nom. Hast thou not heard then of *Perindus* faith and fall?
Cos. No, not a word; but faine would heare.
Nom. And shalt: my tongue is as ready as thy eare;
Meane while leade these away;
Soone as *Dicæus* returnes, I'le overtake you.
Can. I prethee Mr *Priest,* let mee crave one favour; that I may have an *Epitaph* for mee in *Neptunes* church porch, Ile never goe farther.
Nom. Heres no time for *Epitaphs,* away.
Can. Nay, tis soone done, Ile trouble never a poet of them all, I have it already.

> *Cancrone valorous and kind, where art thou,*
> *Cancrone too kind and valorous to live?*
> *Ingulft in Cyclops guts. Readers, why start you?*
> *His life for his master he did freely give.*

SICELIDES

Ungratefull Sicelie that want'st his bones,
Instead of members keeping his memorie in stones.

Short and sweete, Mr *Priest*.
  Scr. *Cancrone*, this is a land voyage, you must leade the way.
  Can. But when wee saile downe the *Cyclops* throat, Ile give you the preeminence.   *Exeunt*.
  Nom. After that haplesse *Nymph* had heard her doome,
As shee was led t[o] th' rocke, i'th' middle way,
Perindus flying fast, calls out [to] stay :
And for he thought his feete too slowly bore him,
Before he came, he sent his voyce before [him].
Stay, stay, *Dicæus*, th'art a man, I see,
And well mayst erre : heavens not more pure then she.
Yet since the doome is past, i'le pawne my breath,
And make your fact lesse hainous by my death :
I'le lose her life in me, and she shall spend
My life in her, so both shall better end.
  Cos. This was no ill newes to the [guiltie] Nymph.
  Nom. Yes, yes : then first she thought her selfe condemnd,
Death in him shee fear'd and in her selfe contemnd.
That law it selfe (says shee) should suffer death,
Which one condemnes, another punnisheth.
True, sayes *Perindus*, my life, my all's in thee,
When thou offendst, why shoul[d] th[ey] punish me?
But briefe to give their words in short contracted,
Was never part of love more lovely acted :
Both loath to live, and both contend to die,
Where onely death strove for the victory.
Meane time I could but weepe, nor I alone,
That two such loves should die, not live in one.
  Cos. Their spotlesse fayth's a cristall, where I see
Too late my cancred hates deformity.
  Nom. At length the law it selfe decides the strife,
That he with losse of his might buy her life.
Then and but then she wept, and to prevent him,
Downe fell shee with a deadly looke and eye,
Acting the prologue of his tragedy,
And wak'd againe, she 'gan to chide and rave,
And vowes to live no further then his grave ;

While he with cheerfull steps the rocke ascending:
Fearelesse beholds his death, that steepe descending,
And boldly standing on the utmost browe,
Thus spake:
Poore life, I never knew thy worth till now,
How thou art over valewed to pay
Her life with thine, gold with base alcumy.
   Cos. Just, just, you heavens, I have set a gin
For them, and now my selfe the first am in.
   Nom. Then turning to his love, thus spake his last:
Farewell *Glaucilla*, live and in thy brest
As in a heaven my love and life shall rest:
Seeke not by death thy selfe from griefe to free,
Remember now *Perindus* lives in thee.
Cherish my heart, which in thy heart doth lye,
For whilst thou liv'st, *Perindus* cannot dye:
So leapt he lightly from the cloudy rocke.
   Cos. Is hee then dead?
   Nom. No: for the guilty sea[s]
With soft embraces wrapt his limbes [in ease];
It seemes the waves moov'd with Sympathy,
Would teach unhumane men humanity.
[And since they could not backe the doome recall]
Though they could not prevent, would ease his fall;
And not consenting to his pious death,
Restor'd him up againe to aire and breath:
Briefly, those two his servants not regarding
Dicæus theatning voyce, and just awarding,
With him tooke up his guilt, and to a shippe
That rides in the haven safe convayd him, there
They left him now reviv'd, themselves were taken
And as the law commands, were doom'd to suffer
The death of slaves: both to be strongly bound,
And in those hils left to the greedy *Cyclops*:
And now the stay is onely in *Dicæus*,
At whose returne they suffer, just they dye,
Who love their master more then equity.
   Cos. O lawlesse love! this [great, this] foule offence,
Which when it prosperd, pleasd my ravish't sence:
With what a d[ir]e aspect, what horrid sight,

SICELIDES

Now done, it fils my soule with guilty fright,
Who ere thou art, if in thy spotlesse brest,
Thy undefiled thoughts doe quiet rest:
Wake them not, and let no blood-hound with thee dwell,
These murthering thoughts are like the mouth of hell,
Into whose yawning 'tis more easie never
To fall, then falne, to cease from falling ever.

Enter Pas.

Pas. Nomicus, thou now mayst let thy prisoners free,
Thalander to *Olinda* now reviv'd,
Perindus to *Glaucilla* are to be married,
And all are brought along with [mirth and] singing,
Hymen the shores, *Hymen* the ecchoes ringing.
Nomicus, seest thou this Nymph? ah couldst thou thinke
That treason, envy, murder, spight and hell,
All hell it selfe in such a heaven could dwell?
This is the knot of all these sorrowes; *Cosma*,
If not for shame, why yet for spight or fashion,
For womans fashion let some teares bee spilt:
A sea of weeping will not wash thy guilt.
  Nom. Great nature, that hast made a stone descry
Twixt meaner natures, checking baser metalls,
Which proudly counterfeit the purer gold,
Why hast thou left the soule of man no touch-stone,
To judge dissemblance, and descry proud vice,
Which with false colours seemes more vertuous
Then vertues selfe? like to some cunning workeman,
Who frames a shape in such a forme [and] stature,
That oft he excells by imitating nature.
He that should looke upon this Nymphs sweete eye,
Would vow't a temple sworne to purity.
  Pas. If murder rest in such a lovely grace,
Here do I vow never to trust a face.
Shall I call backe your Prisoners?
  Nom. Prethee doe:
Our nets, boates, oares, and hookes shall now goe play,
For heaven hath sworne to make this holyday.

PHINEAS FLETCHER

Act. 5. Scen. 6.

*Enter Dicæus, Tyrinthus, Thalander, Olinda,
Perindus, Glaucilla, Alcippus, Chorus.*

Song.
    Hymen, Hymen, come saf[r]on Hymen.
    [That love] for ever constant stands,
    Where hearts are tied before the hands,
    Where faire vertue marries beauty,
    And affection pleads for duty :
    Hymen, Hymen, come saf[r]on Hymen.

  Al. You honour paire of fishers, see where your love,
So full of constant triall now hath brought you,
See, blessed soules, through so many teares,
Turnings, despaires, impossibilities,
Your love is now most safe arriv'd : *Thalander,*
Is this the Nymph, whom heaven and angry hell,
Her cold desires, and colder death it selfe
Would have devoured from thy deserving love?
Thalander, these hands are thine, that heavenly face,
Those starrie eyes, those roses and that grace,
Those corrall lips, and that unknowne brest,
And all the hidden riches of the rest :
They all are thine, thine is the faire *Olinda.*
Yet thou, as thou wast wont, all sad and heavy.
  Tha. Blame me not, friend : for yet I seeme forsaken
And doubt I sleepe, and feare still to be waken.

Enter Pas, with Cancrone and Scrocca.

  Cos. Now is the time of pardon. Ye happie maids,
Your love in spight of all tempestuous seas,
Is safe arriv'd, and harbors in his ease,
And all those stormes have got but this at last,
To sweeten present joyes with sorrowes past.
Blessed *Olinda,* thou hast got a love
Equall to heaven, and next to highest *Jove.*

SICELIDES

Glaucilla, thy losse thou now dost full recover.
Ah you have found (too seldome found) a lover.
Then doe not her too rigorously reprove,
For loving those whom you yet better love.
  Olin. For us, we judge not of your hard intent,
But reckon yo[u] joyes fatall instrument.
  Dicæ. Yet this her penance: *Cosma*, marke thy censure,
Whom most thou shouldest love, thou shalt love never
Dote thou on dotards, they shall hold thee ever:
The best and wisest never shall respect thee,
Thou onely fooles, fooles onely shall affect thee.
Loose now those prisoners; so forward to the temple.
                                        Exit Chorus.
  Can. Ha brave Judge, now Mistris mine, I must confesse [you].
  Cos. This charme begins to worke already,
I love this foole, and doate upon him more,
Then ever upon any man before:
Well, I must be content thus to be curst
And yet of lovers, fooles are not the worst.
For howsoever boyes doe hoote and flout them,
The best and wisest oft have fooles about them.
  Can. I and many a fooles bable too, I warrant thee.
Sweete heart, shall we goe to bedde?
  Cos. What, in the morning?
  Can. Morning? tis night.
  Cos. Thou art a foole indeede, seest not the sunne?
  Can. Why that's a candle or the moone, I prethee let's goe to bed.
  Cos. Content; no time [I count] unfit for play,
Love knowes no difference twixt night and day.
  Can. Nay, all the play's done, gentles, you may goe,
I have another play within to doe.
Riddle me, Riddle me, what's that?

> *My play is worke enough; my worke is play,*
> *I see to worke i'th' night, and rest [i']th' day:*
> *Since then my play and worke is all but one,*
> *Well may my play begin, now yours is done.*
>   *Exeunt.*

PHINEAS FLETCHER

EPILOGUS.

As in a Feast, so in a Comedy,
    Two sences must be pleasd; in both the eye,
In feasts, the eye and taste must be invited,
In Comedies, the eye and eare delighted:
And he that onely seekes to please but eyther,
While both he doth not please, he pleaseth neyther.
What ever feast could every guest content,
When [as each] man each taste is different?
But lesse a Scene, where nought but as 'tis newer
Can please, where guests are more, and dishes fewer:
Yet in this thought, this thought the Author easd,
Who once made all, all rules, all never pleasd.
Faine would we please the best, if not the many,
And sooner will the best be pleasd then any:
Our rest we set in pleasing of the best,
So wish we you, what you may give us : Rest.

FINIS.

APPENDIX
TO
THE POEMS
OF
GILES FLETCHER

[ELEGIES ON HENRY, PRINCE OF WALES]

[From *Epicedium Cantabrigiense*]

[I]

Upon the most lamented departure
of the right hopefull, and blessed Prince
HENRIE *Prince of* WALES.

THe weeping time of Heav'n is now come in,
   Kindely the season clowdes of sorrowe beares,
To smile, ô let it be a deadly sinne
And happy hee, his merry looks forswears,
See heav'n for us is melted into teares:
   O deerest Prince how many hearts wear knowne
   To save thy life, that would have lost their owne?

When thou thy Countreys griefe, weart once her glory,
How was this blessed Isle crown'd with delight;
So long it never knew how to be sorry,
But anchor'd all her joyes upon thy sight;
The musique every whear did freely lite:
   The Sheapheards pip't, and countrey byrds did sing,
   The water-nymphs came dauncing from their spring.

It was the mother then of harmeles pleasure
The Queene of beawty all men came to see,
And poore it could not bee, thou weart her treasure,
Onely it was a little prowde of thee,
Aye mee, that ever so it might not bee!
   The Garden of the world, whear nothing wanted,
   Another Paradise, that God had planted.

APPENDIX

Her happie fields wear dec'kt with every flowre,
That with her sweetest lookes Peace smil'd to see it:
Delight it selfe betwixt her breasts did bowre,
And oft her rustique Nymphs thy coach would meet,
And strow with flowers the way before thy feete.
　But now those flowers wee woont to strow before thee,
　　Dead, in thy grave wee throw them to adore thee.

Sleepe softly, royall Ghost, in that cold bed,
Let deaths pale chambers give thee easie rest,
Whear all the Princely bones lie buried,
With guilded crowns and long white scepters drest.
Ah, little look't they thou shouldst be their guest!
　What makes the heav'ns proclaime such open warres?
　　Wee did not owe thee so soone to the starres.

And yet our vowes doe not thy starres envie thee,
Bathe thee in joyes, wee in our teares will swim:
Wee doe not unto heav'n, or God denie thee,
Onely the Muses begge this leave of him,
To fill with teares their fountaine to the brim,
　And as thou sett'st emparadis'd above,
　　To powre out to thee rivers of their love.

See how the yeare with thee is stricken dead,
And from her bosome all her flowers hath throwne,
With thee the trees their haires fling from their head,
And all the Sheapheards pipes are deadly blowne,
All musique now, and mirth is hatefull growne:
　Onely *Halcyons* sad lamenting pleases,
　　And that Swans dirge, that, as hee sings, deceases.

Heav'n at thy death deni'd our world his light,
Ne suff'red one pale starre abroad to peepe,
And all about the world the winds have sigh'd,
Nor can the watrie-nymphs (so fast they weepe)
Within their banks their flouds of sorrow keepe.
　Suffer us, in this deluge of distresse,
　　Thee, if not to enjoy, at least to blesse.

GILES FLETCHER

Bedded in all the roses of delight
Let thy engladded soule embalmed lie,
Imbrightned into that celestiall light,
Which all Gods saintly Lamps doth glorifie,
Thear boast thy kinred with the Deitie
    Whear God his Sonne, and Christ his Brother greet thee,
And thy too little glorious Sisters meete thee.

But ô thou desert Island, that art found
Cast in the seas deepe bosome by mishap,
As if with our salt teares thou all weart drown'd,
And hadst from heav'n drop't into sorrowes lap;
Desolate house! what mantle now shall wrap
    Thy naked sides? poore widow, made to mourne,
    To whom wilt thou thy sad addresses tourne?

Alas, the silent Angels on his tombe
Can him no honour, thee no comfort sing,
Their pretie weeping lookes may well become
Themselves, but him to life can never bring.
Thee therefore, deerest Prince, from perishing
    Or yet alive wee in our hearts will save,
    Or dead with thee, our hearts shall be thy grave.

HENRIE farewell, heav'ns soone-restored Exile,
Immortall Garland of thy Fathers head,
Mantle of honour to this naked Isle,
Bright drop of heav'n, on whose wish't nuptiall bed
Now all our ripest hopes hung blossomed.
    Farewell, farewell; hearke how the Angels sing,
    On earth our Prince is now in heav'n a King.

G. F. T. C.

APPENDIX

[II]

In fatum summi, & beatissi-
mi Principis HENRICI.

QUò fugis? ah vitâ quondam, dum vita manebat,
    Terris chare magis, nec tam citò debitus astris.
Nondum annosa dies, nec adhuc tibi frigida membris
Sævît hyems, tumulumq́; tuis aptaverat umbris.
Siste fugam superis : quid tam citò divus haberi
Incipis, infelix, & felicissime Princeps?
Quid caput auratis properant tibi cingere stellis
Dii nimium cupidi? quin hìc tibi sceptra, tuisq́;
Seri debentur regnis, Henrice, nepotes.
Ah tibi regnandi ne sit tam dira cupido,
Ut miseros mens sola tuos exosa Britannos,
Aetheriis insueta viis, jam tecta deorum,
Et festinatos cœli deposcat honores :
Hìc priùs in terris pacato numine regnet,
Et tandem sceptris cedat satiata duobus.
    Quanquam (si liceat nostros optasse dolores)
O fortunatos, vel post tua fata, Britannos,
Si patriæ, Princeps, non omni parte perîsses !
Nam siquis tantum nostris Henriculus oris
Luderet aureolus (nobis solatia luctus
Exigua ingentis) qui te tantùm ore referret :
Cujus ab aspectu poteras exire sepulchro,
Atq́; iterum blandis pueri spirare labellis ;
Nec penitus nos Te, nec tu nos funere tanto
Perdideras, nobis sed qui post fata redire
Heu nunquam poteras, poteras post fata redire.
    Sed quid vos, dulces cineres, quid vos fugientes
In superas sequimur revocanti carmine sedes?
Te nigri Soles (quis Solem dicere falsum
Audeat) & flentes lachrymis cælestibus Auræ,
Undantésq́; suis flerunt in vallibus Amnes :
Te Musæ totis luxerunt fontibus ; ipsi
Murmura ducentes imo de pectore Venti
Cum gemitu spirant, spirantibus adgemit Echo.

GILES FLETCHER

Ah miser! ah miseri non debita præda sepulchri.
Ecce dies quoties, quotiésq̨ renatus Apollo
(Te postquam nostro non ampliùs invenit orbe)
Atra nube cadens, heu toto sidere noctem
Excepit, medióq̨ diem deperdit olympo.
I decus, i nostrum, cœlestibus utere fatis.
Et placidé (quando superis adnare necesse est
Littoribus) roseas Zephyri sublatus in alas,
Dive, triumphales cælorum illabere currus.
Non ibi fatorum, properato funere, jussa
Aurea mansuris abrumpunt otia regnis;
Sed tibi sceptra manent nullo peritura sepulchro.
Et, quod gaudebis, medici bene nescia vita.
 Nos tamen interea tumulum, tibi floribus istis,
Heu malé qui terris, nunc te moriente, supersunt,
Spargimus, ecce, tuum, nec te moriente supersint.
Quin ipsi lapides, nostri pia vulnera passi
Mæroris, gelidæ perfusi fletibus auræ,
Hos tibi de duro cantabunt marmore fletus,
Aeternumq̨ dabunt hominum tibi corda sepulchrum.

Carmen Sepulchrale.

Miraris quî Saxa loqui didicere, Viator?
 Cœli depositum conditur hoc tumulo:
Cujus si famam, tacuissent saxa, putares
 Hoc tibi mirandum, non didicisse loqui.
Si sapis, attonitus sacro decede sepulchro,
 Nec cineri quæ sint nomina quære novo.
Prudens celavit sculptor; nam quisque rescivit,
 Protinus in lachrymas solvitur, & moritur.

G. F. T. C.

FRAGMENTARY VERSE TRANSLATIONS

IN

THE REWARD OF THE FAITHFULL

I.

[Boethius, *De Consolatione Philosophiæ* IV. Metr. 1. 25—6.]

    Hæc, dices, memini patria est mihi,
    Hinc ortus, hic sistam gradum.
    O this my country is, thy soule shall say,
    Hence was my birth, & here shall be my stay. (p. 30.)

II.

[*Anthologia Palatina* XI. 53.]

[Τὸ] ῥόδον ἀκμάζει βαιὸν χρόνον· ἂν δὲ παρελθῇ
[Κἂν] μικρ[ῷ] εὑρήσεις οὐ ῥόδον ἀλλὰ βάτον.
    The Rose is faire & fading, short and sweet,
      Passe softly by her:
    And in a moment you shall see her fleet,
      And turne a bryer. (p. 120.)

III.

[*Anthologia Palatina* V. 210. 3—4.]

Ἔστι μέλαινα, τί τοῦτο; καὶ ἄν[θ]ρακες, ἀλλ' ἂν ἐκείνους
θάλψω[μεν], λάμψουσ' ὡς ῥόδα [εἰαρινά].
    She's black: what then? so are dead coales, but cherish,
      And with soft breath them blow,
    And you shall see them glow as bright and flourish,
      As spring-borne Roses grow. (p. 121.)

GILES FLETCHER

IV.

[Boethius, *De Consolatione Philosophiæ* II. *Metr.* VII. 13—4.]

> *Involvit humile pariter & celsum caput.*
> *Æquatq summis infi[m]a.*

> Death and the Grave make even all estates.
> There, high, and low, & rich, & poor are mates.

(p. 203.)

V.

[Boethius, *De Consolatione Philosophiæ* II. *Metr.* VII. 25—6.]

> *Cum sera vobis rapiet hoc etiam dies,*
> *Jam vos secunda mors manet.*

> The poor man dies but once: but O that I
> Already dead, have yet three deaths to die. (p. 206.)

VI.

[Homer, *Iliad*, XIX. 86—7.]

> ἐγὼ δ' οὐκ αἴτιός εἰμι
> Ἀλλὰ Ζεὺς καὶ μοῖρα καὶ ἠεροφοῖτις ἐρινύς.

> It was not he that did them injurie.
> But Jove and Fate, and the night Furie.

(pp. 232—3.)

VII.

[Homer, *Odyss.* I. 33—4.]

> Ἐξ ἡμέων γάρ φασι κάκ' ἔμμεναι· οἱ δὲ καὶ αὐτοὶ
> Σφῆσιν ἀτασθαλίῃσιν ὑπέρμορον ἄλγε' ἔχουσι[ν].

> Men say their faults are ours when their own wils
> Beyond their fate, are authours of their ills. (p. 233.)

APPENDIX

VIII.

[Virgil, *Georg.* II. 475—7, 483, 485—6.]

Me vero primum dulces ante omnia Musæ
(Qu[a]rū sacra fero ingenti perculsus amore)
Accipiant, cælique vias & sidera monstrent:
Sin has non possim Naturæ accedere partes, &c.
Rura mihi, & rigui placeant in vallibus amnes.
Flumina amem, sylvasque inglori[u]s.

No, first of all O let the Muses wings
Whose sacred fountaine in my bosome springs
Receive, and landing mee above the starres,
Shew me the waies of hevē: but if the barres
Of unkinde Nature stoppe so high a flight,
The Woods and Fields shall be my next delight.

(pp. 273—4.)

IX.

[Horace, *Epist.* I. xiv. 43.]

Optat ephippia Bos·piger, optat ara[r]e Caballus.

Faine would the Oxe the horses trappin[g]s weare;
And faine the Horse the Oxes yoake would beare.

(p. 283.)

NOTES

In the following references to the text the lines are numbered from the top of the page, including titles, and, in the case of SICELIDES, *stage-directions and the headings, Act., Scen. and Chorus. Headlines are not included, nor verse-numbers. Side-notes are numbered separately.*

Additional particulars about the editions or MSS. *from which the text and the variants are taken will be found in the Preface to this volume.*

GILES FLETCHER.

CHRISTS VICTORIE, AND TRIUMPH IN HEAVEN, AND EARTH, OVER, AND AFTER DEATH.

A = The First Quarto, 1610.   B = The Second Quarto, 1632.
C = The Third Quarto, 1640.   Qq = The Three Quartos.

The text, unless there is an indication to the contrary, is that of A. *Where the reading of* B *and* C *has been adopted, or an emendation made, square brackets are inserted in the text. In cases, however, of* (1) *repunctuation,* (2) *omission of an apostrophe,* (3) *renumbering of verses, brackets have not been used, but the original form is given in the Notes.*

Variants of spelling in B *and* C *are only recorded when they present some point of special interest.*

p. 5.   The title-pages of B and C are as follow:

B]   **C H R I S T S**
VICTORIE AND
TRIUMPH IN HEAVEN
AND EARTH, OVER
AND AFTER DEATH

A te principium, tibi desinet: accipe jussis
Carmina cœpta tuis, atq, hanc sine tempora circum
Inter victrices hederam tibi serpere lauros.

The second Edition.

CAMBRIDGE:
Printed for FRANCIS GREEN.   1632.

NOTES

C]   CHRIST'S
          VICTORY
             AND
          TRIUMPH,
   In *Heavèn* and *Earth,* over and after
                DEATH

Wherein is } His { Birth.
lively figured }   { Circumcision.
                     { Baptisme.
                     { Temptation.
                     { Passion.
                     { Resurrection.
                     { Assention.

In foure divine Poems.
CAMBRIDGE.
Printed by *Roger Daniel,* for *Richard Royston.*
1640.

p. 5, l. 6. A] *cæpta.*

pp. 7—9. In the British Museum copy of A these pages have been bound by mistake after, instead of before, pp. 10—14.

p. 7, l. 2. A] WORSHIPULL.

p. 9, l. 28. B and C] be fit.

p. 10, l. 13. B and C] whether. l. 25. A] on. B and C] one. l. 28. B and C *omit*] Parables.

p. 11, l. 2. A] μακαριώτερον. l. 16. A] Ghostpel. B and C] Gospell. l. 22. B and C] *Edmond.*

p. 13, l. 25. A] ὀν. B and C] 'Ον. l. 26. Qq] ὄυτοι. Qq] ὄι. A] αὐτὸs.

p. 14, l. 6. B and C] virgin. l. 10. A] Ha'st. B and C] Hast. l. 14. A] broughts. B and C] brought'st. l. 23. B and C] thy song. ll. 24, 25. *Between these* B and C *add:*

Defuncto fratri.
Think (if thou canst) how mounted on his spheare,
In heaven now he sings: thus sung he here.

p. 15, l. 6. B and C] *Jam fletus teneros, cachinnulosque.* l. 16. A] *Ah.* B and C] (*ah!*). l. 20. A] *solem.* B and C] *saltem.*

p. 16, l. 1. A] H'. l. 11. B and C] *clausus.* l. 23. A] *en.* B and C] (*en!*).

p. 18, ll. 1—20. Facing these lines C has an engraving of the Nativity, with the following verses at the foot:

A new way here that prophets text may pass
for truth: the oxe his owner knew, the ass
his masters crib. thus thus incradled lay
your King, your Lord, your Christ; there fix, there stay
thy stoopinge low, dejᵉcted thoughts[.] shall I
since he lay thus depress'd, care where I lie.
                                           Esay: i. 3.

NOTES

On either side of the main engraving is a pastoral scene. On the left is a shepherd boy piping, with his dog by his side, and in the background is a cornfield, and a building which seems to be the inn where the Nativity took place. On the right is another shepherd boy piping, while beyond him there is an old shepherd tending his flock, with his cottage in the background.

p. 19, *side-notes*, l. 12.   A *has a full stop after* guiltie.

p. 23, l. 31.   B and C] flee.

p. 24, l. 6.   B and C] In spirits.   *Side-notes*, l. 4.   A] t.   B and C] it.

p. 25, l. 28.   B and C] th' hastie.

p. 26, *side-notes*, l. 3.   B and C] unthankfulnes.   *Side-notes*, ll. 7—8.   B and C] and remedy.

p. 27, l. 17.   Qq] casts his dead.   *The reading of the Qq may be correct, but the suggested emendation adds point to the antithesis between* quicke *and* dead.

p. 28, l. 12.   A] paint.   B and C] paints.

p. 30, l. 23.   A] thrist.

p. 34, l. 7.   A] despisd'.

p. 36, *side-notes*, l. 5.   A *has a full stop after* sinne.

p. 37, ll. 9—32, and p. 38, ll. 1—4.   Facing these lines C has an engraving of the Circumcision. Below is the reference, LUKE: ii: xxi, followed by these lines :

> View well this sacred Portracture, and see
> what pangs thy Savio^r felt, and all for thee.
> Wilt thou returne a sacrifice may please
> him who hath felt all this! be thou all these:
> Be thou both Preist and knife: react each part
> thy selfe aga^{i}ne. Go circumcise thy heart.

The main engraving has two miniatures on either side of it. On the left side of the page, above, is represented the marriage feast at Cana, with the reference, JOHN: 2. i., and, below, Christ taking hold of Peter when he walked on the sea, with the reference, MATH: 14: 31.; on the right, above, Christ in the Temple in the midst of the Doctors, with the reference, Luk: 2. 46., and, below, the flight into Egypt, with the reference, MATH: 2: 14.

p. 37, l. 22.   A] earrh.

p. 38, l. 6.   B and C] tyrants.   *Side-notes*, l. 3.   A *has a comma after* Men.

p. 39, l. 6.   A] devo'wd.   l. 7.   A] bo'wd.

p. 40, *side-notes*, l. 8.   A *has a full stop after* Mark.   *Side-notes*, l. 12. A *has a full stop after* Attribute.

p. 40, ll. 1—20.   Facing these lines C has an engraving of the Baptism of Jesus by John.   Below is the reference, Mar: i: 9, followed by the lines :

> How many riddlinge thoughts strangly appeare
> Unfolded in this shadow : for first here
> I see the Fountaine in the Streams. I see
> the water wa[s]hd by washing in't. And wee
> through nature black to pitch, and inck are scou^{ur}d
> to snow, while water's on an other pour'd[.]
> I see againe. Ile not say all I can
> least I turne Jordan to an Ocean[.]

276

NOTES

The main engraving has two miniatures on either side of it. On the left side of the page, above, is represented the woman with the issue of blood touching Jesus' garment, with the reference, MAR: 5: 27. In the miniature below the reference has been accidentally omitted, but the scene is apparently the raising of the widow's son at Nain. On the right, above, is depicted the cleansing of the leper, with the reference, MATH: 8: 3, and, below, the healing of the man with the withered hand, with the reference, Mark: 3: 1.

p. 41, l. 30. A] to'. B and C] t'.

p. 42, *side-notes*, l. 4. A *has a full stop after* Psalm. B and C] Psal.

p. 43, ll. 17—34, and p. 44, ll. 1—12. Facing these lines C has an engraving of the Temptation in the Wilderness. Below are the following lines

Tis written. Thus the tempter faught. (And thus
by scriptures wrack'd he oft prevailes on us
                                                thus
*weake flesh and blood) But that he*ˌ*did dare*
by Moses, and the prophets to insnare
the sonne of God; thinck it not strange that he
became confounded in his policie
for sure it could but slender hopes afford
*he by the scriptures should o'recome y*ᵉ *wor*ᵈ.

The main engraving has two miniatures on either side. On the left side of the page, above, is represented the impotent man beside the pool of Bethesda, with the reference, JOHN: 5: 6, and, below, the healing of the man blind from his birth, with the reference, JOH: 9: 1 (the 9 is turned). On the right, above, is the Transfiguration, with the reference, MAR: 9: 4, and, below, Jesus writing on the ground concerning the woman taken in adultery, with the reference, JOH: 8: 6.

p. 44, l. 3. B and C] travelling.

p. 46, l. 5. Qq] Shreechowle. This may be right, but it seems to be a contamination of two forms, both of which exist, Screechowle and Shrikeowle. l. 8. A *has a comma after* grone.

p. 48, l. 29. B and C] Neptunes.

p. 49, *side-notes*, l. 10. Qq *have a full stop after* stood.

p. 50, l. 21. A] flowr's. B and C] flow'rs.   l. 22. A] flowr's-de-luce. B and C] flow'rs-de-luce.   l. 24. A] th'. B and C] the.

p. 51, l. 24. A] amarously.

p. 54, l. 11. A] Phæbus.

p. 55, l. 26. A] virgintie.

p. 57. *The imprint of the second title in* B *is:*

C H R I S T S
T R I U M P H
Over and After
Death.

Vincenti dabitur.

Printed by the Printers to the Universitie of
Cambridge. ANN. DOM. 1632.

277

NOTES

C *omits* this title-page, replacing it by an engraving of the Crucifixion. At the foot of the Cross is the reference, Mat: 27: 37, and below are these lines:

> What you see here does but the picture show
> of sorrowes picture. Miracle of woe.
> Greefe was miscall'd till now, what plaints before
> e're mov'd the bowells of the earth! or toare
> the rocks! nay more: the heav'ns put out their lig^{ht}
> and truc'd with darkness, to avoide that sight.
> Blind Israell! this this your hardness shewes:
> Jewes.
> yee then turn'd stones, whilst thus those stones turn^d

The main engraving has two miniatures on either side of it. On the left side of the page, above, is represented Judas kissing Jesus, with the reference, LUK: 22: 47, and, below, Jesus before Pilate, with the reference, LUK: 23: 1. On the right, above, is the scene of Mary Magdalene anointing the feet of Jesus in the house of Simon the Pharisee, with the reference, LUK: 7: 37, and, below, the Last Supper, when Jesus declares that "the hand of him that betrayeth me, is with me on the table," with the reference, LUK: 22: 21.

    p. 58, *side-notes*, l. 5.   A *has a full stop after* exprest.

    p. 59, l. 18.   A] flowr's.   B and C] flow'rs.

    p. 60, l. 31.   Qq *place inverted commas at the beginning of the line only.*

    p. 61, l. 4.   B and C] whether.   ll. 18 and 22.   A] flowr's.   B and C] flow'rs.

    p. 64, *side-notes*, l. 1.   *A bracketed* 2 *has been inserted to correspond to* 1 *at the beginning of* l. 7 *of the side-notes on* p. 61.

    p. 65, *side-notes*, l. 3.   Qq *wrongly have* 1. *A* 2 *is needed to correspond with* 1 *in* l. 4 *of the side-notes on* p. 64.

    p. 67, *side-notes*, ll. 3 and 6.   A] in.

    p. 70, l. 28.   Qq] shreechowles.   *Cf. note on* p. 46, l. 5.

    p. 72, l. 20.   B and C] funerall.

    p. 73, l. 26.   A] whieh.

    p. 75, ll. 1—16.   Facing these lines C has an engraving of the Resurrection. Below is the reference, MAR: XVI, followed by these lines:

> Forget those horrid stiles of death: see here
> who died, and by his presence there
> imbalm'd the grave. See here who rose: and so
> left hell infeebled, and the powers below,
> and death suppress'd. So that a child (no doubt)
> may safly play wth't, now the Sting's pluck'd out.

The main engraving has two miniatures on either side of it. On the left side of the page, above, is represented the miraculous feeding of the four thousand, with the reference, MAR: 8: 9, and, below, Jesus answering the Pharisees' question about the tribute money, with the reference, MAT: 22: 19. On the right, above, is the scene of the raising of Lazarus, with the reference, JOHN: ii: 43, and, below, the casting forth of the devil out of the daughter of the Syrophenician woman, with the reference, MAR: 7: 26.

    p. 75, *side-notes*, l. 4.   Qq] in.

    p. 76, l. 30.   A] t'is.

NOTES

p. 77, l. 2. A] flowr's. C and D] flow'rs.

p. 79, l. 5. A] flowr's. C and D] flow'rs. l. 10. A] powr's. C and D] pow'rs. l. 11. Qq] interchas't. l. 32. B and C] led.

p. 80, l. 1. B and C] led. ll. 9—16. The number 20 is repeated by mistake at the head of this stanza in the Quartos. From this point, therefore, to the close of the Canto the stanzas have been renumbered. l. 18. A] Greec.

p. 81, l. 18. B and C] Steward. l. 25. A] embowr's. B and C] embow'rs. l. 26. A] flowr's. B and C] flow'rs.

p. 82, *side-notes*, l. 2. Qq] Caritie. l. 23. A] theit.

p. 84, l. 5. B and C] restrain. *Side-notes*, l. 7. A] in.

p. 85, l. 10. B and C] content.

p. 85, ll. 13—32 and p. 86, ll. 1—8. Facing these lines C has an engraving of the Ascension. Below is the reference, MARK: 26: 19, followed by these verses:

> *Tis finished: and hees now gon up on high*
> *rich in the spoyles of hell: in maiestie,*
> *and glorie (and glorie glorious farre*
> *above all words:) each glimpse treads out a starre*
> *dazles the sun: And whether true this bee*
> *here written, follow him, and you shall see.*

The main engraving has two miniatures on either side of it. On the left side of the page, above, is represented the episode of Pilate washing his hands before the multitude, with the reference, MAT: 27: 24, and, below, the scourging of Jesus, with the reference, JOHN: 19: 1. On the right, above, is the crowning with thorns, with the reference, JOH: 19: 2, and, below, Jesus is depicted carrying the Cross to Golgotha, with the reference JOH: 19: 17.

p. 88, l. 23. A] Τέλειον. *After this line* B *and* C *add:* ἔστι τελῶν τὸ τέλος· τέλος ἐστὶ θεὸς τὸ τέλειον.

A DESCRIPTION OF ENCOLPIUS.

p. 89, *side-note*. This is in a different hand from that of Archbishop Sancroft, in which the poem is written. Neither the writer of it, nor Mr Blois, can apparently be identified. *Side-note*, l. 2. MS.] Encolpus. l. 2. *Nisus amore pio pueri &c.* From the *Æneid*, v. 294. ll. 12 and 28. MS.] Encolpus.

p. 90, l. 11. MS.] Encolpus.

PHINEAS FLETCHER.

VERSES OF MOURNING AND JOY.

p. 95, l. 26. The Quarto *omits full stop after*] *Fletcher*.

LOCUSTÆ.

Q = Quarto edition, 1627. S = Manuscript in Sloane MSS., 444.
M = Manuscript at present owned by Mr Dobell.
H = Manuscript in Harleian MSS., 3196.

The text, unless there is an indication to the contrary, is that of Q. *All variants in* S, M *and* H, *except merely of spelling, are noted. Where* S, M

279

NOTES

and H *agree, the spelling used in the variant is that of* H; *where* S *and* M *agree, the spelling is that of* S. *Together with the variants the corresponding passages in* Q *are quoted except in a few cases where the reference is unmistakable.*
  The variations in the arrangement of the paragraphs by Q *and* H *are recorded. This is not done in the case of* S *and* M, *as they differ so considerably from the other two texts in their arrangement, and as* S *does not divide the poem into paragraphs except towards the close.*

  p. 97. There is no title-page in S, M or H. S has at the head of fol. 1, above the dedication to Montagu, in a different hand from the rest of the MS., the title *Phineæ Fletcheri pietas Jesuitica*. At the head of the fly-leaf in H is written in a different hand from the body of the MS. the name *P: Fletcher*. On this and the other entries on this leaf see further the Preface to this volume.

  pp. 99—101. S, M and H *do not contain* the Dedication to Townshend and the Verses by S. Collins. S *has* the following Dedication to James Montagu, Bishop of Bath and Wells:

<blockquote>
Reverendissimo in Christo Patri,
Ecclesiæq, Bathoniensis et
Wellensis Episcopo longè
celeberrimo, Jacobo
Montaguo, domino
mihi colendissimo.
</blockquote>

  Munus (Nobilissime Præsul) iniqua temporum consuetudo a supplicibus extorquet, hoc potissimùm, integritas tua, et nostra (profunda quidem illa) paupertas postulat. Nuperrimè nobis pater, vir tibi notissimus, periit, periit quidem nobis, sibi nunc tandem vivit. viduæ reliquit, quos sustentaret, liberos decem, quo sustentaret planè nihil. In hac orbitabe, patrisq, desiderio, ad illum patriæ patrem confugimus, quanto tu nobis auxilio esse potes, non nescimus, nec potes modò, pro eo quo Rex te semper complexus est favore; sed et pro ea, quam tu semper amplexus es, humanitate, et sanctissimo hoc munere, velis etiam miseris succurrere, orbis opitulari. Orborum preces quàm sint apud Deum efficaces nosti, has tibi, etiam copiosas, devincies; mihi etiam exorandus es, ut carmen hoc Cantabrigiæ nuper inchoatum, inter urbanos strepitus, parentisq, illius quidem exspirantis singultus, hujus verò deflentis lamenta, sororumq, lachrymas confectum (properatum tibi munus) quo soles oculo perlegas.
  Interim qui te maxima Ecclesiæ utilitati ad hanc dignitatem evexit Deus, eidem Ecclesiæ, Principi, Patriæ, bonis deniq, omnibus florentissimum diu conservet.

<blockquote>
Tibi, et dignitati tuæ
devotissimus
Phin: Fletcher
Coll: Regal:
</blockquote>

M *has* the following Dedication to Henry, Prince of Wales:

<blockquote>
Communi Anglo-
rum omnium amori
illustrissimo Wal-
liæ Principi
Henrico.
</blockquote>

  [*After* Henrico *is written apparently by a later hand* div (?), *and in the next line* &, &, &.]

NOTES

O decus, O ævi, et gentis spes maxima nostræ!
Deliciæ Anglorum! fausti faustissima Patris
Progenies! cui Musæ omnes sua munera lætæ,
Cui secat ipsa suas Pallas æqualiter artes:
Cui paria ipse pater Phœbus non invidet arma
Sive libet jaculo contendere, sive potenti
Robora mulcere, et montes deducere cantu,
Si tibi regales indulgent otia curæ,
Accipe, parva quidem, sed non indebita mentis
Munera, quæ canit ignoti nova fistula vatis
Carmina, nascentemq̹ fove (tua regna) poetam.
Non is, non ausus (nec tanta superbia musæ)
Inter Apollineas laurus, palmasq̹ virentes,
Vix raucâ dignos stipulâ disperdere cantus,
Sed salices inter spretas ulvamq̹ palustrem
(Exosas musis salices) miserabile carmen
Integrat, innatosq̹ animi depascitur æstus:
Quà pater externis Chamus vix cognita rivis
Flumina demulcens, Regales alluit hortos,
Templaque submissis veneratur regia lymphis.
 O mihi supremæ maneat pars tarda senectæ,
Dum tua facta licet totum mihi ferre per orbem,
Non me carminibus Linus, non vicerit Orpheus;
Maximus ille licèt, quem jactat Mantua vates,
Maximus ille tamen dicet se carmine victum.
Iam faveas, primoq̹ adsis, Henrice, labori.
Accipe tu trepidantem, atq̹ hanc sine tempora circū
Inter Apollineas myrtum succrescere lauros.
Sic tibi florentem cœli Pater ille juventam
Propitius foveat, sic cùm tibi plenior ætas,
Ipsa tuis Regum meretrix succumbat ab armis
Roma, et septenos submittens diruta colles,
Victa tuos decoret non surrectura triumphos.

H *has* the following Dedication to Thomas Murray, Tutor to Prince Charles, afterwards 13th Provost of Eton:

Optimo et mihi colendissimo
semper viro
Thomæ Murreio.

Quod nonnullis (neq̹ id rarò) Curialibus, id mihi hodie (Vir summe) homini rusticano comtigisse perspicio. Pueritiâ alicui fortasse Heroinæ, Juventutem Magnati, senectam sæpe mendicitati consecrant. Hoc in me certè convenit qui statim aˋ pueritiâ Poeticæ; juvenis cùm essem, Theologiæ, artiū quotquot sunt imperatrici, fidelissimè inserviens, jam nunc opem tuam implorare, et ad mendicorum artes confugere cogor. Nam quod in Poeticæ mercede fieri dolendum, id Theologiæ etiam competere, nunquam satis deplorandum est: Siquis inter Poetas numeratur, qui fœdissimo fabularū contextu Musas publicè stuprare, blanditiisve Asinum Aureum sugillare doctè noverit, huic laurus unâ ferè omnium voce, et præmia satis opima deferuntur. Quòd siquis Simonides adhuc superstes est, qui numinis, cœlique memor, aliquid honesti admiscere audeat, ad deos (ut ab Hierone ille) non sine risu, satis superbe remittitur. Ita sanè inter Theologos qui vitiis Patroni parasitando, in sinus tacitè illabi scitè didicit, qui novi aliquid in fide cōminisci argutèq̹ defendere, qui otiari desidiâ, luxuve torpescere, qui quidvis potiùs quàm Theologum, Pastoremve agere solet, is ferè est, quem admirantur pleriq̹, cui vectigalia Ecclesiæ aut

NOTES

conditionibus non tam iniquis (mox elocaturo) conducere, aut viliùs emere licebit, aut fortè quidem longo tandem obsequio, aut potius servitio demereri. Contra, quos fortiter vociferare, et importunè emendicari pudet, qui non schalâ ad caulas erectam, sed apertas tamen fores (Christi non immemores) expectant, ceu mendicos miniũm merces, non sine increpatione demittimus. Hinc est quòd aut nulla aut perexigua mihi spes affulgeat; cui et vox nunquã importuna, et ingenium minùs quàm hæc ætas postulat inverecundum semper fuit. Huc tamen dura et planè ferrea necessitas usq̃ impulit, ut ad te hominem facie mihi tantùm et famâ notum, semel modò aspectum, nullis officiis devinctum confugerem, stipemq̃ timidus quidem sed non omnino exspes flagitarem. Qui mihi unus succurrere potuit Pater sibi tempestivè, nobis immaturè obiit, qui (liceat quod verum est dicere) patriæ multa credidit, nihil debuit : Patriæ Patrem si appellem, nemo omniũ est, qui mihi auxilio sit, aut subsidio. Hoc igitur quicquid est muneris (ut supplicibus nunc necesse est) ad te deferre certum est ; Musas dico has (da veniam verbo) comẽndicas. Sed liceat mihi obsecro te iisdem versibus nascentis, imò fœliciter crescentis nostræ spei prudentissimum Censorem, quibus suum Poeta Censorinũ affari.

> Donarem pateras, grataque comõdis
> (Censorine) meis æra sodalibus,
> Sed non hæc mihi vis, non tibi talium
> Rei est, aut animus deliciarũ egens.

Verùm ut ille, si

> Gaudes carminibus, carmina possumus
> Donare, et pretium dicere muneri.

Neq̃ diffitendum est, quin ipsa, si accuratiùs inspexeris, parum compta, nec ut curiam decet nitentia, imo certè squalida potiùs, et pædore obsita apparuerint; quippe in luctu meorũ composita, situ diuturno sepulta, et hac tandem necessitate resuscitata, in lucem (tanquam Musarum umbræ) desuetam prodeuntia. Versus enim et malè tornati, neq̃ unquam incudi postea redditi, et multa inter (inimica Musis) negotia descripti sunt. Siquid erratum est, pro humanitate tua ignosces, versusq̃ ipsos, eorũq̃ authorem in tutelam tuam, famulitiumq̃ recipies. Sic te, spemque nostram tibi auspicatò comĩssam, fortunet deus. Sic Carolus noster (ut divinus olim ille puellus) annis, virtutibus, gratiâq̃ apud deum, hominesq̃ quotidie excrescat,

> E familia tibi maximè
> devinctâ, et devotâ,
> natu maximus.
> Phinees Fletcher.

This dedication is followed by the lines addressed in M to Henry Prince of Wales, but here slightly adapted, and now addressed to Prince Charles. The variants, apart from those of punctuation and capitalisation, are as follows: p. 280, l. 45. M] Communi...Henrico. H] Illustrissimo Principi | Walliæ Carolo. p. 281, l. 5. Cui paria...arma. H *omits this line.* l. 10. M] quæ canit ignoti. H] quæ ignoti cecinit. l. 12. M] superbia. H] fidentia. l. 13. M] Inter Apollineas laurus. H] Laurus inter Apollineas. l. 26. M] Iam faveas...labori. H] Tu modo si faveas infanti Carole Musæ. l. 28. M] Inter Apollineas. H] Phœbæas inter. On the dedications in the MSS. and the Quarto see further the Preface to this volume.

p. 102, ll. 1—4. S and M *have the title*] Pietas Jesuitica. H *has no title, but has a headline*] Locustæ. l. 6. H] Janua. S, M and H] Regia. l. 9. S and M] Consurgens. l. 11. S] sternunt. l. 14. S *omits*] è. l. 25. Q] sancti. S, M and H] sacri. ll. 27—8. *Between these lines* S, M and H *add:*

> Et nunc illa quidem gentes emensa supremas
> Imperium terris æquat, cœloq̃ profundo.

NOTES

p. 102, l. 31 and p. 103, l. 1.   S, M and H *omit these lines and substitute:*
  Nunc etiam gentes multâ olim nocte sepultas.
  p. 103, l. 3.   Q] Cocytum.   S, M and H] et manes.   l. 4.   S] Acherunta.
l. 5.   Q, S and H] Nos contrà immemori.   M] At nos læthæo.   ll. 8—9.
Q and H] laboris | Pœnitet, &.   S and M] labores | Vexant, si.   ll. 14—15.
S *omits these lines.*   l. 16.   H *begins a new paragraph here.*   l. 21.   Q]
irrumpere.   S, M and H] invadere.   l. 30.   S. M and H *omit*] heu.   l. 32.
Q, S, M and H] patitur.   If the reading of Q and the MSS. is right, Fletcher's
Latinity is unusually at fault.   The emendation is supported by p. 115, l. 37.
l. 36.   Q] penetúsque.   S and H] penitusq̨.   M] totasq̨.   l. 37.   H *begins
a new paragraph here.*
  p. 104, ll. 3, 6 and 13.   H *begins new paragraphs here.*   l. 4.   S *omits
this line.*   l. 14.   S] repetat.   H] cum mille annos mille addidit annis.
l. 22.   H *does not begin a new paragraph here.*   l. 28.   Q and H] licèt.   S and
M] quanquam.   l. 36.   Q] longo crescentes ordine turbæ.   S, M and H] longoq̨
accrescens ordine turba.   l. 39.   Q] completur.   S, M and H] complentur.
  p. 105, ll. 4—5.   *Between these lines* S, M and H *add:*
  Nomine dissimiles et versicoloribus armis.
l. 8.   Q and H] passim infert milite clades.   S and M] vastabat milite turmas.
l. 11.   Q] Composuere animos omnes.   S and H] Postquam composuere
animos.   ll. 13 and 18.   H *does not begin new paragraphs here.*   l. 15.
M] voluere.   l. 18.   Q] Non secus.   S, M and H] Et velut.   l. 19.   Q]
aut.   S, M and H] et.   l. 27.   Q and M] Palladiis nunc tecti armis.   S]
Palladis instructi telis.   H] Palladiis nunc cincti armis.   l. 35.   M] placeat
tantùm.   l. 40.   Q, M and H] Stygiis.   S] nostris.
  p. 106, l. 1.   Q and H] supplere catervas.   S and M] submittere turmas.
l. 7.   Q and H] sequentes.   S and M] trahentes.   l. 11.   Q] dederat secura,
trahénsque.   S, M and H] præstant secura, trahuntq̨.   l. 12.   Q] tene-
brísve.   S, M and H] penitusve.   l. 13.   S, M and H *have instead:*
  Obscurant, multâq̨ diem caligine miscent.
and add:
  Ut quando exiguâ variatur luce, diemq̨
  Nec totum admisit, nec totum depulit Umbra.
l. 14.   S, M and H] At postquam nebulas.   Q] Phæbus.   l. 15.   Q]
Tratareæ.   S, M and H] Tartareæq̨.   Q] immisso patuerunt.   S] patent
admisso.   M and H] patent immisso.   l. 16.   S, M and H] lucem patitur.
l. 17.   Q and H] imbelles tempus.   S and M] tempus fractas.   l. 19.   Q
and H] prodentia.   S and M] fallentia.   l. 21.   Q, M and H] Sideráque.
S] Stellasq̨.   l. 26.   Q] limina Regum.   S, M and H] Principis aulas.
l. 31.   Q] Gonciliant.   l. 37.   Q] Ac.   S, M and H] Et.   l. 38.   S,
M and H] Dum Superi totum insueti.   l. 39.   H *does not begin a new
paragraph here.*   Q] inspiret.   S, M and H] aspiret.
  p. 107, l. 6.   Q and H] fœti.   S and H] duri.   l. 8.   S and M]
Solus, conciliúmq̨ petam.   ll. 17 and 26.   H *does not begin new paragraphs
here.*   l. 22.   Q] Phæbus.   l. 24.   Q] Succedit nox umbrarum.   S, M
and H] Succedunt trepidi Manes.   l. 25.   Q] Invadit, multáque premit.   S,
M and H] Desertasq̨ premunt multa.   l. 26.   S, M and H] emissæ finibus
auræ.   ll. 31—2.   *Between these lines* H *adds:*
  Turbatove cient ingentes æquore fluctus,
  Navita dum pavitans infidum Nerea diris
  Exagitat, moriensq̨ infaustas devovet artes.

Vol. I   L   283

NOTES

S and M *also have the above lines, but omit* ll. 32—4.　l. 33.　Q] fœto.　H] multo.　l. 37.　Q] illa.　S, M and H] illi.　l. 40.　H *does not begin a new paragraph here.*

p. **108**, l. 1.　S] adjungere.　M and H] annectere.　l. 13.　Q] perenni. S, M and H] furenti.　l. 15.　M] oculis.　ll. 15—6.　S *has*:

  Nunc verbis, nunc ille oculis, nunc fronte minatur,
  Non luxu, vinóve puer, non ille paternâ.

l. 18.　Q and H] Ira.　S and M] arma.　l. 23.　Q, S and H] ferox.　M] quidem.　l. 35.　Q] Iusperata.　l. 36.　H *begins a new paragraph here.* ll. 39—40.　S, M and H *have instead*:

  Exuit, inq̄ manus monachi concessit opimi?

p. **109**, l. 2.　S, M and H *omit*] ut.　l. 7.　Q] Cœpit, & effœtam vix jam. S and H] Cœperat, effœtamq̄ senex.　ll. 8 and 15.　H *begins new paragraphs here*.　l. 17.　Q] albescunt.　S, M and H] rubescunt.　ll. 21—23.　S and H *have instead*:

  Quippe hominum cœliq̄ hostis vilemq̄ faselum
  Miscuit, et primo sementis tempore segnem
  Inspersit segetem, viciasq̄ effudit [(H) infudit] inanes.

l. 25.　Q] Mortiferasq̄.　S, M and H] Infestasq̄.　l. 29.　Q and H] Auspicia impediunt.　S and M] Imperia obsistunt.　l. 30.　Q] Latiis postquam imperium.　S and M] postquam Latiis regnum.　H] postquam Latiis imperium.　l. 33.　S and H] Mox laxis etiam.　ll. 36—9.　S and M *have instead*:

  Iamq̄ nitratorum longus succreverat ordo
  Pontificum, magicisq̄ animos et numine viles
  Obstringens, Latiâ solus dominatur in aulâ.
  Et nunc sceptra potens animis, atq̄ ense superbo

H *has*:

  Nunc etiam longus rasorum accreverat ordo
  Pontificum, magicâq̄ rudem, Stygiâq̄ popellum
  Arte ligans, Latia solus dominatur in arce.
  Et jam sceptra furens animis, et fulmina torquens.

l. 40.　Q] inanes.　S, M and H] inertes.

p. **110**, l. 1.　Q] Projiciens.　S, M and H] Rejiciens.　l. 2.　Q and H] Intonat.　S and M] Fulminat.　l. 14.　S, M and H] flammas.　l. 18. Q and H] Vulpésve.　S and M] ursǽve.　l. 19.　H] lupæ.　l. 20.　Q and H] acuta.　S and H] lippa.　l. 26.　Q] inania ludis.　S, M and H] opaca Mæandris.　l. 35.　Q and H] capit.　S and M] bibit.

p. **111**, l. 5.　S and M *omit this line.*　l. 6.　S] Imperiis umbras. ll. 7—8.　*Between these lines* S, M and H *add*:

  Hic pater accepto castus fovet ære lupanar.

l. 8.　Q] Romulidûm ille.　S, M and H] Romulidumq̄.　l. 16.　Q] Laudat, & incestis.　S and M] Heu malè nutritis.　H] Ah malè nutritis.　l. 39.　Q] sacris.　S, M and H] Reges.　l. 40.　S, M and H *omit this line.*

p. **112**, l. 1.　Q] Superi.　S, M and H] cœlum.　l. 5.　S, M and H] suspendet.　l. 11.　Q and H] ex arbore ramus.　S and M] de stirpe propago. l. 15.　H *does not begin a new paragraph here.*　l. 20.　Q and H] Vincula mox et claustra.　S and M] Jámq̄ specum, jámq̄ æra.　l. 24.　Q and H] ipsos.　S and M] magnos.　l. 34.　Q] ventos properans, Eurósq̄.　S and

NOTES

M] ventos properans, Zephyrósq̧. H] Zephiros properans, ventosq̧. l. 35.
S, M and H] *have instead:*
    Quid toties precibus, festisq̧ accersita votis.
  p. **113**, l. 1. S, M and H] gelido. ll. 15—26. S, M and H *omit this passage.* ll. 27, 31 and 38. H *does not begin new paragraphs here.* l. 29. Q, M and H] vel. S] Aut. l. 30. S and M *have:*
    Armis, et duro sternet mea mœnia ferro.
ll. 30—31. *Between these lines* S, M and H *add:*
    Et super (ah vereor, nec sit mihi credere) victor
    Disjectas super exultet crudelior arces.
l. 37. Q] Dejicere. S, M and H] Projicere. l. 39. H] Defigit. l. 40. Q, M and H] strepitus. S] murmur.

  p. **114**, l. 2. H] incendit. l. 4. Q] sonitus. S, M and H] strepitus. l. 9. Q] residit. S, M and H] sedebat. l. 10. Q] maxime divûm. S, M and H] magne deorum. l. 19. M] Quà fieri id possit. ll. 20—40 and p. **115**, ll. 1—25. S and M *omit this passage.* l. 21. Q] mœnia. H] prœlia. l. 25. Q] nutantia. H] dubitantia. l. 27. Q] labor, at. H] labor est, et. l. 28. Q] citius. H] meliùs. l. 35. Q] atque. H] ac. l. 38. Q] superandus. H] æqandus.

  p. **115**, ll. 1—9. H *omits these lines.* ll. 10 and 25. H *does not begin new paragraphs here.* l. 12. H] facilè vobis. l. 14. H] trunco. l. 26. Q and H] Non. S and M] Nec. Q and H] sero. S and M] paro. ll. 37—8. S and M *omit these lines.* H *omits* l. 38. l. 40. Q, M and H] cultróve. S] ferrove.

  p. **116**, l. 12. Q and H] inflexo. S and M] irriguo. H] Londini. l. 13. Q and H] excurrere. S and M] excedere. l. 16. Q] alte submissas. S and M] alto sublapsas. H] alto submissas. ll. 17, 21 and 27. H *does not begin new paragraphs here.*

  p. **116**, l. 19 (Ipse etiam…) to p. **119**, l. 34 (…pectora Diris). Throughout this passage S and M differ widely from Q and H. They omit many lines found in them, and arrange those common to all four in a very different order. The particulars are as follows. S and M *omit* p. **116**, ll. 19—20. *After* l. 18 *they place* p. **118**, ll. 36—40 (Ipse sacris…) to p. **119**, ll. 1—16 (…quassa triumphis). *After these lines they place* p. **116**, ll. 20—40 (Hîc lapsos …) to p. **117**, ll. 1—33 (…interiúsque recondunt), *though with some minor omissions and variations noted below, in which as a rule they agree with* H. *They omit* p. **117**, ll. 34—40 (Dúmque operi…) *to* p. **118**, ll. 1—25 (…lucémque morantem) *so that* p. **117**, l. 33 *is followed by* p. **118**, ll. 26—33 (Sed quid…Roma). *They omit* p. **118**, ll. 34—5 (Jámque…Senatu) *and* p. **119**, ll. 17—34 (Nox erat…pectora Diris).

  p. **116**, l. 27. S, M and H] Ut primùm numero. l. 35. S, M and H] Pluton. l. 40. H *begins a new paragraph here.*

  p. **117**, ll. 5, 11, 14. H *does not begin new paragraphs here.* l. 9. Q] frequenter. S, M and H] quotannis. l. 13. Q] Ingreditor. S, M and H] Ingredere ô. l. 18. Q] totóque. S, M and H] omniq̧. ll. 19—21. S, M and H *have instead:*
    Hii Stygio devota Jovi, Patriq̧ Latino
    Pectora de totâ excerpunt lectissima gente.

NOTES

ll. 22—3. S, M and H *add between these lines:*
> Ferrea tu proles? an tu magis improba mater?
> Improba tu mater, sed tu quoq̨ ferrea proles.

ll. 26—9. S, M and H *omit these lines.* l. 30. H *does not begin a new paragraph here.* ll. 31—2. S and M *have instead one line:*
> Accelerant, Orco vicini, dirius Orco.

p. 118, ll. 4—5. H *has instead:*
> Ille cado tectus nitroso contrahit artus,
> Cuncta timens, trepidè obliquis speculatus ocellis.

l. 6. H *begins a new paragraph here, and not at* l. 15. l. 20. Q] vicina Lyæo. H] vicinia Baccho. l. 24. H *begins a new paragraph here.* ll. 26—33. H *places these lines between* ll. 16 *and* 17 *on* p. 119 (*their position in* S *and* M *has been mentioned above*). l. 27. Q *and* M] repeto. S and H] memoro. l. 28. Q] repeto celebranda. S] repeto suppressa. M] memoro suppressa. H] memoro celebranda. l. 29. Q *and* H] At. S and M] Sed. S] stupescet. l. 30. Q] Superi. S, M and H] cœlū. l. 34. H *does not begin a new paragraph here.* l. 34. Q] optata. H] propinqua. l. 37. S] superbo. l. 40. Q] incedit. S and H] ingreditur. M] insequitur.

p. 119, l. 3. Q *and* H] placidóque refulgens. S] lætóq̨ effulgens. M] lætoq̨ refulgens. l. 7. Q] roseum commiscuit. S] multum permiscuit. M *and* H] multū commiscuit. l. 16. S, M and H] tremit. l. 20. Q] patulæ lustrans tot. H] latæ perlustrans. l. 23. Q] Qui Phlegetonta, omnes. H] Quiq̨ Styga, et Phlegetonta. l. 30. Q] hinc pœna, hinc præmia pectus. H] pavor trepidantia, spesq̨. l. 31. Q] Sollicitant. H] Corda trahunt. ll. 32—4. H *omits these lines.* l. 40. Q, S and M] imo. H] alto.

p. 120, l. 2. Q *and* H] nuncia clivos. S and M] nuncius ales. l. 4. Q *and* H] Aggressa ambiguo. S and M] Aggressus, dubio. ll. 9 *and* 13. H *does not begin new paragraphs here.* l. 9. Q] at. S and M] hic. H] hæc. l. 11. M *and* H] Londini. l. 12. Q *and* H] impigra turres. S and M] impiger arces. l. 13. Q *and* H] Penniger hic primùm. S and M] Hic primùm volucer. l. 14. Q, S *and* M] fulgescere. H] splendescere. ll. 19—22. H *omits these lines.* l. 19. Q] pleno. S and M] imēnso. l. 22. S and M] gazas. Q] Btitannam. S and M] Britannas. ll. 24—7. H *places these lines, in different order, and with variants, after* p. 122, l. 37. *See note ad loc.* l. 27. Q] Ille modos. S and M] Et numeros. l. 28. H *begins a new paragraph here.* l. 29. Q *and* H] attonito. S and M] egregio. l. 31. Q] Proripiens, suetis. S] Proripuit, solitisq̨. M *and* H] Proripiens, solitis. l. 38. Q] profundum. S, M and H] nefandum. l. 39. Q] bene. S, M and H] probè. Q, S and M] sit. H] est.

p. 121. ll. 3 *and* 7. H *does not begin new paragraphs here.* ll. 4—5. S and M *omit*] dum nubila...aperit. l. 7. Q] rechnas. S, M and H] fraudes. l. 8. Q, M and H] nitroso. S] parato. l. 9. *The* i *in* recondita *is turned in* Q. l. 10. Q] Crimina miranti. S, M and H] Apparent scelera. l. 14. Q] Phæbum. l. 15. H] Apparēt. l. 16. S, M and H] Apparent. l. 18. H *begins a new paragraph here, and not at* l. 23. l. 21. Q] Torvam. S, M and H] Oraq̨. l. 22. S, M and H *have instead:*
> Lumina neglectamq̨ minantem in pectora barbā.

NOTES

l. 29. Q and H] furibundus. S and M] malè-sanus. ll. 31—32. *Between these* S *and* M *add:*

  Non secus inceptam turbant cum visa quietem
  Meus umbras inter, manesq̨ vágata nigrantes
  Sanguineo horrendum somnis sævire flagello
  Tisiphonen, oculisq̨ trucem fulgere cruentis
  Aspicit, anguiferisq̨ comas horrescere vittis
  Jámq̨ fugam parat, atq̨ altos præmittere questus,
  Hærent, incertóq̨ soni cum murmure languent.

l. 32. Q] &. S, M and H] o.   l. 34. S] Servati tanta.
 p. **122**, l. 2. S] tuis.   l. 10. Q] Et lenta æstivo tardas. S] Tardáq̨ producis lento. M and H] Et tarda æstivo lentas. l. 22. Q] fluxis. S, M and H] laxis.   l. 23. H *does not begin a new paragraph here.*   l. 27. H] placidèq̨.   l. 34. S, M and H] nobis clauso.   ll. 37—8. H *between these lines places* p. **120**, ll. 24—7, *in the following order, and with variants in* ll. 26—7.

  Tu mihi, tu labro teretes trivisse cicutas,
  Tu numeros faustus calamo permittis agresti,
  Chamus ubi angustas tardo vix flumine ripas
  Complet, decrepitoq̨ Pater jam deficit amne.

l. 38. Q] pubentem. S, M and H] vestitam.   ll. 39—40 and p. **123**, ll. 1—4. S, M and H *omit these lines, and have instead:*

  Et cui pæne puer prius ipse in patre fovebas,
  In [(M) Iam] sobole agnoscas facilis vestigia cantus.

But p. **122**, l. 39, *and* p. **123**, l. 1, *with variants, and* ll. 2—4, *form in* M *and* H *part of the Dedications to Prince Henry and to Prince Charles, whence* Q *transfers them here.*

 p. **123**, l. 7. Q] Exhaustoq̨ tumens Helicone. S, M and H] Jamq̨ sui non ipsa capax.   l. 9. Q] accinet. S, M and H] audiet.   l. 10. S, M and H *omit*] FINIS.

THE LOCUSTS, OR APOLLYONISTS.

 p. **127**, l. 7. Q *has no stop after* now.   l. 13. Q *prints:*
  Lik't Them and It: forfeit their preservation.
This is unintelligible. In the suggested emendation Them and It *refer to the* Actors, l. 6, *and* their Plot, l. 10.
 p. **128**, l. 14. Q] Faln'e.
 p. **130**, l. 20. Q] hoarse-base-homes.
 p. **135**, l. 5. Q] Loc'kt.   l. 12. Q] drow'nd.
 p. **146**, l. 4. Q *has a mark of interrogation after* mine.
 p. **152**, l. 14. Q] seemes.
 p. **153**, l. 4. Q] Or'e-spread.
 p. **154**, l. 22. Q *has a comma after* sleepe.
 p. **155**, l. 11. Q *omits the asterisk referring to the second side-note.* l. 13. Q] gins. Side-notes, l. 45. Q] himsefe.
 p. **157**, l. 17. Q] tbe.
 p. **160**, l. 1. Q] ha's. Side-notes, l. 8. Q] Baranius. Side-notes, ll. 15—6. Q *has no comma between* Antoninus *and* Sum.

NOTES

p. **161**, *side-notes*, l. 23.   Q *has no stop after* 3.
p. **162**, l. 21.   Q *has a semi-colon after* Baker.
p. **167**, *side-notes*, l. 43.   Q *has no stop after* it.
p. **170**, l. 25.   Q] u *turned in* thoughts.   l. 26.   Q] ptojects.
p. **182**, l. 13.   Q] rheir.   Q] *third* n *turned in* wantoning.
p. **183**, l. 24.   Q] with.
p. **184**, *side-notes*, ll. 1 and 3.   Q *omits stops after* 11 *and* 20.
p. **185**, *side-notes*, ll. 1 and 3.   Q *omits stops after* 12 *and* 16.

SICELIDES.

Q = Quarto edition, 1631.
B = Manuscript in Birch collection, British Museum Additional MSS., 4453.
R = Manuscript in Rawlinson Poetical MSS., 214.

The text is that of Q, though for reasons stated in the Preface it has been necessary to emend it considerably from B and R. Otherwise the same methods have been employed as in the case of the other pieces contained in this volume. Square brackets have not, however, been inserted in cases of (1) *the rectification of misspelt names, full or abbreviated, of dramatis personæ,* (2) *the substitution of an initial capital for a small letter, of Italics for Roman type, or vice versâ in either case.* Every such change, however, has been recorded in the notes. Full stops have been introduced silently after the abbreviated names prefixed to the speeches, and at the end of speeches and of stage-directions.

The variants quoted from the MSS. in the names of dramatis personæ, in stage-directions, in the Prologue, Epilogue, Choruses, and incidental verses are printed in italics as in the case of the corresponding passages in the text.

Where Q and B, or Q and R agree, the spelling used in the variant is that of Q; where B and R agree, the spelling is that of B. Where the reading of B or R has been adopted in the text, it is placed first in the notes.

p. **187**.   R and B *have no title-page.*

p. **189**, *above the list of characters* B *has the following title:* Sicelides: a Piscatorie made by Phinees | Fletcher and acted in Kings Colledge in | Cambridge. It *omits* the heading *Dramatis Personæ.*   l. 2. Q] *Gaucilla.* l. 4. B] *Glaucus and Circe.* Q] *Glaucus.* After the list of characters B *adds, in a larger and perhaps later hand*] *Scene Sicely* 2 *houres.*   ll. 1—25. R *has instead:*

Sicelides

Dramatis psonæ.
Prologus.
Dicæus neptunes Priest.
Nonnius a priest.
Tyrinthius an old man Fath[r] to *Perindus* & *Olinda.*   Grophus [*Tyrinthius* his servant, *added later in different ink*].
Perindus.
Olinda.
Thalander cald *Atyches* sonne to *Glaucus* & *Circes* enamoured on *Olinda.*
Glaucilla a nimph sister to *Thalander.*
Alcippus friend to *Thalander.*
Cosma a wanton nimph.
Conchylio Cosma's page.

288

NOTES

Pas a suitor of *Cosmaes*.
Fredecaldo an old man doting on *Cosma*.
Rimbombo a Cyclops enamoured on *Cosma*
   Scrocca }
   Cancrone } 2 fishermen
Two priests muti
Two nimphs mutæ
Cuma Perindus his page mutus
A Chorus of { fishers
          { singers
                        Chorus
Sequentium est mentio tantum
Glaucus a seagod
Circes
Scilla a scornfull nimph
Mago an Enchanter
Molorcha a seamonster sent by *neptune*

    p. **190**, l. 1. R *omits*] CHAMUS   l. 3. R] *what*. Q and B] *that*. l. 6. Q and B] *assures...agree*. R] *heere tells thee, none will once denye*. l. 7. Q and B] *their*. R] *your*. l. 8. B and R] *Poets*. Q] *Poet*. l. 13. Q and B] *as*. R] *like*. Q] *they'r*. R] *the' are*. l. 15. Q and B] *these*. R] *their, added above the line in different ink*.

    p. **191**, l. 1. B and R *omit*] *SICELIDES*. l. 3. R *adds* mutus *after* CUMA. l. 5. B *omits*] spoyles, and. l. 7. R] comes returne. Q and B] returnes, returne. l. 9. Q and B] While. R] When. Q] n *turned in* and. l. 11. R] y^t drye, now this moist. l. 12. Q and B] this. R] my. l. 15. R] n'ere. l. 16. Q] n *turned in* And. l. 19. R] lawe. l. 21. Q and B] Waves. R] Rocks. l. 26. Q and B] And. R] A. l. 27. Q] plesaure. B] pleasure. R] Solace.

    p. **192**, l. 2. B] with me doth more. Q] with me doth most. R] doth more wth me. l. 3. R] mortalize. l. 6. B] tell; s *added later*. l. 8. Q and B *wrongly give this line to Armillus*; R *is right*. B] Walke I along. Q] Walke along. R] Walke I alone along. l. 11. R] tides I find flit. l. 13. Q and B] or fals all. R] & falls. l. 14. Q and B] or. R] &. l. 15. B and R] ranging. Q] raging. l. 16. B] thee. Q] the. R] thy. l. 17. B and R] Bad. Q] Bud. R] was. l. 18. R] what. Q and R] the. B] thee. l. 19. Q and B] bereav'st. R] berad'st. l. 20. Q] deceivd'st. B] deceavsts; d *added later between* v *and* s. l. 21. B] Therefore although the. Q] Therefore although. R] And therefore though th'. l. 26. R] decree...was. l. 27. R] flight. l. 28. Q and B] Is th'. R] Its y^e. Q and B] that makes that. R] wch that. l. 29. R] Zealous. l. 30. B and R] enmitie. Q] emnity. l. 31. R] tempests. l. 32. Q and B] storme. R] winde. l. 33. R] where. l. 34. R] comes where tis. l. 35. B and R] they. Q] thee. l. 37. Q and B] damped. R] daunted. l. 40. B] with. Q] which. R *is clipped at the foot of the page, and the word is not clear*. B and R] welcome. Q] weleome. R] to.

    p. **193**, ll. 2—5. B *omits*] *Enter, and has* Glaucilla *and* Cosma. R *has instead* Dicæus 2 *other preists*. Olinda *led by two Nymphs*. Glaucilla *and* Cosma. *A chorus of fishers singing*. l. 7. Q and B] *thy countries*. R] *the fishers*. l. 8. Q and B] *seas and rockes*. R] *winds & seas*. l. 10. R] *or*. l. 11. B and R] *these teares thy latest due*. Q] *these tnares they lacest due*. l. 17. R] knowest. l. 19. R *omits*] Olinda. l. 20. Q

289

NOTES

and B] thinke. R] guesse. l. 21. Q] but. l. 22. Q and B] Yeilds. R] Pays. Q *has full stop after* misery. ll. 23—4. *So in* B and R. Q *prints as one line.* l. 23. R] smilest. l. 26. Q] *Gladucilla.* l. 27. R] heavens. l. 28. R] So be...in the. l. 31. R] spend y^t ...wch. l. 32. R] made. ll. 33—4. Q and B *have* Peace...wouldst | Have...reason. R *has one line.*

p. **194**, l. 3. R] embraces. l. 4. R] Nor seest, I see & feele more. l. 5. B] springs. Q *has a semi-colon after* heart. Q and B] then. R] as. R] were now. l. 6. R] wch. R *omits*] me. l. 8. Q and B] heart. R] breast. l. 10. R] narrow a hell. l. 11. Q] *Decæ.* Q *has no stop after* on. l. 13. Q] *Olen. Decæus.* R *omits*] brest. l. 15. Q *has no stop after* rufam. R *omits the line.* l. 17. B and R *omit*] *Enter.* R] *Armillus, Atyches, Perindus.* l. 18. R] this troop. R *omits*] here. l. 26. Q *has no stop after*] *Perindus.* l. 27. Q *has a comma after* passion. l. 32. Q *has a full stop after* depriving. R] all labour priving. l. 33. Q and B] sence. R] feare. Q *has a colon after* overgrieving. l. 36. R] wold faine.

p. **195**, l. 1. B] While. R] Whilest. Q and B] chides. R] checks. R] teare. Q and B] feare. l. 3. R] wch. Q and B] sunnes. R] seas. l. 5. B and R] power. Q] powers. l. 6. Q and B] soule. R] thoughts. l. 8. R *omits this line.* l. 10. R] A my. l. 11. Q *has a comma after* unwelcome. l. 12. Q and B] approach. R] retourne. l. 14. B and R] *Olinda* faire. Q] fayre *Olinda.* l. 18. Q] yes. R] tell the sume. l. 19. Q and B] his. R] her. l. 20. R] rights. l. 21. B] there. Q and R] their. l. 22. B] every flower blowes. Q] every flowers blowe. R] each flower blows. l. 27. Q and B] fragrant. R] frutefull. l. 28. Q] pa'vd. l. 31. R *omits*] little. R] it fully seemes. l. 32. Q] where. l. 35. B and R] one. Q] our. l. 36. R] fruite. l. 37. Q] Mymphs. l. 39. R] Whilest. Q] Nago. l. 40. B] those.

p. **196**, l. 1. B and R] starlike. Q] statelike. l. 6. Q and B] is. R] seemes. Q and B] they chance. R] he canchd. l. 8. Q and B] that. R] the. Q] Herperian. l. 9. R] applies. l. 10. Q and B] the longing. R] of longing. l. 12. B] fine. Q] fitte. R] smooth. Q and B] oaths. R] baths. l. 13. B] works her mind. Q] words hee mind. R] work'd her minde. B and R] ah. Q] ha. l. 14. B] fain'ed. Q] faind. R] fayned. Q *has a comma after* dressing. l. 15. R] the. Q *has no stop after* fruit. l. 19. R] bare. l. 20. R] pay. Q *has no stop after* deserving. l. 21. R] who that. Q *has a comma after*] *Neptune, and a full stop after* tree. l. 22. R] hand. R] *Molorcha.* l. 23. R] *Molorcha.* l. 26. R] Who wold'st pittie y^t. Q *has a full stop after* Thalander. l. 27. R] You. Q *has no stop after* seas. l. 28. Q and B] thy. R] y^t. l. 29. R] But whether. Q] And whither. B] And whether. Q *has a full stop after* going. l. 31. Q and B] And. R] A. l. 34. Q] is. l. 35. Q] impossibie. l. 36. R] certaine death. Q and B] certain. Q *has no stop before* adst. l. 37. B] 'fore. Q and R] for. l. 38. Q *has a full stop after* her.

p. **197**, l. 1. Q and B] die. R] live. R] have her. l. 3. Q] *Atyoh.* l. 4. Q] *Atychcs.* l. 5. R] is. Q and B] was. l. 8. Q] Prest. l. 9. Q and B] the. R] to. l. 10. R] must needs. Q *has no stop after* brother. l. 11. R] ne're. R] thee. Q and B] mee. l. 13. R] shold'st. l. 14. R *adds* Ah my Perindus *before* Can Seas &c. Q *has no stop after* stand. l. 17. B and R] joy. Q] joyes. l. 19. R] I gladly. l. 20. R *omits*]

290

NOTES

Atyches.   l. 21.   Q and B] spirit.   R] fisher.   l. 24.   B and R *omit*] *Enter*, and R *has*] *Armillus, Perindus.*   l. 26.   R] this 'o^r.   l. 29.   R] see.   l. 31.   Q *has no stop after* humanity.   R] desire.   l. 34.   B and R] this perfect.   Q] this.   Q *has no stop after* story.   l. 35.   Q] east.

p. **198**, l. 2.   Q and B] such a tale.   R] such Cause.   l. 4.   R] cloath'd in constancie.   Q and B] in inconstancy.   ll. 5—7.   *In Q these lines are printed as follows:*
> Who hath not heard of *Glaucus* love? haplesse
> Whilst fairest *Scylla* baths him, love inspires
> At once herself she cooles and him she fires.

l. 5.   Q and B] haples love.   l. 6.   R] While beauteous.   R] love him. l. 7.   R] shee flames her selfe.   ll. 8—9.   Q *has no stop after* him, *in either of these lines.*   l. 10.   R] seas.   Q and B] eyes.   R] disdaining.   l. 11. R] flaming.   l. 13.   R] beauties.   l. 14.   R] So stands.   R] zealous. l. 20.   R] Circe the zealous.   Q *has no stop after* now.   l. 21.   Q *omits*] *Per.*   Q and B] his.   R] the.   l. 22.   Q *has no stop after* him.   l. 23. Q and B] reapt.   R] wrapt.   l. 31.   Q *has a comma after* compare. ll. 36—7.   R *omits these lines*.   l. 38.   Q and B] But.   R] Oh.   B and R] sparkles.   Q] sparkle.

p. **199**, l. 4.   Q and B] So on us.   R] Soone as.   l. 8.   Q and B] with just.   R] wthout.   l. 9.   Q and B] an.   R] a.   Q and B] like.   R] little. l. 11.   Q and B] ah.   R] a.   l. 12.   Q] Cea'st.   Q and B] this.   R] 't is. Q and B] hold.   R] wold.   l. 15.   R] Spite of his spite her love his hate exceld, *altered later to same reading as in* Q and R.   l. 16.   R] At last. l. 18.   Q and B] could.   R] wold.   l. 20.   Q *has a comma after*] *Mago*. l. 21.   R] straunge.   Q and B] strang.   l. 22.   R] of a.   ll. 23—5.   Q *has no stops after* pitch *and* lead.   l. 24.   R] eyne.   l. 25.   Q and B] lead. R] dead.   l. 27.   R] leave.   Q and B] have.   Q and B] hell.   B] cell. l. 28.   R] woes her.   l. 29.   R] flatters.   l. 30.   Q and B] I'st.   Q *has a full stop after* possible.   l. 31.   Q *has no stop after* speake.   Q and B] should.   R] might.   l. 32.   R] the kind.   l. 33.   R] Oh who.   R] womans minde.   l. 34.   B] to th'.   Q] to' th'.   R] to the.   R] the wrong. l. 35.   R] fit his smoothing.   l. 37.   Q and B] sole.   R] whole.   l. 38. B and R] imparted.   Q] inparted.   ll. 39—40.   Q *has no stops after* de-parted *and* ranger.   l. 40.   Q and B] in.   R] our.

p. **200**, l. 3.   R] spies *and omits* him.   l. 6.   R] nothing now of him. l. 7.   B and R] wch wth.   Q] with which.   l. 9.   Q *has no stop after* affords. l. 10.   R *omits*] *Exeunt*.   l. 14.   R] *Then pleasing sleepe &* quiet.   l. 15. R] *When neither*.   l. 16.   B and R] *doe*.   Q] *doth*.   l. 18.   R] *nor age*. l. 19.   Q] *prey, no.*   B] *pray, nor.*   R] *prayers, nor.*   l. 22.   Q] *beautous*. l. 23.   R *omits*] *the before just.*   l. 26.   R] *grave.*   l. 27.   R] *Noble... slave.*   l. 28.   R] *vertuous.*   l. 31.   Q and B] *art.*   R] *as.*   l. 32. R] *Sweet doth.*   Q *has a full stop after*] *tart.*   l. 33.   R] *pleasur's sharpe.* l. 34.   R] *Death thought in death.*   l. 36.   R] *hapie are, & know.*   Q *has no stop after*] *teares.*   l. 37.   B and R *omit*] *Exit.*   l. 38.   R *omits*] *Finis Actus Primi.*

p. **201**, l. 2.   R *omits*] *Enter.*   l. 5.   R *omits*] waves.   Q *has a comma after* hell.   ll. 6—7.   R *omits these lines.*   l. 6.   Q *has no stops after* fast *and* toyle.   l. 8.   Q and B] found no.   R] sought some.   l. 9.   R] your dabling.   l. 10.   Q and B] while.   R] there.   Q] fishers.   B and R] servants.   R] on seas &.   l. 11.   R] Send.   l. 12.   Q *has a comma after* No.   Q] arrive's.   l. 13.   R] Shee is.   R] these cliffes.   Q *puts the comma*

291

NOTES

after cliffs *instead of* rockes. l. 14. R] Mycena. l. 15. Q *has a comma after* shores. ll. 16—7. Q *has no stop after* woman *in either line.* l. 17. R] loves. l. 18. R] One for his spritefull witts, ye third for. l. 19. Q and B] Him cause. R] Another because. R *omits*] his. Q *has no stop after* blacknesse. l. 20. R] but more. l. 21. R] b˙b˙bable. l. 22. R] fat Cod. l. 23. B] sop. Q] sow. R] Fop. Q *has no stop after* her. l. 25. R] a other. Q *has no stop after* another. l. 27. R] ah know. Q and B] cue. R] name, *added in different ink.* l. 28. B *has*] *Enter Pas after* l. 26. l. 29. R] Alas poore foole, hee's all *malum Collū.* ll. 30—3. Q *has no stops at the end of these lines.* l. 31. R *omits*] He *and* all. l. 32. R *omits*] that. l. 34. B and R] come, come. Q] come. Q *has no stop after the first* begin.

p. 202, l. 2. Q *has no stop after*] *Pas.* l. 3. B] sea. Q and R] seas. l. 5. B] winds. Q *has no stop after the second* I. l. 5. R] wth netts. l. 6. Q and B] in. R] my. l. 7. Q *has a comma after* tie. l. 13. R] changes in a hower doth proove. l. 14. R] & most. l. 17. R] Fond hope that Anchors in. l. 18. R] And hart thus fir'd in love. l. 19. R] Fond hope fond love, fond thoughts. l. 20. R] winds. l. 22. R] *Exit ad Rupem.* l. 23. Q *has a comma after the first* asse. l. 24. R] Fond thought, fond hart, fond love. l. 27. R *omits*] still. R] ner'e. l. 28. Q *has no stop after* one. l. 32. R] a old. Q *has no stop after* foure-score. l. 33. B and R] left some. Q] left him some. ll. 43—5. *So divided in* B *and* R. Q *prints* Rack't up....flame | And...dwarfes. l. 34. Q and B] cold. R] Coale. l. 35. R] Dwarfe. l. 36. Q and B] though neere. R] ne're. Q *has no stops after* who *and* boyes.

p. 203, ll. 1—5. Q *has no stops after* dancing, sporting, eye, lye, name. l. 1. B] youths. Q and R] youth. l. 3. R] upon his head. B] shours in. Q] showes in. R] showres on. l. 4. R] winters...summers. l. 6. B and R] come. Q] comes. Q] i'st. l. 9. Q] *Conhilio,* with no stop before the name. l. 10. B and R] If. Q] *I,* followed by a comma. Q *has no stop after* white *and* cheeke. l. 12. B and R] oft. Q] of. Q *has no stop after* sleeke. l. 13. B] dares. Q *has a full stop after* it. ll. 14—5. Q *has no stops after* folly, rage, *and* age. l. 16. Q *has no stop after* love. l. 17. Q *has no stop after* lovers. l. 18. R] wavering. Q] waning. R] waving, *altered later to*] wavering. Q *has no stop after*] prove. l. 19. Q] *youth.* ll. 20—1. Q *prints these in Roman type, but they are part of Fredocaldo's "disticke."* l. 21. B] sunnes renew, *altered later to*] sunne renews. R] sunne renews my light. l. 26. R] morning. l. 28. R] My nimble limbs. Q and B] My limbs. l. 30. R] taken. l. 31. B] Rufi. R] Runne. Q *has no stop after* channels. l. 32. Q] Pi'sh. B] P'sh. R] Tush.

p. 204, ll. 1—4. Q *has no stops at the end of these lines.* l. 4. R] very prittie. Q and B] prettie. ll. 4—5. *Stage-direction.* Q and B] *throws downe.* R] *takes away.* l. 5. R *omits*] and *and* ho. Q *has a full stop after* and. ll. 6—8. Q *has no stops after* boy, he, eyes, boy. l. 7. B] Ha ha ha...Ha, hah. R *omits the second* hah, ha, he. l. 8. B] A naughtie. l. 10. B] hah, ha, ha. R *omits*] hah, ha, he. l. 11. *Stage-direction.* R *has*] *Conchylio snatches his verses.* l. 12. R *omits*] A...verse. Q *has no stop after* it. ll. 13—4. Q *prints as one line.* B] If...limbs | come on. R] If...white | Nay...on. l. 13. Q *has a full stop after* and. R *omits*] and. l. 14. R] you will. R] your nimble limbs. Q and B] your limbs. (Cf. p. 202, l. 28.) l. 16. R *omits*] how *and* oh. ll. 17—21. Q

292

NOTES

has no stops at the end of these lines. l. 17. R] After a warme. l. 20.
B and R] My M^rs art. Q] my art. R] sparke. l. 21. Q] *Pises.* B]
Pesces, altered later to] *Pisces.* R] *Piscis.* l. 23. B] *Exit Conchylio.* l. 25.
B and R *omit*] *Enter.* Q] *Allcippus, with no stop before it.* l. 26. R *omits
first* that. B] sunke i'th. R] suncke ith. l. 29. R] Liv'd. Q and B] Live.
l. 30. R] feare. Q and B] fire. l. 33. R] Are felted spoke. B and R]
curelesse. Q] carelesse. l. 34. Q] *Alcipyus.* l. 36. R] in thy.

    p. 205, l. 1. R] my say. l. 6. Q] Is'st; *no stop after* good. l. 9.
B] th' Ecco. ll. 11, 14, 17, 24, 37 and 39. Q *has no stops at the end of these
lines.* l. 12. B and R] preist. l. 17. Q] sayd. B] sedde. R] se'd.
l. 18. R] When thus aloude proclaime. l. 22. R] Straightway the. l. 24.
R] some frees'd, some sreek'd. l. 26. Q and R] his. B] is. Q] shrow'd.
l. 28. R *omits*] the. l. 29. Q and B] panting. R] trembling. l. 30.
B] blest. l. 31. R] him. l. 32. R] cold tell. l. 34. R] who.
l. 36. Q and B] in. R] wch. l. 37. R] to a. l. 38. B] in 'hs. R]
in. l. 39. Q and B] to. R] the.

    p. 206, l. 1. R] No threate no prayer, no plaint. R] hears. Q and B]
feares. ll. 3, 5, 10—2, 14. Q *has no stops at the end of these lines.*
ll. 6—7. R *places these lines after* l. 18. l. 6. R] as though the seas. l. 8.
R] and the. l. 11. R] flight. ll. 13—4. R *omits these lines.* l. 16.
R] at 'his. Q *has a full stop after* arrives. l. 17. R] And there in h's.
ll. 18—9, 21—2 and 24. Q *has no stops at the end of these lines.* l. 22. R]
Th' other. Q] i'th. l. 23. Q and B] he. R] shee. l. 24. B] tother.
Q] t'ther. R] th' other. l. 26. Q and B] to. R] wch. Q *has no stop after*
pawes. l. 29. R] Then *Perindus...that love.* ll. 32, 36, 38 and 40. Q
has no stops at the end of these lines. l. 32. R] conquered hart. Q and B]
heart, *but in* B manlike *has been added later above the line before* heart. l. 33.
B] As hadst thou how, *but* As *has been changed to* Ah *and* seene *inserted later.*
l. 35. Q and B] time. R] beene. l. 36. R] faine wold. l. 37. R] hadst
thou seene when. Q] hast thou seene which. B] had'st thou seene w^ch,
altered later to whĕ. l. 38. R] Now love. Q and B] love forgot. R] had
forgot. l. 39. Q and B] How th' eye. R] Now they. Q and B] did.
R] durst. l. 40. R *omits*] up.

    p. 207, l. 1. Q and B] How. R] Now. R] a fight bold. l. 3. Q and
B] thou wouldst. R] then wold. l. 4. R] There never. l. 7. Q and B]
home the. R] come their. l. 8. R] this conquest. ll. 10—2. R *has
instead*] *Dicæus. Thalander. Olinda. Glaucilla. Cosma. Nomichus. & a
chorus of singers.* l. 11. Q *has no stop after*] *Olinda.* ll. 13—20. R
omits these lines. ll. 15, 17. Q *has no stops at the end of these lines.* l. 21.
Q and B] these armes. R] my hands. l. 26. R *omits*] *Exeunt omnes.*
l. 28. R *has instead*] *Scrocca. Cancrone from fishing wth their boats.* l. 29.
R] harbord. B and R] hold. Q] hol, *and has no stop after* wave. l. 30. R]
we 're. R] uppon a. l. 31. Q *has no stop after*] *Cancrone.* l. 32. R
has instead] *he leaps forth.*

    p. 208, ll. 1—2. R *has*] By your leave, I am sure I swell it, my nose kist
it. l. 3. R] on the. R] & there. ll. 4—7. Q and B] had it...sows-
eare. R] 'At my lot beene to have bine M^r at sea as you are | We had ne're
taken such a voiage | In such a cockboate, in such a fly-boate. l. 8. R]
Come leave her. l. 9. B] shee-boat. R] shee boate. Q] shee boote.
R] I warrant you. ll. 11—5. R *omits these lines.* l. 11. Q *has no stop
after* Sir. Q] on. B] upon. ll. 14—5. Q *has no stops after* rocks sir
and place. l. 16. Q *prints* drinks *in Roman type, and has a full stop*

293

NOTES

after laving.   R *has*] (*Scrocca drinks*) *after* is...laving.   l. 17.   R] Ah this is something better then.   ll. 18—20. R *omits*] seest...in, *and transfers but O those Scyllaes...companie, with variants given below, to after* l. 23. l. 18. Q *has a comma after* in.   l. 19. Q *has no stop after* bandogs. B] how our boate.   Q] our boate.   ll. 20—1.   R *omits*] faith...tub. l. 21.   Q and B] now.   R] come.   Q *has a full stop after*] *Scrocca*. l. 22.   R] ye rest of o^r liquor.   Q] *Sirrah* halfe to this blew-beard. B] Sirrah, halfe this to blew-beard.   R] heer's | Halfe this to.   *The passage seems corrupt in all the versions, and no entirely satisfactory text can be formed from them.*   l. 23.   R] not a drope of it.   ll. 24—5. Q *prints* (puff puff), *but it is parallel to* (bough wough) *in* l. 19. Q *has no stop after* (puff puff).   ll. 24—8.   R *has instead*] *Scr.* And wth all remember *Scyllaes* bandogs, baw, waw, baw. | O how o^r boat bepist her selfe for feare.   *Can.* And I & thou for Companie, heer's to them (*hee drinks. Scr.* You hold your poope to high *Cancrone. Can.* Thou alwaies speakest in my cast. (*he drinks againe.* It beginns to bee a little warmer my witt yeers on.   l. 28.   B and R] witt.   Q] wirt.   l. 30.   Q] *Concrone's*.   R] *is safe*. ll. 32—p. **209**, l. 8.   R *has*] *Can.* Why I prithe *Scrocca*, is it such a straunge thing | For a water man now a days to be poet.   *Scr.* But o *Cancrone* I wonder of all the works y^t ever | thou did'st, thou never thoughest uppon an Epitaph | For thy Grandsire, wch was eaten up by ye Cyclops.   *Can.* Prithee *Scrocca* if thou lovest mee, doe not ming my | Grandsire. Oh those hungry shiteslops y^t eate him up | Crust & crum & killed him too, & that wch greives mee | most of all, hee ne're sent me word who bit of his head. | Yet one drauft more & have at him. | *Scr.* Nay if one draught will doe it, hee shall not want. *Can.* I have it.   *Hee drinks againe.*

       Heere lies Cancrones grandsire, who sance boate,
       Sance seas, sance winds, sailed downe the Cyclops throate.

l. 34.   Q] *Sco.*

    p. **209**, l. 7.   Q] *Here: Full stop after*] boate.   l. 8.   Q] *Sands winde.*   l. 10.   B] Why will grave...o' th'.   R] what willt thou grave a...uppon the.   Q *prints* I'me...yonder *as a separate line.*   R] I am...lies there.   l. 11.   R] all the.   l. 13] Well come lets home. Q and B] your.   R] thy.   l. 14.   R *omits*] at...fire.   Q *has a full stop after* fire. ll. 15—6.   R *omits these lines.*   l. 17.   Q and B] *rockes.*   R] *winds.* Q and B] *I thinke yee'l.*   R] y^w well can.   l. 18.   Q] That.   B *adds after this line*] *Exeunt.*   l. 21.   R *repeats*] Ha, ha, he *three times as a separate line.*   Q] i'st possible?   l. 22.   Q *has a comma after* together.   l. 24. Q and B] snowie.   R] ivorie.   Q and B] blew riveld.   R] bewriv'led. ll. 25—7.   Q *has no stops after* snow, unstrung, bound *and* drie.

    p. **210**, l. 2.   R *omits this line.*   ll. 3—17. Q *prints these lines of prose in doggerel verse form, as follows:* What...little | I'le...catch | A Cods-head... them | Did...sir | Me...soone | I...Peloro | When...bandogs | that...marke | But...side | Right...right | And turned...North | By South | Wellbould woodcocke | without a bias | Come...office | I'le...side | Looke...rocke.   l. 4.   R *omits*] I.   ll. 4—5.   R *omits*] Ile...them.   l. 6.   Q] *Sor.* R] tell thee.   Q *has note of interrogation after* wrong *and full stop after* sir.   B and R *omit*] sir.   l. 8.   Q] *Sor.*   R] I prithe unto thee.   l. 9.   Q *has full stop after* bandogs.   l. 10.   Q and B] That did belong.   R] Why that longed.   l. 11. B] o' th' one.   Q] o' th' on.   R] on the on.   l. 12.   Q *has commas after* the left *and* it left.   R *omits*] it.   R] & then turnd.   l. 13.   R] nor: nor by

NOTES

south.   l. 15.   R *omits*] about you.   R] hold you.   ll. 16—7.   Q and B] this way.   R] heere.   l. 17.   R] I prithee unto thee.   Q *has a full stop after* rocke.   l. 18.   Q *has no stop after* well.   R] tis.   ll. 21—2.   B] are come...side.   Q] come...side.   R] are push'd the cleane contrary way.   l. 23.   R] Looke throuh my.   l. 24.   Q and B] unlac't.   R] fond out. *After* knavery R *adds* I have præoccupied her, *the last word being in different ink.*   l. 25.   B] Circe is.   Q] Circes is.   R] Circes.   l. 26.   Q *has no stop after* I.   R] shee tralac'd a good Grandsire.   l. 28.   R *adds before* She *these words:* Something it was made thee looke so licke a sandie pig: and I am sure.   Q and B] white wand, has.   R] to & fro hath.   l. 29.   R] o' th' eare.   R] on the other.   Q] one the other.   B] on th' other.   l. 31.   B and R] Circe.   Q] Circes.   ll. 32—3.   R *omits*] and wee...way.   l. 33. Q and B] leapt.   R] got.   l. 34.   R *has no stop after* how, *and adds* have wee escaped ye sea monster.   R *omits*] he...cries.

p. 211, l. 2.   Q] cancrone.   l. 3.   Q] *Sirocca.*   R] hee hath.   l. 5.   B and R *omit*] from fishing.   l. 6.   R] hath slaine.   l. 7.   R *omits*] Ah *Scrocca.* Q] *Sirocca.*   O'rke.   l. 8.   R] will let such a wicked worme dwell.   R *omits*] a *after* am.   l. 9.   R] name of him.   B and R *omit*] to mee.   Q *has a comma after* then.   l. 11.   Q] *Ser.*   l. 12.   R] Then let mee stricke.   Q *has no stop after* cold.   l. 13.   R] What bold hardie fisher.   l. 14.   R *omits*] and.   Q and B] and more.   R] before.   Q *has a full stop after* more.   l. 15.   B *has originally*] doe not the Orke, *but* tel *has been added later between* not *and* the.   R *has*] doe tell ye orcke, *with* not *added between* tell *and* y^e *in different ink.*   Q] doe not the *Norke.*   l. 16.   Q] *Ser.*   R] did not eate.   Q and B] did eate, *but in* B not *has been added later.*   l. 17.   Q] *Can.; no stop after* chance.   ll. 18—9. R] The best y^t I can advise is to retourne about ye Cape before.   l. 19. Q] O ke.   l. 20.   Q *puts the bracket after* them, *and has no comma.*   l. 23. Q *has a comma after* labour.   l. 24.   Q] Will ; *no stop after* hand.   ll. 25 and 28.   Q *has full stops after* man *and* mee.   l. 31.   R] *Glaucus es.*   l. 32. R] give.   l. 33.   R] this.   Q *has no stop after* thus.   l. 34.   R] When y^w famous fishers fatall fall uppon ye lande.   l. 35.   R] sea.   Q *has no stops after* seas *and* land.   ll. 36—7.   Q and B *have*] I...measure, | I...elbowes. l. 38.   Q *has no stop after* Saile.   l. 39.   Q *has no stop after* office.   R] By land you must goe.   l. 40.   Q *has no stop after* What, *and has a full stop after* expound.   R] expound it.

p. 212, l. 1.   R] boats.   R] by shoare.   l. 2.   Q *has a comma after* made. B] your S^r.   ll. 2—3.   R] S^r I understand you, but I doe not know your meaning.   l. 4.   B] lift it at.   R] Pull you at ye nose of the boate, i'le pull. l. 6.   R] *Hoh, roh, horcha, corca, fuga Ponto.   Bracketed stage-direction,* ll. 4 and 7.   B] *boate.*   Q] *beates.*   Q] *creept.*   B] *creepe.*   R *omits the stage-direction.*   l. 7.   Q *has no stops after* comes, boate, over.   ll. 8—11. Q *prints these lines in doggerel form as follows:* Ile helpe | Retire...on | These... on | 'Tis...begin | To...scourg.   B and R *have them in prose form.*   l. 8.   Q *has a semi-colon after* helpe.   Q and B] thou.   R] you.   R *omits*] creepe on. Q *places the second bracket after the full stop.*   Q *has no stop after* on on. ll. 9—10.   R *omits*] are...soules.   l. 11.   Q *has no stop after* spent.   l. 11. R] to smell, retire I say thou.   l. 12.   Q and B] *Retire.*   R] *away retire.* l. 14.   R *omits*] Hah, ha, he.   R] fouchs.   l. 15.   Q *has no stop after* me. l. 19.   B and R] ile meete with.   Q] ile with.   R *omits*] yet once.   l. 20. R *omits*] *Exit.*   l. 22.   Q] *Fishers swaine.*   B] *fishers swaines.*   R] *fisher swaine.* l. 23.   R] *you.*   Q *has no stop after*] happines.   l. 24.   R] *sports tast.*   l. 25. R] *your hope.*   Q *has no stop after*] *relishes.*   l. 26.   R] *nets.*   l. 29.   Q *has no stop after*] *play.*   l. 30.   R *adds in different ink*] golden.   Q *has no stop*

295

NOTES

after] shore. l. 31. R] *And thus.* Q *has no stop after*] day. l. 33. R] *& ease.*

p. 213, l. 2. Q and B] *Rap't my.* R] *Cherrish y^r.* Q *has no stop after*] eyes. l. 3. R] *in the sacred.* ll. 4—5. Q *has no stops at the end of these lines.* l. 5. Q and B] *birth.* R] *mirth.* l. 6. R] *of a.* l. 9. Q and B] *run.* R] *Come.* l. 10. R] *glides.* ll. 10—1. Q *has no stops at the end of these lines.* l. 11. R] *o^r brother.* l. 12. R] *& us.* l. 13. R] *If I.* R *omits*] natures, *leaving a blank where the word should occur.* ll. 13—5. Q *has no stops at the end of these lines.* l. 15. Q] *those.* B and R] *these.* B and R] *arts.* Q] *nets.* l. 17. B and R] *low.* Q] *love.* Q and B] *safely.* R] *closely.* l. 18. R] *fortunes.* l. 19. R] *careles.* ll. 19—21. Q *has no stops at the end of these lines.* l. 21. B] *A boat.* Q] *About.* R] *My boate.* l. 23. R] *The streame.* ll. 23—5. Q *has no stops at the end of these lines.* l. 25. Q and B] *skie.* R] *cry.* l. 28. R *omits*] *Enter, and has*] Perindus. Glaucilla. l. 29. Q] *Attyches.* l. 30. R] Methings some power. l. 32. R] through the. l. 33. R] but see it. B] *Glaucilla enters.*

p. 214, l. 1. R] my joy, my hate. l. 2. B and R] whether. l. 4. R] flee me. l. 5. Q *has a comma after* spoyle. l. 6. R] Whom thou hast. Q and B] and. R] all. l. 7. R] When y^w. R] oaths, & prayers. l. 10. R] Who. ll. 10—1. Q *has no stops after* importunity *and* meanes, *and has a comma after* persever. *The interpretation is difficult, and there may be some corruption in* l. 11. l. 12. R] loving lov'd. l. 14. R] am not I. l. 16. B] heaven. l. 19. Q and B] purest. R] surest. l. 20. Q and B] the same. R] shee. l. 21—2. R *has instead one line:* But thou art...wast. l. 25. R *omits*] by. l. 26. Q and B] thus. R] now. l. 27. R] swearst. l. 29. R *omits*] a. R] hath. l. 34. R *omits*] *lah.* l. 35. B] Aye me. R] Ai me. l. 36. R] Ai me more. Q and B] Ah me most. l. 37. R] set thou love. l. 40. R] And laughs & dances. Q] And laughs. B] And laughs and.

p. 215, l. 3. B] whereby refusing. R] where by refuting. Q *has a comma after* diest. l. 5. Q *has a comma after* accept. R *omits the line.* l. 7. R *omits*] *lah.* l. 8. R] *Exit ad villam.* l. 9. B] Act. 3. Sc. 3. *This is merely a scribal error.* l. 10. R *omits*] sola. l. 12. Q *has a full stop after* payd. l. 14. Q *has a comma after* lov'd. l. 18. Q] has. B and R] hast. l. 19. Q *has no stop after* never. l. 20. R *omits this line.* l. 21. Q and B] yce. R] eye. ll. 22—3. *Between these lines* R *has*] Act: 3us. Scen: 3^a. Glaucilla. Olinda wth a glasse. R *omits*] *Enter Olinda.* l. 24. Q and B] winking. R] glorious. l. 25. Q and B] rest. R] sleepe. l. 26. Q and B] thou art. R] you as. l. 29. Q and B] soules. R] loves. l. 31. Q *has no stop after* eare. l. 32. Q *has a comma after* ever, *and no stop after* there. l. 33. R] is never. l. 34. Q *has no stop after* wrong. l. 35. B] I'le tell thee. R] I'le thee. R] I tell thee. l. 36. R] in *and omits* thy. Q and B] is thy.

p. 216, l. 1. R] Thou lovest. Q *has no stops after* lovst *and* Olinda. l. 3. B and R] cheeke. Q] cheekes. l. 4. R] Thou art. R] this. Q and B] thy. l. 6. R] open it. l. 7. R] a other. l. 8. R *omits*] I. l. 9. Q *has a comma after* die. l. 12. R *omits*] I. Q *has no comma after* all. l. 14. R] wilt bee. l. 18. Q *has no stop after* same. l. 19. R] to this towne hee came. l. 23. R] the pray. ll. 23—4. Q *has no stops at the end of these lines.* l. 24. R] said I. l. 26. R *omits*] love. l. 27. R] If then the fish, much more. l. 30. B and R] hate. Q] fate. l. 31.

296

NOTES

R *omits*] he. l. 32. R] holding on mee. l. 33. Q *has no stop after* eare. l. 36. R] Amaz'd of it selfe doth. Q *has no stop after the bracket at the end of the line.* l. 37. Q *has no stop after* dead. l. 38. R] all true love sweare. l. 40. Q and B] send. R] give.

p. **217**, ll. 2—3. Q *has no stops at the end of these lines.* l. 3. R] his prayer, *and omits* thee. l. 4. R] His. l. 5. Q *has no stop after* wind. l. 6. R] his pipe. B] lef. R] a precious. l. 7. Q] cuers. l. 8. Q and B] were wee. R] wart thou. l. 9. R] thou wert. l. 10. Q *has a full stop after* thee. l. 11. R] Why $\overset{2}{\text{Glaucilla}}\overset{1}{.}$ Q *has no stop after* lie. l. 13. R] said hee. l. 14. R] by mee that hee. Q and B] that I. l. 17. B] he. R] hee. Q] be. l. 21. R] finde. l. 22. R] so thou. Q *has no stop after* I. l. 23. R] dying love & lovinge dye. l. 24. R] But ah. l. 27. R] *Typhons.* l. 30. R] wch scorn'd. R *omits*] true. Q *has a comma after* shade. l. 32. Q *has a comma after* to ashes. l. 33. R] thou love...thou then alow. l. 34. R] latly. l. 39. R] hee 's. l. 40. B and R] and loves. Q] and love.

p. **218**, l. 1. R] wold please. l. 4. R] this dangerous. l. 5. R *omits*] *Thalander.* l. 6. B] With thee. Q] With mee. R] Wth this. l. 7. Q *omits*] *Glauc.* l. 8. R] disamore. l. 9. R] knowest thou not the. l. 12. R] t' wold. l. 13. R] temper it. l. 18. R] yet never. R *omits*] *Exeunt.* l. 19. R] *Act:* 3us *Scen:* 4ta. l. 20. R *omits*] *Enter, and adds*] *Freddocaldo.* l. 21. B] mar'le. Q] marle. R] marvaile. l. 23. R] Into those. l. 27. B] t' entertaine. l. 28. Q and B] houre. R] time. l. 29. R] *Freddo: enters.* l. 30. *Added in R on the preceding fol., verso.* Q *has a comma after* boh. l. 31. R] I beshrow. l. 32. Q and B] joynt. R] limm. l. 33. R] hath. l. 34. R *omits*] ha, ha, he. l. 35. R] yor.

p. **219**, l. 2. Q and B] What. R] Wher's y^t. l. 3. R *omits*] doe. B and R] yes. Q] yet. l. 4. Q *has no stop after* her. l. 5. Q] what. R] foole's this. l. 6. Q] I But. B] I but. R] But. ll. 7—10. Q *prints these as three lines, as follows:* I...Fredocaldoe | How ist...shoppe | Should...frost. B *has them in prose form.* R *omits*] I preethee *in* l. 7, *and has* I...possible | that...shop | shold...frost. l. 11. R] Knowest. l. 13. R] hee speaks true. l. 14. R] Maks as good a fire as ye greenest wood. l. 15. R] thou art. R] hast thou. Q and B] hast. l. 16. R] oft, the. Q and B] of the. l. 17. R] frosts...& seare. l. 21. B and R] desire. Q] desires. ll. 24—7. Q *prints these prose lines in doggerel form, as follows:* That...Troy | Now...made | But...*Fredocaldoe* | If...grove | To speake...alone. B *has the same arrangement, except that it has* But...alone *as one line.* R *has* That...Troy, *and the rest in prose.* l. 24. Q *has no stop after* Troy, *and has a comma after* have. R *omits*] wee. l. 25. Q *has no stop after* made. R] wilt thou. l. 26. R] next to. l. 27. Q *has no stop after* grove, *and has a full stop after* alone. l. 28. R] If thou dost...as fine. ll. 30—1. Q *prints these as if they were one line of verse, and with no stop after* dry. l. 30. R] of y^t. l. 32. R *omits second* when. l. 34. Q] besure, *followed by a full stop.* ll. 35—6. Q *prints these in one line.* l. 36. Q] never never. R *omits second* never. l. 37. Q] *Con.* beeleeve. B and R *omit*] *Fredocaldoe* I say beleeve me.

p. **220**, l. 2. Q] parches. Q and B] in. R] wth. l. 3. B and R] vale. Q] valley. Q and B] fuming. R] sliming. l. 5. R] nor fire nor *Phœbus* by. l. 7. R] head's. ll. 8—9. *Between these lines* R *has*] *Act:* 3^s *Scen:* 5^a. | *Armillus Conchylio. It omits*] *Enter Armillus.* l. 10. R] a others.

NOTES

l. 11. R *omits*] Thou...boy. l. 15. R] noe. Q and B] so. l. 16. R] Ih' thou art. R *omits*] my boy, *and adds the stage-direction*] *he gives him money.* l. 17. R *omits*] what, *and adds* Lett me see. l. 20. B and R *omit*] very. l. 21. B] Th' art. Q *puts the colon after* too. R] see your. l. 23. R] you cannot, you cannot. B] shee's now taken up. l. 24. R] *Exit ad domū Cosmæ.* ll. 24—5. *Between these lines* R *has*] Act: 3us. Scen: 6^a. | Armillus. l. 27. B and R] subjects. Q] subject. l. 28. R] of his object. l. 30. B and R] The lillie seemes. l. 33. Q *has no stop after* sure. R *has originally*] the same, *but* selfe *has been added in different ink*. l. 34. R *omits*] And face. l. 35. R] affection. ll. 37—8. R *omits these lines*. l. 40. R] Those *Nymphs...worthy...despecting*.

p. 221, l. 1. Q and B] thus. R] thouh. Q] lovo. l. 5. Q *has a comma after* modestie. l. 8. B and R] These. Q] The. l. 10. Q and B] that both. R] this both. l. 11. R] And if...as some. Q] *Conchylo*. l. 12. R *omits*] but. l. 13. R] as yet S^r so overlaiden. l. 14. R] that you cannot speake wth her. l. 16. Q and B] Love...light. R] It is light. Q] 'tis. B] tis. R] It is. l. 17. R] A other. l. 18. R] hands. l. 19. Q and B] light. R] me light. Q and B] in. R] betwixt. l. 21. R *transfers* Sir *to the end of the line*. l. 23. Q] will. B and R] shall. B] her thither straight. Q] you thither straight. R] her presently. l. 24. Q and B] shee'l...there. R] expect her. l. 26. R] I never failed, trust... it. l. 27. R] never let mee see more. Q] stars. B] shores. R] showrs. l. 30. Q and B] nights. R] lights. B and R] upon. ll. 32—3. Q] *Ar.* Adue | *Con.* Farewell. l. 36. R] the Crab. l. 37. R] bee right. R *places*] *Enter Scrocca after* l. 36. l. 38. R] to ye twin, the Crab. l. 39. R *adds*] *Exit*.

p. 222, ll. 1—2. R *omits these lines*. l. 3. R *omits*] quotha. R] ha that. l. 4. R] for a moment. B] Odoxcombria. Q] Odoxcom. R] Ococombria. *Of these classical transformations of* Odcombe, *the home of* Thomas Coryat, *that of* B *seems preferable*. Q *has a comma after* shooes. B] th' ill. l. 6. Q *has no stop after* on't. R] heede. B and R] towards. Q] toward. ll. 6—8, a bounsing...fish. *Added in* R *on the preceding fol*., *verso*. l. 7. R] a numb^r. Q and B] umber. R] looke *Cancr*. not a whiting. l. 8. B] i' th house. l. 9. R *has only one* along. l. 10. R *omits the second*] the Orke's dead and buried. l. 11. R *omits*] I. R] doth...thereabouts. Q] *within*. B] *Cancro: within*. R] *Cancr: in ostio*. l. 12. R] Hinte finte. B and R] *Neptunes*. Q] *Neptune*. l. 14. R *omits*] what. l. 15. R] speake y^e. R] sea armour. Q] searmore. B] sear-more. l. 16. R *omits*] *Enter...coate*. l. 19. R] Push seest not thou I am busiefied, Can a man. l. 20. Q and R] prettie. B] sweete. R *omits first* why *and* thy. B] is thy. l. 21. Q] *Con*. Q and B] Ino... Ino. R] I ne no...ne ne no. B and R] I tell thee. Q] tell thee. R *omits*] this. l. 22. Q and B] vanquish. R] banish. l. 23. Q *puts the colon after* so. R] yet all...it was. l. 25. B] True. Q] Thus. R] Why true. l. 26. Q and B] I. R] I but. l. 27. R] My slimie Gaberdine, my pich patch poled. Q] if I shuld. B and R] should I. l. 31. Q] *Con*. R *omits*] Why...goe. l. 33. R] Well I'le goe. *Exit ad rupem rufam*. l. 35—6. my scalie gaberdine my orcke apparell had. l. 37. R] & why.

p. 223, l. 1. R] hand to hand my selfe. l. 2. Q and B] *Ataches*. R] *Atyches*. *The spelling* Ataches *has been retained here and in* l. 24, *as it may be one of* Cancrone's *mispronunciations, though on* p. 222, l. 25, *the correct form occurs in one of his speeches*. l. 4. *Between* tortoise *and* has R *adds* have I

298

NOTES

retreived you. l. 5. R] your skin. l. 7. R] This Lob. B and R] lovers. Q] fishers. l. 8. B] triumphing. R] trumping. l. 11. y^r *added after* for *in* R *above the line in different ink.* R] I heere reach forth unto y^r. l. 12. B] droopping. l. 13. Q *has a full stop after* flapmouth. R] flop mouth. l. 14. R *omits*] mee. ll. 15—6. R *omits these lines and* ll. 18—9, surmount...*Cupid.* l. 15. B] lover. Q] loves. l. 20. R] Ha are. l. 21. R] wth. Q and B] for. R] a *Cupid* a faith. R] *Exit ad domum.* Q *has a full stop after* Exit. l. 22. Q and B] very. R] filthy. l. 23. Q and B] master. R] M^{rs}. l. 24. R] & yet y^t same. R] *Atyches*. l. 25. Q and B] on's pate. R] of his cap. Q and B] beleare. R] beleeve. l. 26. R] parlouslie. Q] partly. B] parlsly. Q] so, so, so. B] so so. R] niso niso. l. 27. R] *Now courteous Cupid.* l. 28. R] *upon by.* l. 29. R] *never bared.* l. 35. R] see now if. l. 36. R *omits*] for *before* thou. l. 37. R] to it. l. 38. R] then hee wee might ha goe whistle for o^r netts. l. 39. Q and B] *Cancrone.* R] S^r.

p. 224, l. 1. R *omits*] you. l. 3. R] While, then wee'le have a. l. 5. R *omits*] and. R] scarcy. l. 6. R *omits*] if you come. Q] roche. l. 7. R] Yes, yes I'le goe a-fishing on ye land. R] *Exit ad rupem rufam.* l. 8. R] this dog hath...my lesson. l. 9. R *adds*] good *before* courteous. l. 12. R *has* helpe *at the end of* l. 11. l. 13. R *omits*] Enter...habitt. ll. 14—7, 19—24 and 26—7. Q, B and R *have these mock-heroic lines in prose form.* l. 17. R *omits*] doe ycleape. l. 18. Q and B] vile. R] very. l. 20. R *omits*] And. R] ye bright beams of my deitie. l. 21. R] glister wound thy infant eye. l. 28. R] & cannot tell. B] who. l. 29. R] Ther's. B] enough. R] *Urina, Glaucilla, Lilla.* l. 30. Q and B] Mee thinks that. R] O that same. l. 32. R] verie name. B] very name. Q] name.

p. 225, l. 1. R] word to her for mee. l. 2. R] make all to beleeve thee. ll. 2—3. R *omits*] shee...here. l. 4. Q and B] magicke. R] potent musick. l. 8. R] thine. l. 9. Q and B] zize. R] isize. l. 10. for a...fitt thee. l. 11. R *omits this line.* l. 12. R *omits*] Con. R] sympathize of thine. B] no more but thus. Q] but thus. R] no more but this. l. 18. R] & therefore. Q and B] foote with you. R] feete. l. 19. R *omits*] therefore. l. 20. Q] Con. R *omits*] I. Q and B] and. R] so. l. 22. Q] Can. R] ye y^t. l. 26. Q] Con. R *omits*] I. l. 27. R] sitting there a. l. 28. R *omits*] then. Q and B] the. R] she. l. 30. R *omits*] to her. l. 32. R] thou art inspir'd I see. l. 33. R *omits this line.* l. 34. R *omits*] Con. Q and B] throw. R] doe. l. 36. R *omits*] I die...I lye. l. 38. R *omits* too. l. 39. R] it's. R *omits*] such. l. 40. R] forgot y^t.

p. 226, l. 1. R] teach thee. l. 2. Q *has no stop after* goe. Q and B] follow. R] overtake. ll. 3—7. R *has instead*] Can. Da, Da, Cupid Lett mee see, Legge | Con. Loobie. | Can. Bouh | Con. Booby | Can. Cockshell. ll. 9—10. R *omits* these lines. l. 11. B] our. Q] Ino triumph, Ino triumph. B] I no triumph : in ; in : no triumph. R] ino triumphe, ne, ne, no. l. 12. Q and B] he shall sit [B, set] on a. R] I'le make him set on y^e. l. 13. B] Cosma: fyed. R] Cosmified. l. 14. R] shall goe hard. l. 16. R] *will I.* l. 18. R] *Act^{us}: 3. Scen: 7^a.* l. 19. R *omits*] Enter. l. 20. Q and B] strength. R] or. l. 23. R] restraint of foode. Q and B] restraint. l. 25. Q *has a comma after* shunne *and not after* death. l. 27. Q and B] others. R] lovers. l. 29. B] she liketh all, she likes (loves *added in margin*). R] shee loveth all, shee liks. l. 30.

299

NOTES

B and R *omit*] yet. l. 32. R] o. Q and B] and. l. 33. Q] race. B] course. R] curse.

p. **227**, l. 1. *Before this line* R *has*] *Act:* 3. *Scen:* 8^a | *Cosma. Pas.* l. 2. R] love. l. 5. Q] O monstrous. B] O monster. R] harke! o monster. B and R] woman. l. 6. R *omits*] that. B] blames. Q *has no stop after* ranges. l. 7. Q *has a full stop after* changes. l. 8. Q *has a comma after* course. l. 10. Q and B] dead. R] deale. l. 12. R] beauties. l. 13. R] to th'. Q] toth'. B] to' th. l. 15. R] looses. l. 16. B and R] too short. Q] ah short. ll. 17—8. *Between these lines* R *adds*:

> All as a rose that new unswadled
> From her greene hands displays her virgins head
> Straight to the sun her lovelie breast exposes
> Straight all dissolv'd, & her sweet verdure looses
> Thus beautie in our face, as in this flowre
> Doth spring, bud, blossome wither in a houre.

R *has originally* breasts expose *and* virtue loose, *but they have been altered as above.* l. 18. R] easilie dost. l. 21. R] woldest. l. 24. R] Dost thou not. l. 25. Q and B] Maids, you. R] Mayd if thou. R] heere is your. l. 27. Q and B] found. R] fond. l. 28. R *alone has this line.* l. 30. R] heart. l. 34. R] I. Q and B] we. l. 35. R] or fright. l. 36. B] guip. R] gap. R] are these. l. 37. R] *Glaucilla and Olinda.* l. 38. R] dranke. l. 39. R] day.

p. **228**, l. 1. B] long I have lov'd. Q] long I have long lov'd. R] long have I lov'd. l. 3. Q] the. B and R] that. l. 9. R] lover. R] *Exit ad domum.* l. 10. R] Jona. l. 13. B] y' are. l. 14. R] act y^e. l. 17. R *adds*] *a villa meeting Pas going out.* ll. 18—9. R *omits these.* ll. 22—3. R *has between these lines*] *Act.* 3: *Scen:* 9^a. l. 23. R *prefixes*] *Per.* l. 25. R] good y^e...more expresses. l. 28. R] not enjoy what most contents mee. Q and B] may enjoy what more torments me. l. 29. R] life rather than love I wold. l. 31. R] best. l. 32. R] tormenting. l. 33. R] thou now. l. 34. R] Thou then could'st. l. 34. R *omits*] *Enter Glaucilla.*

p. **229**, l. 1. *Before this line* R *has*] *Act:* 3. *Scen:* 10. *Glaucilla a villa.* l. 3. R *omits*] shame. l. 6. B] beleev'd. Q] beleeve. R] belewed. l. 7. R] unbeleive. l. 9. B and R] those. Q] whose. l. 10. R *omits*] *lah.* l. 13. R] Yon flitting. B] yee never. l. 14. B and R] His love, his words. Q] His words, his love. l. 16. R] rocks...seas. Q and B] rocke...sea. l. 21. Q and B] scurvily. R] securely. l. 23. R] vows. Q and B] vow. R] wch. l. 25. B and R] abusest. Q] deceivest. l. 31. R *omits*] 'tis not hate. l. 33. R] I have. Q and B] view'd. R] prov'd. l. 39. R] doth. l. 40. R] it's.

p. **230**, l. 2. Q and B] winst. R] seek'st. l. 4. Q and B] Take... which. R] Why hold'st thou from mee y^t. l. 5. R] thy. l. 6. R *omits*] grant. l. 7. R] all y^e. l. 9. R] 't is. l. 11. B and R] all. Q] much. l. 14. B] sleepes. R] sleeps. Q] seemes. R] my. Q and B] thy. l. 16. R] wth the. l. 17. B] cur'st. Q and R] cut'st. l. 19. R] 'Tis breifly. R] had. l. 20. R] & yet. l. 23. Q and B] sadness. R] greiving. l. 30. Q and B] ever. R] over. l. 33. R] & thy. l. 34. R] my life but wth thy love. l. 35. Q and B] I had. R] had bine. l. 36. B and R] lifes. Q] life. l. 38. Q and B] live. R] dye.

300

NOTES

p. 231, l. 4. Q and B] cost me.   R] caus'd my.   l. 5.   So had.   l. 6. For y^e.   l. 9.   B and R] thy.   Q] my.   l. 10.   Q and B] where.   R] there.   l. 14.   R *omits*] then.   l. 15.   Q and B] to.   R] see.   l. 17. R] ye bad light all.   l. 18.   R] *Exit ad villam.*   B *has*] *Exit Glaucilla, after* l. 19.   l. 19.   Q *omits*] *Per.* which is prefixed by B and R.   R] what thou wishest *Glaucilla.*   ll. 19—20.   R *has between these lines*] *Act:* 3. *Scen:* 11. | *Perindus.*   l. 21.   R] from mine eyes shutt.   l. 24.   B] to's.   R] finde. l. 26.   R *omits*] But, *and places*] Ent^r *Atych.* after l. 25.   l. 28.   R] This soule...as his.   l. 29.   R] her selfe.   l. 30.   Q and B] his thoughts.   R] her selfe.   ll. 38—9.   *Between these lines* B and R *have* Ai mee.   l. 39. Q and B] he.   R] shee.   R *omits*] I'le...him.   l. 40.   R] all alone.

p. 232, l. 2.   B] spiritt.   R *has*] And y^t wch best befitts a greiv'd spirit. l. 4.   R] Sentinell.   l. 5.   B and R] ever.   Q] never.   l. 7.   R] Whose wages hate.   l. 8.   *Editor emend.*] mine and her foes.   R] mee & her foes. Q] mine and her; for.   B] mine and her for.   *None of these readings is intelligible, and some such emendation as that adopted in the text is necessary.* l. 11.   R *omits*] thou.   l. 12.   B] body's.   R] bodies.   l. 13.   R] bodie's. l. 14.   B] o' the two.   R] of th' two.   ll. 19—20.   *Between these lines* R *adds* Proove mee thy love, what canst thou have on mee?   l. 20.   R *has*] My name *Thalanders* name doth much displease y^{ee}.   l. 21.   R] this name... will ease.   l. 24.   Q] i'st; *no stop after* suspected.   l. 25.   B] hee's alter'd. Q] i'st.   l. 30.   R] 'ere.   l. 31.   R] mine eyes.   l. 32.   mine armes. l. 35.   Q] Ist.   R] I scarcely trust.   l. 36.   R] wth their.

p. 233, l. 3.   Q *omits this line, which is found in* B *and* R.   l. 4.   Q *has a full stop after* love.   l. 5.   B and R] thy selfe, thy love.   Q] thy fame. l. 6.   Q *omits* all the ground, *which is found in* B *and* R.   ll. 7—11.   Of all ...most deare.   Q *omits these lines, which are found in* B *and* R.   *The text given is that of* B *from which* R *has the following variants:* l. 9, B] thy, R] her; l. 10, B] who, R] what; l. 11, R *omits*] If this be true.   l. 13.   R] in & for.   l. 15.   Q] She had one.   B] S'had but one.   R] Sh'had but one. l. 17.   B] Why shuld you thus.   l. 22.   R] Shee thinkes.   l. 24.   Q and B] truth.   R] greife.   l. 25.   R *omits*] *Exeunt.*   ll. 26—38.   R *omits these lines, and has*] *Chorus deest.*

p. 234, ll. 1—28.   R *omits these lines.*   l. 7.   Q and B] *fire.   Editor emend.*] fires.   l. 8.   Q] *kinne.*   l. 12.   Q] the.   B] his.   l. 18.   R] losse.   Q] life.   l. 30.   Q, B and R] *Thalander.*   As Thalander has revealed his identity in the previous Scene, p. 232, l. 20, he here is called for the first time in the stage-directions by his real name, instead of the assumed one, *Atyches.*   But, through force of habit, the printer of Q still prefixes *Aty.* to his first four speeches in this Scene; from l. 7 on p. 235 he consistently uses *Tha.*   R] *Perind: Thalander a villa.*   l. 33.   R] till.   Q and B] while.   l. 36.   Q and B] much.   R] such.

p. 235, l. 2.   R] but could...espye no time.   l. 4.   R] ah.   l. 7.   Q and B] life.   R] selfe.   R *omits*] she was.   l. 9.   B and R] Shee was indeede. l. 12.   R *omits*] liv'd...smiling.   l. 13.   R] exile.   l. 17.   R] more greater.   l. 19.   R] yet thou.   l. 21.   R] torments.   l. 22.   R] ills. Q] all.   B] ill.   R] is sayd.   l. 23.   whether dost.   l. 25.   R *omits*] I seeke.   l. 28.   R] mine armes.   l. 31.   Q *has no stop after* forsaking. l. 33.   R] shall nor can they long detaine mee.   l. 34.   Q and B] time. R] while.   l. 36.   R *omits*] my.   l. 39.   R *omits*] *Exeunt.*

301

NOTES

p. **236**, l. 2. R *has instead*] *Cyclops*. l. 3. R] you mountains. l. 6. R] wch. R] too too. Q and B] too. l. 7. B and R] tygres. Q] tygre. l. 9. R] Oake. B] Oke. Q] Orke. l. 12. R] O heavens. l. 13. Q and B] frame. R] make. l. 14. Q and B] lonely. R] lovely. l. 15. B and R] such a pleasing. Q] so fine a. l. 16. R] in her haire. l. 18. B and R] to. Q] into. Q and B] yce. R] yea. l. 23. Q *omits*] but one, *which is given by* B and R. l. 24. Q and B *omit*] of all, *which is given by* R. l. 28. Q and B] vow, and sweare. R] sweare, and woe. l. 30. B] cliffs. l. 32. R *omits*] *Exit*.

p. **237**, l. 2. R *omits*] *Enter*. l. 5. Q and B] succession. R] supply. l. 6. R] inticing. l. 7. R] rebellious...woman. l. 9. R] by them. ll. 13—4. *Between these lines* R *has*] *Act:* 4. *Scen:* 4. l. 21. R] Since y^t I. l. 22. R] heavens. l. 26. Q *omits*] well, *which is given by* B and R. l. 27. R] in my...you are. l. 28. R] the fire. l. 29. R *omits this line*. l. 31. R *omits*] wood. l. 33. Q] flash it lights desire. B] flash it light desires. R] flashing darts desire. l. 35. R] Before 'tis all...all bee.

p. **238**, l. 1. R] it's. l. 2. Q] Ist. B] I'st. R] Its. R] i'st pleasing. l. 3. R *omits*] *kisses her, and has*] *Pas disguised offers*. l. 5. B] *a kisse on the one side*. R *omits the line*. l. 7. R *omits*] *Armil. Cos. severall waies*. l. 8. R] *Act:* 4. *Scen:* 5. l. 9. R *omits*] *Pas. Fredocaldo*. l. 10. R] times. l. 11. R] to y^e. l. 13. Q and B] My old rivall. R] Are you heere my rivall. l. 14. R] but y^t wch shineth. l. 22. B and R] heard me. Q] heard. Q and B] could dare. R] wold fraye. l. 23. R] *Pas comes*. l. 24. R] *shee*. ll. 25—6. R *omits*] *Enter...apparell, and*] *Exit Pas. It has instead*] *Act:* 4 *Scen:* 6. *Conchy: a domo tired like Cosma*. l. 27. Q] do fit. B] doth fit. R] become. ll. 28—9. R *transposes these lines*. l. 28. R] pittie 't is. l. 29. R] I shold I thinke. l. 30. R] I shold. R] as pittifull a. Q] a pittifull. B] as pittiful. l. 32. R] has. l. 33. R] meete wth. l. 34. R *omits*] *at Fred., and places* She stumbles *after* l. 35.

p. **239**, l. 2. R] sleepe's not. ll. 5—6. R] can'st thinke this file shold love | Cold weather. l. 6. R] shold frost. '. 7. Q and B] faire. R] two. l. 8. Q and B *have only*] Bringe backe my spring ; R *adds*] and me two enemies. *The second word, however, in this addition by* R *is doubtful. It looks as if* mie *had first been written*. l. 9. R] sweet love, so bright. l. 11. R] frost. l. 13. Q and B *have this in two lines :* Fie *Fredocaldo* | Not...aire. R *has* what *instead of* Not. l. 14. R] *Exeunt ad lucum*. l. 15. R] *Act:* 4. *Scen:* 7. l. 18. Q] most. l. 19. R *omits*] *Enter Cosma*. l. 20. Q] that yee are. B] that y' are. R] you are. ll. 24—5. B and R *have these lines in prose form*. ll. 26—8. *So arranged in* R. Q *prints these in two lines, as follows :* I...woods | Too...favor. B *has these and the following line in prose form*. l. 28. R] zealous of the love. l. 30. Q and B] horrid. R] haired. l. 31. Q and B] leave. R] loose. l. 32. R *omits*] All...us. Q and B] *Exit Ar*. R] *Arm: runs away*. l. 33. *Before this line* R *has*] *Act:* 4. *Scen:* 8. Q] you are. B] y' are. R] yo're. l. 34. R *adds the stage-direction*] *Hee discloses himselfe*. ll. 35—8 and p. **240**, ll. 1—4. Q, B and R *have these as follows :* Beshrew...me | Doe...man | whose ...owne | Thou...unknowne | Pish...to me | only...me. l. 37. Q and B] Doe you not. R] Dost thou. l. 38. R] thy love.

p. **240**, l. 1. R] Is like himselfe, a alian to himselfe. l. 2. Q and B] thee. R] mee. l. 3. R] yo'ur foolish...I never. l. 4. B and R] Only to mee. Q] To me only. l. 5. R] passions. l. 8. R] cannot. l. 9.

NOTES

R] wish.   l. 10.   R] might moove.   ll. 11—2.   R *transposes* ranging *and changing*.   l. 14.   R] Nay soft there.   B and R] a dog.   Q] dog.   l. 18. R] night.   Q and B] right, *which has been changed in* B *to* night *by a second hand*.   l. 19.   R *omits*] *Exeunt*.   l. 20.   R] *Act:* 4. *Scen:* 9.   l. 21. R *adds*] *a luco*.   ll. 22—32.   *So arranged in* R.   Q and B *have these in prose form*.   l. 23.   R] in y^e.   l. 24.   R] it were.   l. 26.   R] began. l. 27.   R *omits*] doe.   l. 30.   R] doth.   l. 31.   B and R] what a.   Q] what.   l. 32.   B and R] th' one.   Q] sha'me.   B] th' other.   l. 33.   R] already comes.   ll. 33—6, *stage-direction*.   R *has instead*] *Cancrone ent^e: backward*.   ll. 33—4.   *Between these lines* R *adds to Cancrone's speech:*

    Rudenes & madnes tyed up in one sack
    What meane you?

l. 36.   R *omits*] tell, *which has been added above the line in different ink*. l. 37.   Q and B] disciple.   R] depell.   l. 38.   R *omits this line*.

    p. **241**, ll. 1—2.   Q and B *have*] I...cue | The...already.   R *has*] I...worke, *and omits* already.   l. 1.   Q and B] cue.   R *leaves a blank and then has* g, *as if the missing word ended with this letter*.   l. 4.   B and R] even.   Q] ever. R *omits*] him.   l. 6.   R] O those thy glazing.   l. 7.   R] drowne.   Q and B] drownd.   l. 8.   Q and B] arrowe tree.   R] oracle.   l. 10.   R *omits*] his good. l. 11.   Q and B] abroad.   R] And of his buisines abroade.   Q and B] and.   R] or.   l. 12.   R] love-works.   l. 13.   Q] *goes*.   B] *gets*.   R *omits the line*.   l. 14. R *omits*] thy selfe.   l. 15.   R] revive mee.   l. 16.   B *omits*] bundance of people.   R] bundance of folks, *and omits*] bundance a lookers on.   l. 17. R] to y^e.   l. 18.   B and R] presently.   Q] present.   l. 19.   Q] my.   B and R] to thy.   l. 20.   R *omits*] and say on.   l. 21.   R] I dye, I crye.   l. 22. Q *has a comma after* approaching.   R] *Ent^r Rimbombo a rupe*, *placed between* ll. 21—2.   ll. 23—31.   *So arranged in* R.   Q and B *have these lines in prose form*.   l. 23.   R] rugged.   Q and B] ragges.   l. 24.   R] tasts. l. 25.   R] those woers.   l. 26.   B] speakst.   B] now I find.   R] now I see. Q *omits these words*.   l. 31.   Q and B] coyly.   R] wyly.   l. 32.   Q] you. R] ye time.   l. 33.   Q] Yet.   l. 35.   R] And truth I wish you had.   l. 37. R] of this.   R] unconquerable.   Q and B] unconquered.   ll. 38—41 *and* p. **242**, l. 1.   *So arranged in* R.   Q and B *have these lines in prose form*. l. 38.   R] in sea or land.   l. 40.   B and R] sire.   Q] fire.   Q and B] vow. R] sweare.

    p. **242**, ll. 2—27.   Q and B *have these lines in prose form*.   l. 2.   R] treads not on y^e.   l. 3.   R] But's fled unto.   B] th' hills.   l. 4.   Q and B] to mee.   R] unto thee.   l. 6.   R *omits*] jollie.   l. 7.   R] this or that.   l. 8.   R] & teeth.   l. 10.   R] joy & peace.   ll. 11—2.   R *omits these lines*.   l. 14.   Q and B] thine owne.   R] thine, on y^e.   l. 15. B] *Cyclopps*.   Q and B] can.   R] now.   l. 16.   R] then this.   Q and B] this.   Q and B] live.   R] lifte.   l. 17.   R] ye girdle.   l. 22.   R] light flame.   l. 23.   B] to th'.   Q] to' th.   R] to y^e.   l. 24.   R] Conjure. l. 26.   Q *has a colon after* Not.   R *omits*] no, *and places* say on *at the end of this line*.   l. 27.   Q *and* B] neither.   R] never.   l. 29.   R] there about this.   l. 30.   R] hande.   l. 35.   B] neerer to me, yet neerer.   Q] neerer to mee, yet neere.   R] neere to mee, yet neerer.   l. 36.   R] the filthy. l. 38.   Q and B] upon.   R] of.   l. 40.   Q and B] head.   R] beard.

    p. **243**, l. 2.   R] bee my love.   l. 6.   Q] they are.   B] they be.   R] & they bee.   R] lovers knots.   Q and B] knots.   R *adds*] *Exit, at the end of the line*.   l. 7.   R] I prithee come &.   R *omits marginal stage-direction*]

NOTES

Conchylio...is. l. 8. R] yet before. l. 9. R] That thou. Q and B] thou. l. 11. B and R] *Nymphs.* Q] *Nymph.* l. 12. Q] Satyrs. B] satires. R] starrs. l. 13. B *has*] *Redit Conchylio, at the end of* l. 12. R *omits the stage-direction.* l. 14. B and R] Ha, ha, he. Q and B] O wit! O tree. R] O tree! O wet! l. 15. B and R] eye. Q] eyes. l. 16. R] Thou wich, thou bich. l. 19. R *omits*] fishers. l. 20. R *omits*] in. B and R] bandogs. Q] bandog. Q] *Exit.* B] *Exit Conchyl:.* R *omits*] *Exit.* ll. 22—3. Q and B] bring...country. R] call all the towne uppon mee. l. 27. R *omits the second*] not one. l. 28. Q and B] soken. R] sanke. *Editor emend.*] soken. l. 29. R *omits*] oh, oh. l. 30. Q] *Con.* Q] mans. R *omits*] hey. l. 31. Q] that. B and R] there. l. 32. R] on. l. 34. Q and B] a graft of. R] grifte uppon. l. 35. B] wound up. l. 36. Q and B] a barnacle. R] bansticle. l. 37. R] on thy. l. 39. Q and B] of. R] have. l. 40. R] 9 orkes at once. B] ah, hei, au. R] a ha.

p. 244, l. 1. R] fishted. l. 3. Q and B] helpe to. R] but. R] walking staffe. l. 4. R] true heire. l. 5. R] thy staffe? Marry y^t I will, It is...beate. l. 8. R] knew. Q and B] know. R] defloured. l. 11. *Marginal stage-direction, While...ground.* R *has instead*] *Cancr: falls on his back & falls in a sound.* Q and B] a little. R] a little nearer. R *omits*] oh. l. 13. R] has hee. B] these hands. l. 16. B] and your boate sides are so hard. R] & the boate side is harde. ll. 18—9. Q and B] I tell...row. R] Indeede La, Caron. l. 19. Q] fisher man when I. l. 21. R] Wold I. l. 22. B and R] this tree. ll. 23—4. B] thy captaine. Q] thy captive. R] mee Mee thy captaine. l. 25. Q and B] fast. R] safely. l. 27. R] into y^e. ll. 27—8. R *omits*] did...there *and*] *Cancrone* rises up. l. 30. R *omits*] dead and. l. 31. B and R] foe. Q] for. l. 32. R] a shite-slops of him. I'le ne're studdie. l. 33. R *omits*] how. R] on. l. 34. R] sea-brat. l. 35. R] lips aft^r. l. 36. Q] marke that *Cosma:.* B] marke you that *Cosma*?. R] marke you *Cosma:.* l. 37. I'le turne thy netmaker (sweete fisher) if y^t y^u'lt. ll. 39—40. R] sayd I was any mans undoing.

p. 245, l. 1. B] he that pocketted. Q] that pocketted. R] hee that pocked. l. 3. Q] on. B] upon. R] uppon. l. 4. R *omits*] then. l. 5. B] *Bombelo.* Q and B] porridge. R] pottage. ll. 6—7. R *omits*] and...too. l. 7. R] so I will first mince thy. ll. 7—8. R *adds*] bones... meate *on the preceding page, verso.* l. 8. B and R] fishers boys [B, boyes]. Q] a fishers boy. ll. 8—9. Q and B] O...thee. R] I'le geld thee too. l. 9. R *omits*] shalt. l. 10. R] How like you this S^r. l. 12. R] I'le tell ye a. l. 14. R] The same. *After* head R *adds*] of his owne. ll. 14—5. R *omits*] I...him. l. 15. B] it was. Q] he was. R] It was. l. 16. B and R] goats. l. 19. Q and B] imitate. R] intreat. l. 20. Q] glazing. B and R] glaring. l. 21. R] wood. l. 23. B] furginitie. R] virginitie. l. 24. R] I'le warrant thee. l. 25. R] it on thy sholder. l. 26. R] Rant tararant. ll. 26—8, *stage-direction.* R] *Cancrone fals, ye Cyclops gets his dagger.* l. 28. R] behinde. Rant tararant. l. 29. R *omits*] O. B and R *add*] *Cancrone after* Whineyeard. Q] on 't. B] on it. R] it. l. 30. R *omits*] 'Tis no matter. Q and B] fly. R] leap. l. 31. R] this yeare. l. 32. B] I'me. R *omits*] I am sure. l. 34. B] t'is out, let's. R] it is out, it is out, Let's. l. 35. R *omits*] O. l. 36—7. Q and B *have these lines in prose form.* l. 37. R *adds* Farewell, *and omits*] *Exit.* l. 38. R *transposes* shame *and* scorne. l. 39. R] hills. l. 40. R *omits*] *Exit.*

304

NOTES

p. **246**, ll. 1—33 and p. **247**, ll. 1—8. R *omits these lines.* l. 3. Q] *Orpehus.* l. 22. Q] *Caron.* l. 24. Q] to' th'.

p. **247**, l. 1. B] *hunger.* Q] *longer.* l. 4. Q] *Earth.* B] *love.* l. 7. B] *doest.* l. 10. B *has a semi-colon instead of*] *and.* R] *Thalander wth a torch. Alcippus ad lucum.* l. 13. R] light but. Q and B] light. ll. 20—2. *So arranged in* R. Q and B *have these lines in prose form.* l. 20. Q *omits*] love, *which is given by* B and R. l. 21. R] Wold give. l. 22. R] dotage. l. 22. R] Tell me *Alcippus.* Q and B] *Alcippus.* l. 24. B] Know what is love. R] tell what is love. l. 25. y^t love is. l. 31. R] to. l. 32. Q and B] block. R] blot. Q *has a full stop after* defaces. l. 33. R] grounding. l. 34. R] loving. Q *has a comma after* darts. l. 35. R] me love as surely now.

p. **248**, l. 1. R] it is. l. 2. B] ere's. Q] ere. R] e'r's. l. 4. R] Heer's a. B and R] and I. Q] I. l. 8. B] teares th'. Q] hearts th'. R] tears y^e. l. 9. Q *has a comma after* well. l. 10. Q and B] floodstreams. R] stronge streams. *At the end of this line* R *adds*] *Exit ad lucum.* l. 12. R] These. Q and B] the. l. 14. R] mine harts...mine eyes. l. 16. R] loving. l. 18. R] her first. l. 20. Q and B] infold. R] hold. l. 21. B] you doth. Q] you do. R] thou dost. l. 22. R] sun set. l. 23. Ah never. Q and B] Never. Q *has a comma after* ever. l. 24. Q and B] thou. R] faire. l. 25. Q *has a comma after* were. l. 26. Q and B] dies. R] eyes. l. 27. You...eyes. Q *omits this line which is found in* B *and* R. *The latter has* wee fooles. l. 28. B and R] Once. Q] You. l. 29. R] fearfull. l. 30. R] skies. l. 31. R] yee. l. 35. R *repeats with my before the second*] *Olinda.* l. 37. R *omits*] *He... rocke, and has instead*] musicke. l. 39. R] w^{ch}.

p. **249**, l. 2. R] as one. l. 6. Q and B] then. R] sleepe. ll. 8—9. R *has instead*] *Olinda e rupe. Circe wth a song.* l. 10. R *omits*] *Song.* l. 12. B and R] thou. Q] thon. l. 15. R] altar. l. 17. Q and B] appease. R] please. l. 19. Q and B] tryed. R] true. l. 20. Q and B] spend. R] with. Q and B] weare. R] spend. l. 28. Q and B] firmely. R] freindly. l. 33. R] these. *At the end of the line* R *adds*] *Hee startes up amaz'd.* ll. 34—5. R *omits these lines.*

p. **250**, l. 1. R *omits this line.* l. 3. R *omits the second* where, *and has* whether, whether. B] fly'st. l. 9. B] dream'st. l. 11. R] a light wak't never shall I. l. 13. R] on y^e. l. 15. B] beleeve 't. Q *omits*] Olinda, *which is found in* B and R. l. 16. B *omits*] not. R] thine eyes. l. 17. R] can...mine eyes. l. 18. R] That. l. 21. Q and B] love. R] loe. l. 22. B] this had. Q] this. R] my hand. l. 24. R *has instead*] *Act: 5. Scen: 3 Alcip: a luco.* ll. 25—6. Q] How is this ! have you learnt, have you learnt your mother | *Circes* art to raise the dead ? wonder ? thinke shee lives. B *has*] Howes this,...art | To raise...I thinke shee lives. R *has*] How's this, *omits the second* have you learnt, *and is otherwise as* B. ll. 29—35. *So arranged in* R. Q and B *have these lines in prose form.* l. 29. R] hand and heart. Q and B] cold. R] dead. l. 30. Q *has commas after* for *and* Glaucilla. R] prævented. l. 32. Q] thee love. B] thee thy love. R] & thee my love. l. 34. Q] true *Alcippus.* B] tell true *Alcippus.* R *omits the line.* l. 38. R] we live ? are not wee.

p. **251**, l. 1. R] ah let. l. 2. R] If thou wilt...breaths. l. 3. Q] hand lives. B and R] hands live. *At the end of the line* R *adds*] *hee kisses her.* l. 4. Q and B *omit the second* shee lives, *which is found in* R.

NOTES

l. 5. Q and B] that. R] her. R] breath. Q and B] bread. B and R] hath. Q] both. l. 6. Q and B] with. R] &. l. 10. Q and B] happy. R] blessed. l. 12. Q and B] joy. R] love. l. 13. B and R] thee. Q] you. l. 15. Q and B] rash. R] rude. l. 17. R] wold not. l. 22. R] Think'st thou y^t my. l. 25. R] worshippe. l. 27. Q] *Magoe's.* B] *Magos.* R] *Magus.* l. 33. B and R] Wth. Q] What. Q *has a comma after*] *Thalander, and no stop after* ever. l. 34. R] to live & dye. Q *prints*] *Exeunt* at the end of l. 35. R *has*] *Exeunt ad rupem* at the end of l. 33. l. 36. R] their loves. B] nested. R] rested. l. 38. R *omits*] *Manet Alcippus.*

p. 252, l. 1. R] *Act:* 5 *Scen:* 4. *Alcip:* l. 2. R *has instead*] *Tyrinthius a rupe.* ll. 2—3. *Between these lines* R *has* The morne's scarce wak't, yet as I thinke wee are right, *with which Tyrinthus begins his speech.* l. 3. B and R] fisher. Q] sister. l. 4. R *omits*] sir. l. 6. R *omits*] *Exit Alcippus.* l. 7. R] mee most happy. Q] in. B and R] by. l. 8. R] you heavenly power. l. 9. R] life or. l. 11. B] *Grypus.* R] *Grophus.* R] to the ship, & bring. l. 13. R] In wch I. R *omits*] *Exit Gryphus.* l. 14. R] preservs my hart before. l. 15. R *omits*] seeke. l. 19. R] the Persians. Q and B] seas. R] shoars. l. 20. Q and B] my...the. R] that...y^t. l. 21. Q and B] my. R] y^t. l. 23. Q and B] summers. R] years. l. 24. B and R] long have liv'd. l. 26. R] seem'd. l. 29. Q and B] but... their. R] some...y^e. l. 30. R] to th'. Q] to'th'. B] to' 'th. l. 31. Q] left. B and R] lost. R] the infant. l. 33. Q and B] Beeing. R] Being. l. 34. R *omits this line.* l. 35. R] thy altar. R *adds*] *Ent^r. Pas a rupe.*

p. 253, l. 1. *Before this line* R *has*] *Act:* 5. *Scen:* 5. *Instead of*] *Enter Pas, it has*] *Pas. Tyrinth:*. l. 4. R] What breast. B] yee now. l. 6. R] fear's mine. l. 7. Q and B] can. R] shall. Q *has a mark of interrogation after* rest. l. 8. Q *has a full stop after* brest. l. 9. B and R] Fisher. Q] Fishers. l. 10. Q] little as. B] little that. R] little. l. 11. R] heaven. l. 13. B and R] some where. Q] somewhat. R] seene you. l. 14. R] of y^r. l. 20. Q *has no stop after* daughter. R *adds*] is dead *to Pas' speech, and then has the stage-direction*] *He sounds. It omits* l. 21 *and* l. 22: *Pas*...so. ll. 22—4. Q *prints these lines*: I...and falls | *Tyrinthus*... feete | How...returnes. B *has them as prose.* R *has*] Alas...blow | Thus...now | Loath...returnes. l. 25. R] greifes. l. 26. R *omits*] And. l. 27. R] not love. l. 29. Q] ye. B] y'. R] y^u. l. 30. R *omits*] of. B and R] my. Q] thy. l. 32. Q and B] Ah. R] Ah my. l. 36. R *omits*] With. l. 37. B and R] you. R *omits*] me. l. 38. R] a. l. 39. Q and B] slue. R] show.

p. 254, l. 1. B and R] hates. Q] hated. Q and B] much. R] well. l. 2. R] heavens. l. 3. Q] no lesse. B] not lesse. R] not more. l. 4. B and R] hast thou. l. 5. R *omits*] sir. l. 7. Q] my. B] the. R] a. l. 8. R] Loose first. l. 9. B and R] you are. l. 12. B and R] not. Q] and. l. 13. B] by. Q and R] by a. R] violent or naturall death. l. 14. B and R] refus'd. Q] refuses. R] a. l. 19. B and R] unmanly. Q] unnaturall. l. 20. R] By a. ll. 22—3. Q, B and R *have these as one line.* l. 25. R] Can you tell. l. 27. R] yet now. l. 28. Q] might sooner bee. B] may now be well. R] may well bee now. l. 30. R *omits*] you. l. 32. R] soule. l. 34. R] y^t...from fare.

p. 255, l. 6. R] something. l. 7. Q and B] after. R] next to. l. 9. B] th'. Q] 'th'. R] y^e. l. 11. B] Steale. R] Steals. R] from w^{ch}.

NOTES

l. 13. Q and B] deepe. R] steepe.   l. 14. R] draw. B] to her.   l. 15.
R *omits*] and. Q and B] her. R] their.   l. 16. R] To see y^e.   l. 17.
Q and B] leave. R] loose.   l. 19. B and R] my *Olinda*. Q] my poore
Olinda.   ll. 21—4. *So arranged in* R. Q *prints these in two lines, as
follows*: Pas....teares | Tyr....teare. B *has them in prose form*.   l. 25. B]
still lives. Q] strives. R] yet lives. R] good y^t.   ll. 28—9. R *has in
one line:* Two...I left him sad; but safe.   l. 30. R] Chance happens in a.
l. 31. R *omits*] be.   l. 34. B] *Act.* 5. *Scen.* 4. Q] *Act.* 5. *Scen.* 2. R]
Act: 5. *Scen:* 6. *Cancro:*.   l. 35. R *has instead*] *Scrocca. Nonius a Priest*.
l. 36. Q] thou hast. B] hast not. R] hast thou not. B] t'would.   l. 37.
R] deflowred. R] tell y^u ye truth.   l. 38. R] these.

p. 256, l. 1. R] of it, if wee had bine.   l. 2. ne're.   l. 3. B and R *omit*]
up. B and R] should have. Q] shuld never have. R] to your.   l. 7. ne're.
l. 8.   these many years.   l. 10. Q] *Ctclyops*.   l. 11. R] disgest.
l. 12. B] they'l gest. R] they 'le disgest.   l. 13. R] sure I shold bee.
l. 14. R *omits*] up.   ll. 14—5. Q and B] for...good. R] for so I might
chaunce to see good.   l. 17. Q and B] now; nothing. R] but nothing.
l. 19. R] for it.   l. 22. Q and B] thou. R] to.   l. 24. R] these two my.
l. 26. Q] commeth...must. B] then must wee. R] doe wee.   l. 28. B] that
Rimroco. Q] *Rimronce*. R] y^t *Rimbombo*.   ll. 27—8. R *omits*] about...be.
l. 29. B] heele surely be. R] for being on his.   l. 31. R] dyest to fire.
l. 32. R *omits*] My...sonne, *and has* What my *Perindus*.   l. 34. R] if I had.
l. 35. B] t'wuld. R] I shold.   l. 36. R] to have buffited my M^r to have
drowned. Q] quickly. B and R] quietly.   l. 38. R] *Perindus* if thou.
l. 39. R *omits*] friend.   l. 40. Q and B] thou. R] thou so.

p. 257, l. 1. R] Mantled...us. R] Mancled, Bather many this Preist hath
mancled.   l. 4. R] Cods fish.   l. 5. Q *has a semi-colon after* more.
ll. 6—8. Q, B and R *have these in prose form*.   l. 8. Q and B] danger.
R] mischeife.   l. 14. R] diswade & hinder.   l. 16. Q and B] love.
R] health.   l. 17. R *omits*] the. R] sorrow.   l. 18. R] thy woe.
l. 20. Q and B] you. R] him.   l. 21. R *omits*] master.   l. 23. R *omits*]
had. Q] a bundance. B] boundance. R] aboundance.   l. 26. Q and
B] Why. R] What. B and R] To the. Q] O to the. Q and B] fly. R]
hye.   l. 27. R *omits*] live, *and inserts* will *above the line before* die.   l. 28.
R *transfers* Master, master, master *to the beginning of Can.'s speech in* l. 31.
R] *Exit ad rupem*.   l. 29. R *omits*] him.   l. 30. R *omits*] *Exit Pas*.
l. 32. R] you rocks.   l. 33. R *omits this line*.   l. 34. B] swanne.
Q] swaine. R] swan. B and R] finiall.   l. 36. Q] *Con*.   l. 37. Q
and B] month. R] morninge.   l. 38. R] must I.

p. 258, l. 1. R] *Act:* 5. *Scen:* 7.   l. 2. R *omits*] *Enter*.   ll. 3—10.
Q and B *have these in prose form;* R *partly in prose, partly in verse*.   l. 4.
B and R] 's. Q] is.   l. 6. R] I am.   l. 7. R] that have.   l. 8. B
and R] two. Q] too.   l. 9. R] *Nonius*. Q and B] learne. R] know.
l. 10. R] *Nonius*.   l. 13. Q] *Con*.   l. 15. Q and B] had...cus'd. R]
for had you caus'd. R *omits second* not.   l. 17. Q and B] if he...have.
R] had hee not.   l. 18. Q and B] had not fallen. R] wold not have fall.
R] had not hee.   l. 19. Q and B] if...not. R] had not wee.   l. 20. Q
& were. Q] wee would showe. B] wee'd showe. R] wee wold shew you.
l. 24. R *omits*] then.   l. 26. B] my tong's.   l. 27—8. *So divided in* R.
Q and B *have them in prose form*.   l. 27. Q *has a comma after* away.   l. 28.
Q and B] returnes. R] comes.   l. 29. Q and B] I prethee. R] Good.
Q and B] crave. R] beg.   ll. 30—1. B] I could never get any further.

307

NOTES

ll. 30—4. Q and B] for mee...already. R *has instead*] on my grave, Ile not troble any poet for it, I have made it already. l. 35. Q *has a mark of interrogation after* thou. l. 36. R] valourous & kind. Q *has a full stop after* live.

p. **259**, ll. 1—2. B *has these lines as part of the Epitaph.* Q *prints them in Roman type as if they did not belong to it.* R *omits* l. 1 *and gives to Scrocca* l. 2 *in the variant form:* Instead of his members covering his memorie wth stones.   l. 3. Q] M^r.   B] good M.   R *omits the line.*   l. 4.   *In* R *this line in the variant form*] Cancrone you must leade the way, its a land-voiage *follows* l. 2 *as part of the same speech by Scrocca.*   l. 6.   R *omits*] Exeunt. l. 7. R] After the.   l. 8. Q] to'th'.   B] to'th.   R] to the.   Q] i'th'.   B] i'th.   R] in th'.   l. 9.   B and R] to stay.   Q] stay.   l. 11.   B and R] before him.   Q] before.   l. 12.   R] thou art.   l. 13.   R] not so pure as. l. 14.   R] your doome.   Q *puts a comma after* i'le *instead of* past.   l. 15. R] her fact.   l. 18.   B and R] guiltie Nymph.   Q] Nymph.   l. 20.   R *omits*] shee.   l. 21.   B] That law says shee, it selfe.   R] The law say'd shee, it selfe.   l. 23.   R] say.   l. 24.   B and R] shold they.   Q] shouldst thou.   l. 26.   Q and B] lovely.   R] truely.   l. 27.   Q and B] live...contend.   R] dye, both content.   l. 28.   Q and B] strove for.   R] doth Crowne.   l. 32.   Q and B] hates.   R] harts.   l. 34.   R] shold buy. l. 35.   Q *has a comma after* she.   l. 37.   R] to his.   l. 38.   R] 'ginns.

p. **260**, l. 1.   R] While wth...stipps he.   B and R] rocke.   Q] rockes. l. 4.   R *places* thus spake *at the end of* l. 3.   l. 6.   R] art thou.   Q] pay. B and R] buy.   l. 7.   B] Alchymy.   R] Mechymy.   l. 9.   Q] now. B and R] I.   R *omits*] the first.   l. 13.   Q and B] griefe.   R] life.   l. 15. Q and B] heart.   R] selfe.   l. 16.   R] while.   l. 17.   Q and B] from. R] for.   l. 19.   B and R] seas.   Q] sea.   l. 20.   Q *omits*] in ease, *which is given by* B and R.   l. 21.   Q and B] seemes.   R] seem'd.   Q and B] with.   R] wth a.   l. 22.   R] in human men.   l. 23.   Q *omits this line, which is given by* B and R.   l. 24.   R] the fall.   l. 25.   Q and B] pious. R] pittied.   l. 27.   Q *has a comma after* regarding.   l. 28.   Q and B] awarding.   R] regarding.   l. 30.   B and R] i'th.   R] conveyes.   l. 34. R] for y^e.   l. 35.   Q and B] in.   R] for.   l. 37.   R] That love their M^{rs} more then enmitie.   l. 38.   B] this great, this foule.   Q] this foule. R] this greate, this foule.   l. 40.   B and R] dire.   Q] drie.

p. **261**, l. 1.   Q and B] guilty.   R] horred.   l. 2.   Q and B] if in thy. R] wthin this.   l. 4.   Q and B] and.   R] O.   R] wth them.   l. 7.   R *omits*] then.   ll. 7—8.   *Between these* R *has*] Act: 5. Scen: 8.   l. 8.   R] Pas a rupe.   l. 9.   R] *Nonnius*, thou now must.   l. 12.   Q *omits*] mirth and, *which is given by* B and R.   l. 13.   Q and B] ringing.   R] singing. l. 14.   R] *Nonnius.*   l. 16.   R] should dwell.   l. 17.   R] all o^r sorrow. l. 19.   R] womens.   B] teare.   l. 20.   R *omits*] of.   R] could not.   l. 21. R] desaye.   l. 22.   R] & cheeck the baser.   l. 23.   R] purest.   l. 26. R] Colour.   l. 27.   R] W^{ch} faines a.   B and R] and.   Q] of.   l. 28.   Q and B] excells.   R] passes.   l. 30.   R] sweare 't a temple vow'd.   l. 32. Q and B] never to.   R] I ne're will.   l. 33.   Q and B] your.   R] the. l. 34.   R] I prythee doe.

p. **262**, l. 1.   R] *Act:* 5. *Scen:* 9.   l. 2.   R *omits*] *Enter.*   l. 3.   R] *Glau: Perin: Alcippus a rupe.*   ll. 4—10.   R *omits these lines.*   l. 5.   B] safron.   Q] safe on.   l. 6.   B] *That love.*   Q] *That I love.*   l. 10.   B] safron.   Q] safe on.   l. 12.   R *omits*] now.   l. 18.   R] deserved loves. l. 19.   R] those.   l. 22.   R] all those.   l. 24.   R] thou wert.   l. 26.

NOTES

Q and B] Still to.   R] least I.   l. 27.   R *omits this line.*   l. 28.   R] You.
l. 30.   R] harbor'd.   l. 34.   R] and to y^e.
  p. 263, l. 2.   Q and B] have.   R] a.   l. 4.   Q and B] those.   R] them.
l. 6.   R] you.   Q and B] your.   l. 7.   Q and B] this her.   R] thy.   l. 8.
R *omits*] most.   R] love them never.   l. 10.   R] affect.   l. 11.   R]
respect.   l. 13.   R *omits*] *Exit Chorus.*   l. 14.   Q and B] I.   R] you.
l. 15.   Q and B] This.   R] The.   l. 19.   R] worse.   l. 22.   R] I'le.
l. 23.   R] shall's goe.   l. 24.   R] 'ith.   l. 29.   B] no time I count.
Q] no time.   R] I finde no time.   l. 31.   R] play is.   l. 33.   Q] that.
B and R] this.   l. 35.   R] *i'th'*.   Q] *'ith'.*   B] *ith.*   l. 36.   R] *are all.*
l. 37.   Q and B] *now.*   R] *when.*   l. 38.   R *omits*] *Exeunt.   After this line*
R *adds:*
  Post plausum.
 O ô if you bee gentlemen holde your hands
 for as in a feast, they ende with a west-farianhoge
 So o^r poet will close your stomacks wth an Epiloge.
  Deest Chorus.
  p. 264, ll. 1—18.   *In spite of the statement* Deest Chorus, R *has these lines
in the original hand, but preceded by a blank leaf, and in inverted order.*   l. 3.
Q *has no stop after*] *pleased.*   l. 7.   R] *pleases.*   l. 9.   B and R] *as each.*
Q] *as t'each.*   l. 10.   Q *has a comma after*] *newer.*   l. 11.   Q and B]
where.   R] *when.*   B] *dishers.*   l. 14.   R] *hee please best.*

APPENDIX TO THE POEMS OF GILES FLETCHER.

VERSE TRANSLATIONS IN THE REWARD OF THE FAITHFULL.

  D=Duodecimo edition of *The Reward of the Faithfull*, 1623.
  The accents in the Greek quotations in D *are so confused that they have been silently altered in the text.*
  p. 271, ll. 6—7.   These lines, printed in D in Roman type, have been printed in Italics to conform with the others below.   l. 11.   *D omits*] *To.*
l. 12.   D] Κ' αν μικρὸν.   There is some misprint, but the translation *in a moment,*
l. 15, shows that Fletcher did not use the orthodox reading ξητῶν.   Κἀν μικρῷ=
even in a short time, is the simplest emendation.   l. 18.   D] Ἔστι.   The correct reading, not followed by Fletcher, is Εἰ δὲ.   D] ἄνδρακες.   l. 19.   D]
Θαλψωσης λάμψουσ' ὡς ροδα ρειαρενα.   Here again Fletcher departs from the orthodox reading, Θάλψωμεν, λάμπουσ' ὡς ῥόδεαι κάλυκες.
  p. 272, l. 3.   D] *infirna.*   l. 15.   D] *It was not he.*   The use of *he* to represent ἐγὼ in l. 13 is owing to the couplet being preceded in the prose tract by the words] Sayes great *Agamemnon* alas!   l. 20.   D] ἔχουσι.
  p. 273, l. 3.   D] *Quærum.*   l. 16.   D] *arace.*   l. 17.   D] *trappins.*

CORRIGENDA.

p. 14, l. 6, *for* virgins *read* virgi[n].   l. 13. *for* deigns *read* deign's.
p. 15, l. 20, *for* solem *read* s[alt]em.
p. 16, l. 23, *for* Polluipia *read* Pollui pia.
p. 71, *side-note, between* blessed *and* Joseph *add* Saints.
p. 88, l. 20, *for* sœpe *read* sæpe.
p. 96, l. 12, *for* Ab *read* Ah.
p. 111, l. 1, *for* Jaccho *read* Iaccho.
p. 120, l. 5, *for* cœco *read* cæco.
p. 212, l. 22, for *Fishers* read *Fishe*[r].
p. 219, l. 16, *for* [often] *read* of[t] the.
p. 220, l. 30, *for* Lillies seeme *read* Lilli[e] seeme[s].
p. 227, l. 10, *for* dead *read* dea[le].
p. 263, l. 14, *omit* [you].

WITHDRAWN
from the
Alma College Library